Principles of
HUMAN RESOURCE DEVELOPMENT

Principles of
HUMAN RESOURCE
DEVELOPMENT

Jerry W. Gilley, Ed.D.,

Human Resource Development, University of Nebraska–Lincoln

Steven A. Eggland, Ph.D,

Marketing Education, University of Nebraska–Lincoln

 ADDISON-WESLEY PUBLISHING COMPANY
in association with
UNIVERSITY ASSOCIATES, INC.

READING, MASSACHUSETTS   MENLO PARK, CALIFORNIA   NEW YORK
DON MILLS, ONTARIO   WOKINGHAM, ENGLAND   AMSTERDAM
BONN   SYDNEY   SINGAPORE   TOKYO   MADRID   SAN JUAN
PARIS   SEOUL   MILAN   MEXICO CITY   TAIPEI

The publisher offers discounts on this book when ordered in quantity for special sales. For more information please contact:

Corporate & Professional Publishing Group
Addison-Wesley Publishing Company
Route 128
Reading, Massachusetts 01867

Library of Congress Cataloging-in-Publication Data

Gilley, Jerry W.
   Principles of human resource development / Jerry W. Gilley, Steven A. Eggland.
      p.   cm.
   Includes index.
   ISBN 0-201-09013-9
   1. Career development.   2. Personnel management.   I. Eggland, Steven A.   II. Title.
HF5549.5.C35G55   1989
658.3'124—dc 19   88-30498

Cover design by Hannus Design Associates
Text design by Carson Design, Manchester, MA
Set in 10 point Meridien by Typo-Graphics, Orlando, FL

7 8 9 10 11- CRS- 96959493
Seventh printing, October 1993

Contents

Preface   xi

Chapter 1 • ***What is Human Rsesource Development?   1***
Introduction to HRD   2
What are Human Resources?   3
What is Development?   4
Human Resource Concept   5
Essential Terms Defined   6
The Evolution of HRD   8
The Mission and Purpose of HRD   12
The Components of HRD   13
HRD Learning Activities   16
Are HRD Practitioners Adult Educators?   17
The Human Resource Wheel   17
Roles in HRD   20
Competencies in HRD   21
Professional Identity   23
Conclusion   24

Chapter 2 • ***Individual Development   25***
Evolution of Individual Development   26
Responsibility for Individual Development   27
Roles in Individual Development   28
Competencies in Individual Development   29
New Approaches to Individual Development   32
Learning in the Workplace   32
The Seven Laws of Individual Development   35
1. The Law of the Learning Specialist   36
2. The Law of the Learner   38
3. The Law of the Language   40
4. The Law of the Lesson   41
5. The Law of the Teaching Process   42
6. The Law of the Learning Process   44
7. The Law of Review and Application   45
Conclusion   46

Chapter 3 • **Career Development 47**
Overview of Career Development 48
Career Development and Organizations 51
Career Development Activities 52
The Organizational Components and
   Career Development Activities 53
The Individual Component and
   Career Development Activities 67
Summary of Career Development Activities 71
Application and Utilization of the
   Career Development Process 71
Conclusion 73

Chapter 4 • **Organizational Development 74**
Characteristics of OD 77
Goals and Objectives of OD 78
Principles of Change 79
The Change Agent 80
The OD Process 85
Value of OD 89
Organization Types 90
Individual Development and OD: A Relationship 91
Recommendations for HRD Practitioners 93
Conclusion 94

Chapter 5 • **The HRD Manager 96**
Why HRD Departments Fail in Organizations 97
Role of Manager of HRD 98
Competencies of HRD Managers 101
Characteristics of Effective HRD Managers 102
Responsibilities of HRD Managers 103
Strategies for Designing an HRD Program 103
Planning, Organizing, Staffing, Controlling,
   and Marketing HRD 105
Conclusion 116

Chapter 6 • **The Learning Specialist and Instruction in HRD 117**
Criteria for Selecting Learning Specialists 119
Understanding How Adults Learn 120
The Six-Stage Instructional Process 126
Conclusion 142
Appendix A: Training Style Inventory 143
Appendix B: Philosophical Orientations to Training Style 147

Appendix C: A Scale for Measuring the Degree
    of Learner-Centeredness of a Course   149
Appendix D: The 12 Dimensions and
    Their Associated Items   152

Chapter 7   •   *The Instructional Designer   154*
Subroles of the Instructional Designer   155
Activities of Instructional Designers   159
Competencies for Instructional Designers   163
The Relationship of Instructionsl Designer
    to Manager, Learning Specialist, and Consultant   170
Conclusion   170

Chapter 8   •   *The Consultant   171*
Growth in HRD Consulting   173
Why a Consultant for HRD Programs?   174
The Role of the HRD Consultant   175
Consultant Competencies   180
Internal/External Consultants in HRD   182
Implementing Change   184
Hierarchy of Purpose   186
The Consulting Process   191
Conclusion   195

Chapter 9   •   *Assessing the Need for HRD   196*
Definition of Needs Assessment   197
The Importance of Needs Assessment   198
Why Engage in Needs Assessment?   199
Methods Employed in Needs Assessment   200
Models Useful for Needs Assessment   209
Developing a Training Proposal   210
Conclusion   212

Chapter 10   •   *Program Planning, Design, and Evaluation   213*
The Genesis of Learning Programs
    within Organizations   214
Phase 1. Philosophy of Teaching and Learning   215
Phase 2. Needs Analysis   218
Phase 3. Feedback   219
Phase 4. Program Design   220
Phase 5. Program Development   223
Phase 6. Program Implementation   228
Phase 7. Program Management   228
Phase 8. Evaluation   229

Phase 9. Accountability   237
Conclusion   238

Chapter 11   •   *Marketing and Positioning the HRD Program
within the Organization   241*
The Mission   243
External and Internal Environmental Analysis   245
Objectives and Goals   245
Target Marketing and Market Segmentation   247
The Marketing Mix   250
Product Strategy   251
Concept Life Cycle   251
Portfolio Analysis of Importance
and Application   255
Putting It All Together   258
Place Strategy   259
Promotion Strategy   260
Price Strategy   262
Marketing Plan for HRD Programs   264
Conclusion   265

Chapter 12   •   *The Benefits and Costs of HRD   266*
The Costs of Training   267
The Benefits of Training   269
Models for Cost-Benefit Analysis of Training   270
Cost-Effectiveness Analysis   270
Developmental Opportunity and the
Profit and Loss Statement   274
The Multi-criterion Approach to
Evaluation of Benefits   278
Human Resources Accounting—A Critique   281
Conclusion   282

Chapter 13   •   *Professional Certification and Development   283*
What is Professional Certification?   284
History of Credentialing   285
Support for Professional Certification   286
Significance and Purpose of Professional Certification   287
Professional Certification Activities
in HRD-Related Societies   291
The Professionalization Cube   298
Conclusion   301

Chapter 14 • ***Professionalization of the Field of HRD   303***
The Professionalization Process   305
Competency Studies and Research in HRD   309
Conclusion   324

Chapter 15 • ***Careers in Human Resource Development   325***
What Is the Scope of Human Resource
    Development Activities?   326
Roles and Competencies   326
Opportunities in Human Resource Development   327
The Rewards of Working in HRD   329
Self-Assessment in Preparation for Employment   332
Initial Employment in HRD   340
Developing a Career Path in HRD   341
The Future of HRD   342
Learning More about Careers in HRD   343

Chapter 16 • ***The Future of Human Resource Development   347***
Economic, Political, Sociological,
    and Organizational Factors   348
The HRD Practitioners of the Future   362
Conclusion   364

References   365

Index   379

Preface

During the past forty years, the field of Human Resource Development (HRD) has grown, matured, and developed into an essential component of most organizations. Today, an ever-increasing number of corporations are appointing executive-level positions responsible for the enhancement, advancement, development, and growth of human resources. As a result, the field is being viewed as an important strategic approach to improved productivity, efficiency, and profitability. In addition, many view HRD as a field of professional choice rather than as a "pass through" activity on route to a more prestigious and important professional indentity.

There are many points of entry into the field of HRD. The two most common ones are as a student of the field in an undergraduate, master's, or doctorate program or as a practitioner who has mastered a content or skill area which serves as the basis for training and developing others. Regardless of the orientation or entry into the field of HRD, several fundamental questions must be addressed. The first question that is most often asked is "What exactly is HRD?" The second most common question is "What constitutes the field of HRD?" The third is "What do HRD practitioners do?" and the fourth is "What are the competencies required to be a successful HRD practitioner?" Some people are even interested in the historical and professional development of the field (which is the fifth most-often-asked question). Perhaps the most important, or at least the most personal, question is "What career opportunities are available in the field of HRD?" Finally, people are concerned about the future of HRD and what will influence it as a field (this is the seventh question). The previous questions serve as the foundation of this book. Each is answered carefully, honestly, and fully.

This book serves as an overview for students in HRD programs as well as HRD practitioners who desire to enhance their understanding of the field in which they participate.

In Chapter 1, What is HRD?, we begin by providing a comprehensive overview of the field of HRD (Question 1). In the next three chapters, the component of HRD which includes individual development, career development, and organizational development is examined (Question 2). This section of the book concludes by providing a working relationship among these three areas and provides several recommendations for implementation. The next four chapters examine the four fundamental roles performed by HRD practitioners: manager of HRD programs and/or departments, learning specialist, instructional designer,and consultant. For each of these roles, several subroles are identified and examined as well (Question 3). The fourth section of the book examines the competencies required of HRD practitioners (Question 4). They include: instruction, needs assessment, cost benefit analysis, program design, development and evaluation, and marketing of HRD programs within organizations. The book next examines the historical and professional development activities of the field of HRD (Question5). Included in this section is an overview of the eight major studies conducted in the field during the past twenty years as well as the professional development and certification activities of several major HRD-related associations and societies. The last section of the book addresses students' and practitioners' concerns regarding career opportunities and the future of the field (Questions 6 and 7).

In addition to these seven areas of concern, the book is designed to serve as an "overview" of the field of HRD rather than as an in-depth analysis of any one area, and it is from this perspective that the book was written. Each chapter or section could have had more detail but there are several books dedicated to the topics identified in each chapter or section. It is hoped that this work will serve as a foundation to professional awareness and knowledge and that further study and inquiry will result. Finally, this book was written to provide a consistent point of reference, view and flow which is often missing from traditional edited books and/or handbooks available for the field.

We would like to acknowledge the contribution of Michael A. Miller, Chair and Professor of Supervision at Indiana University-Purdue University at Fort Wayne, in the analysis and review of this book. We would like to also thank Bart Beaudin of Colorado State University for his constant support and encouragement during this project and Fred Otte, Georgia State University, for serving as an example of academic excellance for the field of HRD which we used as a standard when writing this book. Each of these individuals helped us to crystalize our thoughts, meaning, and intent. In addition, we would like to thank Tom Hudson and Marsha Phelps, research graduate assistants at the University of Nebraska-Lincoln, for their contributions and assistance. Finally we would like to thank both our families for their support, love, and patience during this project. To M. Gail, Andrea, Robert, Melissa, Shannon, and Michael Gilley, and to Erik and Erin Eggland, a special thank you.

CHAPTER 1

What Is Human Resource Development?

Objectives

After completing Chapter 1, readers should be able to

- define HRD and related terms.

- describe the evolution of the field of HRD.

- identify and describe the mission of HRD.

- describe the three fundamental types of learning activities.

- distinguish between HRD practitioners and adult educators.

- describe the Human Resource Wheel and separate HRD from HRM.

- identify the four primary roles in HRD.

- identify the unique competencies needed for each of the primary roles.

- identify and distinguish among the three identities of HRD practitioners.

Human resource development is a dynamic and evolving field in the world of business. It is the goal of this publication to provide a resource through which HRD practitioners and students can understand the field and grasp its simplicity. It is within that simplicity that an appreciation of the complexity of HRD can be realized. An introductory book such as this should only provide an overview; other more focused publications will provide the crystallization. For example, when entering a community for the first time, its landmarks, citizens, and complexity often seem overwhelming to the newcomer. But after familiarizing oneself with its uniqueness, its roads, streets, buildings, and people, it does not appear as threatening or complex. In fact, if given time, even the most alien community can take on the characteristics of "home."

The same is true for a new professional field. We have tried to simplify HRD in such a way that it becomes less complicated to the newcomer. If, after studying the following chapters, readers feel better able to understand the field, its areas, roles, unique competencies, and relationships to other human resource areas, then the book has indeed accomplished its mission. But one must remember, it is the HRD practitioners themselves who will ultimately provide the learning activities and insights through which the performance improvement of others will occur. Thus, it is their responsibility to master their craft in order for others within the organization to master theirs. Simultaneously, our goal is to provide the details, descriptions, and facts necessary to enable the HRD practitioner to develop an individual development strategy for becoming more professional in the field.

INTRODUCTION TO HRD

Many people accept new career assignments and challenges without fully understanding the duties required in the new role. In fact, people often expect to develop the knowledge and skills required for the job as they participate in the daily activities. This sometimes results in mistakes and loss of productivity and efficiency. This, of course, reflects upon the image and reputation of a field and its practitioners. Consider the following example:

> After 15 years with the organization, I get reassigned to the Human Resource Development Department. My regional vice-president tells me it's a promotion for the excellent way I've performed. In fact he said, "the display of your abilities and talents

convinced upper management that you should be training others. . . ." I realize I have managerial potential, but what is this training function anyway? Fifteen years. . . . Am I ready to train others?
What will my duties be? What competencies will I need? How
does HRD fit in with the rest of the organization? What is Human
Resource Development?"

Does this sound familiar? These are very real and often unanswered questions that newly promoted HRD practitioners face every day. Where can one
turn for information regarding the field of HRD?

From another perspective, that of a student considering HRD as a career,
many things must be examined. One of the most important components of any
career is the roles and activities one will encounter. The role of an HRD practitioner is very diverse, and it often requires that a number of subroles be managed simultaneously. One might expect to serve as an internal consultant to
upper management regarding the organization's learning programs and at the
same time design a systemwide career development program for employees.
Many HRD practitioners become the managers of HRD departments and also
serve as the organization's "learning" representative. Still others specialize in
instruction or instructional design.

HRD practitioners perform several different activities and duties. For example, one might expect to design, develop, and implement learning programs
and training activities. This would include conducting a needs assessment as
well as an evaluation of programs and learners. One might prepare cost/benefit
statements or help market and position HRD within the organization. Regardless of one's orientation, this book will serve as a reference for HRD students,
practitioners, managers, and academics interested in a better understanding of
the principles of HRD.

The question remains, *What is human resource development?* Many people feel
it is a question that is impossible to answer, given the complex nature of the
practice of HRD. It is made even more difficult because the field is changing
rapidly. A clear definition will provide a framework on which to base decisions
regarding the roles and competencies of practitioners as well as the activities
that should be incorporated in HRD programs.

The very term "human resource development" provides us with clues as to
its meaning. Obviously, it is related to the development of people, but calling
people "human resources" reveals an organizational orientation just as "financial resources" and "capital resources" do. Thus, HRD is about the development of people *within* organizations. Therefore, to properly define HRD, let's
examine the terms "human resources" and "development" more closely.

WHAT ARE HUMAN RESOURCES?

Today's organizations consist of three types of resources, physical, financial,
and human. *Physical resources* are machines, materials, facilities, equipment,
and component parts of products. These are often referred to as *fixed corporate*

assets. Physical resources are very important to the health of the organization because they provide it with stability and strength. Also, because they are tangible and can be seen, they provide the public with a measure of the organization's success. A corporate headquarters building is an example of this type of resource (Gilley, 1989).

Financial resources refer to the *liquid assets* of an organization. They are the cash, stock, bonds, investment, and operating capital. Like physical resources, financial resources are important to the organization's ability to react to opportunities for growth and expansion. They also reflect its overall financial stability and strength. This is determined by comparing the assets (physical and financial) with the liabilities (debts) of the organization. A positive outcome is referred to as *net worth.* Net worth is the figure that banks, investors, and the public use to determine the financial health of an organization.

Human resources refer to the people employed by an organization. Measuring the value of human resources is difficult because it is hard to use standard and traditional measures such as fixed and liquid assets. As a result, human resources cannot be depreciated as physical resources can, or used to reflect the net worth of an organization as financial resources are. Human resources, however, are just as important as physical and financial resources. But, unfortunately, corporate executives and managers often overlook this fact, because human resources cannot be used to reflect the prosperity of the organization.

One measure that corporate executives and managers should consider when determining the importance of human resources is the cost of replacing valuable employees, for example, the cost of recruiting, hiring, relocating, lost productivity, training, and orientation. Another measure is the knowledge, competencies, skills, and attitudes of the members of the organization. Corporate executives and managers need to place a value on these intangibles. In other words, a well-trained, highly skilled, and knowledgeable employee is more valuable to an organization than one who is not. This value is ultimately reflected in increased productivity and efficiency, as well as in the employee's attitudes toward work and the organization. Organizations are aware of the value of human resources, but they often fail to consider them in their asset portfolio. As a result, many do not recognize the importance of HRD programs, nor do they realize that improved knowledge, competencies, skills, and attitudes are necessary to improve the overall efficiency and effectiveness of the organization (Gilley, 1989).

WHAT IS DEVELOPMENT?

When examining the term "development" two questions should be addressed: (1) What is meant by the development of people? and (2) What type of development really occurs within an organization? (Gilley, 1989)

Development of people refers to the advancement of knowledge, skills, and competencies, and the improved behavior of people within the organization for both their personal and professional use. This reflects a focus on the individual (individual development). It also reflects a philosophical commitment to the professional advancement of people within the organization (career development). Finally, development of people within an organization is directed at performance improvement in order that the organization can benefit—greater organizational efficiency, more effective competitive practices, and greater profitability (organizational development). These are the three components of HRD (see below).

Development, individual or organizational, cannot occur unless people participate in activities designed to introduce new knowledge and skills and to improve behaviors. This, of course, can be accomplished through daily work experience, but this is a hit-or-miss approach that requires more time with no guarantee of results. It could even mean the development of inadequate or inappropriate knowledge, skills, and behaviors. This is what human resource development is all about—the introduction of organized activities designed to foster increased knowledge, skills, and competencies and improved behavior. Simply stated, HRD refers to learning and to the activities that bring about desired change (Gilley, 1989).

From an organizational perspective, however, it is not enough to simply increase the knowledge, skills, and competencies of employees and improve their behavior. These organizational efforts must result in *performance improvement* that will enhance the organization's competitiveness and efficiency. Performance improvement, therefore, is the ultimate goal of HRD. In summary, then, we can define HRD as "organized learning activities arranged within an organization in order to improve performance and/or personal growth for the purpose of improving the job, the individual, and/or the organization."

HUMAN RESOURCE CONCEPT

In addition to defining HRD, we need to place HRD into a context that will reflect its relationship to the overall human resource function. Nadler (1986) calls this the Human Resource Concept. The Human Resource Concept refers to the holistic view of the human resource process (see Figure 1.1). The Human Resource Concept begins by separating human resources into three broad categories: human resource utilization, human resource planning and forecasting, and human resource development. Each has a different purpose but all contribute and are essential to the human development and performance improvement formula.

Human resource utilization refers to the placement and utilization of human resources within an organization. This includes promotions, appraisal, transfers, and compensation. Human resource planning and forecasting refers to the forecasting of future human resources and the appropriate planning for their recruitment, selection, training, and career advancement. Human resource development refers to the preparation through learning activities of human

Figure 1.1   Human Resource Concept

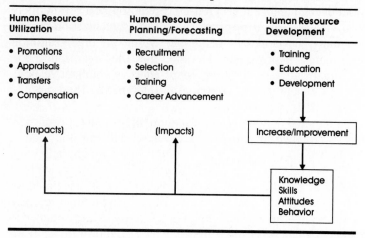

resources for current jobs (training) and future work assignments (development) as well as individual enhancement (education). These are referred to as the three focus areas of human resource development—training, development, and education. The desired outcome of each area is the advancement of knowledge, competencies, and skills and attitude acquisition, utilization, and improvement.

ESSENTIAL TERMS DEFINED

In addition to human resource development, there are several other important terms that will be used throughout this book:

Adult education: a process whereby learning activities are engaged in for the purpose of bringing about change or growth for the adult in a formal or informal educational setting.

Andragogy: the art and science of helping adults learn.

Career development: an organized, planned effort comprised of structural activities or processes that advances employees within an organization and results in their optimal utilization.

Change agent: the person responsible for the inductions of interventions designed to bring about organizational change.

Consultant: the person who actually provides consulting services to an HRD department, whether internally or externally. This term should be used to describe someone who provides a specific learning program external to the organization.

Education: learning provided to improve performance on a future job or to enable one to accept more responsibility and/or new assignments.

Development: learning that is not job-related, although it may have some impact on a present or future job.

Human resource accounting: accounting among other resources, for an organization's employees, that is, measuring both their cost and their value.

Human resource management: the recruitment, selection, maintenance, development, and utilization of, and accommodation to, human resources by organizations.

Human resource planning: the process of analyzing an organization's human resource needs under changing conditions and developing the activities necessary to satisfy these needs.

Individual development (training and development): identifying, assessing, and arranging planned learning efforts that help in the development of the essential competencies that enable individuals to perform current jobs.

Instructional designer: the person responsible for the development, design, writing, and planning of instructional programs and learning materials.

Learning specialist (instructor): the person responsible—traditionally referred to as trainer—for the implementation and/or facilitation of learning experiences so that individuals learn.

Manager of HRD: the person responsible for the operations of the HRD department within an organization.

Organizational development: a systemwide process of data collection, diagnosis, action planning, intervention, and evaluation aimed at: (1) enhancing congruence between organizational structure, process, strategy, people, and culture; (2) developing new and creative organizational solutions; and (3) developing the organization's self-renewing capacity (Beer, 1983).

Pedagogy: the art and science of teaching children.

Training: learning that is provided in order to improve performance on the present job.

THE EVOLUTION OF HRD

Since before the industrial revolution, eight environments have been utilized to enhance human learning: individual, family, community, church, school, college, workplace, and media. During the past several decades the importance of each has changed drastically. (See Figures 1.2, 1.3, and 1.4.)

During the preindustrial period the family, community, and church were paramount in human learning. However, as the demand for better trained personnel grew (industrial period), the learning environment emphasis shifted away from the home to the school. As we enter into the information age, the human learning environment continues to change. It is perceived that the workplace, media, and individualized studies will evolve as principal delivery systems for learning.

The earliest form of training, often referred to as vocational education, was provided by the apprenticeship system in colonial America. Apprenticeships were designed principally for the education of the poor. During this period, the workplace was not viewed as a primary environment for human learning (see Figure 1.2).

In the early to mid-nineteenth century the focus of the country began to change (Figure 1.3). By the end of the century, Frederick Winslow Taylor, a Pennsylvania steel company engineer, had developed a managerial concept known as *scientific management.* He believed that industry could increase productivity through the elimination of wasted effort. Taylor's theory includes job design, worker selection and training, and the separation of planning from performance.

Taylor believed that there was "one best way" to do a job and any other method would result in inefficiency. He also believed that the physical and mental attributes required to accomplish a task should be identified and employees should be trained to meet those requirements. Taylor introduced the idea that extensive preparation should precede actual work. Finally, Taylor concluded that management is responsible for job design, selection, training, and planning. It was during this period of the Industrial Revolution that HRD began to gain in strength and influence as more and more employees were trained in the "one best way" to do a job.

The Hawthorne studies (1920), conducted by Elton Mayo, a researcher for the National Research Council, have had a profound effect on modern-day organizations as well as HRD. Mayo's principal discovery was that all organizations are made up of informal groups and that this affects the efficiency and effectiveness of production. Another important discovery of his was that the amount and quality of attention given to employees affects their production output.

During the 1950s the human relations movement lost much of its influence because of misapplications and misrepresentations. However, it did serve as a stepping-stone for the behavioral sciences as well as for HRD.

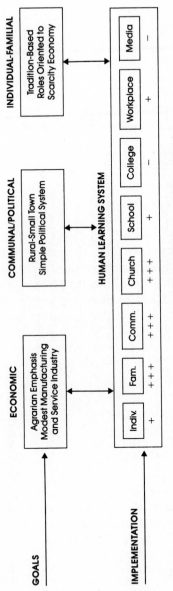

GOALS

ECONOMIC
Agrarian Emphasis
Modest Manufacturing
and Service Industry

COMMUNAL/POLITICAL
Rural-Small Town
Simple Political System

INDIVIDUAL-FAMILIAL
Tradition-Based
Roles Oriented to
Scarcity Economy

HUMAN LEARNING SYSTEM

Indiv.	Fam.	Comm.	Church	School	College	Workplace	Media
+	+++	+++	+++	+	–	+	–

IMPLEMENTATION

- High Indoctrination-Low Intentional Learning
- Traditional Institutional Domination
- Embedded System Management
- Formal Learning as Terminal Activity
- Curriculum Narrowly Defined
- System Inadequate to Changing Goals in Mid-19th Century

Figure 1.2   Preindustrial paradigm

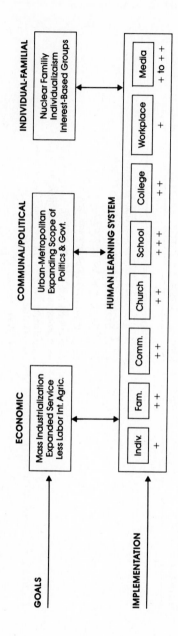

Figure 1.3   Industrial paradigm

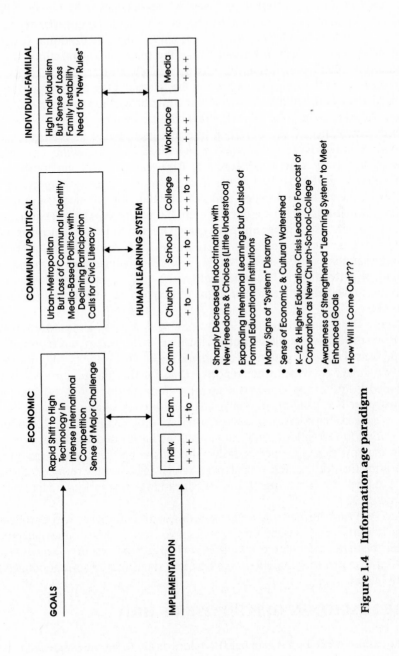

GOALS

ECONOMIC

Rapid Shift to High
Technology in
Intense International
Competition
Sense of Major Challenge

COMMUNAL/POLITICAL

Urban-Metropolitan
But Loss of Communal Indentity
Media-Based Politics with
Declining Pariticipation
Calls for Civic Literacy

INDIVIDUAL-FAMILIAL

High Individualism
But Sense of Loss
Family Instability
Need for "New Rules"

HUMAN LEARNING SYSTEM

Indiv.	Fam.	Comm.	Church	School	College	Workplace	Media
+ + +	+ to –	–	+ to –	+ + to +	+ + to +	+ + +	+ + +

IMPLEMENTATION

- Sharply Decreased Indoctrination with
  New Freedoms & Choices (Little Understood)
- Expanding Intentional Learnings but Outside of
  Formal Educational Institutions
- Many Signs of "System" Disarray
- Sense of Economic & Cultural Watershed
- K–12 & Higher Education Crisis Leads to Forecast of
  Corporation as New Church-School-College
- Awareness of Strengthened "Learning System" to Meet
  Enhanced Goals
- How Will It Come Out???

Figure 1.4   Information age paradigm

During the fifties and sixties, fostered by the behavioral science movement in management, the attitude of organizations toward human resources began to change. The writings of Herzberg, Rogers, Maslow, Drucker, McGregor, Likert, and Argyris have had a tremendous impact on this movement. The "tension" between workers and management—caused by the organizational structure and interpersonal relationships—became the focus of organizations. It was believed by management that this friction severely retarded productivity and organizational efficiency. Management also felt that if the energy spent trying to reduce tension could be harnessed, it could be applied to more profitable areas. Another by-product of the behavioral science movement was management's acceptance of the power of informal groups and its realization that human resources were as important to organizational profitability as financial resources and raw materials (Figure 1.4). It is because of the behavioral science movement that HRD has had such a dramatic impact on today's organizations.

During the past two decades, and aided by the philosophical shift that has taken place, human resource development has emerged as a professional field in its own right. HRD programs have gained tremendous momentum as management better appreciates its human resources. In addition, the serious nature of international competition today has forced management to reexamine employee performance. The result has been a much greater emphasis on the training, development, and education of employees, the three focus areas of HRD.

Today, the American Society for Training and Development (1986), which supports the evaluation of the human learning environment, has reported that 79 percent of all those who need training to get jobs get some of that training in the workplace. It was further reported that, for the 5.8 million individuals enrolled in industry-sponsored degree programs during 1984, business and industry spent $29 billion annually. ASTD reported this figure for formal training to exceed that for formal and informal training combined—$200 billion. According to Dervarics (1985), organizations have discovered that they can train employees in job-specific skills without the participation of traditional education institutions. Because of these trends, an increasing number of teachers are seeking employment in noneducational institutions (McLagan & Bedrick, 1983).

ASTD (1986) further reported that 6 out of 10 employees had enrolled in new training programs in the previous two years. Eighty-nine percent of America's largest companies maintain a chief human resource executive. In 1986, the expenditure of HRD, $210 billion, rivals that of formal education, $238 billion.

THE MISSION AND PURPOSE OF HRD

The mission of HRD, that is, what HRD does, is (1) to provide *individual development* focused on performance improvement related to a current job; (2) to provide *career development* focused on performance improvement related to

INDIV.
DEVEL.
CAREER
DEVEL.
ORGANIZATION
DEVEL.

future job assignments; and (3) to provide *organizational development* that results in both optimal utilization of human potential and improved human performance, which together improves the efficiency of the organization. Efficiency is measured by increased organizational competitiveness and/or profitability.

The purpose of HRD, on the other hand, is to bring about the changes that cause the performance improvements that will ultimately enhance the organization. Nadler and Wiggs (1986) referred to this as "making a difference." In other words, learning is transferred to on-the-job performance, reducing costs, improving quality, and increasing the competitiveness of the organization.

A need can be defined as the difference between "what is" and "what should be." To reduce the gap between poor performance ("what is") and improved performance ("what should be"), managers of HRD and their staff have to sort out and isolate the circumstances and identify possible ways to solve the problem. Solutions are often activities that improve job competencies and skills or employee motivation. Sometimes, however, employee performance can be less than acceptable, and for a variety of reasons that have little or nothing to do with job competencies or skills or employee motivation. In these situations, HRD programs should not be held accountable. For example, a salesperson closes a very difficult client, only to discover that the only merchandise left for sale is the floor model, which the customer does not want. The result is a lost sale, not because of poor sales training but because of operational realities. The salesperson's performance is measured according to production (closed sales); little consideration is given to inadequate management or operational conditions. In many cases the HRD department is blamed for not properly preparing the sales staff.

Lawrie (1986) identified four purposes of HRD:

1. Training new employees
2. Training employees to perform new duties and responsibilities
3. Improving competencies and skills of employees in current positions
4. Preparing employees for upward mobility and personal growth

THE COMPONENTS OF HRD

There are three fundamental component areas of human resource development: individual development (personal), career development (professional), and organizational development. The importance of each component will vary from organization to organization according to the complexity of the operation, the criticality of human resources to organizational efficiency, and the organization's commitment to improved human resources. But all three have one focus—individual performance improvement. Since individual performance improvement is the heart of an HRD program, HRD can be described as the "area of congruence" among the three components (see Figure 1.5).

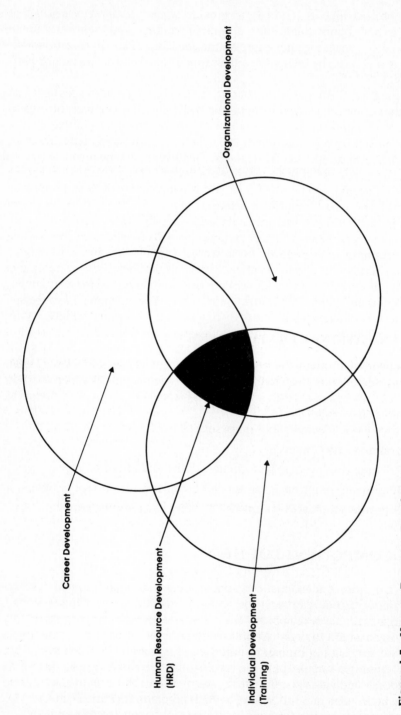

Organizational Development

Career Development

Human Resource Development (HRD)

Individual Development (Training)

Figure 1.5   Human Resource Development

INDIVIDUAL DEVELOPMENT

Individual development refers to the development of new knowledge, skills, and/or improved behaviors that result in performance enhancement and improvement related to one's current job (training). Learning may involve formal programs, but is most often accomplished through informal, on-the-job training activities.

CAREER DEVELOPMENT

Career development focuses on providing the analysis necessary to identify the individual interests, values, competencies, activities, and assignments needed to develop skills for future jobs (development). Career development includes both individual and organizational activities. Individual activities include career planning, career awareness, and utilizing career resource centers. Organizational activities include job posting systems, mentoring systems, career resource center development and maintenance, using managers as career counselors, providing career development workshops and seminars, human resource planning, performance appraisal, and career pathing programs.

ORGANIZATIONAL DEVELOPMENT

Organizational development is directed at developing new and creative organization solutions to performance problems by enhancing congruence among the organization's structure, culture, processes, and strategies within the human resources domain. In other words, the organization should become a more functional unit as a result of a closer working relationship among these elements. The ultimate goal of organizational development is to develop the organization's self-renewing capacity. This refers to the organization's ability to look introspectively and discover its problems and weaknesses and to direct the resources necessary for improvement. As a result, the organization will be able to regenerate itself over and over again as it confronts new and ever-challenging circumstances. This occurs through collaboration of organizational members with a change agent (an HRD practitioner), using behavioral science theory, research, and technology.

STRATEGICALLY,

individual development is directed at a short-term orientation to performance improvement, which results in a lower level of organizational enhancement. Simply stated, this means improved knowledge, skills, or behaviors that affect single jobs or groups of jobs. Career development is more long term than individual development and is more complex. It has a greater impact on organizational efficiency because it is directed at providing employees with a continuous developmental approach reaching ever-increasing levels of competency, which impacts the total operation of the organization. Organizational development, however, by its very nature, provides the highest level of organizational efficiency, but it also requires the greatest skill as well as the most commitment to human resource improvement. Organizational development often requires a more comprehensive analysis of performance difficulties. This approach will incorporate a variety of techniques to improve performance, which may not necessarily include learning activities and/or programs.

HRD LEARNING ACTIVITIES

HRD can best be described as a comprehensive learning system designed to enhance individual performance for the purpose of improving organizational efficiency. As such, HRD includes three types of learning activities: on the job, off the job, and through the job (see Chapter 2).

On-the-job learning activities are used when individual instruction is appropriate. An example of this would be on-the-job training (OJT). On-the-job learning activities do, however, include workshops and seminars designed for group participation. They are usually conducted by HRD learning specialists or highly qualified and experienced managers. Again, the purpose is to enhance performance through the acquisition of increased knowledge, skills, competencies, and/or improved behavior.

Off-the-job learning activities include college and university courses as well as workshops and seminars conducted by outside consultants and instructors. These are used to supplement internal organizational learning activities and/or to provide specialized learning that cannot be provided by internal HRD practitioners. An example would be a program on team building or interpersonal dynamics using outside resources away from the organizational setting.

Finally, *through-the-job* learning activities manifest themselves as new job assignments and/or duties that foster growth, development, and confidence. They include job rotations and job enrichment programs designed to increase knowledge, skills, and competencies and/or improve behavior. Because these types of activities are focused on providing *new* experience and *increased* responsibilities, they are often not viewed as learning activities. Properly organized and arranged, however, they can serve as the foundation for a comprehensive and complete career development program. Included in this approach is individual analysis of knowledge, competencies, skills, values, and interest. Career planning has also become a part of this approach by returning to the employee the responsibility of career advancement and mobility. The organization becomes an active participant by providing challenging assignments designed to foster interest and commitment.

All three types of learning activities (on, off, and through the job) have as their purpose increased knowledge, skills, and competencies and improved behavior, all of which should result in performance improvement.

ON
OFF
THROUGH
THE
JOB

ARE HRD PRACTITIONERS ADULT EDUCATORS?

For the past several decades, HRD practitioners and adult educators have examined and debated their relationship. Many HRD practitioners are uncomfortable with being identified as "adult educators"; and many adult educators resist being referred to as "trainers." Much time, energy, and money has been spent discussing and studying the relationship between the two fields, but little if any agreement has been reached.

Today practitioners in each field, HRD and adult education, continue to view their professions as separate disciplines built on different bodies of knowledge, approaches, and methodologies (Gilley, 1987). This has prevented an open exchange of ideas and information regarding adult learning theory, program and curriculum design, classroom methodologies, and other approaches to enhancing adult learning and change. Such an exchange would help practitioners in both fields to grasp a better understanding of how adults learn. By helping each identify the useful elements of the other, open exchange would also shed some light on the similarities between the two.

Adult education programs are established to advance or increase knowledge level, competence, or skills, and the individual participants are the main beneficiaries. Human resource development programs have the same *purpose*. They also share with adult education the five components of program and curriculum design: (1) identification of need and knowledge through assessments, (2) program design and development, (3) sequencing of programs, (4) presentation of material or concepts, and (5) program and learning evaluation (see Figure 1.6). However, HRD programs are established primarily for the benefit of the organizations that sponsor and support them, rather than the individual participants. This is a simple and often overlooked difference, but it is the major reason for the separation—both attitudinal and physical—between the two fields, and its emphasis has meant the neglect of an obvious and major similarity: Adult educators and HRD practitioners are all in the business of advancing the skills and increasing the knowledge and improving the behavior of *adults,* whoever the intended beneficiary might be. Because all too often the focus is on the differences, many HRD practitioners know very little about adult learning theory and the other theories of the adult education field. Some lack a fundamental knowledge and understanding of the characteristics of adult learners and of the techniques of program and curriculum design that foster change and improvement of performance. They do not fully appreciate the special classroom methodologies they should use when they are working with adult learners (Gilley, 1987).

THE HUMAN RESOURCE WHEEL

In 1983 the American Society for Training and Development (ASTD) completed a study entitled "Model for Excellence." It is commonly referred to as the McLagan Study, for Patricia McLagan who was the project manager. In an

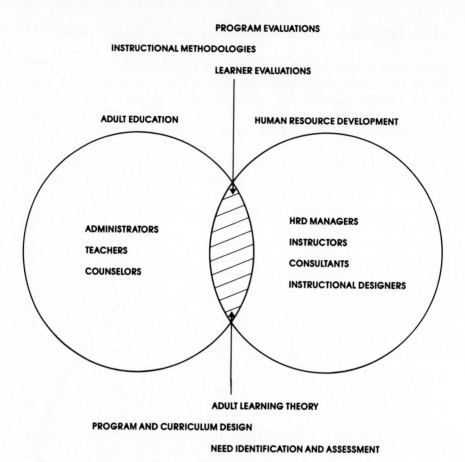

Figure 1.6   Relationship between HRD and adult education

attempt to better define and understand the field of human resources, the study developed the Human Resource Wheel. At that time nine separate but related areas were identified. Each represented a special area of the whole field of human resources.

1. Training and Development
2. Organizational Development
3. Organizational/Job Design
4. Human Resource Planning
5. Selection & Staffing
6. Personnel Research and Information Systems
7. Compensation/Benefits
8. Employee Assistance
9. Union/Labor Relations

Then, in the summer of 1987, the ASTD Competency and Standards Task Force, again under the direction of Patricia McLagan, began to reexamine the Human Resource Wheel as well as the remainder of the study. It was the recommendation of the task force members to add Career Development to the wheel and change the name of Personnel Research & Information Systems to Human Resources Information Systems. Another major recommendation was to separate the wheel into two primary areas of focus. One, the field of Human Resource Development (HRD), would consist of Training & Development, Career Development, and Organizational Development. The remaining seven would comprise the other, the field of Human Resource Management (HRM) (see Figure 1.7). HRD would represent the learning and development orientation of both the individual and the organization. HRM would represent the selection, management, planning, forecasting, compensation, and staffing of vital human resources within the organization.

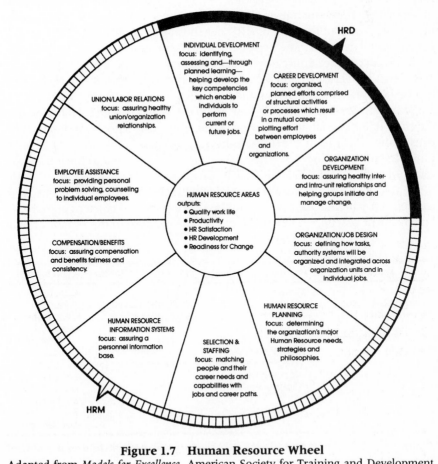

Figure 1.7   Human Resource Wheel
Adapted from *Models for Excellence,* American Society for Training and Development. Reprinted by permission. All rights reserved.

ROLES IN HRD

Another outcome of the Model for Excellence Study was the identification of roles in Training and Development. Training and Development, according to the study, includes people who perform a mix of roles. Fifteen roles emerged, after several rounds of reviews and questionnaires completed by experts in and around the field.

It is important to remember that the earlier 1983 ASTD study focused upon Training and Development. It did not attempt to describe the roles unique to the field of HRD. This is often overlooked by many practitioners, academics, and students. In fact, many practitioners mistakenly refer to the study as an HRD competency study rather than a Training and Development competency study. It is essential that these groups understand the difference in focus between HRD and Training and Development. HRD includes individual, career, and organizational development, while Training and Development means simply individual development. This may appear to be a minor point, but advancement of the field of HRD depends upon a clear understanding of the terms that describe these two disciplines. As mentioned above, in 1988, the Model for Excellence Study (known as the Competency and Standards Study, 1989) was expanded to include career development. Thus, it is now considered to be an HRD competency study.

For the purposes of this book, four broad categories will be used to describe the roles in HRD: managers, learning specialists, instructional designers, and consultants. Each of the 15 roles from the McLagan Study are incorporated under them (see Figure 1.8). The relationship of the 15 roles to the four broad categories will be explained in detail in Chapters 5 through 8.

The role of *manager* of an HRD department consists of four separate but overlapping components. Each is vital to the development of efficient and proper management practices. They include: (1) management of the organizational

Manager	Learning Specialist	Instructional Designer	Consultant
-Evaluator	-Evaluator	-Evaluator	-Evaluator
-Manager of Training & Development	-Group Facilitator	-Instructional Writer	-Group Facilitator
-Marketer	-Instruction Writer	-Media Specialist	-Industrial Development Counselor
-Program Administrator	-Instructor	-Need Analyst	
-Strategist	-Media Specialist	-Program Designer	-Instructor
	-Need Analyst	-Task Analyst	-Marketer
	-Program Designer	-Theoretician	-Need Analyst
	-Task Analyst		-Strategist
	-Transfer Agent		-Task Analyst
			-Transfer Agent

Figure 1.8   HRD Roles and subroles (including those identified in the Model for Excellence)

learning system; (2) operational management responsible for the planning, organizing, staffing, controlling, and coordinating of the HRD department; (3) strategist responsible for long-term planning and integrating of HRD into the organization; and (4) marketing specialist responsible for the advancement of HRD within the organization. (See Chapter 5.)

Learning specialists (instructors) are responsible for presenting the information that is associated with learning programs and training activities. At the same time they must identify learning needs and develop appropriate activities and programs to address those needs. Finally, they must be able to evaluate the effectiveness of the programs and activities and determine their effects on the organization and learners. (See Chapter 6.)

The *instructional designer* will design, develop, and evaluate the learning programs and training activities but will seldom implement them. This separates this role from that of the learning specialist who develops but also implements such programs. Instructional designers are generally employed full-time by large organizations that can afford such specialization. They are often the organization's media specialist, instructional writer, task analyst, and evaluator. (See Chapter 7.)

The role of *consultant* in HRD is one of the most complex and difficult. Consultants range from technical experts for instruction and program design to facilitators who solve problems to bring about change. Consultants may be internal or external to the organization. A variety of factors usually determine the appropriate selection of a consultant (see Chapter 8).

Regardless of whether the tasks in HRD are divided fifteen ways or four, we need to look at them in terms of the four broad categories within the field of HRD. This way we pinpoint the persons who are to develop learning activities that bring about performance improvement and increased organizational efficiency. They, in turn, can better focus upon the essential roles unique to their area. Moreover, once their roles are clearly delineated, organizations can create professional development programs for them, which will result in enhanced competencies and skills for each role. This type of self-improvement and growth can only increase the professionalism of the individual HRD practitioner and enhance the field of HRD in general (see Chapter 13).

COMPETENCIES IN HRD

Another important output of the 1983 McLagan Study was the identification of 31 competencies necessary for excellent performance in the Training & Development field (see Figure 14.3, p.321). Most of these skills and competencies are required in developing learning activities and programs that center around individual and organizational needs and deficiencies. Five fundamental skill areas emerge from the list, each vital to HRD practitioners: (1) needs assessment, (2) program design, development, and evaluation (including individual evaluation), (3) marketing of HRD programs, (4) cost/benefit analysis, and (5) facilitation of learning. The first four will be examined in detail in Chapters 9 through 12; facilitation of learning is covered in Chapter 6.

NEEDS ASSESSMENT.

HRD practitioners must be proficient in designing and conducting needs assessments *prior* to designing and developing the learning programs and training activities. There are four reasons for this: (1) to identify specific problem areas in the organization; (2) to identify specific learning deficiencies to serve as the bases of programs and activities; (3) to determine the bases of future learner evaluations; and (4) to determine the costs and benefits of the programs and activities in order to get organizational support. (See Chapter 9.)

PROGRAM DESIGN, DEVELOPMENT, AND EVALUATION.

At the heart of all learning programs and training activities is their design, a blueprint from which to construct all learning in the organization. Without a properly designed program, learning will not be consistent, nor will desired results become evident. HRD practitioners wise enough to develop the competencies and skills they need will design and develop effective programs and activities and will be able to evaluate outcomes accurately. (See Chapter 10.)

MARKETING OF HRD PROGRAMS.

Many HRD programs are severely reduced during financially difficult periods. Often they are eliminated altogether. HRD practitioners should therefore develop a clear understanding of and appreciation for marketing. By doing so they can improve the overall image of the program, the field, and its practitioners and help position HRD as a serious and vital component of the organization's strategic future (see Chapter 11).

COST-BENEFIT ANALYSIS.

Cost-benefit analysis is often used as a means of justification or evidence of impact. It provides upper management with information they understand and moves the evaluation of HRD effectiveness from qualitative to quantitative. (See Chapter 12.)

FACILITATION OF LEARNING.

HRD practitioners need to develop teaching skills and an ability to facilitate learning in a variety of settings. They must also understand how adults learn and know how to evaluate learning and behavioral change. These competencies are essential to each of the four fundamental role categories in HRD; thus, this competency area is considered one of the most important in the field.

PROFESSIONAL IDENTITY

Another way of studying HRD is to look at how practitioners align themselves with the field. According to Nadler (1986), HRD practitioners can be viewed as (1) professionally identified, (2) organizationally identified, or (3) collaterally identified.

HRD practitioners who are *professionally identified* view HRD as their profession. Professionally identified HRD practitioners have been active participants for at least two years. They are also active in various professional societies. They often seek elected offices and pursue other ways of increasing their identification with the HRD field. Still another way of indicating an intention to remain and develop in the field is by enrolling in academic study. This trend is evident by the number of universities now offering degrees and/or programs in HRD. There were 100 in 1979; in 1987 there were over 250.

Organizationally identified HRD practitioners are those people who have been moved to the department from another unit in the organization. Organizations will often assign an employee not previously in HRD to the unit, but it is not their intent nor the employee's to remain in HRD permanently (as indicated in our example). In many cases, this type of assignment is viewed as "developmental"; an employee who performs well in the HRD unit will be considered ready for advancement to another assignment within the organization. In some situations professionally identified practitioners may resent this, since this type of individual lacks their professional dedication and interest in the HRD field. Actually this is a prime opportunity for professionally identified practitioners to help an organizationally identified practitioner to understand what HRD is and how it relates to performance improvement and organizational efficiency. Thus, the time an organizationally identified practitioner spends in the HRD unit should be viewed as a learning experience.

Collaterally identified employees are ones who do not actually work in the HRD unit yet have HRD (learning) responsibilities. Many line supervisors and managers, for example, are expected to improve employee performance using learning activities—usually on-the-job training (OJT) but often including developmental learning experiences to increase performance. Many times these individuals serve as subject matter experts, or even as internal consultants for the HRD unit. They also rely on the learning activities and programs provided by the HRD unit and thus represent a vital user group for the unit. Regardless of their indirect identification with HRD, these employees are performing an essential HRD activity and must be included in the organization's HRD formula.

Each organization must determine for itself the optimum mix of HRD practitioners, as well as their appropriate identification. The size, complexity, and evolving nature of the business, the importance and criticality of human resources to the efficiency of the organization, and the structure of the organization all help determine the ideal mix. Some organizations will view the whole HRD department as an excellent unit for developing vital skills necessary for executives. Others may believe that only the professionally identified HRD practitioners can serve their needs. Nonetheless, all three identifications are present in all organizations, and all have a need for the increased knowledge, skills, and competencies that can be developed through an effective HRD unit.

CONCLUSION

Most organizations that maintain HRD programs focus on individual development activities (training). However, an ever-increasing number of them view career and/or organizational development as an essential part of the mix. These three components are covered in Chapters 2, 3, and 4. The roles performed by HRD practitioners are examined in Chapters 5 through 8. Chapters 9 through 12 provide a comprehensive overview of the competencies (skill areas) needed to adequately develop learning activities that foster performance improvement. So that readers may fully appreciate and understand the evolutionary process and historical antecedents of HRD, an in-depth analysis of its empirical foundations is provided in Chapters 13 and 14. Finally, the human resource areas related to HRD are examined in Chapters 15 and 16.

CHAPTER 2

Individual Development

Objectives

After completing Chapter 2, readers should be able to

- identify the evolution of individual development.

- determine the responsibility for individual development.

- differentiate among the roles in individual development.

- identify and describe the competencies needed in individual development.

- differentiate among the different approaches to individual development.

- identify and describe the three domains that are applicable to individual development.

- list the implications of new approaches to individual development for HRD.

- identify, describe, and differentiate among the seven laws of individual development.

Individual development focuses on the importance of personal growth and development through learning programs and/or training activities. Employees are able to develop knowledge, competencies, skills, and appropriate behaviors for current jobs. Many refer to this process as "training." However, individual development is broader than that. It includes communication, interpersonal skills, and other areas of personal development in addition to training. Learning occurs in both formal and informal settings, while training usually occurs on the job. In addition, individual development activities include *all* types of learning programs and training activities. Training refers primarily to skill development. Another difference is that all employees, including executives and senior managers, can engage in individual development. Training, on the other hand, is viewed as being for new or less competent employees. Finally, the delivery systems in individual development include computer-based training, interactive video, instructor-led training, satellite programs, and individual self-directed learning as well as on-the-job training.

EVOLUTION OF INDIVIDUAL DEVELOPMENT

In the fifties there was a growing concern over the "little effect" formal training had in bringing about improvements in organizations. Many mistakenly viewed training as an activity directed at organizational development only. This idea was based on the "critical mass theory": Get enough people to take training courses and, surely, the organization will improve. Because this concept embraced the supply-side theory of organizational development, training became very costly. This idea also encouraged participation in programs that were not based on individual needs or specific organizational problems. Supervisors, managers, and employees alike soon lost their enthusiasm for organizational training programs.

During the sixties and seventies, however, a few training programs began to focus on individual needs and on the impact learning systems had on the organization. But they were the exception rather than the rule. As well, management was beginning to see the usefulness of behavioral objectives and evaluation schemes. During the late seventies and early eighties, those in the field began to turn their attention to the professional development of practitioners. Several studies emerged. The Pinto-Walker Study (Pinto & Walker, 1978) and the Model for Excellence Study (McLagan & Bedrick, 1983) provided guidance for the field. Their outcome, as well as that of other research conducted during this time, was the professionalization of practitioners and the development and establishment of professional standards for the field of HRD.

Now practitioners began to examine the purpose of their HRD learning programs and training activities and the basis for each. As a result, they understood that each program or activity must be based on the needs of the learners as well as on the needs of the organization. In addition, practitioners understood that, to address those needs, clearly stated learning objectives and activities must be developed. The final outcome was that today more and more practitioners focus their efforts on designing programs that are needs oriented, and that make a difference in the organization.

Individual development has evolved to include more than skill development. It now includes personal growth and development that one can apply to a current job. Programs are directed at all employee levels and utilize several different delivery systems. In addition, many organizations have developed self-improvement skills that not only are appropriate to employees' current jobs, but are transferable to a variety of job settings.

RESPONSIBILITY FOR INDIVIDUAL DEVELOPMENT

The purpose of individual development is to increase employee knowledge, skills, and competencies and/or to improve behaviors in current jobs while at the same time addressing the immediate need of the organization as well as that of the employee. Clearly, then, the responsibility for individual development would appear to be that of the supervisor. In many organizations, however, responsibility is delegated to the HRD learning specialist who is skilled in learning theory, program design, and delivery. This role confusion often creates conflict between the supervisor and the HRD practitioner, because the supervisor may not be given credit for the improved employee performance that results from learning. Moreover, supervisors are often held accountable if production declines or performance worsens. Supervisors need to be rewarded in some way for the improvement in their employees' performance. If they are not rewarded, they are often not supportive of individual development programs, nor the HRD practitioners who represent them.

There is another reason why HRD practitioners need to seek the support of supervisors: often performance improvement is not immediately evident. This is especially true in learning programs and training activities that are aimed at attitudinal change. In these programs results may not be apparent for several months. Supervisors may even discourage employees from attending learning programs and training activities, causing future barriers between HRD learning specialists and supervisors as well as negative perceptions of HRD itself. Responsibility for individual development should be a shared effort.

ROLES IN INDIVIDUAL DEVELOPMENT

HRD practitioners often perform several roles simultaneously. This is indeed the case when they focus on individual development activities. The roles that are often integrated are learning specialist, instructional designer, and consultant. The HRD manager is usually not involved in individual development. Because instruction is the principal focus, in individual development, the role of *learning specialist* is a critical one. This person will perform needs assessments, will develop instructional strategies, and will select appropriate methods of instruction. He or she will also deliver instruction and evaluate learning programs and training activities during individual development. Each task is equally important and should be treated accordingly by the learning specialist.

The *instructional designer* is responsible for designing, developing, and planning learning programs and training activities that improve performance and ultimately increase organizational efficiency. This role includes the development of evaluations that measure the results and/or impacts of learning. In career development (the subject of Chapter 3) the focus is on developmental activities; in organizational development (Chapter 4), on process. But in individual development it is the well-designed learning program or training activity that is the crucial factor. This, then, becomes the fundamental responsibility of the instructional designer.

It is important to remember that, while learning specialists also design and develop programs, they deliver the programs they create. This is not the case for instructional designers. They design the programs but others deliver them to the learner. In many cases, the learning program or training activity is presented through computer- or video-assisted instruction, rather than by the instructor. Either way, the instructional designer is not directly involved in the delivery of instruction.

In many cases, a *consultant* is hired to deliver learning programs and training activities to employees through workshops and training sessions. In some situations, consultants are used to provide on-the-job training in both formal and informal settings. In either case, they are viewed as vital to individual development. They may also perform many of the same activities as the learning specialist. Sometimes consultants are used to determine the most appropriate job design for employees. This is still a part of individual development because it is focused on the employee's current job and the knowledge, skills, and competencies needed to perform the job in the most efficient manner.

COMPETENCIES IN INDIVIDUAL DEVELOPMENT

Individual development activities also require HRD practitioners to possess competencies and skills in needs assessment, instruction, program design and development, and evaluation. In addition, HRD practitioners must possess an understanding of formal (structured) and informal (unstructured) on-the-job learning activities. Finally, a basic knowledge of self-directed and incidental learning is required. All of these competencies and skills are essential in developing effective, change-oriented learning programs and training activities.

NEEDS ASSESSMENT

Constructing questionnaires to determine training needs, identifying needs through interviews and formal discussions, and conducting analyses of job requirements should occur prior to developing programs and activities. In addition, HRD practitioners should assess job performance both before and after the programs and activities are carried out in order to measure the results or impacts of training and to determine to what extent training will affect future performance. Finally, HRD practitioners must evaluate the needs they identify as a way of determining program priorities. (For more on Needs Assessment, see Chapter 9.)

INSTRUCTION

Another primary activity of HRD practitioners during individual development is instruction. This, of course, means conducting the learning programs and training activities, but it also includes on-the-job training as well. On-the-job training activities can be informal (unstructured) or formal (structured). Informal ones are those conducted daily in organizations. A supervisor, manager, or HRD practitioner provides simple job-related information in a nonstructured, matter-of-fact manner. For example, a new employee in a fast-food restaurant is told how to greet customers by a supervisor as the two work together. The information shared is not a part of formal training required by the organization but is based on the insight and experience of the supervisor. It may or may not be shared with all employees because it is a spur-of-the-moment sharing activity. It is done as a way of helping the new employee learn the tricks of the trade. On the other hand, formal, structured, on-the-job training activities are offered to all employees equally in order to provide continuity among employees. These activities are designed to provide the correct or exact procedures for conducting a particular job. They are very detailed and require many hours to complete. They are considered structured because there is a proper order required, and they are often sequenced with other training activities. Such formal training should include learning objectives and activities designed to bring about appropriate behaviors, skills, or competencies. To provide realism they are often conducted at the work station or job site. This gives employees a chance to practice job skills and provides immediate feedback on performance.

As instructors, HRD practitioners must also train managers and supervisors in how to train others. This important function is often overlooked. However, its impact on the organization and the employees can be significant because more people get involved in the individual development function. Another function is the establishment and maintenance of a library of training resources and materials. Finally, HRD practitioners must be able to use various methods of instruction effectively. Ones that appear to be appropriate are behavior modeling, simulation and games, demonstrations, discussion, lecture, and small group techniques (see Chapter 6).

In 1988 the International Board of Standards for Training, Performance and Instruction (IBSTPI) published a list of 14 competencies for instructors. Known as *The Standards,* the list provides instructors and their organizations with criteria for developing learning programs. They serve as a means for measuring the current skills level of instructors as well as learners' performance. They represent the most comprehensive listing of competencies yet published for instructors in HRD (see Table 2.1).

Table 2.1   IBSTPI's 14 Core Competencies for Instructors

1. Analyze course materials and learner information.
2. Assure preparation of the instructional site.
3. Establish and maintain instructor credibility.
4. Manage the learning environment.
5. Demonstrate effective communication skills.
6. Demonstrate effective presentation skills.
7. Demonstrate effective questioning skills and techniques.
8. Respond appropriately to learners' needs for clarification or feedback.
9. Provide reinforcement and motivational incentives.
10. Use instructional methods appropriately.
11. Use media effectively.
12. Evaluate learner performance.
13. Evaluate instruction.
14. Report evaluation information.

© *International Board of Standards for Training, Performance, and Instruction (1988). Reprinted from* Instructor Competencies: The Standards, Vol 1 *(1988) p. 6, by permission of International Board of Standards for Training, Performance, and Instruction.*

Program Design and Development

A third activity performed by HRD practitioners is that of program design and development. It is a multistep process that fosters the creation of learning programs and training activities that increase knowledge, skills, and competencies and improve behavior. The desired outcome is improved employee performance resulting in improved organizational performance. Competencies needed in this area are more fully covered in Chapter 10.

Several components of this process should be considered. Under *design* they include

1. Establishing learning objectives for the program.
2. Creating programs that satisfy specific needs.
3. Determining program content and training activities.
4. Determining program structure.
5. Determining appropriate sequences of programs and activities.
6. Deciding whether to use an existing program, to purchase an external program, or to create a new one to satisfy needs.
7. Identifying equipment and supplies required for programs and activities.

Under *development* they include

1. Evaluating alternative instructional methods.
2. Developing training materials.
3. Developing criteria for selecting progarm participants.
4. Developing exercises and tests for measurement.
5. Developing self-assessment tools.
6. Preparing scripts for films and videotapes.
7. Preparing artwork and copy slides and overheads.

EVALUATION

The final activity HRD practitioners must perform is evaluation, both program and learner. The ultimate purpose of evaluation is to determine the impact that a particular learning program or training activity has on the learner as well as on the organization. Evaluation includes the design and development of valid and reliable instruments and administration of achievement tests, aptitude tests, and questionnaires. HRD practitioners need to keep abreast of EEO/Affirmative Action and OSHA regulations related to individual development programs.

Learning evaluations, both pre-test and post-test, measure learning. Reaction evaluations are designed to determine participants' feelings and attitudes toward individual development activities. Behavior evaluations determine changes in employee behavior or performance action. A fourth type is called a result of impact evaluation. This is designed to determine the ultimate outcomes of learning or training on the individual and the impact on the organization.

Behavior and result evaluations are best used when the cost of training is high and there is a way to measure the change in behavior and/or quantify the results. Reaction and learning evaluations are best when training costs are low and it is important to determine the emotional responses of learners or if learning has occurred. Both are easy to develop and manage compared to the behavior and result evaluations, which are much more complicated and difficult to administer and manage. Each of the four types has its place in the evaluation-scheme, and it is the HRD practitioner's responsibility to decide when one would be more appropriate than another.

NEW APPROACHES TO INDIVIDUAL DEVELOPMENT

Much of individual development has been based on a behavioristic concept of human performance and learning (Marsick & Watkins, 1986). As a result, program design has focused on measurable, observable skills directed at performance improvement. This orientation stresses the importance of learning for the purpose of increased productivity and organizational efficiency. Marsick and Watkins argue that an uncritical acceptance of these models will insure that HRD practitioners are part of the problem rather than the solution. While performance improvement is an extremely important focus of learning systems, greater attention needs to be paid to informal modes of learning. Carnevale and Goldstein (1983) point out that a large percentage of learning is informal and occurs through consultation with peers, in small work groups, through coaching and mentoring relationships, and by means of networking opportunities.

Marsick and Watkins (1986) added that it is not enough for HRD practitioners to understand how to develop human resources to meet needs as defined by and for existing production systems. They must also assume the lead in creating learning environments in which employees can become active, empowered participants, both in satisfying their own needs and in improving the organization in the future. This approach requires a new understanding of both the workplace and the individual as well as organizational learning in the workplace. Morgan and Ramirez (1983) recommend that a concept known as *action learning* be adapted for today's organizational learning system. Action learning is concerned with empowering people to become critically conscious of their own values, assumptions, actions, beliefs, and attitudes through self-analysis and examination. The goal of this approach is to help people become active participants in the creation of their reality. Thus, there is a consistency between who they are and the real world in which they operate.

According to Marsick and Watkins (1986), organizations must also be willing to shift their orientations in order to adjust to ever-changing realities. To accommodate this shift, organizations must be willing to provide environments that foster teamwork rather than competition. They must be willing to focus on mutual shared responsibilities instead of relying on the traditional hierarchical structure so common today. Also, organizational leaders need to embrace multiple views of reality rather than a single corporate view. This will encourage greater cooperation among employees as well as loyalty. These shifts provide a climate for organizational change and increased employee participation.

LEARNING IN THE WORKPLACE

According to Mezirow (1985), there are three domains of learning that are applicable to learning in the workplace: (1) instrumental learning, (2) dialogic learning, and (3) self-reflective learning. Each is essential in the enhancement of human performance and potential.

Instrumental learning is what commonly takes place when people learn how to do their job better. Knowles (1986) referred to this as "training," but it is best described as on-the-job training of an informal nature. In this type of learning, people identify a problem, formulate a course of action, try it out, observe the effects, and assess the results. Learning is generally prescriptive.

Dialogic learning takes place in the work setting when employees learn about the culture of the organization: its taboos, unwritten rules, myths, heroes, and heroines (cited in Marsick and Watkins, 1986). It is also dialogic learning when employees learn to interpret policies, procedures, goals, and objectives within the specific meaning framework of the organization and the people with whom one works. The purpose of this kind of learning is increased understanding, the sharing of meaning, not problem solving in the conventional sense. This type of learning best identifies with individual development.

Self-reflective learning is directed at personal change. Often undervalued and unrecognized in favor of demonstrated performance, self-reflective learning is central to one's ability or motivation to learn about the organization or the job. This type of learning takes on additional salience in managerial development, since many of the abilities needed by middle and higher level managers are moderated by a manager's view of the world and his or her place in it.

Self-reflective learning takes place through a process Mezirow (1981) identified as "perspective transformation." Individuals reconstitute the meaning perspective by which they order their understanding of themselves and their world. This enables them to obtain further insight into their own values and belief systems, as well as achieve greater self-assurance and self-esteem. Learners better understand themselves and their role within the organization.

The introspection process just described is often referred to as *critical reflectivity*. It is essential to both dialogic and self-reflective learning. It can also be important to instrumental learning, although it is not often encouraged in current learning models. The notion of critical reflectivity can expand HRD practitioners' ways of understanding and designing learning programs and training activities without rejecting the need for appropriate skill training to meet instrumental learning needs. Figure 2.1, a model for learning in the workplace, takes into account each of the three types of learning: instrumental, dialogic, and self-reflective. The model provides suggestions as to their roles in learning systems (cited in Marsick and Watkins, 1986).

IMPLICATIONS OF NEW APPROACHES FOR HRD

Three fundamental implications for HRD result from the adoption of new approaches of learning systems. First, HRD programs and organizational learning environments should not be confined to or based on a single learning approach (behaviorism). Rather, an eclectic approach enables a variety of situations and circumstances to be accounted for and adjusted to.

Learning the Job: Productivity
Learning the Organization:
  A. Commitment, job satisfaction
  B. Team relationships, including networking, coaching, mentoring, role modeling, power and politics, status hierarchy
  C. Philosophy and goals of the organization, roles, rules and how they are interpreted, negotiated, and modified in specific situations

Learning about Oneself in the Workplace:
  A. Confidence building or undermining
  B. Competence building or undermining
  C. Identification with the organization
  D. Dealing with authority
  E. Coping with unfair treatment, rejection, ambiguity, failure, or competition
  F. Coping with personal tragedy
  G. Progress within the organization
  H. Changes in values, belief system, or self-concept
  I. Dealing with discrepancies between personal values and those of the organization
  J. Changes in orientation toward the job, the organization, or career or role

---

Figure 2.1   A model for learning in the workplace
Model developed by Mezirow, Marsick, and Brookfield, 1986.

The second implication is that individual learning cannot be examined in isolation from group and organizational learning. Finally, HRD practitioners must develop new approaches to designing learning programs and training activities in order to capitalize on changes that enforce and include emerging orientations for work and learning (Marsick & Watkins, 1986).

FROM INDIVIDUAL TO ORGANIZATIONAL LEARNING

To allow for self-reflective learning, the culture of the organization must be transformed. Argyris (1982) implies that a self-reflective learning system requires that the organization allow individuals to publicly express vulnerability, make what are considered "mistakes by peers," and take risks in exploring themselves as they confront difficult, unworkable, and ambiguous problem situations. He believes that organizational change is thus inevitable, and lists the attributes organizations need to achieve a new competence:

1. A capacity to reaffirm the organization as a learning system by such things as learning new roles, embracing error, acknowledging uncertainty, and spanning information boundaries.

2. A capacity to learn new interpersonal skills including active communications, to encourage open communication, and to use intuition and feelings as valued information.

3. The creation of an effective corporate climate.

4. The establishment of an environment that enables and empowers individuals to be responsible, productive, and creative.

Argyris concludes by saying that organizations face unprecedented and unavoidable uncertainty. Management responses to uncertainty require a new organizational culture that performs like a learning system (cited in Marsick & Watkins, 1986).

THE SEVEN LAWS OF INDIVIDUAL DEVELOPMENT

Individual development has laws as final as the physical laws of growing organisms. Such laws are a process in which definite forces produce definite results. Individual development, in the simplest sense, occurs through communication of experience. Experience may consist of facts, truths, and ideas or may be taught by the use of words or by signs, objects, actions, or example. Whatever the substance, the mode, or the aim of the learning program or training activity, the act itself, fundamentally considered, is always substantially the same. It is a communication of experience.

If any act of individual development is to be considered complete, it will be found to contain seven distinct elements or factors:

- Two persons—a learning specialist and a learner.
- Two mental factors—a common language or medium of communication and a lesson, truth, or skill to be communicated.
- Three functional acts or processes—that of the learning specialist, that of the learner, and a final or finished process to evaluate and fix the result.

Each of these should be present, regardless of the length of the session. None of them can be omitted and no others need be added. They combine to make up the individual development-learning process. In order to make certain that these seven are properly blended, seven laws of individual development must be followed:

1. A learning specialist must know the program, lesson, subject, skill, or truth to be taught.
2. A learner must attend with interest to the program, lesson, or subject.
3. The language used as a medium between the learning specialist and the learner must be common to both.
4. The information, truth, or skill to be mastered must be explicable in terms of information or truths already known by the learner—the unknown must be explained by means of the known.
5. The teaching process must be arousing, using the learner's mind to grasp the desired thought or to master the desired skill.
6. The learning process must turn one's own understanding of a new idea or truth into an overt habit that demonstrates the new awareness.
7. The evidence of individual development must be reflected through a reviewing, rethinking, reproduction, and applying of the material, information, truth, or skill that has been communicated. (Adapted from *The Seven Laws of Teaching* by John Milton Gregory, 1978 [first published in 1884].)

If each of these laws is present, the process of individual development will be complete. Absence of any one of them will result in failure to learn.

1. THE LAW OF THE LEARNING SPECIALIST

Simply stated, the law of the learning specialist is "what the learning specialist knows, he or she must teach." This seems too obvious even to consider, yet many violate it. The word "knowledge" stands central to this law. Knowledge is the material with which the learning specialist works. Without it there is no learning. The uninformed learning specialist and his student is like the blind leading the blind with only an empty lamp to light the way.

But the law of the learning specialist goes deeper still. Truth must be clearly understood before it can be vividly felt. A learning specialist who only half knows the subject is lifeless; one who fully understands its truths will be fired with enthusiasm. The latter unconsciously inspires the learner and instills questions and interest. This is often referred to as a "passion" for the subject, which can be very contagious.

A learning specialist's ready and evident knowledge helps give the learner needed confidence. In the same way, a well-prepared learning specialist awakens in his or her learners the active desire to study further. Thus, it is not enough to possess great knowledge. One must also have the ability to inspire learners with a love of learning. Only then will the learner become independent and truly self-directed.

RULES FOR THE LEARNING SPECIALIST

Several rules should be followed to insure that this law is not violated. Each will help the learning specialist to master the art of instruction and foster interest and desire on the part of the learners.

First, prepare each lesson by fresh study and review. This sharpens one's understanding and deepens one's awareness. It also provides you with a fresh start for each session or workshop. Unwarranted biases and misconceptions toward the learners will be forestalled. Remember, only fresh conceptions inspire learners to their best efforts.

Second, illustrate new ideas, concepts, truths, and facts in terms of the everyday experiences of the learners. In other words, provide a familiar frame of reference by presenting new information in terms and symbols the learner understands. This communicates a sensitivity to where the learner is. An appreciation for the knowledge and skills the learner already possesses reflects a respect both for the learner and for the contribution the learner can make to the learning situation. Active participation and involvement will result. To do this, the learning specialist must study the material until it is completely understood.

Third, discover the "natural order" of material or information to be presented. In every program or activity there is a natural path from the simplest ideas and steps to the more complex. Material must be presented in this fashion in order to insure understanding.

Fourth, whenever possible relate the material to the lives of the learners. This will foster involvement and help learners identify with the concepts and truths being taught. This is especially true with human relations skills and communication training as well as other interpersonal skills training. The practical value of the material, concepts, and truths lies in the ability of a learning specialist to foster such a relationship.

Fifth, set aside a definite time for study for each session or lesson, in advance of the instruction. This will help you gather fresh insights, interest, and illustrations prior to the actual performance. It is often helpful to develop a plan of study, but never hesitate—when necessary—to study beyond the plan. Answering the "what," "how," "who," and "why" of a lesson is a recommended outline to follow.

Sixth, learning specialists should not limit themselves to the training aids at hand. It is important to use whatever is necessary until real understanding is accomplished. In fact, it is a good idea to prepare several additional training aids, even if they are not used. Proper preparation will prevent misunderstandings and misapplication of concepts, truths, ideas, competencies, and skills.

Seventh, it is important to remember that complete mastery of just a few ideas is better than an ineffective smattering of many. Learn to focus on the central ideas and concepts and develop strategies to present them. The "All-American" presentation is not necessary for meaningful learning to take place.

Finally, learning specialists should not deny themselves the help of some good books on the subject of the lesson. A multitude of opinions and beliefs will aid in the shaping of a presentation. It may be necessary to buy, borrow, or beg such materials, but they are essential to well-developed and properly designed learning programs and training activities. In their absence, write down your thoughts on the lesson. Expressing ideas this way often helps expand one's thinking and clears up areas of confusion and uncertainty.

VIOLATIONS AND MISTAKES

Discussion of this law would be incomplete without mention of some frequent violations. The very best learning specialists may spoil their most careful and detailed work by thoughtless blunders. Being aware of some common violations and mistakes will help you minimize errors and maintain your credibility. They include the following:

- The very ignorance of the learners regarding the topic or lesson may tempt the learning specialist to neglect careful preparation and study.

- Many learning specialists maintain that it is the learners' responsibility, not theirs, to study. This type of indifference and lack of preparation will discourage serious study on the part of the learners, which seriously hampers learning.

- Many learning specialists who have not mastered the material conclude that they can make it through the session with random talk and an occasional story. Many even fill the time with unrelated exercises or videotapes and films that are not closely related to the learning objectives.

- Many learning specialists attempt to hide their lack of knowledge or preparation by presenting an array of high-sounding phrases that are beyond the comprehension of the learners. Others claim they possess deep insights through extensive study and research but lack the time to properly prepare for the session and are unable to provide it for the learners.

These are a sample of a few learning specialists who fail to prepare and who lack knowledge. Many of them also lack the power and enthusiasm necessary to produce the desired results in the learners.

2. THE LAW OF THE LEARNER

Attention means the direction of the mind upon some object (Gregory, 1978). It may be external, as when one watches carefully the operation of a machine or assembly procedures; or it may be internal, as when one reflects on the meaning of some idea or recalls some past experience. There are three types of attention that are present in learning situations: (1) passive attention, (2) active attention, and (3) secondary passive attention. Each is important from the point of view of teaching and learning (Gregory, 1978).

Passive attention is the primitive, instinctive, basic type of attention. The learner simply follows the behest of the strongest stimulus. It involves no effort of will, because the individual is letting the forces around him control the cognitive function.

Active attention, a distinctively human type of attention, requires people to separate stimuli and consciously select the one that is appropriate. The characteristics of the human mind can control stimuli rather than be controlled by them. People can look beyond the immediate environment into the future. The learner is an active participant in this process.

Secondary passive attention is similar to passive attention in that the subject or object is so attractive and interesting in and of itself that it demands little or no effort to study it. However, it is different from passive attention because the person is focused upon the material and is persistent in his or her efforts to understand and comprehend the concepts, ideas, facts, and truths. Generally speaking, we learn best and most easily when we are absorbed in our work. Under this condition, learning is so fascinating that it simply carries us along with it.

It is obvious that the attention most desirable to cultivate is the secondary passive type. It results in pleasant and effective study on the part of the learner and improves the probability that learning will occur. The implication is that materials must be presented in such a way as to motivate interest. Learners must work with a fixed purpose; in other words, they must think. Learning specialists and training materials may be full of vital information, but learners will get from them only as much as their power of attention enables them to. This requires secondary passive attention, which enables people to work with maximum efficiency.

There are two primary hindrances to attention: *apathy* and *distraction*. Each of these must be addressed by learning specialists in order to minimize their effects. Apathy refers to the lack of desire to study a topic, perhaps because of a bad learning experience in the past or a fear of one's abilities. Advanced math and statistics are examples. Distraction is when one's attention is divided among a variety of stimuli. Under this condition the responsibility of the learning specialist is to isolate the negative or unproductive stimuli and neutralize them.

RULES FOR THE LEARNING SPECIALIST

Several rules should be followed:

1. Never begin a training session until the attention (active) of the learners has been secured.
2. Pause whenever attention is interrupted or lost; wait until it is completely regained before you begin again.
3. Never completely exhaust the attention of the learners.
4. Adapt the length of the exercise to the ages and physical conditions of the learners.
5. Appeal whenever possible to the personal interests of the learners.
6. Use a variety of instructional methods to arouse the attention of the learners.
7. Identify sources of distraction and reduce them to a minimum.
8. Make the presentation as attractive as possible, using illustrations, graphics, and training aids.
9. Use third-party stories, dialogue, and analogies whenever possible to illustrate the point.
10. Maintain and exhibit a genuine interest in the subject or topic through fresh study and review.
11. Prepare before the session several thought-provoking questions.
12. Maintain appropriate eye contact with the learners and use appropriate voice inflection and body language (Adapted from Gregory, 1978).

VIOLATIONS AND MISTAKES

Many learning specialists violate the law of the learner by failing to gain their attention before they begin the session. They might as well start before the learners enter the room, or continue after they leave. Some continue after the learner's power of attention has been exhausted and when fatigue has set in. Others kill the power of attention by failing to utilize fresh inquiries or new ideas and illustrations. Some even enter the learning environment with old notes and materials that immediately turn off the learners. Perhaps the worst mistake is to make little or no attempt to discover the interests, tastes, and experiences of the learners, presenting material learners already understand. Boredom sets in and a negative attitude toward the specialist—and toward learning—develops.

3. THE LAW OF THE LANGUAGE

Language has been called the vehicle of thought. It is made up of words and symbols whose meaning is based upon common experiences and understandings. Instruction will not be complete unless it is done in a plain, intelligent language common to the learners. This means that expression of thought should be in their language, not mere repetition of ready-made definitions of someone else. In training this is extremely important, because much of the information is highly technical and is a language unto itself. Learning specialists who must present technical material should know technical language.

RULES FOR THE LEARNING SPECIALIST

Several rules for this law should also be followed by the learning specialist:

1. Use the simplest and fewest words that will express the desired meaning.
2. Study carefully and constantly the language of the learners.
3. Test the learners' understanding of the words frequently to make certain that they are not being incorrectly used.
4. Use short sentences of the simplest construction.
5. Use illustrations to help the learners understand the meaning of words and symbols.
6. If the learners fail to understand, repeat the idea or thought in other language, or use an analogy or example.
7. Identify the terms, symbols, and language that the learners are familiar with prior to the session and adjust the program accordingly.
8. Encourage the learners to communicate during the program. This will help you determine the level of learner understanding as well as identify specific language or words used (Adapted from Gregory, 1978).

VIOLATIONS AND MISTAKES

Many learning specialists have no proper appreciation of the wonderful character and complexity of language. They simply take language for granted. They are also fooled by learners who look interested and perceive that they thoroughly understand, when in reality they do not. The misuse of language is another common violation. Many learning specialists never attempt to determine if they are using the words or symbols correctly.

Many learners do not ask for explanations or examples, and learning specialists assume that they understand the information or ideas. Because learners have not asked any questions is not a signal to move forward. It could indicate that learners are seriously confused. Learning specialists should test for understanding prior to moving forward.

Many learners are entertained by the manner of the learning specialist and so fail to hear the words spoken. They are passively attentive and appear to be mentally involved; however, they are not. It is common to look directly at an instructor yet be somewhere else mentally. There may be a more pressing matter at home or at work that is occupying one's attention. It is the learning specialist's responsibility to determine if this is the case and to find ways to minimize the situation.

4. THE LAW OF THE LESSON

All learning programs and training activities must begin somewhere. If the subject is completely new, then identify a point at which to begin, one that in some way likens the new material to something the learner knows. This could be a familiar experience, a related topic, a procedure, or a process. Or it could be an example or story that provides a common framework on which to build the program (Gregory, 1978).

All learning programs and training activities should be based on an identified set of learning objectives. These objectives should be the criteria for the selection and development of all learning experiences. Once determined, the objectives and experiences should be prioritized and sequenced in an appropriate order to properly link one fact or concept to another, remembering that simple and concrete ideas lead naturally to general and abstract ideas. Each step must be fully mastered before the next is taken. If not, the learners may find themselves proceeding into unknown areas without proper preparation.

Presentation, then, means the sharing of information that links the known to the unknown. Unless this approach is followed, communication between the learning specialist and the learner is impossible.

RULES FOR THE LEARNING SPECIALIST

Again there are several rules that apply to this law that help foster its application.

1. Discover what the learners know of the subject, topic, and material; this is the starting point.
2. Utilize the learners' knowledge and experience.

3. Relate every lesson—as much as possible—to former lessons as well as to the experiences of the learners.

4. Arrange the presentation so that each step of the lesson leads easily and naturally to the next.

5. Use illustrations that the learners can identify with.

6. Encourage the learners to make use of their own knowledge.

7. As much as possible, choose the problems that you assign to the learners from their own activities and interests.

8. Encourage the learners to find illustrations from their own experiences and to share them with fellow learners (Adapted from Gregory, 1978).

VIOLATIONS AND MISTAKES

It is not unusual for learning specialists to let learners participate in programs they are inadequately prepared for, by previous personal or academic experience. This can create a great deal of frustration and stress; it can also result in their failure to meet the learning objectives. More importantly, it can cause bad feelings toward the HRD program and its practitioners.

Too many times learning specialists fail to thoroughly familiarize the learners with elementary facts and definitions. They incorrectly assume a certain level of knowledge or skill, which, for many programs and courses, results in an inappropriate point of entry.

Another common error is the failure to relate the present material to previous material. Learners cannot make the connection between different thoughts, ideas, and/or concepts. They often view various sections of present material as separate because there is no attempt to integrate them. In addition, present material is often not connected to material yet to come. This creates problems for future applications and relationships.

Many learning specialists fail to motivate learners. By not fostering an attitude of discovery they create a situation in which learners are not prepared for secondary passive attention and so miss many opportunities to grow and develop. Or they may present too much material, which exceeds the learners' ability and power to understand and apply the concepts or information. They also provide too little time for practice and mastery of skills or competencies.

In many cases, every step of a process, skill, or procedure is not always thoroughly understood before the next is attempted. Thus, the new process, skill, or procedure is being used or applied prior to mastery of the previous process, skill, or procedure, which results in inadequate understanding and development.

5. THE LAW OF THE TEACHING PROCESS

It is often believed that learning cannot take place without a teacher or learning specialist. This is of course not the case. People can learn without a teacher or learning specialist. In fact, true teaching is not teaching that "gives knowledge" but teaching that stimulates learners to gain knowledge for themselves. In other words, one might say that those who teach best are those who teach least (Gregory, 1978).

Since the primary aim of learning is to acquire knowledge, or to develop skills and competencies or to change behaviors or all three, it could be said that learners who are taught without having to do any studying for themselves are like those who are fed without being given any exercise: they will lose both their appetite and their strength (Gregory, 1978). Thus, the responsibility for learning should shift from the learning specialist to the learner, if growth and development are to occur.

Learning specialists must, however, present the material or information in such a manner that it motivates the learners to become absorbed by it. Anything less will result in inadequate preparation, development, and growth. Learning specialists must stimulate the minds of the learners and challenge their abilities and skills. Only then can a learner become truly self-directed.

RULES FOR THE LEARNING SPECIALIST

Like the other laws, this one also suggests some practical rules for instruction.

1. Adapt lessons, materials, and assignments to the ages, experience, preparation, and skills of the learners.

2. Consider carefully the subject, material, and/or lesson to be presented, and identify its points of contact with the lives, interests, and experiences of the learners.

3. Excite the learners' interest in the subject, lesson, and/or material through statement of inquiry or thought-provoking questions.

4. Consider it a principal responsibility to awaken the minds of the learners and to not rest until each learner demonstrates his or her mental activity and involvement.

5. Place yourself frequently in the position of the learners and join in their search for additional information and knowledge.

6. Repress impatience with a learner's inability to grasp concepts and ideas or to master skills.

7. Allow learners time to sort out the material and gain understanding.

8. Repress the desire to tell all you know or think about the subject, lesson, or topic.

9. Encourage the learners to ask questions when they are confused or puzzled.

10. Allow learners the time to answer questions or complete exercises on their own.

11. Be dedicated to beginning each session in a manner that stirs interests and activity (Adapted from Gregory, 1978).

Violations and Mistakes

Many learning specialists neglect these rules, which often kills the learners' interest and enthusiasm for learning. They then wonder why the learners are not excited and motivated to learn. Some learning specialists have an inappropriate and impatient attitude toward the learner regarding their abilities, skills, and level of comprehension. Others criticize the learners' lack of memory. Still others have an overdemanding attitude toward learners.

The result of impatient instruction is that learners only comprehend enough to be able to recite in a prompt fashion, instead of thoroughly learning and understanding the material. Thus, true understanding is negated and never obtained.

6. THE LAW OF THE LEARNING PROCESS

It should be pointed out that learning is not memorization and repetition of the words and ideas of the instructor (Gregory, 1978). The learners should strive for a deep understanding of the memorized words. But they should also be able to apply the information, concept, idea, or skill learned. In fact, the learning process is not complete until this last stage has been reached. Prior steps aid in illuminating learners' understanding as they progress in their work, but the law of the learning process demands this final stage. Both learning specialist and learners must constantly direct their efforts to this purpose.

Rules for the Learning Specialist

The rules that follow from this law are useful for the learners as well as the learning specialist.

1. Help the learners form a clear idea of the work to be done.
2. Ask the learners to express in words or in writing the meaning of the session or lesson as they understand it.
3. Answer the questions of the learners in a nonthreatening manner.
4. Strive to make the learners self-directed and independent investigators.
5. Seek constantly to develop in learners a profound regard for truth as something noble and enduring (Gregory, 1978).

Violations and Mistakes

The most common violations and mistakes occur during this step. They are perhaps the most fatal of all, since each results in the loss of learning. The first mistake is the failure of the learning specialist to insist on original thinking by the learners. Second, practical applications are persistently neglected. Third, many learners are left in the dark because of a lack of well-thought-out instruction or directions. In many cases, learners fail to question the learning specialist or material; they blindly assume that they are correct and accurate. This can cause serious difficulties when learners attempt to apply inaccurate information on the job.

7. THE LAW OF REVIEW AND APPLICATION

This law seeks to insure that knowledge, skills, competencies, and behaviors are best developed when learners have the opportunity to review, rethink, reproduce, and apply each. Its purpose is to perfect, confirm, and render each ready and useful. Review, however, is more than repetition. A machine may repeat a process, but only an intelligent human being can review it. Repetition implies rethinking of an idea, concept, or truth for the purpose of deepening one's understanding. This includes new associations and conceptualizing.

A review is not a separate event added to the instructional process but rather an important part of the process itself. It is an essential condition of good instruction. Not to review is to leave the work half done. Any exercise that recalls material to be reviewed may serve as a review. One of the best and most practical forms of review is to pose some realistic problem or circumstance and then give learners the opportunity to apply the new information, knowledge, skill, competency, or behavior to the problem or circumstance. Such a contrived situation is safer and more secure than an actual situation on the job, and allows for mistakes that otherwise might cost the organization hundreds of dollars.

RULES FOR THE LEARNING SPECIALIST

Consider the following rules for this law.

1. Realize that reviews are a part of the instructional process.
2. Establish a set time for review.
3. Get into the habit of providing a review at the completion of each lesson as well as after each section or at the close of a topic or subject.
4. Integrate old material into new material.
5. Never omit a final review.
6. Seek comprehensive and complete groupings of material.
7. Identify as many applications as possible.
8. Demand that learners rethink material and information into a personal understanding and orientation (Adapted from Gregory, 1978).

VIOLATIONS AND MISTAKES

The most obvious violation of this law is to totally neglect the review process. This is a sign of a poor learning specialist. The second most common error is to conduct an inadequate review. This is often the result of an impatient or hurried learning specialist who is often more concerned with getting through the material than with enabling the learners to grow and develop.

Another mistake is to delay all reviews until the end of the program when most of the material or ideas have been largely forgotten. In this circumstance, the review is simply an example of poor relearning with little interest or value to the learners. A final mistake is to make the review merely a lifeless restatement of facts, concepts, ideas, and information provided earlier in the program.

CONCLUSION

The focus of individual development is acquiring knowledge, developing competencies and skills, and adopting behaviors that improve performance in current jobs. Other critical approaches should also be considered, such as reflection and incidental learning. These two mean that organizations undergo a radical transformation. In order for HRD practitioners to utilize individual development to its fullest capacity, seven laws should be followed and critical violations and mistakes avoided.

CHAPTER 3

Career Development

Objectives

After completing Chapter 3, readers should be able to

- identify the purposes of a career development program.

- identify six factors required to maintain a successful career development program.

- identify three planning processes related to career development and the responsibilities of the employee and the organization during each.

- identify the responsibilities of the employee and management related to a career development program.

- discuss the five-step implementation process of career development.

- identify and explain career development activities of an organization.

- identify and explain career development activities of the employee.

Many performance problems are career related; employees often feel trapped, stagnated, or overlooked in their present jobs or occupations. Many find little pleasure in them, which contributes to increased stress and lowered output. These workers do not work up to their full potential and often fail to meet organizational expectations. Either they have lost their occupational mission in life, or they have been unable to identify their vocational purpose.

To further complicate matters, many supervisors are reluctant to approach employees about performance problems. They hold their breath, look the other way, cross their fingers, and hope that somehow the situation will work itself out. But it is the supervisors who are still held accountable for their subordinates (Gilley and Moore, 1986).

OVERVIEW OF CAREER DEVELOPMENT

By providing a more systematic way to reduce performance problems for both the subordinate and the supervisor, career development programs have become vital to business and industry. According to Kaye (1984), career development is now an accepted HRD strategy among training and development administrators, personnel officers, and organizational consultants. It allows and encourages employees to examine future career paths, and its programs help them analyze their abilities and interests in order to better match their personal needs for growth and development with the needs of the organization. What is more, management, can increase productivity, improve employee attitudes toward work, and develop greater worker satisfaction through effective career development programs. In addition to reducing performance problems, the career development process can also promote more efficient allocation of human resources and greater loyalty among employees.

In sum, *career development* can be defined as an organized, planned effort comprised of structured activities or processes that result in a mutual career plotting effort between employees and the organization. Within this system, the employee is responsible for career planning and the organization is responsible for career management (Gutteridge & Otte, 1983).

Organizations have two primary motives for implementing career development programs: (1) to develop and promote employees from within and (2) to reduce turnover. Career development programs communicate strong employer interest, something employers want in order to maintain a positive recruiting image. Furthermore, a successful career development program is not viewed as a separate activity or entity but is integrated into the organization. There are six integrative activities that can be adopted by HRD practitioners: (1) forecasting future organizational needs, (2) utilizing performance appraisals, (3) job announcements and posting, (4) career pathing for employees, (5) training and development, and (6) the development of consistent compensation practices.

It should be pointed out that HRD practitioners cannot assist employees adequately unless the organization offers the right kinds of challenging career development activities (Cross, 1983). Top management must also develop an appropriate awareness and appreciation of career development. Otherwise, career development will continue to proceed in a piecemeal fashion.

An effective career development program will focus on long-term results, will account for the diversity of people, and will use methods other than the traditional classroom approach. Suggested alternatives include experience-based training, monitoring activities, self-directed learning projects, and involvement in professional organizations and associations. For best results, the HRD practitioner will have to identify the needs and career goals of the employees and then plan career development activities accordingly. To insure success, Hanson (1981) has identified several guidelines for HRD practitioners to follow:

1. Start small and design a specific program in response to a particular need.

2. Integrate the program into ongoing personal activities or programs.

3. Obtain top level management support.

4. Encourage time management and lobby for support.

5. Develop an evaluation process and communicate measured results.

6. Continue to explore alternatives and maintain flexibility.

In other words, career development should center around needs related to personal activities and interests, be flexible, develop appropriate evaluation procedures, and have the support of top management.

In career development, the employee is responsible for *career planning* and the organization, more specifically the HRD practitioner, is responsible for *career management*. These two separate but related processes combine to make up the organizational career development process. Figure 3.1 illustrates this interface. Career planning is a process of setting up employee career objectives and developing activities that will achieve them. Career management refers to specific human resource activities, such as job placement, performance appraisal, counseling, training, and education. All three processes make up a system of organizational career development that serves as a framework on which HRD practitioners can design future career development programs.

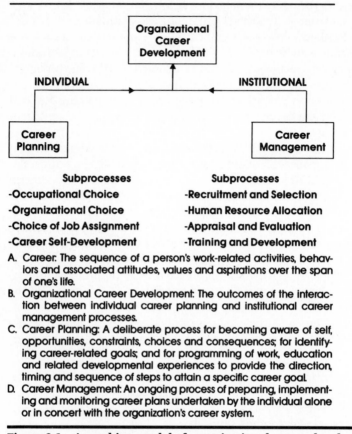

A. Career: The sequence of a person's work-related activities, behaviors and associated attitudes, values and aspirations over the span of one's life.
B. Organizational Career Development: The outcomes of the interaction between individual career planning and institutional career management processes.
C. Career Planning: A deliberate process for becoming aware of self, opportunities, constraints, choices and consequences; for identifying career-related goals; and for programming of work, education and related developmental experiences to provide the direction, timing and sequence of steps to attain a specific career goal.
D. Career Management: An ongoing process of preparing, implementing and monitoring career plans undertaken by the individual alone or in concert with the organization's career system.

Figure 3.1   A working model of organizational career development

Reprinted from Gutteridge, T. G. & Otte, F. L. (1983) Organizational Career Development: State of the Practice. *Washington, D.C.: ASTD Press. p. 7.*

From the point of view of the employee, career planning is also a personal process, with the following outcomes: (1) broad life planning, (2) developmental planning, and (3) performance planning (Walker, 1980; see Figure 3.2). In *broad life planning,* interests, abilities, experiences, aptitudes, and values are analyzed, resulting in improved self-concept and projected self as related to careers. The employee is primarily self-reliant; however, HRD practitioners can help formulate this process by providing employees with career information and by utilizing appropriate evaluation instruments and personality assessment tools.

Developmental planning focuses on a realistic evaluation of future career options and opportunities and the creation of activities that will prepare individuals for future jobs and future career decisions. There is a natural relationship here between the employee and the organization; both work collaboratively in the successful identification and realization of career development. At this

Planning Inputs	Input Sources Personal	Planning Results
Experience, education, strengths, aptitudes, abilities, interests, values, desires, etc.	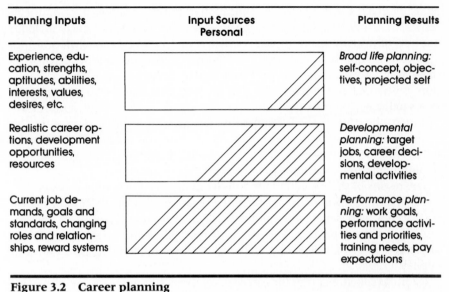	*Broad life planning:* self-concept, objectives, projected self
Realistic career options, development opportunities, resources		*Developmental planning:* target jobs, career decisions, developmental activities
Current job demands, goals and standards, changing roles and relationships, reward systems		*Performance planning:* work goals, performance activities and priorities, training needs, pay expectations

Figure 3.2   Career planning
Reprinted from J. Walker, Human Resource Planning, *New York: McGraw-Hill, 1980.*

point the HRD practitioner intervenes as change agent, actively designing development activities and providing necessary career information to help employees make career decisions.

Performance planning centers around the identification of specific job demand goals and priorities and the reward expectations of current job assignments. Specific training needs, performance activities, priorities, and explanations, as well as financial compensation, are identified, and the result is successful completion of stated objectives and goals. In this stage of career planning, the employee must rely primarily on the organization for effective performance planning, which becomes an HRD activity. But some HRD practitioners lack the skill, and employees as well as organizations must then assume responsibilities that are inappropriate. The result is inadequate long-range life planning and serious shortages of qualified human resources within the organization.

CAREER DEVELOPMENT AND ORGANIZATIONS

Career development programs vary in their purpose, approach, ideology, and philosophy. The attitude of the individual, the organization's commitment to career development, and different theoretical orientations contribute to this diversity.

According to Reynierse (1982), a marriage between the organization and the individual is essential in career development. He contends that organizations engage in developmental planning, the process of assessing appropriate goals, objectives, and the proper allocation of physical, financial, and human resources, while employees engage in career/life planning which includes analysis of personal goals, competencies, and a realistic evaluation of future opportunities. Both organizations and employees need to conduct three types of analyses: needs, skills, and potential. Needs analysis refers to the examination of personal and organizational needs. Skills analysis, on the other hand, refers to the evaluation of an employee's competencies while the organization examines the competencies required within each job classification as well as those needed throughout the organization. Potential analysis is conducted when both the employee and the organization project their future competency requirements and determine areas of deficiency or weaknesses.

The results of these evaluations will determine the "matching process" between the two principals. HRD practitioners can then blend career information (employee) with developmental plans (organizational) as a way of improving the matching process. This can also provide needed insights for future implementation of career development activities by both organization and employees.

It can be concluded that for career development programs to be successful the employees and organization must work together as a team. In addition, the HRD practitioner must be responsible for the organization and management of the program as well as the identification and development of the career development activities deemed appropriate. The HRD practitioner must be aware of the various career development theories available in order to establish a philosophical/theoretical orientation to career development. This will aid in the selection of career development activities as well as enable HRD practitioners to make generalizations and assumptions about career development. The HRD practitioner must also work as a mediator between the employee and the organization in the career development process. He or she should indoctrinate managers regarding the importance of career development while encouraging employees to become responsible for their careers. Other responsibilities include: establishing mentoring systems and career resource centers; designing career development workshops; becoming acquainted with job posting systems and career pathing programs; conducting employee interests, values, and competency analyses; utilizing performance appraisals as a learning and training tool; becoming involved with human resource planning and forecasting; and developing managers as career counselors. Each of these responsibilities can be carried out through career development activities, which we examine in detail in the next section.

CAREER DEVELOPMENT ACTIVITIES

Employees and organizations alike engage in essential career development activities to improve the effectiveness of career development. The amount of time spent and the degree of importance placed on these activities together enhance harmony between the employees and the organization. This harmony is known as the *area of career development congruence* (see Figure 3.3), and the goal of career development, for both employees and organizations, is to increase this area. This will result in improved human resources and therefore enhanced organizational efficiency. All of this can be accomplished through the effective identification and utilization of career development activities. Each of the activities engaged in by the organization and by the individual will be examined in the next two sections. This will provide insight into how they fit within the career development process. Following is a five-step approach to the utilization of career development by HRD practitioners.

THE ORGANIZATIONAL COMPONENT AND CAREER DEVELOPMENT ACTIVITIES

Organizations are accountable for the management of career development programs and the activities employees participate in. The integrative approach to career development includes the future forecasting of organization needs using performance appraisals and the development of career pathing for individuals.

The type of career development activities organizations choose to offer should be challenging, comprehensive, and flexible. They are an essential component in the HRD formula and can enhance the total HRD program.

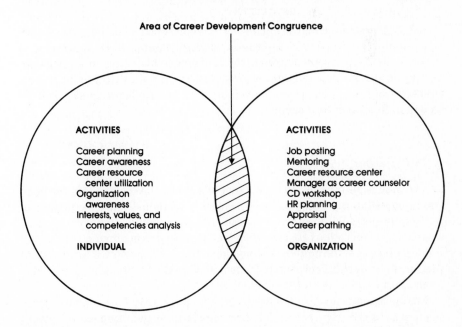

Figure 3.3 Individual/organizational career development relationship

Organizational activities designed to enhance career development include: (1) the establishment of a job posting system, (2) the development of mentoring activities, (3) the development of career resource centers, (4) the training of managers as career counselors, (5) the planning and implementing of career development workshops, (6) human resource planning and forecasting, (7) utilizing performance appraisals, and (8) developing career pathing programs.

According to Zenger (1981), the organization maintains several fundamental responsibilities regarding career development:

1. Agree that career pathing is a vital part of the organization.
2. Prepare career paths for employees.
3. Maintain an efficient, complete job posting system.
4. Train managers as career counselors.
5. Provide assessment testing.
6. Communicate the organization's philosophy.
7. Reward managers who develop people and establish mentoring programs.
8. Provide career workshops for employees to explore career development issues.
9. Establish a human resource forecasting system.
10. Develop an effective performance appraisal process.
11. Establish career resource centers.

The HRD practitioner is the organization's representative in the career development process; thus, the identification, implementation, and management of each of the eight career development activities is his or her responsibility. These persons should, therefore, actively participate in the career management functions of the organization, as well as help develop learning systems designed to foster behavior change.

JOB POSTING SYSTEM

Job posting is an organized process that allows employees to apply for open positions within the organization. They can respond to announcements and postings of positions and then be considered along with external candidates. Individual qualifications are considered, and employees are then screened. If it is determined that the employee is qualified, then an interview is arranged. At this point, he or she is measured against, or compared with, other applicants, in an effort to select the most qualified.

Such programs have been adopted widely, principally for nonmanagerial, salaried positions. One reason for their popularity is their implicit openness. All employees who consider themselves qualified can be considered for positions. Office and clerical personnel as well as administrative and technical positions utilize this system. Many organizations incorporate job posting systems as part of affirmative action programs.

An *employee request system* is a variation of the job posting approach. It allows employees to select a position or positions he or she is interested in and considered qualified for, regardless of whether or not a vacancy exists. The personnel office then reviews qualifications, experience, and the educational level of the employee to determine qualifications for the position requested. If qualified, and if no position is currently available, then the request is placed in an inventory as a target position for the employee. When a vacancy does occur, the employee is automatically considered a candidate. If not, the employee could qualify for specific training or continuing education in order to develop the skills, competencies, and/or knowledge needed in the future.

HRD practitioners should be aware of the types of positions that become available within the organization, even though job posting activities are often viewed as a function of the personnel department. They can then identify employment trends and anticipate future training needs. Second, being aware of the job posting system communicates to upper management a sincere interest in the organization. Third, HRD practitioners can then encourage employees to analyze position announcements and openings, communicating to them the interest of the HRD department in the advancement of their careers. This is the kind of positive feedback that will improve the image of the HRD department and help reposition it within the organization.

MENTORING SYSTEM

The primary purpose of a mentoring system is to introduce people to the inner network of the organization, which may assist them in their career advancement. Mentoring systems help clarify the ambiguous expectations of the organization, provide objective assessment of the strengths and weaknesses of new employees, and provide a sounding board for participants. Newcomers indicate they like mentoring programs because they reduce much of the initial entry shock and ambiguity in joining a new group. Organizational leaders and managers as well as HRD practitioners also like it because it allows them to observe mentors and new employees more closely. Mentors can develop talents and skills in human relations and upper management can observe which employees have the ability to grow within the organization. Moreover, mentoring serves to instill additional loyalties and commitment to the organization on the part of both the mentor and the employee.

Research conducted by Phillips-Jones (1983) revealed nine features critical to the success of a mentoring program: (1) top level management support, (2) integration of the mentoring program into the total career development program, (3) volunteer participation in the mentoring program, (4) keeping each phase or cycle of the program short, (5) careful selection of mentors and mentees, (6) provision of an orientation for participants, (7) allowance for flexibility, (8) preparation for challenges, and (9) guidance in monitoring system.

Mentoring programs can be very formal, which allows organizations to build strong dyadic relationships among employees. On the other hand, they can be very informal, designed to serve as an orientation to a new organization, environment, or culture. Regardless of the degree of formalization, this type of program should be based on the specialized needs of the organization and its employees. HRD practitioners should start small, making certain that positive results are accomplished initially.

The characteristics of a good mentor include personal qualities, position placement, and processing skills (Grote & Stine, 1980).

- Personal Qualities: A good mentor is perceived as open, perceptive, personally successful, possessing of outstanding expertise, and able to maintain good credibility.

- Position Placement: They maintain high status within the organization and have an appropriate network of contacts.

- Processing Skills: Good mentors should maintain a good self-concept and be open to disagreements and have good interpersonal skills. In addition, they should be able to encourage growth and risk taking.

The development and management of a mentoring system is again a responsibility of the HRD practitioner. First, mentors must be recruited, screened, and trained by the HRD practitioner. Perhaps the most important function that the latter performs in the mentoring process is the matching of mentors and mentored. A mismatch could result in turnover, or the retarded growth of the new employee. In addition, a bad experience for the mentor could result in his or her lack of interest in future relationships. It could also prevent other managers and supervisors from participation in future mentoring activities.

CAREER RESOURCE CENTER

Career resource centers have been multiplying in businesses and industries during the past decade. Mainly, the centers serve as a means for employees to obtain information regarding their careers. There are four groups within the organization that utilize career resource centers. The largest group are those who are focusing on degree-related educational activities including a full range of academic degrees: A.A., B.S., M.S., M.B.A., and Ph.D. In addition are those employees who are interested in noncredit courses and seminars as well as self-study courses designed to increase competency and knowledge. Employees engaged in training activities and education courses also take advantage of career resource centers. The second largest group of users seek information on career planning. This includes persons interested in developing job finding techniques and career opportunities within as well as outside the organization. Those interested in developing specialized skills or enhancing interpersonal relationships often want to develop additional understanding of human relations and supervision. They comprise the third group utilizing career resource centers. This group has increased during recent years due to the emphasis on personal development and advanced job efficiency. Managers and supervisors who want to improve their own skills make up the fourth group. Major concerns regarding motivation, productivity, human relations, communication, and listening skills are often areas of extreme interest for this group.

According to Kaye (1981), a career resource center returns the responsibility of career development to the employee. The center offers self-directed, self-paced learning, and provides resources without creating dependence on the organization. However, career development works only if employees accept responsibility for their own careers. One of the fundamental goals of career development is to help facilitate career decision making, which helps to develop career exploration and evaluation competencies. Career resource centers are viewed as a way of accomplishing this goal.

In research conducted by Moir (1981), the primary services provided at career resource centers are educational information (25 percent), career planning (20 percent), and personal growth (20 percent). Job-finding skills (10 percent) and management/supervision training (15 percent) were other services provided (see Figure 3.4). HRD practitioners should adjust career resource center material to accommodate these services.

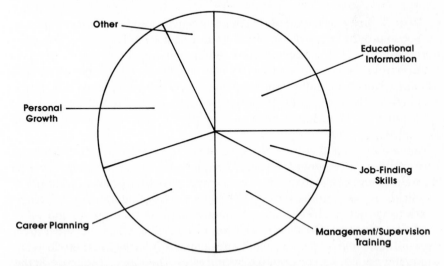

Figure 3.4   Distribution of services provided by the career resource center
Adapted by permission from Moir, E. "Career Resource Center in Business and Industry." Training and Development Journal 35 (2). Copyright 1981 American Society for Training and Development

Educational Information. Educational information includes general educational references, nontraditional programs, financial aid information, and occupational guides. Occupational guides include information regarding occupational classifications and definitions. These guides include comprehensive descriptions of job duties, salary ranges, future job prospects, numbers of people employed, and training required to enter the respective field. These references can be used in the process of career exploration to make intelligent plans based on a broad knowledge of available choices. They can also be used as job placement tools to match job requirements to worker skills.

Since many employees use career resource centers to obtain education information, education material provides profiles of accredited institutions. In addition, they include detailed descriptions of programs, academic requirements, admission requirements, expenses, financial aid programs, student activities, and faculty data.

Because encouraging employees to leave their jobs to attend an institution of higher education would inevitably result in extensive employee turnover, HRD practitioners should obtain a complete listing of college catalogs within their geographical area. This would provide employees with an awareness of the diversity of local academic and vocational programs and serve as an alternative to and complement for other educational information.

If the academic advancement of employees is a goal of the organization, HRD practitioners should provide information as a necessary first step. A commitment to provide this type of resource material communicates the importance of advanced training and education and reveals the organization's commitment to individual improvement.

Career Planning Activities. Career planning activities and decision making can also be improved by providing career resource material. This type of information assists in selecting career options and in preparing for a career.

Career planning is the employee's counterpart to the company's overall human resource planning process. Since career planning is an individualized activity, it is important to provide materials that are self-directed and self-regulated. The materials listed accomplish this objective without creating dependency.

Another resource that can enhance a career resource center in an HRD department is a career guidance series. This type of material consists of several separate listings designed to provide a comprehensive overview of selected career fields. A career guidance series provides the latest information related to salary range, job prospects, advancement opportunities, training, and other important concerns. Since each selection is directed at a field or career area, these listings provide more in-depth and complete information than do occupational guides or career resource information. The Career Guidance Series (Arco, Simon & Schuster) and The Chronicle of Guidance (McGraw-Hill) are examples of comprehensive and excellent selections for a career resource center (Gilley, 1985).

One final resource needed in an HRD career resource center is the Counselor's Guide to Occupational Information. This document provides an annotated listing of government publications. The first section includes information about occupations, including job descriptions, entry requirements, advancement opportunities, job outlooks, and earnings. Other sections include materials on overseas jobs, special programs for minorities, women, and vocations, educational and financial aid, job search information, career education statistics, and bibliographies useful to career counselors. This single document represents a reservoir of occupational information available through the federal government (Gilley, 1985).

Career resource materials can immeasurably enhance employee's career plans by improving awareness of the career options, personalities, values, interests, and competencies. These resources can also improve employee's self-esteem by improving their understanding of themselves (Gilley, 1985).

In addition, many discover that their present career paths are already aligned with their perceived goals, values, interests, and skills. This discovery does much to reinforce past career decisions. Career resource materials often assist in this discovery.

Finally, before a career resource center is created, HRD practitioners should

1. Secure top administrative support.
2. Identify the needs of the population and organization the center will serve.
3. Locate the existing resources in the organization and coordinate the center with them.
4. Determine the necessary facilities, room space, and staff to run the center.
5. Determine the criteria and sources for selecting material and name the categories of materials (Moir, 1981).

HRD Practitioners' Responsibilities. HRD practitioners are responsible for the identification of occupational guides, educational references, career planning guides, and computer programs related to career selection. In addition is the management of the career resource center, as well as its design and layout. Another often-overlooked duty is the promotion of the center to managers and supervisors. Otherwise, managers and supervisors would fail to fully comprehend the importance of such centers. Employees should also be recruited to use the center, and HRD practitioners should develop workshops designed to promote the advantages of career resource centers in career planning and development (Gilley, 1985).

MANAGERS AS CAREER COUNSELORS

As a move toward excellence, organizations have made career development programs an important and vital activity of the human resource domain. Career planning efforts have expanded rapidly during the past 10 years, especially in business and industry. The main aim has been to help employees analyze their abilities and interests to better match personal needs for growth and development to the needs of the organization. Career planning is a critical tool by which management can increase productivity, improve employee attitudes toward work, and develop greater worker satisfaction. Moreover, the relationship between employee and the organization is at the heart of career development programs (Kaye, 1984).

Because of this vital relationship, organizations tend to take two approaches when establishing career development programs. They employ career development specialists or relinquish career development responsibilities directly to managers and supervisors (Jones, Kaye, & Taylor, 1984). The latter alternative appeals to many organizations because of its simplicity and cost benefits. It can also be argued that the supervisor's impact on a worker's career is greater than any other organizational factor. Thus, top managers and line supervisors are held responsible for helping in this matching relationship between employee and employer, for it is they who control the opportunities and organizational rewards. They also bring several unique advantages to the career counseling role. Managers and supervisors

- benefit from having practical experience.
- can make realistic appraisals of organizational opportunities.
- can use information from past performance evaluation to make realistic suggestions concerning career planning.
- can evaluate external economic opportunities pertaining to business.
- have experienced similar career decisions and can be empathetic toward the employee (Gilley & Moore, 1986).

Many managers hesitate to offer career counseling to subordinates because they lack formal training in psychology and counseling and feel inadequate in the role. In addition, most managers have been promoted to positions with supervisory responsibility because of technical abilities and skills, not necessarily because of interpersonal competencies. Thus, when confronted with difficult and complex problems, managers sometimes lack the competencies and abilities to correctly address them. The organization, however, will not release supervisors from their management responsibilities. Thus a catch-22 develops, which is difficult to escape. As a result, the transition from technician to mentor is difficult and often frustrating (Gilley and Moore, 1986).

A case report may be helpful. It concerns what managers did in one medium-sized manufacturing firm in its quest to identify stressful cases of poor productivity, low morale, and other dysfunctional outcomes. A supervisor in an assembly division with 24 workers noted that only one subordinate deviated from all four key outcome indicators. Through one-to-one counseling by this boss, a job mismatch came out, indicating an employee need for greater independence where more self-control could be exercised. Subsequently, a transfer for this worker showed that all four of the desired organizational results improved, with a subsequent reduction in this person's stressors and a much enhanced opportunity to stay with the firm and develop.

Research and experience show that most managers already possess many of the necessary interpersonal and human relations skills used in the career counseling process. Present skills can be further developed through training and study. Training provided by the HRD department can include identifying and labeling counseling techniques, reading self-help books on the subject, and practice with subordinates.

Since most of a supervisor's time is spent with subordinates, peers, and supervisors in verbal interactions, career counseling is seen as an important HRD task used to assist development of more effective communication and interpersonal skills. Below are listed seven activities managers can engage in to develop their skills as career counselors (Gilley & Moore, 1986). These activities can be utilized by HRD practitioners as well.

1. Develop a knowledge of occupational information and career source material.
2. Develop an understanding of the different career theories and their applications.
3. Enroll in college classes related to counseling theories, human relations, and counseling techniques.
4. Subscribe to professional journals that publish articles on career development.
5. Understand the elements of an effective relationship and how to build them.
6. Develop good listening and questioning skills.
7. Learn to respect the confidentiality of employees.

Fostering these skills will greatly enhance a supervisor's effectiveness and increase personal growth and development. Managers can also utilize such interpersonal abilities during performance appraisal interviews and other formal evaluation reviews. Indirectly, then, pursuing the career counseling role provides managers the opportunity to develop or enhance essential relationship skills, which can be used throughout a career and can increase potential. In the final analysis, furthering interpersonal skills through the career counseling role will benefit the organization while simultaneously advancing managerial competence (Gilley and Moore, 1986).

In addition to counseling, managers maintain eight different roles associated with career development:

1. Communicator—one who promotes a two-way exchange between him/herself and the employees.
2. Appraiser—one who evaluates an employee's performance and provides feedback.
3. Coach—one who gives instruction or skill training.

4. Mentor—one who serves as a sponsor to facilitate an employee's career growth.

5. Advisor—one who directs and supports an employee's career growth.

6. Broker—one who serves as an agent for the employee.

7. Advocate—one who intervenes on behalf of the employee for benefits, promotions, and elimination of obstacles.

8. Referred Agent—one who identifies resources to help an employee with a specific problem (Leibowitz & Schlossberg, 1986).

Regardless of whether career specialists are hired or managers are utilized as career counselors, the HRD department is responsible for the results of such facilitating activities. Therefore, career specialists as well as managers must be well trained as career counselors. Skills and competencies needed to perform as career counselors should be provided by HRD practitioners.

CAREER DEVELOPMENT WORKSHOPS AND SEMINARS

A favored form of career development enhancement is workshops and seminars designed to encourage employees to take responsibilities for their careers. Employees can reflect on their present occupation in order to determine their level of satisfaction. Thus, workshops and seminars are excellent vehicles for orienting employees to career/life planning, a major component of career development.

According to the "self-analysis" approach to career development, workshops and seminars seeks to address several basic questions:

- Where are you in your career and your life?
- What are your goals, interests, values, choices, and skills?
- Where do you want to be in your career in the future?
- What are your career options?
- What knowledge and skills do you need to attain your goals?
- How do you plan to gain knowledge and skills?
- Is your plan realistic? What are the obstacles? What obstacles are self-imposed?
- What is your commitment to developing your career?
- What support do you have? What resistance?
- How do you plan to maximize support and minimize resistance? (Hanson, 1982)

Once these questions have been addressed, participants can begin to develop appropriate plans of action designed to improve their current career options. Each participant is also encouraged to develop his or her own definition of career success, thereby personalizing the career development process. Moreover, it increases the person's ownership of responsibilities, the principle purpose of career development workshops and seminars.

Another aspect of career development workshops and seminars involves focusing on the alternatives available. This phenomenon is called "constructive coping"—that is, confronting tasks and developing appropriate responses in order to enable growth and development. The process includes

- Diagnosing the problem—which improves the person's understanding of the situation that is causing stress.

- Diagnosing oneself—which improves one's understanding of oneself, including needs, feelings, and available resources.

- Selecting a coping response—the development of a plan of action to cope with stressful situations.

- Diagnosing the effects of coping response—evaluating whether the plan of action accomplished its purpose and whether the problem has been solved. (Hanson, 1982)

This process is also a stress management technique; therefore it can also be incorporated in other forms of professional development.

Career development workshops and seminars also focus on the assessment of skills and competencies. This information serves as the foundation for future training and development activities sponsored by the HRD department. In addition, an employee may not be utilizing skills and competencies effectively because of his or her current position and/or situation. The employee is then encouraged to investigate other occupation and/or career areas. Indirectly, career exploration is becoming another focus of career development workshops and seminars.

Evaluation of current career development workshops and seminars serves as a means for improving and upgrading future workshops and seminars. Four types of evaluation can be administered: (1) evaluations of participants' reactions to the workshop, (2) evaluation of participant's learning, (3) evaluation of changes in behavior on the job as a result of the workshop, and (4) evaluation of the results (positive or negative) of new attitudes, skills, or knowledge that developed during the workshop (Kirkpatrick, 1975).

Both the development and evaluation of career development workshops and seminars is the responsibility of the HRD department and HRD practitioners. While this is a favored form of career development enhancement, it is often overused, which greatly reduces its impact. To prevent this from happening, HRD practitioners are encouraged to blend workshops with other career development activities. This enables the HRD department to maintain a dual approach while providing other alternatives to employees. This tends to meet the needs of more employees and provides variety to the career development process.

HUMAN RESOURCE PLANNING

Human resource planning has been a function of the human resource management department since the origin of the modern industrial organization. In fact, in some organizations, human resources has become as important as financial and physical resources. This has come about because of a shortage of the experienced and tested personnel needed to progress to senior executive responsibilities, the substantial cost of relocating employees, the high cost of recruiting talented managers and executives, shortages of specialized technical personnel needed for business expansions, and the cost of implementing employee layoffs or reducing the labor force. As a result, the HRD department is becoming more involved in the proper allocation and development of human resources. This includes human resource planning as well as training and development.

The HRD practitioners should also engage in developmental planning, based upon corporate goals and objectives and the proper allocation of physical, financial, and human resources as a part of their human resource planning responsibilities. Human resource planning is viewed as a process, not merely as a part of the personnel staff function. It is viewed as a process of analyzing an organization's human resource needs under changing conditions and developing the activities necessary to satisfy these needs. From this definition, human resource planning is a two-step process consisting of need forecasting and program planning. From the analysis of needs, priorities can be determined and human resources can be allocated to satisfy existing future needs through either performance management or career management. By determining the future human resources required and future human resources available, the HRD department can determine their surplus or deficiency of personnel.

PERFORMANCE APPRAISAL

The oldest technique used to improve individual production and performance is the appraisal. The principal purpose of a performance appraisal is to assess past performance, which serves as a foundation for future decisions. The focus of a performance appraisal is on the review of the past, utilizing judging methods, ratings, and/or descriptions established by the organizations. Supervisors and managers are the primary evaluators, and past accomplishments are viewed as the basis of the review. This is known as the *evaluation approach.*

There is another approach to performance appraisal—the *developmental approach.* Its purpose is to motivate and direct individual performance as well as career development efforts. The focus is on future planning; counseling and interaction between the manager and employees is the primary methodology. Emphasis is placed on goal setting as well as review. The supervisor, manager, and employee share equal responsibility in this type of appraisal process. The basis of the review is future goals and plans for future development. The developmental approach is better suited than the evaluation approach for integration into the career development activities that HRD practitioners are responsible for (Walker, 1980).

Performance appraisals are now being viewed as a form of needs assessment, as a means of gathering information for future training programs and learning activities. More specifically, performance appraisals are a tool HRD practitioners can use to guide and direct future growth opportunities for employees. This should aid in the development of a person's career as well as enhance communications and understanding. Therefore, HRD practitioners as well as managers should develop the most appropriate technique to bring about the desired results.

Several appraisal techniques can be used by an HRD practitioner, but their selection should be based on the specific need of the organization and the preferences as well as the abilities of the HRD practitioners. They include

- Narrative appraisals—open-ended interaction regarding individual performance.
- Goal setting and review—identification of goals mentally, followed by comparison of performances against those goals.
- Rating scales—performance is measured against predetermined factors.
- Checklists—performance is rated against a list of normative factors.
- Critical incidents—examples of good and bad performance are identified by the appraiser as they occur and are maintained until review.
- Ranking—relative performance is completed by the appraiser. Individual or group consensus is required (Walker, 1980).

HRD practitioners and managers can utilize any or all of these techniques or use them in combination as a means of evaluating employee performance. Once the weaknesses have been identified, then the HRD department can begin to develop programs and activities as a way of overcoming deficiencies.

CAREER PATHING PROGRAM

In an effort to enhance the skills, competencies, and knowledge of employees, many HRD practitioners and organizations use career pathing activities. One of these activities is the sequencing of work experiences, usually different job assignments, in order to provide employees with the opportunity to participate in many aspects of a professional area. For example, in order for a salesperson to move up the ladder to regional manager, it is important that he or she understand all aspects of the job. Therefore, a career path in sales might include a period of time in sales, account supervision, and district management. By experiencing each of these related but different occupations, the employee can develop a better understanding of the broad role of regional manager.

Three types of career paths exist today: historical, organizational, and behavioral. The characteristics of each are presented in Table 3.1.

Table 3.1   Three Kinds of Career Paths in Contrast

Historical	Organizational	Behavioral
Past patterns of career progression; how the incumbents got where they are	Paths defined or dictated by management to meet operating needs; progression patterns that fit prevailing organizational needs	Paths that are logically possible based on analysis of what activities are actually performed on the job
Actual paths created by the past movement of employees among management jobs	Paths determined by prevailing needs for staffing the organization	Rational paths that could be followed willingly
Perpetuates the change: way careers have always been	Reflects prevailing management values and attitudes regarding careers	Calls for change; new career options
Used as basis for promotions and transfers	Usually consistent with job evaluation and pay practices	Used as a basis for career planning
Basis is informal, traditional	Basis is organizational need, management style, expediency	Basis is formal analysis and definition of options

Reprinted from J. Walker, Human Resource Planning, *New York: McGraw-Hill, 1980.*

Historical career paths are informal paths that have always existed in organizations and are usually represented by the past paths of incumbent senior managers (Walker, 1980, p. 318). This approach utilizes promotions and transfers as a tool for upward movement. It represents the traditional approach to career advancement, yet most managers fail to see that their current position represents a formal career path approach. In some organizations there is a socialized approach to upward mobility. "If I had to, so do you." This reflects the historical approach to career pathing.

Organizational career paths is an approach defined by management. The paths are pragmatic in nature and are reflected in business plans, needs, and the organization structure. They represent the prevailing values of management. Job description, job evaluation, and compensation practices are reflected in this form of career pathing (Walker, 1980).

Finally, *behavioral career paths* represent a logical sequence of the positions that could be held by an employee based on an analysis of what people actually do in the organization. This approach matches the needs of the employee to the goals of the organization. It is an excellent approach for and the basis of career planning. It allows for mobility across functions, geographic lines, and organizational lines in an effort to obtain a logical basis for career pathing as well as career development (Walker, 1980).

The primary role of the HRD practitioner in a career pathing program is to help management identify which of the three approaches would be most appropriate for the organization. Another responsibility is to help employees recognize that career paths do indeed exist and that they are responsible for the management of them. In addition, the HRD practitioner has an obligation to bring together the employees and management in order to better facilitate career pathing programs.

THE INDIVIDUAL COMPONENT AND CAREER DEVELOPMENT ACTIVITIES

An equal partner in the enhancement of harmony in organizational career development is the individual employee. Let's now turn our attention to the important career development activities that individuals engage in to increase knowledge and competence.

The activities of a truly comprehensive career development program will, in addition to assisting employees plan careers, help them to enhance self-awareness and awareness of other career areas. They can improve their decision-making skills and learn how to analyze the organization in order to determine career opportunities and options.

There are several career development activities employees can participate in. They include: (1) career planning, (2) career awareness, (3) using career resource centers, (4) becoming aware of different career opportunities and options within the organization, and (5) engaging in interests, values, and competencies analysis (see Figure 3.3). These activities return much of the responsibility of career development to the individual; for example, (1) assuming full support for the management of their careers, (2) determining abilities, interests, and strengths and desire for work, (3) becoming acquainted with the organization, (4) maintaining a broad outlook of career development, and (5) aggressively pursuing career opportunities (Zenger, 1981).

CAREER PLANNING

Career planning is the process of setting individual career objectives and creatively developing activities that will achieve them. Career planning can also be seen as a personal process, consisting of three criteria: (1) broad life planning, (2) development planning, and (3) performance planning (Walker, 1980; see Figure 3.2). The HRD practitioner, however, has an obligation to encourage as well as provide for the utilization of career planning on the part of employees. Career planning is the employee's counterpart to the organization's overall human resource planning activity.

According to Zenger (1981), there are three main barriers to the implementation of career planning programs: (1) lack of role clarity in the organization in terms of career planning responsibilities, (2) lack of skilled HRD practitioners in career planning and related issues, and (3) the peripheral nature of career planning (Zenger, 1981). These barriers indicate the need for additional evaluation by the organization, the development of a philosophy regarding career planning, an assessment of the organization's, including HRD practitioners' and managers' responsibilities, additional training, and a long-term commitment to the concept of career planning.

Techniques in career planning include counseling, workshops, self-development materials, occupational information, and assessment programs. An organizational orientation toward career planning is essential to successful career planning programs. The principal purpose of the workshops is to encourage employees to take responsibility for their careers. This should be the primary responsibility of the HRD practitioner.

The challenge of career development lies in equipping the employee with necessary knowledge about self and reality. Although the perception is that it is the employee who is ultimately responsible for his or her own career, the organization is an equal partner in career planning.

Today many forces are encouraging organization-sponsored career planning programs.

1. Affirmative action programs.
2. Women, mid-career employees, and college recruits are seeking career planning assistance.
3. Highly talented candidates demand organizations demonstrate that career advancement opportunities exist.
4. Corporate growth and development results in a need for more qualified human resources.
5. A competitive environment, especially with the Japanese, demands more and more of employees. This in turn demands more support and rewards from organizations.

As a result, career planning has been a higher priority in organizations during the past decade. HRD practitioners should examine each of these forces carefully and determine the impact that each has on the organization. Once this has been accomplished, HRD practitioners can prepare for and react to the future pressures applied to HRD programs from external as well as internal groups. The end result will be a better understanding of why career planning is so vital.

According to Walker (1980), there are nine reasons for offering career-planning programs:

1. Desire to develop and promote employees from within.
2. Shortage of promotable talent.
3. Desire to aid career planning.
4. Strong expressions of employee interest.
5. Desire to improve productivity.

6. Affirmative action program commitment.

7. Concern about turnover.

8. Personal interest of unit managers.

9. Desire for positive recruiting image (p. 335).

Also, organizations want to avoid unionization. HRD practitioners should understand that any or all of these reasons may be present in their organization. Regardless of the number of reasons for career planning, the ultimate responsibility of the HRD department remains the same: the enhancement of human resources within the organization. This includes career development as well as career advancement, and HRD practitioners must utilize career planning in the development process. This, of course, is based on the assumption that as employees improve and grow the organization benefits.

CAREER AWARENESS

That employees are ultimately responsible for the development of their own careers is obvious. Employees control decisions such as whether to remain in the organization, whether to accept specific occupational assignments, whether to perform at acceptable levels, and even whether to engage in personal growth activities through training or professional continuing education. The role of the HRD practitioner is to provide the means and the information to assist in personal career decision making. But he or she must also develop a climate and culture that is conducive for growth, one that encourages career development. Employees, in turn, should take advantage of that climate and be aware of the important components of career development. They need to construct plans that will enable them to accomplish their career goals, analyze potential career areas, and determine if they possess the skills, competencies, and knowledge necessary to be considered serious candidates for such positions. In addition, employees should attend career development workshops. In these workshops employees learn the essentials of career planning and can determine how much support the organization is willing to provide in future career development. They also get the feedback they need on the "attitude" of the organization toward career development. Career awareness includes knowing what occupational guides, education materials, career planning guides, and other occupational information is available at the career resource center (see p. 70).

It is important to remember that, as with career planning, the HRD practitioner is responsible for developing and providing the *means* for career awareness—selecting career analysis instruments, developing management of career resource centers, and introducing career pathing programs. As a result, the employee and the HRD practitioner become equal partners in the career awareness activity.

CAREER RESOURCE CENTER UTILIZATION

Most career resource centers provide occupational guides, educational references, career planning guides, and computer programs aimed at assisting employees in determining their career interests, values, and competencies. These materials increase the effectiveness and efficiency of career planning and provide employees with alternative approaches to career development.

HRD practitioners must develop, maintain, and manage their organization's career resource center. The center will have a profound effect on the operational budget of the HRD department, something the HRD practitioner must take into account. However, there is a low-cost alternative, the office of a local college or university career development and placement department (Kahnweiler, 1984). These offices will often provide training in career pathing and occupational analysis. Many colleges and universities view this service as a means of attracting highly qualified adult students and as a part of their outreach program to the local community, state or region. In addition to providing occupational information, colleges and universities offer excellent career counseling services as well as vocational testing programs. These services provided by organizations are usually limited in their focus. HRD practitioners should encourage employees to utilize local college and university career development and placement offices whenever possible.

ORGANIZATION AWARENESS

Another responsibility of the employee in career development is to become aware of the career opportunities available within their present organization. By maintaining an accounting of job postings and the organization's financial condition, the HRD department can communicate the type and degree of career openings presently available as well as the future trends of the organization. In large organizations that provide mentoring activities, employees can learn much about the history, culture, and philosophy of their organization from managers, supervisors, and corporate officers. In addition, employees should identify the types of positions the organization has the greatest need for. They can then determine if they have the interest and/or the skills for them. If not, HRD practitioners can, for example, arrange additional training and education so they can be more competitive with other employees.

During performance appraisals and evaluations, employees need to discuss their career goals with HRD practitioners and management. This communicates a sincere interest in career advancement. Also during performance appraisals employees should request information on the future direction of the organization and ascertain if their personal career focus is consistent with the organization's.

The HRD practitioner who identifies future organization needs and communicates them to employees will greatly enhance their organization awareness. This person should become more active in performance appraisals because they are so important in identifying training and development needs. He or she can also create and design career development workshops to orient employees to the organization and to stress the type of training available, as well as the opportunities that exist within the organization.

INTERESTS, VALUES, AND COMPETENCIES

Several computer programs have been developed that are aimed at assisting employees in determining their career interests, values, and competencies. These programs also provide additional occupational information that complements written resource materials available at career resource centers. "Discover" (ACT) is an example of a program dedicated to improving individuals' awareness of themselves and their career options (Gilley, 1985).

The Strong-Campbell Interest Inventories, The Self-Directed Search (Hollands), and VISTA (ACT) are examples of interest inventories designed to provide employees with important information about their career interests, values, and competencies. These tests are easily administered and can provide the vital baseline data essential in career planning and career enhancement.

The ultimate selection of interest inventories and values and competencies analysis instruments is the responsiblity of the HRD department and its practitioners. It is therefore extremely important that HRD practitioners become aware of the many inventories and instruments available and determine those that are most appropriate for their organization (Gilley, 1985).

SUMMARY OF CAREER DEVELOPMENT ACTIVITIES

The degree of career development congruence between the individual and the organization depends on their cooperation when career development activities are implemented. A cooperative and harmonious attitude dedicated to the development of a mutually beneficial relationship will increase the effectiveness and efficiency of career development programs. A pseudo attempt will only result in a smaller area of congruence (see Figure 3.3). Without a high degree of cooperation, the effective use of career development activities is restricted and the overall development of human resources is diminished. Once the principals accept their respective responsibilities, congruence increases.

APPLICATION AND UTILIZATION OF THE CAREER DEVELOPMENT PROCESS

Career development programs can be greatly enhanced if HRD practitioners utilize a five-stage approach (see Table 3.2). The process begins with an *employee orientation* in which individual career responsibility is stressed. This should be accomplished through a workshop sponsored by the organization.

Table 3.2   A Five-Stage Approach to Career Development

Stage	Individual Activities	Organizational Activities
1. Orientation	Career responsibility	Workshop
2. Who am I?	Career analysis Test taking	Manager as career counselor
3. How am I viewed?	Self-analysis	Performance appraisal

4. What are my options?	Organizational
	  awareness
	Utilizing career
	  resource centers
		Job posting
		Career resource
		  centers
		Human resource
		  planning

5. How do I accomplish
  my goal?
	Career planning	Manager as career
		  counselor
		Mentioning
		  Career Planning

Printed from Gilley, J. W. (April 1988) issue of Personnel Administrator, *copyright 1988, The American Society For Personnel Administration, Alexandria, VA*

Another way to obtain more career harmony is to utilize the manager (as career counselor) to point out and promote the idea that career development is primarily the responsibility of the individual.

The second stage is *individual self-analysis.* In this stage the employee answers the question, "Who am I?" Career awareness is the principal purpose here. The principal activities are use of the manager as career counselor and test instruction designed to determine one's interests, values, and competencies related to career development.

Stage three is the *reality check.* The employee determines "How am I viewed?" by the organization. Performance appraisal is the fundamental activity organizations use to provide feedback to the employee regarding this question.

The next stage seeks to determine the *options* that are available to the employee. During this stage, employees develop organization awareness and seek out alternatives within or outside of the organization through the career resource center. At this point, HRD practitioners reveal the organization's human resource planning needs so employees can determine how they fit into the organization. The HRD practitioner should also encourage employees to examine job posting announcements and utilize the career resource center. In addition, mentors and managers (as career counselors) should also be consulted about career options.

Finally, employees should turn their attention to developing a plan of action for accomplishing their *career goals.* Career planning is their principal activity during this final stage. At the same time, the HRD practitioner should engage in mentoring and career pathing activities and utilize managers as career counselors to aid them in developing their career plans. The HRD department can sponsor career workshops throughout all five stages; however, they often rely too heavily on them as a principal way to assist employees in career development.

CONCLUSION

At the conclusion of this chapter, HRD practitioners should understand that the primary purpose of career development is to help employees analyze their abilities and interests to better match personnel needs for growth and development to the needs of the organization. Second, HRD practitioners should be able to identify the factors in maintaining a successful career development program. Three types of planning related to career development have been discussed: broad life planning, development planning, and performance planning. HRD practitioners should incorporate each of these into the career development program. Next, HRD practitioners should be able to identify their general responsibilities in the area of career development as well as their specific responsibilities to their employer and the organization. They should also be able to identify methods for improving the harmony between the individual and the organization related to career development. Finally, HRD practitioners should be able to apply career development to the organizational setting.

CHAPTER 4

Organizational Development

Objectives

After completing Chapter 4, readers should be able to

- identify the 13 characteristics of organizational development (OD).

- distinguish between the micro and macro view of OD.

- define the term "organizational development."

- list the goals and objectives of OD.

- identify the principles of change and their impact on the OD process.

- identify the purpose for a change agent in OD.

- describe the roles of a change agent.

- describe the relationship between the change agent and the client system.

- identify the value of change agents.

- describe the OD process and the change agents' responsibilities during each phase.

- identify the value of OD to the organization.

- identify the four types of organizations that change agents must interact in.

- describe the relationship between individual development and OD.

- list the recommendations of a linkage between ID and OD.

Organizational development (OD) has emerged as a management function on both the internal and external organizational fronts. Internally, employees demand rehumanization of the workplace and greater participation in decision making, resulting in greater control over their work lives. This causes change within the organization. Externally, economic changes and pressures have forced organizations to adjust to a new marketplace. To meet this challenge, organizations have had to implement changes and take risks. They can no longer maintain the status quo. Many believe that a manager's success in bringing about substantive and positive changes depends to a great extent on his or her skill in OD. HRD practitioners have been principally responsible for enhancing management's awareness of and skills in OD.

The goal of organizational development is personal, professional, and organizational growth. This growth is guided by a change agent, who acts primarily as a catalyst in the dynamic process of OD. OD is a planned process as well, one that occurs within the organization over a long period of time. This process involves an action-research orientation in which the scientific method is applied to practical organizational problems. The objective is to develop the problem-solving capabilities of the organizational participants. Organizational development is also inclusive. In order for an intervention to be effective, all members of the organization must be involved.

Organizational development, then, is viewed as a planned, data-based approach to change, involving goal setting, action planning, implementation, monitoring, and taking corrective action when necessary. It is problem solving oriented in that it applies theory and research from a number of disciplines that solve organizational problems. OD is also a systems approach—both systemic and systematic—closely linking human resources and organizational potential to technology, structure, and management process. As such, it is an internal part of the management process, not something done to the organization by outsiders. OD is not a "fix-it" strategy, but rather a continuous process, an on-going way of managing organizational change processes that, over time, become a way of organizational life (Phelps, 1988).

Therefore, organizational development can be defined as a systemwide process of data collection, diagnosis, action planning, intervention, and evaluation aimed at (1) enhancing congruence between organizational structure, process, strategy, people, and culture; (2) developing new and creative organizational solutions; and (3) developing the organization's self-renewing capacity (Beer,

1985). It occurs through collaboration of organization members working with change agents (HRD practitioners) using behavioral science theory, research, and technology. This definition reveals that OD focuses on the overall efficiency of the organization, the development of an innovative approach to problem solving, and the establishment of a "survivalistic attitude" in an ever-changing environment of technological advancement and cultural change.

As a result, OD is concerned with long-term changes in the culture, technology, and management of a total organization or at least a significant part of the total organization (Laird, 1986). It is useful to think of OD as a philosophy as well as a collection of methods for organizational improvement. Both are characterized by an emphasis on collaborative participation in data collection, diagnosis, planning, intervention, and evaluation in order to improve the entire organization.

Organizational development also relies on learning as a way to bring about change. However, the focus is on the overall human system within the organization, rather than on the individuals within the system. From this vantage point, OD can be viewed as a "macro perspective" of overall organizational efficiency. In other words, the OD process assumes that the principal beneficiary of any learning activity (training, education, development), operational and structure change, attitudinal enhancement, and cultural improvement is the organization itself; the employees are the secondary benefactors of such actions (Gilley, 1989).

While this is the generally accepted view of OD, it fails to account for the fact that all organizations are made up of a myriad of individuals; and regardless of the intervention type and the changes the organization makes, it is the people in the organization who must carry them out or act upon them.

A macro perspective of improved organizational efficiency must take into consideration that changes cannot occur, nor can performance improve, without each member of the organization improving respective skills, competencies, knowledge, and attitudes. Organizations are not separate entities unto themselves. They are comprised of people who identify and accept a common set of organizational goals and objectives for the benefit of others outside the organization. In exchange, each organizational member receives financial compensation as well as other intrinsic rewards. This is based on the assumption that organizations do not run themselves, people do. It is also based on the belief that individuals release their personal power and control to other organizational members so that the organization runs more efficiently. Without this compliance, organizations could not maintain control or operate efficiently.

While it is understood that organizations consist of capital and physical resources as well as human resources, it is the latter that manages and controls the former. In any organization there is a hierarchy where certain individuals are perceived to be more valuable to the overall operation of the organization than others. While this remains a constant, it should be noted that top management would be at a loss if support staffs failed to function efficiently or disappeared altogether. In fact, the modern organization would grind to a certain stop within a few months if their secretarial and computer personnel decided to collectively boycott the organization (Gilley, 1989).

Of course, most organizations believe that they would survive if employees elected to leave. As a result, they often operate with a "revolving door" philosophy based on supply-side economics where the supply of qualified personnel exceeds the organization's demands. It is this philosophy that helps embrace the macro view of improved organizational efficiency: Improved performance is desired only as a means of improving the operations of the organization. It is not a way to enhance employees' skills, competencies, knowledge, and attitudes. Finally, the "revolving door" philosophy fosters the attitude that the employees exist for the organization. Therefore, the organization has control over the movement, distribution, and development of its employees. Many organizations recognize that this practice is not necessarily the most efficient approach to the management of human resources, yet they still practice it in everyday operations (Gilley, 1989).

CHARACTERISTICS OF OD

Several characteristics of OD are common. Margulies and Raia (1978) identified the following thirteen characteristics:

1. OD involves a total organizational system.
2. OD views organizations from a systems approach.
3. OD is supported by top management.
4. OD employs third-party change agents.
5. OD is a planned effort.
6. OD uses behavioral science knowledge.
7. OD is intended to increase organizational competence and health.
8. OD is a relatively long term process.
9. OD is an ongoing process.
10. OD relies on experiential as opposed to didactic learning.
11. OD uses an action research intervention model.
12. OD emphasizes the importance of goal setting and action planning.
13. OD mainly focuses on changing the attitudes, behaviors, and performance of organizational groups or teams rather than individuals.

Organizational development is not effective unless members of the entire organization are involved. This includes top level management support as well as managers and supervisors. OD views the organization as a system in that it consists of inputs such as financial, physical, and human resources used to produce outputs such as products and services. Improved organizational efficiency, which is the principal goal of OD, is related to the proper utilization of the organization's resources (inputs) in the production of improved outputs.

Organizational development employs a third-party change agent who is responsible for introducing new and innovative ideas that result in improved organizational efficiency. They use behavioral science knowledge such as humanistic concepts of management and leadership, participative management, and interpersonal skills to bring about change. They also use experiential learning that focuses on shared experiences, group participation, and application of learning. In addition, change agents often use an action research intervention model, which places a strong emphasis on developing specific insight interventions in collaboration with management, following intensive data gathering and diagnosis.

It is a long-term process because it requires that several members of the organization possessing different orientations develop a common view of the organization and its future. It also requires an agreed-upon approach to change, which also takes time to facilitate. It requires an understanding of strategic planning which emphasizes the importance of goal setting and action planning.

The purpose of OD is to increase organizational competence and health. This is done primarily through changes in attitudes, behaviors, and performance of group members rather than by focusing on individual change. Finally, OD should be an ongoing process, not a single event conducted to foster instant success.

GOALS AND OBJECTIVES OF OD

The overall goal of the OD effort is generally to improve organizational performance in terms of efficiency, effectiveness, and health. The first two of these measures are fairly tangible and objective, but health refers to such subjective aspects of the organization as morale, creativity, and climate or atmosphere. Furthermore, McGill (1977) reported that "organizational health is a function of the character and quality of the relationship between the individual and the organization" (p. 5). This is characterized in three important ways. First, it effectively integrates individual and organizational goals. Second, individual and organizational problem-solving capacities are maximized. Finally, the climate encourages individual and organizational growth (Phelps, 1988).

Neilsen (1984) sees the primary objective of OD at the organizational level as initiating a *collaborative* form of organization (see page 90 below for a comparison of types of organizations). Such an organization is characterized by (1) structures and policies that facilitate understanding of and commitment to organizational goals; (2) reward systems that emphasize group performance while still recognizing individual contributions; (3) measurement systems that are used as imperfect yardsticks for measuring progress toward objectives, not as rigid performance criteria that become ends in themselves; and (4) participative staffing and human resource development procedures that analyze individual career aspirations reflective of both the organization's long-term needs and the present and future competencies the individual brings to the organization.

The collaborative form of organization may evolve most naturally under philosophies of leaders who believe that their followers are basically committed to the welfare of the organization and that every member is potentially a valuable resource for promoting the organization's welfare (Phelps, 1988).

It is important to remember that an OD effort is not a separate or single event but rather a series of events interacting over an extended period of time. The intent of OD is not to make decisions for management, but merely to help clarify their choices. Cummings (1980) cites the value of informed choices as those most pertinent to OD. In other words, OD must help organizations generate valid data about the state of the organization relative to its environment. OD must also help organizational stakeholders clarify desired outcomes. In addition, OD must help organizations make strategic choices based on a diagnosis of the current state and desired outcomes (Phelps, 1988).

PRINCIPLES OF CHANGE

Bowers and Franklin (1977) identified three fundamental principles of organizational change. They reported that unless these principles are honored in the OD process, constructive change cannot occur. They are the Principles of Congruence, Predisposition, and Succession.

The *Principle of Congruence,* simply stated, means that the treatment (i.e., action or intervention) must be selected, designed, and varied to fit the structure and function of the organization attempting the constructive change. This implies that a tailored intervention is better suited for the organization than the "off-the-shelf" approach that many consultants advocate (Phelps, 1988).

The *Principle of Predisposition* states that there are certain points in the organization where changes are most likely to succeed. Change should be introduced at these penetration points and be allowed to spread to the rest of the organization. Some refer to these as entry points; Lippitt and Lippitt (1986) refer to them as leverage points. They report that these points in the organization may be either most receptive to the change, or they may have the ability to influence others to accept change (Phelps, 1988).

The *Principle of Succession* holds that change is accomplished indirectly, not directly, by a process wherein some things are changed in order to change other things. In other words, some changes can only occur after barriers and obstacles are removed in the culture. Thus, it is important to accomplish "minor" successes along the way in order to insure that the ultimate change occurs.

In addition, Cummings (1980) reported the need for a new model of OD that would integrate three traditional perspectives regarding organizations and change: political, technical, and cultural. The first traditional perspective views organizations as political entities that can only be changed by the exercise of power or by bargaining among powerful groups. The second adopts a rational-economic or technical perspective. It prescribes change strategies based on empiricism and entailed self-interest. Here, the focus is on acquiring and applying knowledge useful for effective performance of organizational tasks. In the third perspective, organizations are seen as cultural systems based on values with shared symbols and shared cognitive schemes linking individuals together in a common organizational culture. Change, then, comes by altering the norms, values, and cognitive schemes of the organization members.

THE CHANGE AGENT

Regardless of which perspective one adopts, successful change requires a change agent, typically a consultant from outside the organization, to facilitate the OD process. The change agent (an HRD practitioner) is a critical component in the success of the entire undertaking. Bowers and Franklin (1977) identified the change agent as a "transducer between scientific knowledge regarding organizational functioning and the change process, on one hand, and the particular situation on the other" (p. 13).

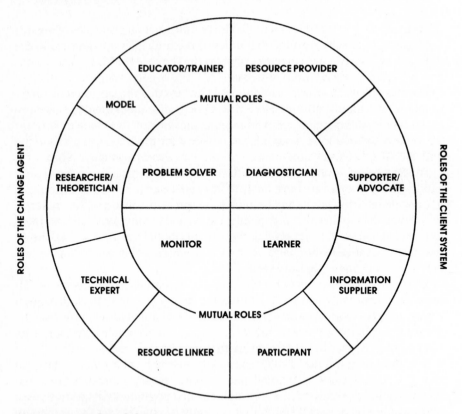

Figure 4.1 Roles of change agents

Reprinted, by permission of the publisher, from OD for Operating Managers, M. E. McGill, Figure 4:4, copyright 1977, AMACOM, a division of American Management Association, New York. All rights reserved.

ROLES OF CHANGE AGENTS

Change agents perform a variety of roles during the OD process, each designed to maximize the effectiveness of interventions as well as improve communications and relationships. Figure 4.1 illustrates the different roles a change agent plays, as well as the roles of the client system. This diagram also reveals the mutual roles that are played by each party.

The change agent can be viewed as a problem solver or as a monitor of the OD process. At the same time, the client system functions as a learner in the OD process or as a diagnostician of itself. The change agent and client system can also function in one of several independent roles that are based on the situation and/or the need of the organization.

In 1983, White and Wooten identified 10 separate stages of the OD process, the purpose of each, the roles that the change agent and the client system play during each stage, and the dilemmas that result from each stage (Table 4.1). This reveals the essential activities that change agents and client systems must participate in, as well as the various roles identified in Figure 4.1. It is important to note that each of the roles are revealed during the 10 stages of the OD process.

Neilsen (1984) adds that the change agent may help set up task forces to address items on the project agenda or may assume an active role in helping client groups improve their interaction through process consulting. This involves intervening in group operation as well as interacting. In organizational development, the HRD practitioner (consultant) models behaviors and provides insights that help organization members deal with problems in areas such as patterns of communications, members' roles and functions, problem-solving and decision-making styles, group norms, leadership and authority relations, and intergroup competition and cooperation (Phelps, 1988).

It is possible for the change agent (HRD practitioner) to be a member of the organization undertaking the OD process. A comparison of the roles of the external versus the internal change agent is provided by Mclean (1982). He envisions the external consultant as providing conceptual stimulation and world views and acting as sounding board and counselor, resident guru, and firefighter. The roles of internal consultant, on the other hand, are more likely to include that of tactician, loner, trainer, and cultivator—that is, a medium for introduction and translation of ideas and a sensor of the climate, gathering information and feeding it back to the external consultant and/or appropriate organizational member (Phelps, 1988).

To summarize, then, the apparent role played by the external change agent can be that of an educator, visionary, and prophet, providing organizational members new ways of seeing and broadening the field of vision. External change agents view themselves primarily as links between a body of knowledge and a client system in potential areas of intervention (Bower and Franklin, 1977).

First, an external change agent interprets and imparts information to the client system in order to motivate management to change, to tell what changes

Table 4.1   Change Agents and Client System Roles in the Organizational Development Process

Stage	Purpose	Role of Change Agent	Role of Client System	Dilemmas
Initiation	First information sharing	To provide information on background, expertise, and experience	To provide information on possible needs, relevant problems, interest of management and representative groups	Misrepresentation of the consultant's skill base and background Misrepresentation of organizational interest
Clarification	Further elaboration of initiation stage	To provide details of education, licensure, operative values, optimum working conditions	To provide a detailed history of special problems, personnel, marketplace, internal culture, and organizational politics	Inappropriate determination of who the client is Avoidance of reality testing Inappropriate determination of value orientation
Specification/agreement	Sufficient elaboration of needs, interest, fees, services, working conditions, arrangements	To specify actual services, fees to be charged, time frame, actual work conditions	To specify whose needs are to be addressed, goals, objectives, and possible evaluative criteria or end-state outcomes	Inappropriate structuring of the relationship Inappropriate definition of change problem Collusion to exclude outside parties
Diagnosis	To obtain an unfiltered and undistorted view of the organization's problems and processes pinpointing change targets and criteria	To collect data concerning organizational problems and processes, and to provide feedback	To assist change agent in data collection	Avoidance of problems Misuse of data Distortion and deletion of data Ownership of data Voluntary consent Confidentiality
Goal setting/action planning	To establish the specific goals and strategies to be used	To agree mutually with the client system on the goals and strategies to be used	To agree mutually with the change agent on the goals and strategies to be used	Inappropriate choice of intervention goal and targets Inappropriate choice of operative means Inappropriate scope of intervention

Systems intervention	The intervention into ongoing behaviors, structures, and processes	To intervene at specific targets, at a specific depth	To invest the energy and resources required by planned intervention	Assimilation into culture Inappropriate depth of intervention Coercion vs. choice, freedom, and consent to participate Environmental manipulation
Evaluation	To determine the effectiveness of the intervention strategies, energy, and resources used, as well as the change agent-client system relationship	To gather data on specified targets and report findings to the client system	To analyze the evaluation data and determine effectiveness of the intervention	Misuse of data Deletion and distortion of data
Alteration	To modify change strategies, depth, level, goals, targets, or resources utilized if necessary	To make alteration to meet original goals, or to develop new mutual goals and strategies with client system	To make known needs and expectations, and to provide the context for a modification of the original agreement, if necessary	Failure to change and lack of flexibility Adoption of inappropriate strategy
Continuation/ maintenance	To monitor and maintain ongoing strategies, provide periodic checks, and continue intervention based on original or altered plans and strategies	To specify the parameters of the continuation of the maintenance of the relationship	To provide or allocate the resources required to maintain or continue the intervention	Inappropriate reduction of dependency Redundancy of effort Withholding of services
Termination	To have the change agent disenfranchise self from the client system and establish a long-term monitoring system	To fulfill the role agreed on in previous stages and evaluate overall effectiveness from feedback from the client system	To determine the organization's state of health, and whether it has developed the adaptive change process	Inappropriate transition of change effort to internal sources Premature exit Failure to monitor change

Source: Adapted from White, L. P. and Wooten, K. C. "Ethical Dilemmas in Various Stages of Organizational Development." Academy of Management Review 8, no. 4, 1983, p. 695.

are needed, and to help them learn how to make needed changes. It is extremely important that the change agent facilitate understanding and acceptance of the information (and model for change) among management and organization participants. These are key elements in the change agent's role and activities during the diagnostic phase of the OD process (Phelps, 1988).

Second, as the OD process moves into the therapeutic or actual implementation phase, the change agent's activities and emphasis shift from facilitating understanding and acceptance to supplying information on possible activities, helping organizational members cope with attitudinal shifts, and handling defensive reactions (Phelps, 1988).

Third, if change is to occur within the organization, participants will need the awareness that arises from identifying the discrepancy between "what is" in the organization versus "what should be." They will also need the knowledge and methods that will bring about the actual change. In this phase, the change agent's emphasis shifts to facilitating group members' acquisition and perfection of skills. At this point, participants begin to rely less on the change agent. Problem solving, giving and receiving personal feedback, listening, leadership, goal setting, resolving conflict, and diagnosing group processes are some of the most common areas of training designed to enhance skills in organizational members. During the implementation phase the change agent also gives intermediate, informal feedback to change participants regarding progress toward achieving desired goals (Bower and Franklin, 1977).

COMPETENCIES OF CHANGE AGENTS

A complex and varied set of competencies and skills are needed by change agents. Neilsen (1984) identifies three basic categories of competencies needed: interpersonal, conceptual, and technical. Interpersonal skills are at the heart of the communication process, which is so essential in consultant/client relationships. It also structures the management process between the consultant and client, which enables the consultant and client to develop mutual acceptance and positive regard. The change agent must also generate in clients a sense of security when trying out new and unfamiliar behaviors. The consultant must be able to foster mutual respect through active listening and interviewing skills. And finally, the consultant must respect the personal boundaries and values of the client and vice versa (Phelps, 1988).

Conceptual skills form the resource for managing content of the OD process. This involves the capacity to guide the client's attention to problems, opportunities, and ways of thinking about organization that are consistent with productive and important change. According to Neilsen (1984), "every OD practitioner needs a theory to guide and direct his or her behavior, one that he or she is continuously testing and elaborating, both for professional development and for understanding the situations one encounters" (p. 79).

Technical skills relate to the change agent's ability to conduct the wide variety of programmed procedures available for implementing the OD process at the individual, group, or organizational level. This involves not only selecting and modifying established procedures, but also developing new ones to meet the specific needs of a particular client. It requires good presentation skills, execution skills, and the ability to respond to unforeseen contingencies.

Finally, blending interpersonal, conceptual, and technical skills into the management of a total project requires integrative skills. These relate to the ability to conceive, sell, and manage a total OD project in order to respond to the client's needs and, at the same time, reinforce OD values (Neilsen, 1984).

VALUES OF CHANGE AGENTS

French and Bell (1976) found that change agents subscribe to a set of values that constitute four primary beliefs of applied behavioral scientists:

1. The belief that the needs and aspirations of human beings are the reason for an organized change process.
2. The belief that work and life can become more meaningful if employees are allowed to participate in decisions affecting their organization.
3. The belief that improved organizational effectiveness can be accomplished by employing action research techniques.
4. The belief in the democratization of organizations through power equalization processes.

McLean (1982) adds that developing an approach that is internally consistent—that is, based on theories validated in the consultant's personal experience and congruent with his or her values, skills, abilities, and personality—may be the single most important precursor to the success of a change agent.

THE OD PROCESS

Most models of the OD process were divided into two overall phases: first, a broad-based educative scheme—considered necessary to the second phase, consisting of specific activities and activities of a more problem-solving nature (McLean, 1982). According to Bowers and Franklin (1977), at least four elements are involved in the OD process: a model, a goal, an activity, and feedback. The diagnostic phase of OD, which we discuss below, is a goal-setting system, while the intervention phase is, in effect, an adaptive-control system or midcourse correction activity. The evaluation phase, in the form of feedback, completes the loop as the entire sequence of phases in the OD process recycles.

Similarly, McGill (1977) describes the OD process in terms of consecutive cycles of plan-action-evaluation/plan-action. He views it as a managerial process which has no end. Specific OD activities change as problems are solved and new issues emerge. As organization members become increasingly competent in OD skills, consultants detach themselves from the process and the organization assimilates OD as a continuing function. It is a sort of monitoring behavior that scans the environment for change or improvement opportunities. Activating change or improvement does not require a specific problem, nor does it stop when a solution has been found (cited in Phelps, 1988).

Although the phases as defined vary slightly from one theoretical model to another, most OD theoreticians generally agree on six: (1) problem identification, (2) the relationship phase, (3) the diagnostic phase, (4) the solution identification phase, (5) the intervention phase, and(6) the feedback (evaluation) phase.

PROBLEM IDENTIFICATION

The OD process begins when organization decision makers discover that there is a need or problem within the organization that is affecting productivity, morale, attitudes, or the organization's combativeness. The need, as we pointed out in an earlier chapter, is the difference between "what is" and "what should be," and the gap is the problem that must be resolved. Most organizations strive to obtain a state of equilibrium, by narrowing the gap between "what is" and "what should be."

McLean (1982) pointed out how extremely important it is to identify the problem correctly when he stated, "We fail more often because we solve the wrong problem than because we get the wrong solution to the right problem" (p. 81). In other words, for successful change, begin with a rigorous measurement of the current situation and how the organization is presently functioning. This information provides the material for a correct diagnosis, the basis for a proper design for change.

THE RELATIONSHIP PHASE

According to Neilsen (1984), the decision to start an OD project requires that change agents carefully consider four criteria: (1) the match between client needs and what OD has to offer; (2) the match between project demands and client influence, resources, and organizational readiness; (3) the match between OD values and the client's management philosophy; and (4) the match between the personalities of the change agent (consultant) and the client.

Lippitt and Lippitt (1986) report that the establishment of the consultant-client relationship is perhaps the most critical element in determining the success of a change effort. Rooted in Lewin's three-phase model of change (i.e., unfreezing, moving, and refreezing), Lippitt and Lippitt essentially add only two, both of which concern the client system/change agent relationship. Neilsen (1984) reiterates its importance by suggesting that particular attention be paid to establishing as well as stopping the relationship.

An important part of establishing the relationship between the OD consultant and the client system is defining the roles and expectations of the different parties involved. Four primary groups can be identified, all of which are essential to the change effort. First are the *outside consultants* who guide and coordinate the overall change project, organize information collected from the members of the system, and plan and lead many of the training activities. Second are the *internal resource persons* who are responsible for developing and facilitating the information needed for critical organizational decisions. Even though they remain members of the organization, they are effectively separated from it by virtue of their access to information that cannot be shared with supervisors. A third group is the *managers* who must commit themselves, in terms of both time and money, to the activities required to support the OD effort. The final group consists of *nonmanagerial personnel,* who make commitments to work with the other three, the consultants, internal resource persons, and managers, in improving the organization (Bower and Franklin, 1977).

At the very heart of it all lies the issue of control. In defining the relationship between consultants and the client system there must be a clear understanding of who will make what decisions and how they will be made. The balance of power between managers and consultants must be established at the outset. According to McGill (1977), power can be shared in one of three ways. It can be (1) consultant-centered (power rests with consultant), (2) client-centered (power rests with client—in fact, the client dominates the relationship, deciding on the demand for, the design of, and the delivery of the consultant's knowledge and skills), or (3) mutually shared (client and consultant share the power equally). Under the last model, client and consultant are mutually responsible for diagnosing needs and generating and choosing solution alternatives. Except for the manager's ultimate veto, effective power is weighted in favor of neither the client nor the consultant (McGill, 1977).

THE DIAGNOSTIC PHASE

In diagnosing problems and setting goals, primary emphasis has been on the processes of change. Little attention has been paid to the development of theoretical models prior to the initiation of change activities. In the diagnostic phase it is important to develop a sound methodology. To do so requires that

- a theoretical orientation be selected that is an appropriate model of organizational behavior, change, and design.
- a comprehensive assessment be made of all functional systems.
- all functional areas and hierarchical levels be represented.
- change potential be predicted, by identifying all aspects of the system that can be altered by an appropriate intervention.
- change orientation be identified, one that focuses on the well-being of the client system, not the consultant.
- one be able to distinguish among the different actions to be taken by the client system and their implications (Bower and Franklin, 1977).

The diagnostic process involves data acquisition, data organization, and evaluation or interpretation of the organized information. Data may be verbal or numeric and, as a general rule, should be gathered more frequently in less stable organizations. The diagnostician may gather data directly or indirectly through interviews, questionnaires, and observations and/or by analyzing organizational documents such as policy and procedure manuals, job descriptions, performance evaluations, and the operating records of the company (Phelps, 1988).

THE SOLUTION PHASE

Change agents must be able to identify the sources of problems and match appropriate solutions to the problems. This requires a comprehensive analysis of the current state of the organization (diagnostic phase). This analysis precedes, and will in fact determine, the appropriate treatment or intervention. Therefore, change agents must be familiar with the myriad of intervention strategies available and categorize them in a meaningful fashion. Once this has been done, it is time to identify the most appropriate and powerful intervention possible. Of course, this should be based on the type of problem identified during the diagnostic phase. Many times the solution identification phase is overlooked as an important part of the OD process. Often it is included in the intervention phase. It should remain separate, since matching an appropriate intervention to an identified problem is just as important as the intervention itself.

THE INTERVENTION PHASE

The action that is taken by the change agent is generally referred to as intervention. It is defined as any strategy, approach, program, learning activity, or organized improvement designed to bring about a meaningful improvement in the organization and/or its human resources. This could include changes in beliefs, feelings, relationships, processes, and structure so that improved efficiency can be facilitated.

During intervention and implementation several factors are significant in successful organizational change. Top-level managers must be involved in and committed to the change effort. The individuals must also be involved in order to understand the need for change and how it affects them. Involving these organizational members should increase their commitment to change—they may lack the knowledge and skills necessary to identify and solve problems. It is also an excellent way for outside consultants and HRD practitioners to provide the training that results in the growth and development of human resources.

Once an intervention has been implemented, the change agent monitors its progress and determines if adjustments are needed. It is essential that consultants and client communicate effectively during this phase. Failed communication may result in failure of the intervention and a missed opportunity for meaningful change to occur.

Intervention can be threatening to members of the organization who see "change" as something to fear. Therefore, consultants must look for signs of resistance and "gatekeeping" on the part of employees and react accordingly. Gatekeeping refers to retaining or holding information vital to others in the organization. This requires that the change agent be skilled in observation techniques and interview skills so that problems can be detected in the early stages.

THE FEEDBACK (EVALUATION) PHASE

McGill (1977) indicated that the results or performance of OD is ultimately assessed through three categories of measures. These measures may be (1) product-oriented, relating to OD's direct contribution to profit; (2) product/ process-oriented, relating to OD's contribution to production and profit; or (3) process-oriented, relating to measuring performance in nonproductive, nonquantifiable terms and usually dealing with the quality of organizational processes (p. 36).

Bowers and Franklin (1977) define two types of evaluation: (1) summative and (2) formative. Summative evaluation is geared to an assessment of overall outcomes of the OD effort and to a decision to continue or terminate the process. Formative evaluation, on the other hand, is intended to provide feedback for program improvement and to facilitate choosing among possible modifications. Evaluation of an OD intervention should be developmental—that is, formative. It should be used as the basis for constructively modifying the OD effort in the future, not simply as a basis for keeping it alive or, alternatively, completing the process (Phelps, 1988).

VALUE OF OD

The optimal value of OD is indeed in the improvement of an organization in terms of its efficiency and productivity. However, OD is of value to the organization in several other ways (Margulies and Raia, 1978); For example:

1. OD provides opportunities for people to function as human beings rather than as resources in the productive process.

2. OD provides opportunities for each organization member, as well as the organization itself, to develop to full potential.

3. OD increases the effectiveness of the organization in terms of all of its goals.

4. OD allows an environment to be created in which it is possible to find exciting and challenging work.

5. OD provides opportunities for people in organizations to influence the way in which they relate to work, the organization, and the environment.

6. OD enables each person to be treated as a human being with a complex set of needs, all of which are important in his or her work and life.

Another way of examining the value of OD is to determine its underpinnings. These underpinnings reflect the growing importance of the humanistic point of

Figure 4.2   Underpinnings of organizational development

Reprinted from E. H. Neilsen, Becoming an OD Practitioner, 1984, p. 17. Reprinted by permission of Prentice-Hall Inc., Englewood Cliffs, NJ.

view and the transition to participatory management. Figure 4.2 reflects the values underlying OD strategy and this transition.

Neilsen (1984) reported that "OD is most likely to succeed . . . with organizations whose members are mature, psychologically healthy adults, who are committed to the organization's welfare and who have important resources to offer, and whose leaders are willing to risk experimentation to enhance individual and organizational health" (p. 22). However, many believe that the ultimate value lies in the OD process. As a process OD allows organizations and their members to *become* mature, psychologically healthy, and committed to the organization. They also believe that OD as a process encourages the development of personal skills and competencies the organization can utilize in its effort to remain competitive and productive. Thus, OD's principal value is that it allows the development of people as well as organizations.

ORGANIZATION TYPES

Organizations can be divided into four types—passive, pyramidal, competitive, and collaborative—according to how they view their employees and/or the relationship of the employees to the organization.

Passive organizations do not view employees as important and they are not committed to their welfare. This type of organization does not rely on the talents, abilities, and skills of its employees to solve problems and make essential contributions. This orientation cannot be conducive to OD and its benefits unless it severely alters its passive attitude toward employees.

Pyramidal organizations believe that most employees are committed to the welfare of the organization but only a few have important talents, abilities, or skills to offer. This represents a tall, hierarchical orientation with many levels and layers. OD often occurs at a specific level in this type of organization. A systemwide approach is not appropriate because most employees are not viewed as critical.

Competitive organizations consist of many talented and skilled employees with only a few being loyal to the organization. In this type of organization the employees often have a higher level of education and many years of experience. Most are able to find employment in a number of competing firms, placing extreme pressure on management and organizational leaders. OD can be fostered in competitive organizations if it enables employees to become actively involved. One of the purposes for OD in these companies is to improve organizational loyalty and commitment.

Collaborative organizations view employees as important and committed. They allow employee participation in most if not all aspects of the organization. The organization's culture fosters loyalty and involvement. OD is an ongoing process and is encouraged and supported. In fact, the goal of OD is to develop cultures that utilize employees' talents, abilities, and skills and encourage commitment the way competitive organizations do.

INDIVIDUAL DEVELOPMENT AND OD: A RELATIONSHIP

Many HRD practitioners fail to see the connection between individual development (training) and OD. These terms are often used interchangeably, which leads to increased confusion and the misapplication of each. It is, therefore, necessary to arrive at an acceptable understanding of the relationship between these two concepts in order to increase understanding and thus the effective use of each concept.

Regardless of the type of learning that takes place in an organization (training, education, or development), the focus remains the same: The "employees" are engaged in activities that enable them to perform more efficiently on either present or future job assignments. Therefore, the common element in each learning activity is the individuals. They are the ones who are participating in learning and who receive the greatest benefit. The implication of this is that training (individual development) is at the heart of OD. This is a "micro" perspective of organizational development. A micro perspective maintains that each employee contributes to the overall efficiency of the organization through increasing skills, competencies, knowledge, and attitudes. As stated earlier in this chapter, the macro perspective maintains that the organization is the principal beneficiary of learning interventions and change. The individual employees are viewed as secondary in the development process.

Because there are both micro and macro views of improved organizational efficiency, organizations generally maintain both an individual development process and an organizational development process. This is often counterproductive because the two processes are competing for limited capital resources aimed at improving performance and the efficiency of the organization. It also creates an unhealthy environment in that two completely different philosophies are oriented toward the same goals and objectives. This increases ambiguity and confusion over how important and worthy human resource development is. Moreover, it continues to communicate to upper management a lack of an agreed-upon approach to human resource enhancement.

The answer to this dilemma is not in the approach or approaches used to obtain improved organizational efficiency but in the commonality of the micro and macro perspectives. Their principal commonality is the improved performance and personal growth of the individual employee. This is essential if the organization is to improve and realize the benefits of operational efficiency. It must be understood that this is more than the application of the three types of learning activities implied by individual development, it is a commitment to the advancement and enhancement of the employees' career potential, thus, their career development (Gilley, 1989).

On the other hand, it is also more than the improvement of the organization. Organizations cannot actually improve unless the employees in respective management and leadership positions improve. For example, organizations are perceived as more efficient when employee performance improves, but the reality is that the improved performance is a direct result of individual employees increasing their skills, competencies, knowledge, and/or improving their behaviors. The efficiency of the organization has improved only because the individual employee has improved. It is also argued that operational changes improve organizational efficiency, but it is the employees who implement the changes and make the new structure work better. The same concept may be applied to quality circles. The philosophy behind quality circles is that the employees are in a better position than management is to identify operational problems, but they lack the official authority to make the changes needed to improve performance and efficiency (Gilley, 1985).

Therefore, the micro and macro perspectives of improved organizational efficiency maintain one commonality: the "individual employees" and their respective improvement. Since organizations are made up of a myriad of individuals, improvement must begin with each of the respective members of the organization. Then and only then will performance improve, and the organization will operate more efficiently (Gilley, 1989).

This commonality can be best understood if another HRD concept is applied, the concept of career development. This idea may be confusing since many HRD practitioners view the process of career development as separate from individual development and OD. It becomes clearer if we examine career development more closely. For example, the primary purpose of career development is to help employees analyze their abilities and interests to better match personal growth and development to the needs of the organization. Let us illustrate what we mean by this. *First,* career development was defined in Chapter 3 as an organized, planned effort comprised of structural learning activities or processes that result in a practical plotting effort between employees and organizations. This definition implies that learning activities are necessary. In fact, each of the three learning activities identified as a part of the individual development process—training, development, and education—can be applied to the career development process. For example, training is necessary for employees to learn the basic abilities they need to remain on the job. Development activities are necessary as a means of career advancement and mobility. Educational activities are necessary so that employees can personally develop to their maximum potential (Gilley, 1989).

Second, within the career development system, the employee is responsible for career planning and the organization is responsible for career management. These two separate but related processes combine to make up the organizational career development process (see figure 3.1 on page 50). A marriage between the organization and the individual employee is essential in career development. Organizations engage in developmental planning, the process of assessing appropriate goals and objectives, and the proper allocation of physical, financial, and human resources. Employees engage in career/life planning, which includes analysis of personal goals and competencies and a realistic evaluation of future opportunities (Gilley, 1989).

Both organizations and employees need to conduct three additional types of analyses which will determine the "matching process" between the two principals. They are: needs, skills, and potential. Once the matching process is completed, the organization should have identified its human resource needs and can begin to develop learning activities designed to prepare employees accordingly. The organization could improve operational efficiency as well. This, however, is not perceived to be a micro perspective of improved organizational efficiency because it involves both the organization and the employee in the process of learning. That is, the career of the employee is greatly enhanced and at the same time the organization benefits from the improved performance. As a result, the purposes of both the micro and macro perspectives have been met.

Career development programs are a critical tool through which organizations can increase productivity, improve employee attitudes toward work and the organization, and develop greater work satisfaction. Organizations want to develop and promote employees from within and reduce turnover, in an effort to eliminate the "revolving door" philosophy so common in organizations today. In addition, they want to communicate to employees that they are deeply interested in their development, an image that serves as a positive recruiting tool.

It can be concluded that for career development programs to be successful, the employees and the organization must work together as a team. In addition, the HRD practitioner must be responsible for the organization and management of the program as well as the identification and development of career development activities deemed appropriate. Each of the key players (top management, HRD practitioners, managers, employees) must meet their responsibilities regarding career development. The result will be a stronger linkage between individual development and organizational development (see Table 4.2).

RECOMMENDATIONS FOR HRD PRACTITIONERS

HRD practitioners must relate to a variety of people in order for career development to become the linkage between ID and OD. This group includes top level management, supervisors, and employees. In addition, they must assume

Table 4.2 Career Development Responsibilities

Player	Responsibilities
Top management	Policy development related to career development programs. Commits financial resources to career development program. Provides opportunities for others to collaborate.
HRD Practitioner	Guidance and information. Leadership and development. Program liaison.
Manager	Support and advice as career counselor. Feedback through performance.
Employee	Responsibility for career. Career planning. Undertakes needs analyses. Identifies training and development needs. Implements results.

Reprinted with permission from J. W. Gilley, Performance Improvement Quarterly 2(1), copyright 1989 National Society for Performance and Instruction.

many different roles, such as administrator, developer, provider, counselor, and manager of career development programs, if they are to become meaningful to employees as well as to the organization. At the same time, HRD practitioners must inform and update others in the organization while they work with supervisors and managers in the roles of mentor and counselor.

While all of this is taking place, HRD practitioners are, in a carefully balanced way, facilitating, coordinating, and monitoring employees' career development activities. HRD practitioners are also emphasizing the importance of career development to employees so that they will assume responsibility for initiating and implementing their own career development activities. These activities will assist them in developing the skills, competencies, knowledge, and attitudes that are appropriate for improved organizational efficiency. Again, the linkage between the micro and macro perspectives will have been met.

It is important to remember that if there were not clear and separate lists of responsibilities as identified in Table 4.2, HRD practitioners would become responsible for the entire career development process and the process would never become the bridge between ID and OD. In addition, without a clear understanding of their responsibilities, many employees would only participate in career development programs as a requirement and would thus never accomplish their personal career potential.

CONCLUSION

Improved organizational efficiency can only be accomplished when the employees within the organization develop the skills, competencies, knowledge, and attitudes to perform at the highest level possible. This can be done through training, but efficiency would be limited because the organization is only indirectly impacted (the micro perspective.) It can also be accomplished through organizational development, but then the individual employee is often overlooked (the macro perspective). Thus, without a commitment to improved performance on the part of employees, changes that improve organizational efficiency are only short lived. Independently, the micro and macro perspectives of organizational efficiency have weaknesses. Thus, a link between the two processes is necessary. Career development is that linkage. By viewing improved organizational efficiency from an individual perspective (micro) while remaining dedicated to the overall enhancement of the organization (macro), HRD practitioners can provide learning and planning activities that can enhance careers that develop the skills, competencies, knowledge, and attitudes of employees that are needed for organizational efficiency.

Career development is a linkage that enables organizations to meet the needs of their employees, while also accomplishing their own goals and objectives. The importance of human resources is recognized and management knows that the HRD program maintains a consistent approach to human resource growth and enhancement. This type of human resource development is also consistent with other types of strategic planning so vital to the modern organization.

(The authors would like to acknowledge the efforts of Marcia K. Phelps, Coordinator of Cooperative Education and Internships at the University of Nebraska, Lincoln, for her research and contributions in the development of this chapter.)

CHAPTER 5

The HRD Manager

Objectives

After completing Chapter 5, readers should be able to

- define the role of HRD manager.

- describe why HRD programs fail in organizations.

- identify and describe the five separate but overlapping components of the role of HRD manager.

- list the essential competencies required for HRD managers.

- identify the characteristics of effective HRD managers.

- describe the responsibilities of HRD managers.

- identify and describe the eight strategies for HRD managers for designing cost-effective and reputable HRD learning programs and training activities.

- identify, describe, and distinguish among the planning, organizing, staffing, controlling, and marketing phases of management of HRD departments.

The learning specialist, instructional designer, and consultant in HRD direct their efforts at the advancement of knowledge, competencies, skills, and attitudes in order to improve the productivity of employees as well as the efficiency of the organization. Each of these roles has as its primary purpose the development of learning programs and training activities that bring about such changes. The manager is focused on the administration and management of the learning system within the organization through the planning, organizing, staffing, controlling, and marketing of the HRD department. This role is better known as the "manager of HRD."

This chapter will discuss each of these essential activities. It will also address the purposes of the HRD department, the role and subroles of the manager of HRD, the strategic design of the HRD department as an operational unit within the organization, and the characteristics and leadership of the manager of HRD.

WHY HRD DEPARTMENTS FAIL IN ORGANIZATIONS

During strong economic periods, HRD departments grow and expand and are considered essential to the extended growth of the organization. But when economic growth turns soft, HRD programs and its practitioners are the first to see the swiftness of the corporate ax. The question that remains unanswered is "why?" Brim-Donohoe (1981) believes that there are two reasons for such action: (1) The manager of HRD has failed to demonstrate the need for the function, and (2) he or she has failed to establish viable programs that enable employees to develop required competencies and skills that allow the organization to remain competitive. Other reasons are also cited. They include: (1) HRD departments are not viewed as a part of the strategic planning process. (2) HRD departments fail to adequately measure their impact on the effectiveness and efficiency of the organization. (3) HRD departments fail to communicate those impacts to organizational decision makers if they are known. (4) Learning is not viewed by organizational decision makers as an essential competitive advantage in the marketplace. (5) Human resources are not viewed as being as vital to the organization as are capital, financial, and physical resources. (6) A supply-side mentality for human resources is predominant among organizational decision makers, which reflects the "replace them later" approach to financial management, especially during periods of economic instability. (7) The overall image of HRD departments and their programs within the organization is poor.

The second question that is often left unanswered is "Who is responsible for this situation and how can it be reversed?" An examination of the principal duties of the various HRD roles clearly provides the answer. For example, instructional designers are responsible for planning, designing, and developing learning programs and training activities that improve skills and competencies of employees. On the other hand, learning specialists primary responsibility is to deliver and facilitate the programs and activities. Neither is in a position to alter or change the effectiveness of the HRD department within the organization, except on a case-by-case basis through learning programs.

Internal consultants do have the position power and influence to alter opinions regarding the importance of the HRD department because they are not generally viewed as executive-level positions. External consultants fail to maintain the organizational identity to effect such changes.

Manager of HRD is the only HRD role that maintains both the opportunity and the position power to bring about needed changes within the organization regarding the importance of human resources and the role that the HRD department plays in the development of such resources. Only this role can demonstrate the need for a comprehensive learning system that is designed to develop human resources, something that is vital to the growth, development, and competitiveness of the organization. This role is the only one that has access to essential decision makers and that can influence their beliefs regarding the value of HRD. Finally, it is the only role that is viewed as a "true" part of the management function of the organization and treated accordingly.

ROLE OF MANAGER OF HRD

The role of manager of HRD consists of five separate but overlapping components referred to as subroles. Each is vital to the development of an efficient and properly managed HRD department. They include: (1) evaluator of the HRD program's impacts and effects on organizational efficiency, (2) management of the organizational learning system, (3) operational manager responsible for the planning, organizing, staffing, controlling, and coordinating of the HRD department, (4) strategist responsible for long-term planning and integrating of HRD into the organization, and (5) marketing specialist responsible for the advancement of HRD within the organization through well defined and effective networks. Sredl and Rothwell (1987) developed a simplified model of managing the HRD department that reflects each of these five subroles (see Figure 5.1).

EVALUATOR

The HRD manager is the principal evaluator of the impact of the HRD program on overall organizational efficiency. Within this subrole, the manager is responsible for the design, development, and implementation of program evaluations as well as cost/benefit programs. Each of these is used to determine the effects of learning on the employees and the organization. HRD managers are also

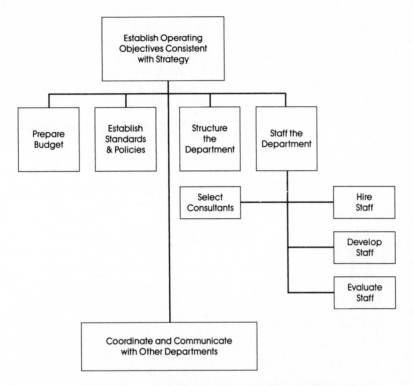

Figure 5.1   A simplified model of managing the HRD department
Reprinted by permission of Stredl and Rothwell, The ASTD Reference Guide to Professional Train-ing Roles and Competencies, *1987, The HRD Press.*

responsible for the evaluation of career development programs and organiza-tional development activities. The evaluation of the effectiveness of learning specialists, instructional designers, and consultants is another part of this sub-role. In summary, the HRD manager is accountable for the evaluation of all aspects of the HRD program, its results, its effectiveness, its impacts, and its practitioners.

MANAGEMENT OF THE ORGANIZATIONAL LEARNING SYSTEM

HRD is about improved performance and productivity through increased knowledge, competencies, skills, and attitudes. In other words, HRD is about learning, its effects on employees, and its impact on the organization. The man-ager of HRD is the person responsible for the management of learning within the organization and the development of programs and activities that foster growth.

The manager of HRD should possess knowledge of program planning and design, as well as knowledge of how to evaluate learners, programs, and in-structors. A manager of HRD should also be able to deliver or facilitate learning programs and activities. In addition, he or she must know how to assess the impacts that HRD is having on the organization and be able to effectively communicate such results to organizational decision makers.

A knowledge of adult learning theory and appropriate instructional strategies is desirable. An understanding of on-the-job, off-the-job, and through-the-job learning activities is also needed. Finally, an HRD manager must understand the importance of career development and organizational development and how they contribute to learning and development and when it is appropriate to incorporate them into the learning system.

OPERATIONAL MANAGER

This role is often viewed as the primary role of a manager of HRD. It consists of the five basic elements of management—planning, organizing, staffing, controlling, and marketing. Each of these elements will be addressed in detail later in this chapter. Some of the areas that will be examined include

1. Importance of strategic planning to the HRD department
2. Staff recruitment, selection, hiring, evaluation, and development
3. HRD budget development and control
4. HRD policies, procedures, and standards
5. Financial management
6. Management of equipment and facilities
7. Material development and management
8. Supervision of staff and operation
9. Program schedule
10. Environmental maintenance

It is important to note that the major part of any manager's time is devoted to these activities.

ORGANIZATIONAL INTEGRATION OF HRD

The manager of HRD must develop long-range plans included in the broad human resource strategy of the client system. This includes the development of an organizationwide HRD program that is a part of the everyday operations of the organization. It is not enough to be a component of the organization; HRD must be integrated into the fabric of the organization as well.

As a strategist, an HRD manager must identify the department's strengths and weaknesses and develop plans for their continued development or elimination. A manager must also identify external threats as well as opportunities that the HRD department will be confronted with. In addition, an HRD manager must identify forces or trends impacting HRD; for example, the impact of technological developments on instructional strategies and delivery systems. A manager must develop guidelines and plans for implementing long-range plans and determine alternative directions for HRD. Finally, a manager of HRD must be able to identify and implement cost/benefit analyses that measure the impact of HRD on the organization.

Regardless, an HRD manager must function first as a member of the management team and second as an advocate of performance and productivity improvement through learning. As an organization member, HRD managers must be able to demonstrate that the HRD department is a worthwhile part of the organization. Its importance should be equal to other organizational departments and viewed as such.

MARKETING SPECIALIST

In order to build and maintain supportive internal/external relations, the HRD manager must become a part of the organizational management team by attending meetings, making presentations, serving on a variety of committees, and writing articles and professional papers about the importance of HRD to organizational enhancement. In addition, he or she must be constantly available to all individuals and groups within the organization. HRD managers must also build and develop networks that communicate the importance of HRD and support its continued development. Chapter 11, Marketing and Positioning the HRD Program Within the Organization, is an excellent resource for managers to follow in their quest to improve the image of their program and department.

COMPETENCIES OF HRD MANAGERS

According to the ASTD Model for Excellence (McLagan & Bedrick, 1983), several competencies are required in order to perform as a competent HRD manager. They include

- Organization-behavior understanding
- Delegation skill
- Cost/benefit-analysis skill
- Intellectual versatility
- Feedback skill
- Data-reduction skill
- Presentation skill
- Relationship versatility
- Industry understanding
- Organization understanding
- Futuring skill
- Group-process skill

- Negotiation skill
- Training-and-development-field understanding
- Adult-learning understanding
- Computer competence
- Career-development knowledge
- Personnel/HR-field understanding

Of these competencies, the first four are the most important for the HRD manager. The last four are the least important.

CHARACTERISTICS OF EFFECTIVE HRD MANAGERS

Nadler and Wiggs (1986) identified the characteristics of effective HRD managers. Each is viewed as essential to the development of a comprehensive and competent HRD program. *First,* HRD managers must have the ability to plan HRD activities that foster training, development, and education. These activities should be targeted at the needs of employees, supervisors, line managers, customers, and nonemployees of the organization. *Second,* they should be able to establish goal priorities for the HRD activities over a one-to-five-year time span. In other words, HRD managers must be futurist with respect to appropriate HRD activities. *Third,* HRD managers must have the ability to identify the most appropriate organizational structure and location for HRD. *Fourth,* HRD managers must possess effective communication skills which they use to direct the HRD staff as well as to communicate with organizational leaders. *Fifth,* as a means of establishing good internal and external data sources, HRD managers must be able to identify and develop effective HRD management information systems.

Sixth, HRD managers should develop a mission-oriented position description for the professional HRD staff. In addition, HRD managers must be able to develop internal training, development, and education activities by which to foster ongoing growth for the HRD staff. *Seventh,* effective HRD managers must practice what they preach. For example, many HRD programs advocate participator management techniques and open-minded leadership. If the HRD manager of such programs fails to demonstrate these skills in his or her daily operation it will result in very low acceptance and credibility. *Eighth,* HRD managers must be technically competent but also practical and application oriented. *Ninth,* effective HRD managers must build confidence in their HRD staff by allowing them to become a part of the decision-making process and by providing opportunities for greater involvement and responsibility. This is often referred to as delegation of duties or responsibilities. By allowing such opportunities, HRD managers are communicating their faith and trust in members of the HRD staff, which builds confidence. It also builds a team orientation that strengthens the entire department.

RESPONSIBILITIES OF HRD MANAGERS

HRD managers must be ready to prepare organizations for a different and more challenging labor force: for example, older workers with many more years of experience than was the case in the past; a better educated work force that is less willing to accept the values, beliefs, patterns, and goals of the organization; an overall decline in the work ethic among all classes of labor; and greater emphasis on quality-of-life issues rather than the "company"-goals-at-all-cost mentality. These are but a few of the many changes that face organizations to which the HRD manager must respond.

Through all of this HRD managers must be able to demonstrate the effectiveness of their programs and show how their efforts contribute to the overall effectiveness of the organization. There needs to be progress in reducing absenteeism, accidents, tardiness, errors, turnover, and client complaints and employee grievances, while at the same time increasing the employees' knowledge, competencies, skills, and attitudes. Efforts need to be concentrated in increasing productivity and performance while eradicating improper employee selection.

STRATEGIES FOR DESIGNING AN HRD PROGRAM

Lawrie (1986) identified for managers of HRD an eight-point strategy for designing cost-effective, reputable learning programs that can survive economic crises and internal/external changes affecting the organization.

1. Establish a written HRD philosophy. There should be a written HRD philosophy that states unequivocally that effective human resource development can improve performance (i.e., change behavior, produce results, increase productivity). This provides a framework for the HRD program. It also provides a common objective for each of the members of the HRD staff on which to focus their efforts. It will serve as a guide for the program's planning and implementation.

Components of an HRD philosophy should include: (1) an assessment of the employees and an explanation of what each employee needs to contribute to their own growth, (2) a comprehensive statement of the importance of HRD to the organization and its future growth and development, (3) a position statement outlining the HRD staff view of the training-learning process and the instructional strategies the department will use, and (4) a statement on the relationship of the HRD program to the overall organization and essential decision makers and supporters.

2. Establish HRD policy. A policy statement should answer questions regarding implementation of release time for training, tuition reimbursement, eligibility requirements, and standards of employee participation. An HRD policy should also include a statement regarding the purposes and long-range outcomes of participation. Attainable learning objectives and corresponding time frames, organizational structure, authority and funding sources, provisions for periodic review and revision, utilization of needs assessment data, and record-keeping procedures need to be addressed as well.

3. *Obtain support of top management.* HRD programs can only make a difference if management accepts and encourages the utilization of learning as a means to increase productivity and improve performance. Top-level management must be involved in planning and implementing HRD learning programs. This support is often difficult to obtain, not so much because of management indifference or lack of concern but because of a lack of awareness of the potential impact that HRD can have on performance and productivity improvements.

Yeomans (1982) defined top-management support as a continuing commitment backed by words and deeds over a long period of time. He also identified eight ways to obtain top-management support:

1. HRD managers must start thinking of HRD as part of the business.

2. HRD managers must learn the organization and the business they are in.

3. HRD managers must design and develop learning programs and training activities that line managers want.

4. HRD managers must involve top-level management in the HRD function through the feedback phase of program design (see Chapter 10, Program Planning, Design, and Evaluation in HRD) and use them as subject matter experts when appropriate.

5. HRD managers must design and develop programs that are practical and applicable.

6. HRD managers must understand the concept of return of investment and be able to demonstrate how their department is utilizing it in their daily operations.

7. HRD managers must make some hard-nosed decisions such as saying no to training requests that represent problems that learning cannot solve.

8. HRD managers must adopt an impact strategy rather than an activity strategy. In other words, HRD programs should be based on the impacts and outcomes of training instead of on the number of programs offered and a body-count orientation.

4. *Integrate HRD into the long-range organizational plan.* HRD programs must become a meaningful part of the organization's long-range planning. If it is not, then the learning programs and training activities may not be related to the needs of the organization. This will prevent the HRD program from having a positive impact on the organization. As a result, both the organization and HRD will suffer.

5. *Conduct extensive needs assessments.* HRD programs must address the needs of the employees as well as the organization. In order for learning programs and training activities to be effective, they must be based on the employees' needs or the organization's needs or both. HRD managers must make certain this is

the procedure that is followed and that the HRD staff understands this simple but fundamental orientation.

6. *Encourage collaboration.* HRD managers should encourage collaborative efforts as a means of obtaining maximum efficiency. This also allows different and divergent perspectives to be incorporated into the HRD program. This will insure that other departments and divisions are properly represented by the HRD department. It will also help build supporters for the programs who can be called upon during periods of economic uncertainty.

7. *Establish criteria for participation in HRD programs.* It is important to set a selection criteria by which employees are chosen to participate in HRD programs. This accomplishes two objectives. *First,* it communicates a higher standard of involvement and commitment on the part of the employee. *Second,* it forces supervisors and line managers to make a greater commitment to conduct employee interviews and performance reviews, to identify performance deficiencies, and to assist employees in developing individual developmental plans. Increased management involvement will mean increased credibility for HRD and a greater return on the organization's investment.

8. *Be introspective but focus on results.* HRD managers must seek feedback from supervisors, line managers, top-level managers, and employees as well as their staff regarding the quality of their programs, the status of their relationship, barriers to effectiveness, and the level of involvement expected of the HRD department. Both positive and negative findings must be reported. This information must be incorporated into future programs. Regardless, the focus of all HRD programs must be on results, and special attention should be given to obtaining such information. It should also be communicated to essential decision makers as a way of advancing the image of HRD.

PLANNING, ORGANIZING, STAFFING, CONTROLLING, AND MARKETING HRD

The management process involves a group of similar functions performed by HRD managers, regardless of the type of organization. These functions are planning, organizing, staffing, controlling, and (marketing). Figure 5.2 shows the approach these functions follow. The sequence in which the parts are treated and their relationship reflect the essence of the management function.

PLANNING

Planning charts a course of action for the future. It aims to achieve a consistent, coordinated set of operations that will yield desired results. Planning is the primary task of management. It must come before any of the other managerial functions because it determines the framework in which they are carried out.

Planning is basically an intellectual process that involves decision making. It requires a mental predisposition to think before acting, to act in the light of facts rather than guesses, and to do things in an orderly way. There is no substitute for the hard cognitive action that planning demands.

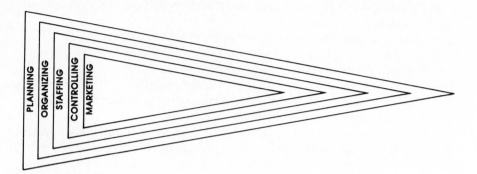

PLANNING ORGANIZING STAFFING CONTROLLING MARKETING

Figure 5.2   The management process

HRD managers must plan before they can intelligently perform any other function. This is not to imply that once HRD managers have gone through the planning process they will not have to plan again. Remember, the five managerial functions overlap, which means that one function affects the other and so on. Although HRD managers must plan before they can organize, staff, control, or coordinate, it is conceivable that because of the overlap they can begin to perform the next function even if the prior one has not been completed.

Because planning is concerned with the future, for the HRD manager, the task of planning is never completed. One of the characteristics of planning is that it is economical. It minimizes costs. Planning makes for purposeful and orderly activities. In other words, all efforts are directed toward a desired result, unorganized approaches are minimized, activities are coordinated, and duplication is eliminated. Facilities are used to their best advantage and guesswork is eliminated. Failure to plan may cause the loss of important economic opportunities.

Another characteristic of planning is that it enhances commitments. This is evident when a working relationship is achieved among the HRD manager, the HRD staff, and other organizational members for the purpose of planning. There is an old saying that sums up this concept, "People support what they create."

Planning is a long-term proposition and has far-reaching implications in that it looks at the operation of the HRD department in an analytical way. It helps traditional organizations that focus on short-term profits to consider the importance of HRD programs and activities and their future effects. Long-range planning will place a premium on research and development, expansion and diversification of learning programs, executive training programs, and many other programs such as career development, which represents a current expense but constitutes an improved future.

A good plan consists of five specific elements:

1. Clearly defined objectives.

2. It is comprehensive, but clear to the staff as well as to other organization members.

3. A hierarchy of plans that focuses on the most important areas first.

4. It is economical, considering available resources.

5. It is flexible, allowing for changes without serious delays and difficulties.

The essence of planning is informed anticipation of the future. Planning takes place against an intelligent background of information, premises, and assumptions regarding the future condition, all of which have a bearing on the organization.

ORGANIZING

Organizing is based on the goals and objectives established through the planning process. It reflects the HRD manager's thinking on the structure of and the relationship among the various parts of the HRD program as well as those of the organization. A classic discussion of organizing should include division of labor, authority, span of control, and structure of the HRD department (formal and informal).

Sredl and Rothwell (1987) identified four questions that must be addressed when considering the issue of "how the HRD department should be organized."

1. How will the tasks, duties, and responsibilities of the department be divided?

2. How much authority will be delegated
   a. to whom?
   b. on what matter?

3. How many positions will report to each supervisor?

4. How will jobs be grouped? (p. 291)

The first question addresses the issue of division of labor; the second, authority; the third, span of control; and the fourth, departmental structure.

Division of labor refers to the way work is divided. This includes (1) difficulty of tasks or duties and (2) number of tasks or duties. The ultimate goal is to strike a balance between these two. Often, division of labor is centered around areas of specialization. This provides for highly skilled and well trained human resources. If such resources are not available, the HRD manager must provide the needed knowledge, competencies, and skills through training or career development activities.

Authority refers to the degree of individual decision making that is allowed without the approval of higher authority. Again, this is based on the experience and competency of current HRD practitioners within the department. It also depends on the leadership style and orientation toward authority of the HRD manager. The type of organization and its mission or function will also help determine the authority structure within the HRD department. In addition, training or career development activities may be needed in order to develop highly independent HRD practitioners.

Span of control refers to the number of individuals reporting to one HRD manager. HRD managers who refuse to delegate authority may become overloaded because each subordinate must consult prior to taking action. This provides for consistent action on the part of the department but less will be accomplished. On the other hand, HRD managers who delegate authority will develop a larger span of control. It should be pointed out that the complexity of subordinates' duties and tasks and their level of competency, ability, skill, and attitude will help determine the appropriate span of control of the department. This, of course, will vary from organization to organization.

Departmental structure refers to the ways jobs and work groups are organized (Johnson, 1976). Four common approaches include: entrepreneurial, functional, divisional, and project (Sredl & Rothwell, 1987). Under *entrepreneurial structure,* one person is in charge of the HRD department and its practitioners. Job specialization is low because each member of the department performs several roles. It is most appropriate in small departments or when a small span of control is desired. Figure 5.3 reflects this type of structure. Figure 5.4 reflects a *functional structure.* In this situation, the HRD department is divided into areas of specialization by (1) activities such as needs assessment, instruction, evaluation, or design or (2) types of training provided such as executive training, management training, technical training, and others. A supervisor is assigned to each functional area.

In addition to function, the HRD department is further organized by location or division (see Figure 5.5). A supervisor is responsible for either functional duties or geographic duties or both. *Divisional structure* is often used in large organizations or in organizations that prefer to subdivide by geographical location, such as retailing or sales organizations. Figure 5.6 illustrates the most complex,

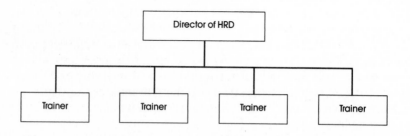

Figure 5.3   Entrepreneurial structure
Reprinted by permission of Sredl and Rothwell, The ASTD Reference Guide to Professional Training Roles and Competencies, *1987, The HRD press.*

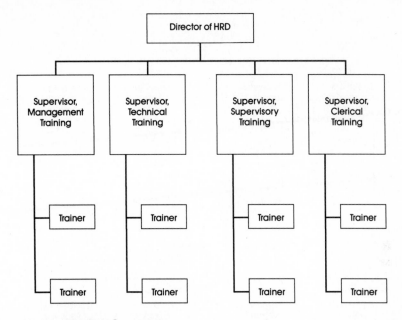

Figure 5.4   Functional structure
Reprinted by permission of Sredl and Rothwell, The ASTD Reference Guide to Professional Training Roles and Competencies, 1987, The HRD Press.

project structure. In this situation a supervisor is in charge of HRD projects in addition to function and location. In many cases, individuals outside the HRD department are temporarily assigned to project teams to prepare or provide training. This provides HRD managers with an excellent opportunity to communicate the importance and value of HRD to outside members of the organization who can facilitate future support. It also provides a fresh perspective and valuable insight regarding the role of HRD.

STAFFING

Staffing is the function that supplies people to run a planned and organized system. It supplies the human resources to fulfill the HRD mission and vitalize the department. Traditional organizational theory requires that staffing occur only after tasks and task relationships have been established. Thus, the nature of the work is divided and people are found to do it. As a result, staffing includes not only recruiting, selecting, and hiring but also placement, training, appraisal, and compensation of HRD practitioners.

Recruitment. This is a process of attracting qualified practitioners for existing or anticipated openings. Often, this refers to an external search for qualified personnel, but internal searches should also be considered. External recruitment

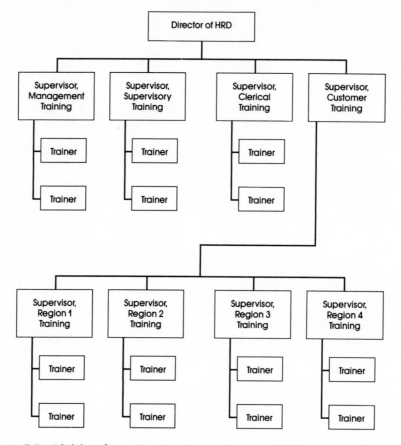

Figure 5.5   Divisional structure
Reprinted by permission of Sredl and Rothwell, The ASTD Reference Guide to Professional Training Roles and Competencies (1987), The HRD Press.

can include structured and organized internship programs as well as cooperative education activities. Advertising in newspapers and trade publications, college recruitment, employment agencies, and search firms and referrals from one's own network are other external recruitment activities. Internal recruitment focuses on targeted personnel through job posting systems, referrals, and human resource planning activities.

Regardless of the type of recruitment strategy HRD managers use, finding qualified and competent HRD practitioners is a very difficult and time-consuming activity. It requires that HRD managers be able to identify qualified candidates and also know the field of HRD in order to make informed decisions. There are a number of qualified candidates available, but knowing where to find them is part of the problem. This is why a knowledge of the field of HRD is so necessary.

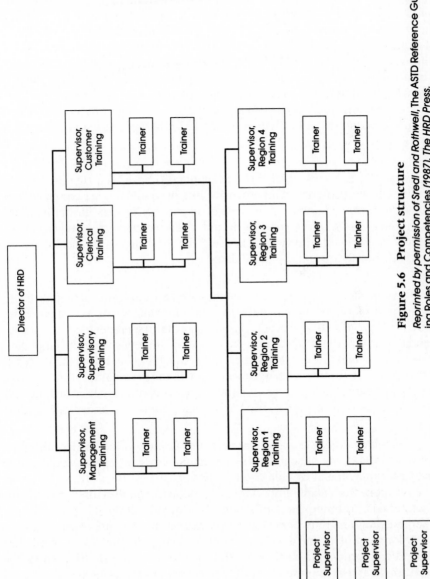

Figure 5.6   Project structure
Reprinted by permission of Sredl and Rothwell, The ASTD Reference Guide to Professional Training Roles and Competencies (1987), The HRD Press.

Selection. Once an appropriate recruitment strategy has been identified, it is important to identify selection criteria prior to job posting or advertising for positions. This insures qualified applicants and helps prevent a rush of under-qualified, unqualified, or overqualified applicants. Ultimately it aids in the hiring and future placement of HRD practitioners. For example, if an HRD department needs an instructional designer with experience in CBT, include this information in advertisements and job announcements to preclude any false hopes on the part of prospective candidates. Ads and announcements that with-hold information, however unintentionally, create bad public relations and a poor image for the HRD department as well as the organization as a whole.

Four questions should be addressed: What are the job requirements? How is the job currently being performed? What are the future job requirements? What skills are needed for the current job and higher level positions in the depart-ment? Each of these questions should be addressed early in the selection pro-cess. In addition, Suessmuth (1978) identified several additional criteria. These are presented in detail in Chapter 6, The Learning Specialist and Instruction in HRD.

Hiring. Hiring occurs when the best candidate(s) have been identified, based on the selection criteria. Comprehensive lists of candidates are compiled and the list is narrowed down to the most qualified. The process further includes examining work samples, conducting and scoring screening tests when appro-priate, employment interviews, choosing the most qualified, and follow-up procedures with unsuccessful candidates.

Placement. Once an HRD practitioner has been hired it is critical that he or she be properly placed in order to utilize the new hire's talent to its fullest potential and maximize growth and development opportunities. Proper placement is es-sential to a smooth transition into the new environment so that the employee better understands the organizational culture and his or her role in the HRD de-partment. How the new employee will relate to the personality, attitudes, and style of current employees is something else to consider when making the placement decision, as well as critical communication links and opportunities.

Management of Staff (Training, Appraisal, and Compensation). The recruitment, selection, and hiring of qualified HRD practitioners is critical to the success of the HRD function and will ultimately determine the future of HRD within the organization. But equally important is the growth and development of HRD practitioners. Training programs must be properly designed, performance appraisal programs must be effective, and compensation programs must be ade-quate for the growth and development of competent, highly skilled, and dedi-cated HRD practitioners. As the HRD staff grows and matures, so does the HRD department and its importance to and impact on the organization.

CONTROLLING

Controlling is the process that checks performance against standards. It makes certain that HRD goals and objectives are being met. Controlling is closely related to planning, an example of the overlapping nature of the total HRD management system.

There are many misconceptions about the controlling function. One of the most serious is that controlling is only concerned with events after the fact. One reason for this is that controlling is often the last function to be addressed in management textbooks. This gives the impression that it occurs after all the other functions have been performed. It is important to remember that the control function occurs simultaneously with all other functions in a system. Control decisions affect plans, for example, just as planning decisions affect control. In the process of planning, HRD managers set goals and objectives and these become the standards against which performance is checked and appraised. If there are deviations between achievements and goals, HRD managers have to take corrective action. This action itself entails new plans and new goals and therefore new controls.

Control is the element in the functional management system that insures that performance carries out the prescriptions of plans. Planning, organizing, and staffing are preparatory steps for getting work done. Controlling makes certain that it gets done. Without controlling, HRD managers could not do a complete job of managing. There are four separate but equal components of the controlling function: budget control, policies, procedures, and standards.

Budget Control. Of all the available control devices, the budget is probably the most widely used. Budgets express the plans, objectives, and programs of the HRD department in numerical terms. The preparation of a budget is a planning function, but its administration is a controlling function, in that, to exercise control, budgetary standards are set to which costs of operations must be compared and adjusted. By setting standards, progress of actual performance can be measured against planned performance. Budgetary standards provide HRD managers with the information they need to choose the course of action that will assure the desired results.

Budgetary plans generally cover all phases of the HRD operation and for a definite period of time. The most common way for organizations to organize the HRD unit is to provide a budget for its operation. This is often referred to as the *budget item center* approach (Nadler & Wiggs, 1986). At the beginning of each fiscal year, the HRD department is provided with a budget that reflects the operational expenses of the unit. This includes salaries, benefits, travel, program design and delivery costs, materials, equipment, consultant fees, and other costs. Under this method, HRD managers know exactly what financial resources are available to them. Each operating division, including the HRD unit, shares in the administrative overhead of the organization. Under this approach, other divisions will tend to participate in HRD programs because there is no additional cost. In fact, they can recover their other expenditures by sending their employees to learning programs and training activities. There is a disadvantage to the budget item center approach. Because funds are controlled by the organization and not by the HRD unit, there is less motivation on the part of the unit to identify and respond to the real learning needs of the organization and its employees.

Another budgetary approach, the *cost center* approach, allows the HRD unit to charge the respective organizational units for HRD services. At the end of the fiscal year, the HRD unit will report its budgetary performance in terms of a break-even, a surplus or a loss. Under this approach, the HRD department begins the fiscal year with little in the way of budget allocation. But as the year progresses, HRD managers have a better idea of the HRD activities that are needed and can plan accordingly. Historical accounting becomes extremely important because it provides a pattern of operation that HRD managers can use to make critical decisions (Nadler and Wiggs, 1986).

There are several advantages to this approach. Divisions are directly accountable for the services they receive. Specific organizational and employee needs are identified and programs can be developed, designed, and delivered to meet them. There is no actual cash exchanged. Funds are transferred from one account to another. The cost center approach reflects a more accurate picture of the true cost of the HRD unit, and it forces HRD managers to be aware of the cost of programs and activities and to cut out unnecessary ones.

There are disadvantages. Line managers must plan ahead for HRD, often a very difficult task. Many cannot anticipate needed HRD services, and/or are not properly trained to determine costs and benefits. They have to maintain more flexibility in their budget in order to take advantage of HRD when it is needed.

The *profit center approach* is the last form of budgetary control. It is very similar to the cost center approach except for two fundamental differences: (1) there is an element of profit and (2) programs and activities are sold both internally and externally (Nadler and Wiggs, 1986). An example of the latter is the Arthur Andersen & Co., which markets learning programs to over 50,000 internal employees. It also markets similar and often identical programs and activities externally through its Educational Consulting Division.

The advantages and disadvantages of this approach are the same as the cost center approach except for one notable exception. Under this approach, HRD managers may tend to play it safe and only offer programs and activities that will result in short-term benefit. This prevents them from focusing on the development of the entire organization. Being unwilling to risk purchase of more expensive long-term programs and activities could weaken the HRD unit over time and place it in the unfavorable position of having inadequate services to offer during economically difficult periods. Clearly the type of budgetary approach the HRD manager chooses will impact the organization greatly. Selection, therefore, should be done with great care.

Policies. Policies are broad statements of desired action intended to insure co-ordination within the HRD department or between HRD and other departments. Newman (1980) identified seven components of a comprehensive HRD policy:

1. A statement of department purpose
2. Basic objectives
3. The philosophy that guides practice
4. General practice (e.g., scheduling evaluation)
5. Use of facilities
6. Budgeting methods
7. Record-keeping

The HRD policy statement should reflect the relationship of the HRD department to the overall HR function and to other departments, organizational plans, and career management. To be concise it should reinforce the purpose of HRD, why HRD is needed, and what HRD is accountable for.

Procedures. If an HRD policy statement answers the question, "Why is HRD needed?" then procedure statements answer the question, "How is the HRD unit to be run and how are HRD activities to be handled?" For example, how do you handle a request to attend an internal course? How can an employee obtain assistance for college tuition? These are examples of areas in which specific procedures are required. It is important to remember that although the HRD manager may decide to delegate many of these decisions to others in the unit, he or she is still responsible for their execution.

Standards. These are broad statements of practice and reflect the desired level of quality. Sredl and Rothwell (1987) identified several standards, examples for HRD managers to consider:

- Training should contribute to improvements in employee knowledge, skills, attitudes, or abilities.
- Training should indicate the amount of knowledge, level of skills, and type of attitudes or abilities that participants should have before they attend the training.
- Training should indicate the amount of knowledge, level of skill, and type of attitudes or abilities that the participants should exhibit following the training experience.
- Training should be designed by people competent both in the subject and in principles of training.
- Training materials should be tested before they are used.
- Training materials should be critiqued by third-party experts on the subject matter and experts on the principles of training.

- Trainees should be informed about training objectives and other necessary information before the training experience.
- Instructors should be competent in the subject matter and the instructional methods used.
- Training directors or sponsors should screen participants to ensure that only those with necessary prerequisite knowledge, skills, and other qualifications will attend sessions (p. 301).

Policies, procedures, and standards are important controlling devices which can help shape the HRD department. They should be established based on the organizational strategic plan, but individually developed, to improve the unit and the services it has to offer.

MARKETING

In Chapter 11 much of the focus is on the marketing strategies that foster increased utilization of HRD, as well as on the enhancement of the image of HRD. At this point readers should refer to Chapter 11 to fully appreciate the complexity, comprehensiveness, and importance of the marketing function to the HRD manager.

CONCLUSION

HRD manager is one of the most important roles within HRD. The manager of HRD is indeed the organizational representative and serves as the official leader of the HRD unit and its staff. More importantly, the future of HRD in many organizations depends on the performance of the HRD manager. In fact, the competence and skill of this single person in the execution of his or her duties and tasks could determine the success or failure of the HRD unit in the organization.

CHAPTER 6

The Learning Specialist and Instruction in HRD

Objectives

After completing Chapter 6, readers should be able to

- describe the roles and subroles of a learning specialist in HRD.

- identify the three primary orientations of learning specialists.

- identify and prioritize the criteria for selecting learning specialists.

- distinguish among the different learning theories and identify the most appropriate one for their situation.

- identify the principles, characteristics, and assumptions of adult learning.

- identify the three types of learning for which learning specialists are responsible.

- identify the six stages of the instructional process in HRD.

- critique the importance of content and experience in learning.

- identify the four essential training styles and discuss their similarities and differences.

- identify the importance of a supportive and comfortable learning climate.

- identify the 10 techniques that can assist learning specialists in the development of a supportive and comfortable learning environment.

- determine the learner-centeredness of various kinds of instructors.

- identify the two models of needs assessment.

- write appropriate learning objectives and prepare adequate lesson plans.

- identify the appropriate methodology to be used in learning settings.

- describe the importance of experimental learning and identify the four stages of an experiential exercise.

- identify and distinguish among the four types of evaluation.

- identify the elements that an evaluation is intended to critique.

Three terms are often used interchangeably to describe the HRD practitioner who instructs. They are instructor, trainer, and/or facilitator. They may mean the person responsible for the dissemination of information or the person responsible for the utilization of the learners' experience. We prefer to use the term *learning specialist* (Nadler, 1986), which includes both.

In HRD, several roles are critical; however, none more so than the role of learning specialist. These HRD practitioners are responsible for a presentation of information that will ultimately impact the growth and development of employees. Simultaneously, they must identify learning needs and develop appropriate learning activities to address those needs. They must also be able to establish a learning environment that is conducive to sharing and exchanging important information. In addition, learning specialists must be able to develop learning objectives and select appropriate instructional methodologies that will foster increased knowledge, skills, and competencies and improve behaviors and attitudes on the part of learners. Finally, learning specialists must be able to evaluate the learners; the programs, to determine their effects on learners; and the impact that learning has on the organization.

A learning specialist is the ultimate "delivery agent" of the learning system (Laird, 1986). He or she is also the principal "change agent" in the learning environment, responsible for increasing knowledge, skills, and competencies and/or improving behavior. As manager of the learning process, the learning specialist performs several subroles. They include

- Evaluator
- Group Facilitator
- Instruction Writer
- Instructor
- Media Specialist
- Needs Analyst
- Program Designer
- Task Analyst
- Transfer Agent

Each of these subroles can also be clustered under three primary orientations: Facilitator of Learning, Program Planning and Design, and Analyst.

Facilitator of Learning	Program Planning and Design	Analyst
Group Facilitator	Instruction Writer	Evaluator
Instructor	Program Designer	Needs Analyst
Media Specialist		Task Analyst
Transfer Agent		

In this chapter we focus on Facilitator of Learning, with a brief overview of Analyst. Program Planning and Design will be addressed in detail in Chapter 7, The Instructional Designer in HRD, and in Chapter 10, Program Planning, Design, and Evaluation in HRD. Within Chapter 10, a comprehensive discussion of the analyst orientation will be presented.

Instruction in HRD is many times referred to as "stand-up training." This description is very narrow and certainly does not accurately describe the role. Today, organizations are less concerned with platform skills, although they are important, and more concerned with the facilitation of learning in others. The emphasis today is on questioning, listening, and providing feedback in order to bring about change in the learner. It is not enough simply to be a subject matter expert; learning specialists must understand how adults learn. They must also follow an instructional approach that fosters increased knowledge, skills, and competence and/or improved behavior. In the remainder of this chapter, these two major topics will be addressed in detail. But first we will say something about the selection of learning specialists.

CRITERIA FOR SELECTING LEARNING SPECIALISTS

Many organizations have difficulty with the selection of learning specialists. Some are selected because they possess superior knowledge and understanding of their job. Others are selected because they demonstrate the ability to relate well to people and can maintain an empathetic approach to people management. Still others are selected because of their platform skills and powers of persuasion. Regardless of how learning specialists are selected, they are responsible for learning and behavior change and therefore must be able to facilitate learning in an interesting and enthusiastic manner, so that learners become responsible for increasing their own knowledge, skills, and competencies and/or for improving their behavior.

In order to improve selection, Suessmuth (1978) established 10 criteria for selecting learning specialists. He rank-ordered the criteria from the most important to the least important. He also indicated that the first four criteria are "musts." That is, no one is hired unless all four are met. The remaining six are nice to have but if they are not present the applicant is not automatically ruled out.

Criterion 1.   Wants to be a trainer (wants to lead others).

Criterion 2.   Relates well to others—a highly subjective criterion but essential, since working with people is what teaching is all about.

Criterion 3.   Intelligence—must be able to quickly adapt and adjust to learners' answers and the context of the information being taught.

Criterion 4.   Knows what he or she wants in a job—self-actualization rather than security and money.

Criterion 5.   Willing to change self—changeable. Since change in others is the primary purpose of training, the learning specialist must be willing to demonstrate change or growth.

Criterion 6.   Outgoing, enthusiastic, flair—the ability to make learning enjoyable and exciting.

Criterion 7.   Analytical—if teaching from a manual, this skill is not necessary, but will be, if the learning specialist is asked to analyze who, what, and how he or she will teach.

Criterion 8.   Self-awareness—this criterion relates to Criterion 5 because it reveals a person's self-knowledge. Awareness is essential, because being aware of anything is the first step in the change process.

Criterion 9.   Secure within self—being satisfied with oneself is important because it demonstrates internal congruence, an attribute needed in more managers, supervisors, and employees.

Criterion 10.   Experience—not in teaching, which is expected of all learning specialists, but in the subject matter they are teaching.

Each of these criteria can be used to select learning specialists. However, it is important to remember that each organization must determine which ones are more appropriate to its needs and select accordingly.

UNDERSTANDING HOW ADULTS LEARN

Learning specialists are the ones primarily responsible for adult learning in organizations. Thus, it is important that they examine how adults learn. But first we need an acceptable definition of learning: Learning can be defined as knowledge obtained by study and/or experience; the art of acquiring knowledge, skills, competencies, attitudes, and ideals that are retained and used; a change of behavior through experience. The last tells us that learning includes change. Learning specialists are change agents who are responsible for bringing about desired change in adult learners. This fosters improved performance so that organizations can function efficiently and realize improved profits. Another result of this change is the personal growth and development of employees.

Unfortunately, how learning occurs—or better yet, how change takes place—is not a subject totally agreed on by researchers and scholars. Today, there are several theories of how learning occurs, each with a different view of or orientation to the "nature of the human being." In the paragraphs that follow we examine several learning theories, as a basis for finding out how people learn.

Behaviorist Theory: This theory equates the human being with the machine, that is, as with the machine, an input is introduced (stimulus), which is controlled (how the input is processed—known as operant conditioning), and a predetermined output (response) results. Accordingly, the purpose of learning is to produce prescribed behaviors—how one should perform. This is the so-called stimulus-response theory fostered by E. L. Thorndike, E. R. Guthrie, Clark Hull, and B. F. Skinner.

Cognitive Theory: This theory equates the human being with the brain, in that the one thing that separates human beings from other living things is their capacity to think critically and solve problems. This theory maintains that the purpose of learning is to lead the brain to engage in critical thinking and problem solving.

Gestalt Theory: This theory is also in the cognitive realm, but involves the whole personality. Advocates of this theory believe that the whole is more than the sum of its parts—a *gestalt*. According to this theory, the psychological organization of the individual tends to move always in one direction; always toward a good gestalt, an organization of the whole which is regular, simple, and stable (This & Lippitt, 1983). Another part of this theory is the Law of Pragnanz as a law of equilibrium. When confronted by learning situations, tensions develop and disequilibrium results. The individual moves away from equilibrium; however, at the same time the individual strives to move back to equilibrium. In order to allow the individual to move back to a state of equilibrium or a more stable state, the learning situation should be structured so as to possess good organizations (e.g., simple parts presented first; or difficult parts presented next, so that the learner can group each).

Humanistic Theory: This approach maintains that all people are unique and possess individual potential. It also maintains that all people have the natural capacity to learn; thus, the purpose of learning is to encourage each individual to develop to his or her full unique potential.

Each of these theories prescribes its own preferred approach to learning. The behaviorist theory prescribes programmatic instruction and behavior modification, computer-assisted instruction and repetition. The cognitive theory fosters didactic instruction, rote memorization, and standardized testing of correct solutions to identified problems. The gestalt theory prescribes organized and systematic instruction beginning with a simple concept and moving toward the more complicated. The humanistic approach maintains and advocates the discovery model, underlining learning projects and self-directed inquiry and learning.

Andragogy: Another learning theory, which is based on the humanistic orientation, is known as andragogy. Andragogy, derived from the Greek word *Anere* for "Adult" and *agogus* meaning "leader of" refers to the art and science of helping adults to learn. According to Knowles (1985), adults learn differently from children; and HRD learning specialists should understand that their trainees or learners, not being children, should not be treated as such. The andragogical theory of learning makes several assumptions—about adults as learners, program design and instructional methodologies, and approaches used by learning specialists.

Synergogy: Synergogy derives from a Greek word *synergos,* that is, "working together." Working together means shared teaching. Mouton and Blake (1984) report that synergogy is different from other learning theories in three ways:

1. It offers meaningful direction through learning design and instruments.

2. It relies on a team rather than an individual or group approach.

3. It is based on the gestalt theory of learning, that is, the whole can be more than the sum of its parts.

ADULTS AS LEARNERS

Many researchers who document that adults learn in a variety of ways agree that their primary learning style is either visual or interactive (James & Galbraith, 1984). Oral and print media receive low to middle rankings for adult learning preference.

Also, most adults seek out learning experiences in order to cope with specific life-changing events, and they are certain to engage actively in any learning that promises to help. The theory of andragogy maintains that adults want to participate actively in the assessment of their own needs and in planning their own learning activities. Adults also want to participate in the establishment of the goals and objectives for their learning, as well as in the evaluation of their learning.

In addition, the more time that passes before adult learners can apply training, the less impact the training appears to have on actual job performance. This is especially true when a person is attempting to adjust to new responsibilities that come with promotion or transfer. Therefore, timely training is extremely important to adult learners.

Usual HRD practices often contradict these assumptions. Many learning specialists rely on lecture or reading for the delivery of information; neither one is the most appropriate for or preferred learning styles of adults. Many, if not all, training programs take place because the organization deems them necessary or important—not because the needs of their employees demand them. This is contrary to andragogy's basic assumption that adult learners want to participate actively in their own learning.

PROGRAM DESIGN

When designing training programs, learning specialists should pay attention to the research. Studies indicate that adults tend to be less interested in and less motivated by survey courses (Gilley, 1987). They prefer courses that cover single theories and simple concepts and that emphasize the practical application of those concepts. Adult learners also tend to be slow to adopt new information that conflicts with their existing values and beliefs. Therefore, it is essential to provide several examples, case studies, and third-party stories—as well as periods of discussion and interaction—in a training design. In many cases, adults are more willing to accept differing and divergent opinions once they have had an opportunity to express their displeasure with an idea or concept that is contrary to their beliefs (Gilley, 1987).

Adults often perceive their self-esteem to be on the line in classroom situations, and they tend to feel personally at fault when they make errors. Thus, training programs and activities should be designed to minimize personal embarrassment and such feelings of inadequacy.

Ron and Susan Zemke (1981) point out another fact that trainers should consider. Adults prefer self-directed and self-designed learning projects seven to one over group learning activities directed by a professional instructor. In addition, when designing their own learning activities, adults often select several media and want to control the pace as well as the starting and stopping times. Remember, self-direction does not mean isolation. Learners should not be abandoned by learning specialists. In fact, most self-directed learning activities incorporate as many as 10 or 12 resources, and even adult learners need assistance in the management of such projects.

INSTRUCTIONAL METHODOLOGIES AND APPROACHES

In adult classroom situations, the key to learning is an environment that is comfortable both physically and psychologically and that fosters interaction and exchange. Long lectures without opportunities for interaction, unproductive periods, and a lack of practical application of the idea or concept are high on the adult learner's list of unpleasant and unacceptable conditions. In addition, adults bring a great deal of experience into training sessions, but trainers tend not to use this reserve of knowledge when introducing new information or concepts. They also fail to rely on this knowledge base when further explanation and examples are required, depriving learners of the opportunity to learn from dialogue and exchange with their peers.

Because of the lack of available time, many HRD learning specialists tend to use approaches that maximize their control and allow for the greatest amount of content to be presented in the shortest possible period of time. They mistakenly equate the quantity of material presented with the degree of learning, and adult education research simply does not document or support such leaps of faith. Ironically, experienced trainers are best able to establish control and obtain the desired learning when they respect their learners as being interested and capable, and when they relinquish much of their control. As a result, they gain the kind of "facilitative" control that greatly affects and improves adult learning.

Finally, new knowledge should be integrated with previous knowledge. This requires an assessment of the learners' current levels of competence and knowledge. Such assessment may reveal needs and areas of weakness that can be improved through training, but it should be used primarily to identify existing levels of competence and knowledge on which to build. Using this approach helps foster the learner's active participation, which can in turn facilitate learning.

Principles of Adult Learning

According to Cross (1982), people working in adult learning situations should apply four fundamental principles. *First,* present new information only if it is meaningful and practical. If theory is introduced, it should be linked with a practical application. This approach should reduce any resistance to learning such material.

Second, present information in a manner that permits mastery. Adults maintain the ability to learn throughout their lifetime. In fact, many studies document that the ability to learn only diminishes slightly until the age of 55, and then continues to diminish at only a very moderate rate. However, because of reduced physical abilities such as eyesight and hearing, adults may require greater amounts of time to comprehend concepts and information.

Third, present only one idea or concept at a time—to help adults integrate it with their existing knowledge. In addition, minimize competing intellectual demands in an effort to increase comprehension. It is important to remember that the principal goal of learning activities is the development of knowledge, skills, competencies, and attitudes that can help adults in the successful resolution of existing problems that will result in improved performance. Therefore, the issue is not which method is used or even how rigorous the process is, but simply the development of the desired competence, skills, knowledge, and/or attitudes.

Fourth, use feedback and frequent summarization to facilitate and foster retention and recall. Because of the lack of time available for training, these activities are often overlooked or greatly deemphasized. Failure to incorporate feedback and summaries into training could result in incorrect application of the material or a failure to apply it.

According to Donaldson and Scannell (1986), there are several additional underlying principles that will help us understand how adults learn. They include

1. Learning is a self activity.

2. People learn at different rates.

3. Learning is continuous and a continual process.

4. Learning results from stimulation to the senses.

5. Positive reinforcement enhances learning.

6. People learn best by doing.

7. "Whole-part-whole" learning is best.

8. A supportive learning environment improves learning.

9. Training must be properly timed.

Davis (1984) identified several useful characteristics of adults that can be used when learning specialists design and/or deliver learning activities. He pointed out that adults are

1. People who have a good deal of first-hand experience.

2. People who have set habits and strong tastes which affect learning.

3. People who have some amount of pride.

4. People with very tangible things to lose in a learning setting (e.g., reputation, respect).

5. People who have developed a reflex toward authority such as a resistance to authority.

6. People who have a great many preoccupations outside a practical learning situation.

7. People who are bewildered by options.

8. People who have developed group behavior consistent with their needs.

9. People who have established rational framework consisting of values, attitudes, and tendencies.

10. People who have developed selective stimuli filters.

11. People who respond to reinforcement.

12. People who are supposed to appear in control and who therefore display restricted emotional responses.

13. People who have strong feelings about learning situations.

14. People who need a purpose for existence.

15. People who can change.

16. People who have a past that can positively influence learning.

17. People who have ideas to contribute.

Each of these should be incorporated into a learning situation in order to enhance learning.

TYPES OF ADULT LEARNING

Many researchers and scholars believe that learning, to be truly understood, cannot be described by a single process or theory. They believe that there are actually three types of learning, each with its own separate learning or training strategy: knowledge learning, skill learning, and attitude learning.

1. Knowledge learning includes recognition, comparison, correlation, integration, creation, and storage of data and information.

2. Skill learning involves repetitions, practice, or habit. It also includes all procedures, operations, activities, methods, and techniques involving repetition—skill is a method or technique, while knowledge is the information supporting it.

3. Attitude learning includes the formation of values, emotional responses, interests, preferences, likes, and dislikes. These are the elements that result in behavior (Davis, 1984).

By separating learning into three types, needs can be illustrated rather simply. The inadequacy (or lack) of a certain behavior may be explained in four ways:

1. The learner has incorrect or inadequate knowledge.

2. The learner lacks the skill to use the knowledge he or she has.

3. The learner does not want to acquire knowledge or skill.

4. Any combination of the above.

From this information a set of learning objectives can be established as a means for grouping the different types of learning required to produce a particular behavior or set of behaviors (Davis, 1984).

THE SIX-STAGE INSTRUCTIONAL PROCESS

Regardless of the learning theory an individual embraces or the type of learning being addressed, there should be a systematic instructional process that accounts for each of the principles of adult learning as well as for the characteristics of and assumptions about adult learners. In an HRD instructional process, six stages are needed (see Figure 6.1). Each stage maintains different purposes and outcomes. The instructional process in HRD should start with a *philosophy*. It is during this stage that learning specialists establish their orientation to learning. This means selecting a learning theory that will reflect the desired approach and determine the necessary activities.

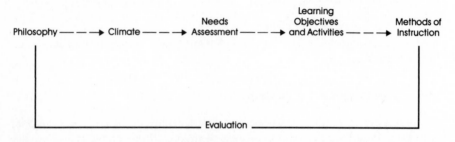

Figure 6.1   The instructional process

The next is the *climate* stage, which can be friendly or formal, and learner-centered or teacher-centered. It reflects the learning specialist's efforts to produce a comfortable and supportive learning environment. The *needs assessment* stage is the third. It is during this stage that the learner's needs are discovered. These needs should then become the bases of *learning objectives and activities*. Programs are shaped through well-written learning objectives and properly designed or selected learning activities. This becomes the fourth stage in the instructional process. Once learning objectives and activities have been identified, appropriate *methods of instruction* can be selected, as well as instructional techniques and instructional aids. This represents the fifth stage. The sixth stage is *evaluation*. It is during this final stage that HRD learning specialists will evaluate the program, the presenter, and the learner to determine (1) the reaction of learners to the program, (2) if learning occurred, (3) if behavior changed as a result of learning, and (4) if training resulted in organizational improvement. The six stages of the instructional process will be examined in more detail in the following sections.

PHILOSOPHY (STAGE 1)

Most learning specialists maintain preferences, orientations, and perceptions of how adults learn. Based on these, they select and apply learning activities, methodologies, and materials and establish learning environments. They also identify appropriate evaluation schemes and determine the needs of learners. One's preferences, orientations, and perceptions of how adults learn are often referred to as a personal philosophy of learning. This philosophy guides and directs all discussions and activities related to learning and greatly impacts the teaching-learning process.

As a way of understanding one's philosophy of teaching-learning, it is important to determine (1) one's view of instructional *content* and of the importance of the learners' professional and personal *experiences;* and (2) one's attitude toward instructor control and how people process information, often referred to as cognition. Based on these two analyses, a learning specialist can identify his or her personal philosophy of the teaching-learning process. Finally, a personal philosophy serves as a filter for each of the subsequent five stages of the instructional process and will greatly impact each. It is, therefore, essential that it be identified and understood (Gilley & Dean, 1985).

Many training programs and learning activities, however, are developed without considering the relationship between instructional content and the learner's experience. Also, learning specialists develop materials and learning exercises and select teaching methods without having adopted a philosophical orientation to the teaching-learning process. These two fundamental errors can result in inadequate and inappropriate course design and learner underachievement. Consequently, the cost of training increases because valuable human resources are not effectively managed or utilized.

The etymology of the word "education" can provide insight into the nature of the training-learning process. The Latin root *(educare)*, from which the word education derives, has two meanings, in-filling and drawing out. The in-filling process includes the inculcation and formation of ideas. The drawing-out aspect includes activities and experiences (Chadwick, 1982).

The in-filling process refers to the presentation of ideas, facts, concepts, theories, and data, utilizing methods that minimize the interaction between trainer and learner. The principal goal of this process is to increase the learners' reservoir of knowledge.

The drawing-out process refers to the application of ideas, facts, concepts, theories, and data, utilizing the background of the learner. This process emphasizes the interaction between the learning specialist and the learner. The learning specialist provides circumstances, games, activities, projects, and group discussions that require application and input from the learner. The principal goal of this process is to increase the learners' ability to apply newly acquired knowledge (Gilley & Dean, 1985).

For the past several decades learning specialists have debated their role. Are they disseminators of information (in-filling)? Or, are they facilitators of learning (drawing-out)? This dichotomy can be seen as a continuum anchored by the two extremes. Depending on their philosophical orientation toward the teaching-learning process, learning specialists identify with one extreme or the other, or with some point along the continuum (see Figure 6.2).

However, a realistic definition of education includes both the dissemination of information (in-filling) and the facilitation of learning (drawing-out). Thus, content and experience are partners in the teaching-learning process. Therefore, it is inappropriate to arrange content (in-filling) and experience (drawing-out) along a single continuum. Instead, their working relationship should be reflected. The fundamental assumption of this working relationship can be illustrated by constructing two continuums, one horizontal and one vertical. The horizontal continuum reveals the importance of content in the teaching-learning process, while the vertical continuum reveals the importance of experience (see Figure 6.3).

Five primary instructional styles can be illustrated using this model. Each style reflects the learning specialist's philosophical orientation toward the teaching-learning process. Learning specialists, by identifying an orientation

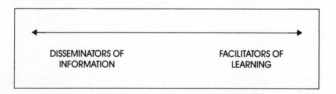

DISSEMINATORS OF INFORMATION   FACILITATORS OF LEARNING

Figure 6.2   The instructional role continuum

Reprinted with permission of J. W. Gilley and R. Dean, Performance and Instruction 24(10), copyright 1985 National Society for Performance and Instruction.

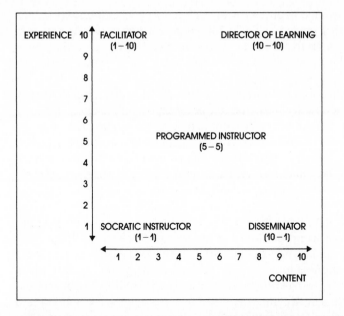

Figure 6.3   The two continuums of the teaching-learning process
Reprinted with permission of J. W. Gilley and R. Dean, Performance and Instruction 24(10), copyright 1985 National Society for Performance and Instruction.

strategy, can develop learning activities and programs that reflect their view of the teaching-learning process more consistently. This can improve the design of learning activities and programs and assist in the selection of appropriate teaching methods (Gilley and Dean, 1985).

The following instructional styles reflect different integrations of content and experience. They are: Socratic Instructor, Disseminator, Programmed Instructor, Facilitator, and Director of Learning. (The numbers in parentheses reflect the degree of importance of content and experience, respectively.)

Socratic Instructor (1–1). This style of instruction is often valued for its intrinsic intellectual satisfaction, since neither content nor experience is emphasized (Kaye, 1977). Philosophical issues are often addressed using this style. Gratification is received through cognitive exchanges, but few new ideas or facts are purposely presented. According to Kaye (1977), this style requires very intelligent students and instructors in order to be effective. Courses utilizing this style are very difficult to design because few, if any, learning objectives are stated.

Disseminator (10–1). This style of instructor assumes that learning is principally a process of disseminating information and memorizing. The most common method of presentation is lecturing. Disseminators often use a few examples to demonstrate application. The experience of the learner is minimized and learners are expected to absorb ideas, facts, concepts, and/or theories and demonstrate their understanding and comprehension by successfully completing examinations. Presently, this is the style primarily adopted in most learning institutions.

Programmed Instructor (5–5). Instructors who use this style attempt to integrate content and experience. However, the amounts of content and experience used are moderate, and this limits the amount of learning. Critics of this middle-of-the-road approach contend that content and experience are at a level too low to be useful to most learners. Therefore, learning takes place at the lowest common denominator of the audience, and deep awareness and understanding are not likely.

Facilitator (1–10). The experience of the learners is personalized using this style. New ideas, facts, concepts, and theories are not emphasized. The learner must possess an adequate understanding or have relevant experiences in order for meaningful awareness to occur. The primary focus of this approach is to deepen the learners' existing knowledge level and to crystallize the learners' experiences. When this is accomplished, the learners' experiences become a source of knowledge and a benchmark for comparisons. Classes are often active and interesting, and are most effective when basic knowledge exists.

Director of Learning (10–10). Instructors aspiring to this style believe that content and experience are equal partners in the teaching-learning process. This style differs from programmed instruction in that the emphases on content and experience are equally paramount and are at the highest possible level. Directors of learning must be masters of several teaching methods and experts in the discipline. By focusing simultaneously on content and experience, the director of learning can demonstrate concern for the learner and for the material, and promote a healthy relationship between them.

Learning specialists can utilize this model by adopting its philosophical assumptions and by arranging learning activities to reflect appropriate degrees of content and experience. This model can assist learning specialists in the selection of appropriate teaching methods. Also, by being aware of the relationship between content and experience, learning specialists can construct programs that reflect a proper blend of both. Finally, the model provides learning specialists with a philosophical orientation toward the teaching-learning process. It allows them to make generalizations and discriminations about the learning process, and subsequently a very complex task is simplified. Also, this awareness will enable them to maintain consistency in course design and program development (Gilley and Dean, 1985).

The background and knowledge of learners varies greatly but their combined experience represents a gold mine of information and data. Too often learning specialists approach learning situations with unnecessarily low assumptions regarding learners. They never tap the rich reservoir available to them.

Lindeman (1926, p. 1) stated, "The resource of highest value in education is the learner's experience." If the experience of the learner is to be used as a resource, the instructor must be willing to balance presentation of materials with discussion and sharing of relevant experiences (Zemke & Zemke, 1981). Learning activities and programs that present new ideas and concepts (in-filling) and also apply and examine those ideas and concepts (drawing-out) provide the learner maximum opportunity to develop new competencies and awarenesses. When this approach is utilized, learning becomes a pragmatic activity.

Many HRD learning specialists, unfortunately, cannot identify their own personal training style or orientation. To aid them in doing so, Brostrom (1979) designed an instrument that provides information regarding learning specialists' philosophical orientations to learning. (See Appendix A for a copy of the instrument.) By using this instrument, the learning specialist can identify the importance of control in learning situations (locus of control) and preferences regarding the manner by which learners process information (cognition) (see Figure 6.4). The four philosophical orientations in the Brostrom model—behaviorist, structuralist, functionalist, and humanist—are contrasted in Appendix B.

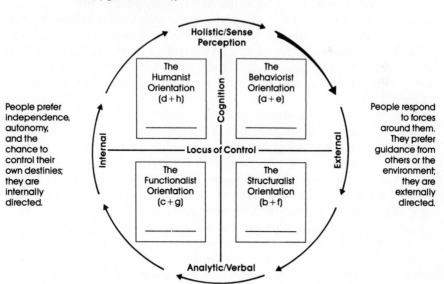

People deal with wholes, not parts — intuitively, emotionally, physically. They move spontaneously, "unpredictably," instinctively, unconsciously, non-lineally (right-brain activity).

People prefer independence, autonomy, and the chance to control their own destinies; they are internally directed.

People respond to forces around them. They prefer guidance from others or the environment; they are externally directed.

People's minds work "rationally," intellectually, scientifically. Information is processed systematically, sequentially, for storage (memory) and retrieval (language) (left-brain activity).

Figure 6.4   Brostrom model
Reprinted with permission from Richard Brostrom, Park City, UT.

The instrument (Appendix A) is designed to determine your training-style orientation. Fifteen questions are asked and you are to rank one of four statements as you perceive it applies to you. The total numerical response determines your training-style orientation. For example, the behaviorist orientation is indicated by your response to statements labeled A or E, while the humanist orientation is D or H, functionalist is C or G, and structuralist is G or F. Regardless, each orientation maintains a different orientation to teaching-learning, different assumption regarding learning, different interpersonal style, strengths, and limitations. These are detailed in Appendix B. This information can provide a better understanding of yourself and of others in a learning situation. It is useful for discussion regarding the selection of instruction methods, learning activities, and proper organization and design.

CLIMATE (STAGE 2)

Once having determined the most appropriate orientation to teaching and learning and selected the optimal mix of content and experience, the learning specialist can turn his or her attention to the establishment of an appropriate learning environment. The learning specialist must first recognize the importance of having a functional working relationship with learners. It is important to work toward an environment in which a free exchange of ideas and feelings is encouraged. Learners will feel secure and recognize that the lines of two-way communication are open. Such an environment is considered to be nonthreatening, comfortable, conducive to sharing, and even nurturing for employee development. A sharing environment goes beyond the superficial to demonstrate a deep concern for the well-being of learners and is dedicated to the improvement of interpersonal relations. Such conditions comprise what is termed "climate."

In order to establish a climate that will foster learner innovation, participation, and development, learning specialists must work to develop an attitude that is empathetic, accepting, and understanding. By treating learners' points of view with respect, and by observing their behavior, learning specialists can deepen their knowledge of their learners. In addition, direct eye contact and a relaxed posture during verbal exchanges help convey interest in learner needs. This aids in building bridges in the relationship process. Moreover, there are 10 interpersonal techniques that can be adapted to help improve the abilities needed in learning specialists (see Table 6.1).

In 1976, Boydell designed a 48-item instrument which can help determine a learning specialist's learner-centeredness by measuring the relationship between control and climate (see Appendix C). The control dimensions are the sum of average scores on dimensions 1–5, related to goals, homogeneity, sequencing, control, and evaluation; the range here is from −60 to +60. The climate dimensions are the sum of average scores on dimensions 7–10 related to instructor-learner relationship, group climate, instruction, and feeling. The range is from −48 to +48 (see Appendix D). Four types of climates result accordingly:

Table 6.1   Counseling Techniques for a Proper Learning Climate

Approach	Aim
1. Active Listening	Hearing and clearly understanding what is being said, by concentrated involvement in the communciation process with the employee.
2. Reflecting	Mirroring the subordinate's message content with an estimate stating what his or her feelings and attitudes are believed to be.
3. Paraphrasing	Demonstrating an understanding of a worker's ideas by restating them in your words.
4. Clarifying	Getting employee elaboration on feelings or attitudes to benefit understanding.
5. Interpreting	Dealing with cause and effect relationships, apparent from your own knowledge and the worker's comments, to allow grasping of implications.
6. Questioning	Using inquiry to help pull together the pace of interaction.
7. Silence	Intentional pauses that help adjust the pace of interaction.
8. Encouraging	Supportive statements or gestures that let the employee know you can accept or empathize with his or her approach as being worthwhile.
9. Tentative Analysis	Partial conclusion based on initial public testing of one idea expressed by the worker.
10. Summarizing	Tentative overall conclusion of what has transpired in the interaction to check levels of agreement and understanding by the participants.

Reprinted from J. W. Gilley and H. A. Moore, Personnel Administrator (March 1986), copyright 1986 The American Society for Personnel Administration, Alexandria, VA.

1. *Friendly learner-centered*—learners set their own goals; good, warm, supportive feelings and climate.
2. *Friendly traditional course*—instructor sets goals; climate warm, supportive.
3. *Nasty traditional course*—instructor sets goals; bad, nasty, unfriendly relationships, climates, feelings.
4. *Sour T-group*—learners set goals; bad, nasty, sour, unfriendly feelings (see Figure 6.5) (cited in Suessmuth, 1978).

The learning climate can also be affected by lighting conditions and ventilation. It is also affected by the degree of isolation provided. This refers to whether or not the environment is sufficiently removed from the workplace so the learner is not interrupted by outside distractions and/or contact with fellow employees. An insulated environment enables learners to concentrate fully on the learning activities, experiences, and/or program. A final consideration related

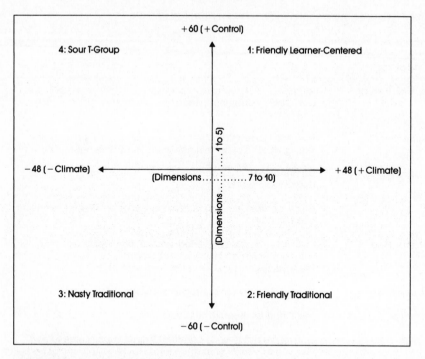

Figure 6.5   Learner-centered scale (Suessmuth, 1978)

Reprinted from P. Suessmuth, Ideas for Training Managers and Supervisors, *San Diego, CA: University Associates, Inc. 1978. Used by permission. Adapted from T. Boydell,* Experimental Learning, *Manchester, England: Manchester Monographs, Manchester University.*

to climate is the room arrangement. If a formal, lecture-oriented, and conservative environment is needed, the room should be set up accordingly. However, if an informal environment that will foster sharing is desired, then barriers such as tables and podiums should be removed. The room should be set up to reflect a comfortable, supportive environment in which information can be exchanged.

NEEDS ASSESSMENT (STAGE 3)

Too often training programs are begun in organizations simply because management perceives that a problem exists. In many cases little attention is given to the reasons why training should be offered as a solution to organizational difficulties. There are at least four reasons why it is important to assess need. First, it gives HRD learning specialists a place to begin. Second, it provides necessary directions. Third, it answers the question "why," and fourth, it authorizes continuation or gives learning specialists permission to stop.

There are two primary models of needs assessment. The most popular is the *problem analysis model.* It begins with a problem statement, followed by a systematic process of moving from the problem statement to a series of learning needs that are then ranked in order of priority. The purpose of this method is to determine the difference between "what is" (current condition or behavior) and "what should be" (desired condition or behavior). The second model is the *competency model* approach. It begins with the development of a competency model. Subsequent steps lead to a specification of what must be learned in order to meet the standards of the model. As with the problem model, the identified needs are then ranked in order of priority. This approach makes the assumption that there is a desired set of competencies that can be measured. Both the problem analysis and competency methods can be used to determine organizational as well as individual needs.

Several other types of methods exist to determine exact needs. Each of these is examined in detail in Chapter 9, Assessing the Need for HRD. It is very important to understand that learning activities and programs should be based on a comprehensive needs assessment. Failure to comply with this simple rule may result in the development of a host of programs and learning activities that fail to address the weaknesses and problems of an organization.

LEARNING OBJECTIVES AND ACTIVITIES (STAGE 4)

The identification of training needs reveals to learning specialists what must be accomplished as a result of training, but it does not tell them "how to get there." A set of instructional objectives, however, does. Two types of learning objectives exist—general and specific. A *general learning objective (GLO)* describes what the participant (learner) is expected to know or to do or how he or she is to behave as a result of the learning activities. A *specific learning objective (SLO)* describes as precisely as possible what the learner will be able to know or do or how he or she will behave as a result of a learning activity or series of activities. A well-written SLO should (1) identify the type of learning the program wishes to accomplish, (2) describe the observable behavior that will demonstrate that learning occurred, (3) identify an acceptable level of performance for the learned behavior, and (4) describe the condition under which the performance will be measured (Davis, 1984).

Both types of learning objectives are directed at three behavioral domains: (1) the psychomotor (skills), (2) the affective (attitudes, feelings), and (3) the cognitive (knowledge). These parallel the three types of learning that exist in organizations: training, development, and education. Each domain cites distinct levels of behavior from which a GLO and an SLO can be written (see Table 6.2).

Writing learning objectives (GLO and SLO) is a very difficult task because so many of the words and phrases we use are open to misinterpretation. Consider, for example,

To know   To believe

To understand   To have faith in

To appreciate   To realize

To enjoy   To grasp the significance of

Table 6.2   Domains and Levels of Behavior for Determining Learning Objectives

Psychomotor Domain

1. Perception. Becoming aware of objects, qualities, or relations through the sense organs.
2. Set. Preparatory adjustment or readiness for a particular kind of action or experience.
3. Guided Response. Overt action of a learner under the guidance of an instructor.
4. Mechanism. Desired response becomes habitual.
5. Complex Overt Response. Performing a motor act that requires a complex movement pattern.

Affective Domain

1. Receiving. Willingness to receive information: receptivity to a concept, an idea, or an issue.
2. Responding. Participating in discussion, reading, or other activity: reacting in some way.
3. Valuing. Attaching worth or value to a particular object, phenomenon, concept, skill, or behavior.
4. Organization. Bringing together different values, resolving conflicts between them, and building an internally consistent value system.
5. Characterization by a Value. Allowing one's value system to control one's behavior and determine one's life-style, resulting in behavior that is consistent and predictable.

Cognitive Domain

1. Knowledge. Remembering previously learned material: recall of material from specific facts to complete theories.
2. Comprehension. Grasping the meaning of material: being able to translate material from one form to another, to interpret material, and to estimate future trends.
3. Application. Using learned material in new and concrete situations: being able to apply rules, methods, concepts, principles, laws, and theories.
4. Analysis. Breaking material down into its component parts: being able to identify parts, to analyze relationships between parts, and to recognize organizational principles involved.
5. Synthesis. Putting parts together to form a new whole: being able to produce a unique communication (speech or other presentation), a plan of operation (research proposal), or a set of abstract relations (scheme for classifying information).
6. Evaluation. Judging the value of material for a given purpose: judgments based on definite criteria.

Knowledge, understanding, and appreciation, as objectives, are difficult if not impossible to measure. The best way to communicate objectives like these is to describe the desired behavior of the learner in words that are specific enough to preclude individual interpretations. These words are called "action words." The examples in Table 6.3 can be used to write general as well as specific learning objectives. They describe specifically what the learner must do at each level of behavior under the cognitive domain (Table 6.2). Such words should include the type of learning, the observable behavior that will demonstrate that learning did occur, the level of performance, and the conditions under which learning will be measured.

Table 6.3   Specific Behaviors in the Cognitive Domain

1. Knowledge Level

count	list	recall
define	name	recognize
draw	point	record
identify	quote	repeat
indicate	read	state
tabulate	trace	write

2. Comprehension Level

associate	compare	compute
contrast	describe	differentiate
distinguish	estimate	extrapolate
interpret	classify	compare

3. Application Level

apply	calculate	solve
illustrate	practice	use
utilize	complete	demonstrate
employ	examine	order

4. Analysis Level

group	relate	transform
summarize	construct	detect
analyze	infer	separate
explain	investigate	divide

5. Synthesis Level

arrange	combine	create
design	develop	formulate
generalize	construct	integrate
organize	plan	prepare
prescibe	produce	propose

6. Evaluation Level

appraise	assess	critique
determine	evaluate	grade
judge	measure	rank
recommend	specify	estimate
rate	select	test

Lesson Plans. According to Donaldson and Scannell (1986), a lesson plan is simply a blueprint that identifies the basic five Ws (who, what, where, when, and why). This includes the audience (who), the content (what), the location (where), the time consideration (when), and the objective (why). In selecting the lesson format it is important to determine (1) the frequency of use of the knowledge or skill, (2) the complexity of the task performed, (3) the time available for the lesson, and (4) the number of people performing the task (Suessmuth, 1978). Once the lesson format has been determined, instructional techniques can be selected.

A typical lesson plan should also include classroom requirements, training aids, equipment, supplies, handouts, and references. To structure a lesson plan, time, content, notes, and audiovisual requirements should be coordinated. This information will enable the learning specialist to know exactly the time new information or content is to be delivered. It also provides for detailed notes regarding content and appropriate audiovisuals.

METHODS OF INSTRUCTION (STAGE 5)

If major-league pitchers are to have a long career in baseball, they must develop several different pitches. Early in their career, many pitchers possess only a blazing fastball. This pitch serves them well but, as hitters get adjusted to it, they must counter it by mastering other "out" pitches. So they develop curveballs, sliders, change-ups, and even splitfinger fastballs as a means of controlling hitters and to extend their careers. The same thing is true with learning specialists. When they first enter the field of HRD many possess an abundance of subject matter knowledge and rely on this to make up for their lack of competency in and knowledge of training and learning. With time, however, this knowledge is blended with a new set of skills and a command over instructional methods.

In baseball, pitchers understand that getting hitters out will depend on throwing the right pitch at the right time. Success in training also depends on using the most appropriate method at the right time. According to Randall (1978), the selection of an instructional method depends on the following factors:

1. the subject
2. the objectives
3. the size of the group
4. the equipment available
5. the time available
6. the best way to present the subject
7. the group's knowledge of the subject
8. the kind of participation wanted

Again, in baseball, keeping the batter off balance (that is, he is looking for a curveball and the pitcher throws a fastball), will improve a pitcher's chances of getting the batter out. In training, using a combination of instructional methods will provide a change of pace and help maintain interest. It will also help emphasize the different facets of the subject and make the sessions more stimulating and effective.

There are several different instructional methods to select from, each with its distinct advantages and disadvantages. The following commonly used methods will provide a change of pace. Space prevents a more lengthy discussion of each.

- Lecture: one-way communication, a series of facts or information about a particular subject.

- Buzz group: a large group discussion allowing questions and feedback.
- Role play: permits learners to create situations and play a role of one or more individuals.
- Case study: an actual presentation, either written or verbal, of an incident that did or could have happened in a related area.
- Games: simulations made competitive.
- Demonstrations: a "show-and-tell" technique used to illustrate a point or a feature of something.
- Nominal group techniques: problem-solving group techniques designed to get someone to participate.
- Brainstorming: designed to elicit as many ideas and responses as possible about a problem.
- Question-and-answer session: enables learners to obtain needed and vital information through inquiry.

Selection should be based on the personality of the learning specialist. This will improve mastery and will also help insure that the method is presented in a lifelike and natural manner. Finally, it is better to use a few methods at a mastery level than a myriad of methods at only a marginal level.

EXPERIENTIAL TECHNIQUES

Another instructional approach is to use structural exercises or experiential learning. These experiential exercises are designed to utilize the experiences of the learners. Many learning specialists, however, prefer simply to expose learners to knowledge, using such traditional content-oriented techniques as the lecture. These disseminators do not use experiential exercises for three reasons: (1) they do not know when it is appropriate to use the exercise, (2) they do not know how to plan and design such an exercise, and (3) they are unsure about how to achieve closure following the exercise (Dean & Gilley, 1986). Others do not include experiential techniques simply because they do not know what the exercises are. Many do not recognize experiential learning as a valid method of formal instruction because their training was only in traditional, content-oriented approaches. Others recognize the value of the experiential approach, but they lack the vigor to expend the energy they need to design and present experiential exercises.

Thiagarajan (1980, p. 38) has suggested that experiential exercises are appropriate for five specific learning objectives: (1) to develop highly complex cognitive skills such as decision making, evaluating, and synthesizing; (2) to positively impact on the learners' values, beliefs, or attitudes; (3) to induce empathy (understanding); (4) to sharpen human relations interactive skills such as interpersonal communication skills; and (5) to unlearn negative attitudes or behaviors. The learning objectives that are established should be specific and achievable (cited in Dean and Gilley, 1986).

To implement an experiential exercise, four distinct stages are involved, from the inception of an idea to the product of an exercise (see Figure 6.6). The model is designed to assure that all aspects of the learning package concept will be included in the four sequential stages. Stage 4, actually conducting the exercise, also continues sequentially. The model is designed for an individual learner or a group of learners. Conducting the exercise requires that five elements of Goodstein and Pfeiffer's (1986) experiential learning package be incorporated for groups, and four elements be included for individuals. Briefly, the group cycle requires: (1) experiencing (doing the activity); (2) publishing (sharing reac-

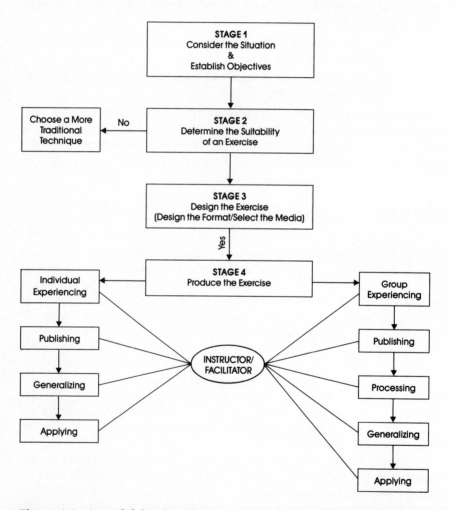

Figure 6.6   A model for the selection, design, and use of experiential exercises

tions, observations, and emotions from the activity); (3) processing (discussing the group dynamics that occurred during the activity); (4) generalizing (inferring principles from the activity that relate to the real world); and (5) applying (planning more effective behavior for actual use in the real world). Processing, the third element in the cycle, has been omitted from the model for individual learning, since individual learners are not considered in group interaction.

During the learning activity, the role of the learning specialist is not a passive one. He or she, as facilitator, guides the individual learner or the group through each element of the learning cycle. According to Steinaker and Bell (1979, p. 33), the learning specialist acts as the catalyst at the exposure stage. "The learner's acceptance of the teacher's guidance through the experience is now more crucial than before, since it begins to involve changes in behavior and in the perception of what is right for the individual."

It is important for learning specialists to understand that a meaningful experiential exercise should contain each of the elements in the model. Use of the model by those who now avoid the technique will motivate them to explore the world of experiential learning. In addition, it should provide clear guidance to learning specialists who are looking for a systematic approach to the selection, design, and use of experiential exercises. Adopting experiential exercises as one approach to learning will help learning specialists become better equipped to handle the educational challenges of the present and the future.

EVALUATION (STAGE 6)

Why is an evaluation necessary? One reason is to see if the needs identified in Stage 3 were addressed and to determine if the learning objectives in Stage 4 were met. Another reason is to improve the learning activity or program. This can be accomplished through learners' critiques and suggestions. In addition, learning specialists are often asked to defend or justify the continuation of a certain program. If they can produce objective data that reflect the worth of a program, the reviewer will be able to quickly recognize its value to the organization.

Evaluations should be designed to critique learning activities or programs from four essential elements: the program, the learner, the learning specialist, and on-the-job results. The process of evaluation should begin with data collection using questionnaires, interviews, tests, and observations. Next, the information collected must be analyzed and interpreted and conclusions drawn. These interpretations and conclusions, which should be recorded, serve as the basis for future program decisions.

When evaluating programs, learning specialists should check the program design against the learning objectives, and measure the value and usefulness of the program content. Learners should be asked to evaluate the learning specialist in several areas, ranging from holding their interest and stating clear objectives to classroom management and presentation skills. According to

Kirkpatrick (1976), four types of evaluation should be conducted to evaluate the learner:

1. Reaction: How well did the learner like the program?
2. Learning: What principles, facts, and techniques were understood and observed by the learner?
3. Behavior: Did the training bring about a direct change in a behavior?
4. Result: Did the organization improve (profits, efficiency) as a result of training?

Results can also include sales volume, direct cost reduction, work quality, accident rate, absenteeism, turnover rate, customer complaints, public relations, and new customers. In summary, evaluation of learning is done as a way to critique each element of the program for the purposes of improving it, justifying it, and reviewing it. (See Chapter 10 for more information.)

CONCLUSION

Instruction in HRD begins with an understanding of the roles and subroles that the instructor—the learning specialist—must balance. The learning specialist must also maintain an appreciation of the various learning theories and of certain assumptions about and characteristics of adult learners. These will serve as a focus for the teaching-learning process. A six-stage instructional process can be followed as a means of enhancing learning. It begins with the philosophical orientation of the learning specialist, which serves as a filter for each of the subsequent stages. This systematic approach provides for the development of an appropriate learning environment or climate, assessment of needs, identification of learning objectives, selection of methods of instruction, and evaluation of the program. Each of these stages is designed to foster increased knowledge, skills, and competencies and to improve behavior, which will result in improved organizational efficiency and profitability.

APPENDIX A

Training Style Inventory

Richard Brostrom

Instructions: For each of the following fifteen phrases printed in italics, rank the four statements given in the order that completes the phrase to your best satisfaction. Give your *most* favored statement a rank of *4;* your next favored, *3;* your next, *2;* and your *least* favored statement, a rank of *1*. Place your ranking for each statement in the square to the right of that statement.

1. *In planning to conduct training, I am most likely to*
   - survey the problem and develop valid exercises based on my findings. [c]
   - begin with a lesson plan—specify what I want to teach, when, and how. [b]
   - pinpoint the results I want and construct a program that will almost run itself. [a]
   - consider the areas of greatest concern to the participants—and plan to deal with them regardless of what they may be. [d]

2. *People learn best*
   - when they are free to explore—without the constraints of a "system." [h]
   - when it is in their selfish interest to do so. [g]
   - from someone who knows what he or she is talking about. [f]
   - when conditions are right—and they have an opportunity for practice and repetition. [e]

3. *The purpose of training should be*
   - to develop the participants' competency and mastery of specific skills. [a]
   - to transfer needed information to the learner in the most efficient way. [b]
   - to establish the learner's capacity to solve his or her own problems. [c]
   - to facilitate certain insights on the part of the participants. [d]

4. *Most of what people know*
   - they have acquired through a systematic educational process. [f]
   - they have learned by experience in trial-and-error fashion. [e]

- they have gained through a natural progression of self-discovery rather than some "teaching" process. [h]
- is a result of consciously pursuing their goals—solving problems as they go. [g]

5. *Decisions on what to be covered in a training event*
   - must be based on careful analysis of the task beforehand. [a]
   - should be made as the learning process goes along and the learners show their innate interests and abilities. [d]
   - should be mutually derived, by the learner and the teacher. [c]
   - are based on what learners now know and must know at the conclusion of the event. [b]

6. *Good trainers start*
   - by gaining proficiency in the methods and processes of training—how to teach—and then bringing in the content. [f]
   - by recognizing that learners are highly motivated and capable of directing their own learning—if they have the opportunity. [g]
   - by mastering the field themselves and becoming effective "models" for the learners. [h]
   - by considering the end behaviors they are looking for and the most efficient ways of producing them in learners. [e]

7. *As a trainer, I am least successful in situations*
   - where learners are passive, untalkative, and expect the trainer to do all the work. [d]
   - that are unstructured, with learning objectives that are unclear. [a]
   - where there is no right answer. [b]
   - when I am teaching abstractions, rather than concrete, specific ideas. [c]

8. *In a training event, I try to create*
   - the real world—problems and all—and develop capacities for dealing with it. [g]
   - a learning climate that facilitates self-discovery, expression, and interaction. [h]
   - a stimulating environment that attracts and holds the learners and moves them systematically toward the objective. [e]
   - an interesting array of resources of all kinds—books, materials, etc.—directed at the learners' needs. [f]

9. *Emotions in the learning process*
   - are utilized by the skillful trainer to accomplish the learning objective.

      a

   - have potential if the trainer can capture the learners' attention.   b
   - will propel the learner in many directions, which the trainer may follow and support.   d

   - provide energy that must be focused on problems or questions.   c

10. *Teaching methods*
    - should be relatively flexible but present real challenges to the learner.

       g

    - should be determined by the subject.   f

    - must emphasize trial and feedback.   e

    - must allow freedom for the individual learner.   h

11. *When learners are uninterested in a subject, it is probably because*
    - they do not see the benefit.   c

    - they are not ready to learn it.   d

    - the instructor has not adequately prepared the lesson.   b

    - of poor planning.   a

12. *Learners are all different:*
    - some will learn, but others may be better suited for another activity.

       h

    - the best approach is to teach the basics well and put learners on their own after that.   g
    - with an effective training design, most tasks can be mastered by the majority of learners.   e
    - an experienced teacher, properly organized, can overcome most difficulties.   f

13. *Evaluation of instruction*
    - is done by learners regardless of the instructor; the instructor should be a sounding board.

       d

    - should be built into the system, so that learners continually receive feedback and adjust their performance accordingly.   a

- is ultimately decided when the student encounters a problem and successfully resolves it.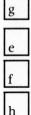

- should be based on pre-established learning objectives and done at the end of instruction to determine learning gains.

14. *Learners seem to have the most regard for a trainer who*
    - taught them something, regardless of how painful.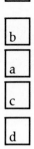
    - guided them through experiences with well-directed feedback.

    - systematically led them step-by-step.

    - inspired them and indirectly influenced their lives.

15. *In the end, if learners have not learned,*
    - the trainer has not taught.

    - they should repeat the experience.

    - maybe it was not worth learning.

    - it may be unfortunate, but not everyone can succeed at all tasks.

Reprinted with permission from Richard Brostrom, Park City, UT.

APPENDIX B

Philosophical Orientations to Training Style

	Behaviorist	Structuralist	Functionalist	Humanist
Orientation to Teaching-Learning	New behavior can be caused and "shaped" with well-designed structures around the learner.	The mind is like a computer the teacher is the programmer.	People learn best by doing, and they will do best what they want to do. People will learn what is practical.	Learning is self-directed discovery. People are natural and unfold (like a flower) if others do not inhibit the process.
Basic Assumptions	Training designers select the desired end behaviors and proceed to engineer a reinforcement schedule that systematically encourages learners' progress toward those goals. Imaginative new machinery has made learning fun and thinking unnecessary. Learners often control the speed.	Content properly organized and fed bit-by-bit to learners will be retained in memory. Criterion tests will verify the effectiveness of teaching. The teacher "keeps people awake" while simultaneously entering data—a much envied skill.	The learner must be willing (or motivated) by the process or the product, otherwise it is useless to try teaching. Performance "on-the-job" is the true test. Opportunity, self-direction, thinking, achieving results, and recognition are important.	"Anything that can be taught to another is relatively inconsequential (Rodgers) Significant learning leads to insight and understanding to self and others. Being a better human is considered a valid learning goal.
Key Words and Processes	·stimulus-response ·practice ·shaping ·prompting ·behavior modification ·pinpointing ·habit formation ·reward and punishment ·teaching machines ·environmental design ·successive approximation ·sensitizing ·extinction ·taken economy ·mastery	·task analysis ·lesson planning ·information mapping ·chaining ·sequencing ·memory ·audiovisual media ·presentation techniques ·standards ·association ·evaluation ·measuring Instruments ·objectives ·recitation	·problem solving ·simulation ·"hands on" ·reasoning ·learner involvement ·reality-based consequences ·achievement ·failure ·confidence ·motivation ·thinking ·competence ·discipline ·recognition ·feedback ·working	·freedom ·individuality ·ambiguity ·awareness ·spontaneity ·mutually ·openness ·interaction ·experiential learning ·congruence ·authenticity ·listening ·cooperation ·feelings

(Continued)

APPENDIX B (*CONTINUED*)

	Behaviorist	Structuralist	Functionalist	Humanist
Interpersonal Style	Supportive: emphasis on controlling and predicting the learner and learning outcomes—cooperative, stimulus-response mentalities are valued. Process is product centered.	Directive: planning organization, presentation, and evaluation are featured. Process is teacher centered.	Assertive: a problem-focused, conditional, confrontational climate—striving, stretching, achieving. Process is task oriented and learner centered.	Reflective authenticity. Equality and acceptance mark relationship. Process is relationship centered.
Strengths	"The Doctor": clear, precise, and deliberate, low risk, careful preparation, emotionally attentive, complete security for learners, a trust builder, everything "arranged", protective, patient, in control.	"The Expert": Informative thorough, certain, systematic, stimulating, good audiovisual techniques, well rehearsed, strong leader, powerful, expressive, dramatic, entertaining.	"The Coach": emphasizes purpose, challenges, learners, perform and make mistakes, takes risks, gives feedback, builds confidence, persuasive, gives opportunity and recognition.	"The Counselor": sensitive, empathic, open, spontaneous, creative, non-evaluative, accepting, responsive to learners, facilitative, interactive, helpful.
Limitations	"The Manipulator": fosters dependence, overprotective, controlling, manipulative "for their own good", sugar coating, hypocritical agreeing, deceptive assurances, withholds data.	"The Elitist": preoccupied with means, image, or structure rather than results; ignores affective variables, inflexible (must follow lesson plan), dichotomous (black or white) thinking, superior.	"Sink or Swim": ends justify means, loses patience with slow learners, intimidating, insensitive, competitive overly task oriented, opportunistic, return-on-investment mentality.	"The Fuzzy Thinker": vague directions, abstract, esoteric, unconcerned with clock time, poor control of group, resists "teaching", appears unprepared.

Reprinted with permission from Richard Brostrom, Park City, UT.

A Scale for Measuring the Degree of Learner-Centeredness of a Course

This questionnaire is designed to obtain your views about the nature of this course. It consists of 48 statements; in front of each statement there is a space for a number.

Please put a number in the space in front of each statement, according to the following scales.

+ 3 if the course definitely or nearly all the time was like this.
+ 2 if the course, generally or most of the time, was like this.
+ 1 if the course, over-all, was something like this.
− 1 if the course, over-all, was not really like this.
− 2 if the course, generally or most of the time, was not like this.
− 3 if the course definitely or nearly all the time, was not like this.

_____ 1. The teaching-learning process involved the learner discovering things for himself.

_____ 2. People felt free to speak and express their opinions.

_____ 3. Each course member attended the same sessions.

_____ 4. Ideas, concepts, procedures, etc. were presented by the instructor as facts, as proven, as valid ways of doing things.

_____ 5. The goals of the course were set by the learners, based on their own important issues.

_____ 6. A large number of different learning methods were used.

_____ 7. The instructor evaluated the course by the extent to which participants found it useful.

_____ 8. Course members formed real friendships with the instructor.

_____ 9. Issues of values, emotions or feelings were avoided.

_____ 10. The course was based on a pre-planned content or syllabus.

_____ 11. The sequence or order in which things were learned was largely determined by the learners themselves.

_____ 12. The course was controlled by the instructor.

_____ 13. At any one time, all course members would be doing the same thing.

_____ 14. The teaching-learning process involved instructor explanation with learner grasp.

_____ 15. Different learning methods were used to suit the requirements of different learners.

_____ 16. The instructor judged the course by the extent to which he felt participants successfully learned the laid-down content.

_____ 17. The instructor presented ideas, concepts, procedures, etc., as speculative, not definitely proven or known for certain to be true.

_____ 18. The instructor often admitted his own uncertainties, weaknesses and problems.

_____ 19. There was much exploration and discussion of values, feelings and emotions associated with the subject matter.

_____ 20. There was little variety in the learning methods used.

_____ 21. Everybody, participants and instructor, had an equal say in the way the course was run.

_____ 22. At any one time, different learners or groups of learners would be doing different things.

_____ 23. There was little trust and support throughout the group as a whole.

_____ 24. The order in which things were learned varied according to the requirements of individual participants.

_____ 25. The course members had very little to say in deciding what was taught on the course.

_____ 26. The instructor judged the course according to the feelings of the participants.

_____ 27. The emphasis was on presenting neat, cleared up end results of thinking and research.

_____ 28. People were discouraged from becoming emotional.

_____ 29. The course was run by a cooperative group of learners and instructor.

_____ 30. The sequencing, or order in which things were taught, was fixed in advance.

_____ 31. The content was not determined in advance, but evolved during the course itself.

_____ 32. The instructor measured the effectiveness of the course according to the extent to which participants acquired the specific knowledge and skills.

_____ 33. The emphasis was on the generation of knowledge, rather than passing it on.

_____ 34. The instructor made all the decisions about the way the course was to be run.

_____ 35. It was stressed that to many problems there is no 'right' answer and that each individual must solve problems in the way that he/she thinks is best.

_____ 36. The instructor quite often discussed his out-of-work life and activities with course members.

_____ 37. The instructor stuck to his favorite learning methods and used these whenever possible.

_____ 38. Emotional issues were brought out into the open and discussed.

_____ 39. The instructor avoided talking about his own thoughts, feelings and emotions.

_____ 40. Each participant went through the same sequence of learning.

_____ 41. The relationships between learners and instructor were formal, based largely on role or status.

_____ 42. The instructor never discussed his own problems with course members.

_____ 43. Individual participants were able to 'do their own thing' if they wished.

_____ 44. Facts, ideas, concepts etc., were presented, put over by the instructor to the learner.

_____ 45. The instructor treated the participants as his friends and equals.

_____ 46. Participants did not really respect each other's views and opinions.

_____ 47. The instructor did not really care what happened to participants.

_____ 48. There was much cooperation and teamwork in the course.

Reprinted from P. Suessmuth, Ideas for Training Managers and Supervisors, *San Diego, CA: University Associates, Inc. 1978. Used by permission. Adapted from T. Boydell,* Experimental Learning, *Manchester, England: Manchester Monographs, Manchester University.*

APPENDIX D

The 12 Dimensions and Their Associated Items

Dimension Title	Instructor-Centered	Learner-Centered	Item Numbers
1. Goals	Goals set by the instructor in advance to meet needs that he has identified.	Goals set by the learners, with assistance by the trainer, to meet the learner's diverse needs as they evolve.	5, 10,* 25,* 31
2. Homogeneity	All learners go through the same learning experiences; at any one time all learners attend same sessions, do the same things.	Wide variety of activities; at any one time, various learners will be doing different things to suit their own needs at that point in time.	3,* 13,* 22, 43
3. Sequencing	The sequencing, or order in which things are taught, is fixed in advance by the instructor according to his preferences and programming planning techniques.	The sequencing is very flexible; it is not determined in advance, but according to felt needs of learners. Similar items may be learned in different sequence by different learners.	11, 24, 30,* 40*
4. Control	Decisions made by the instructor, who maintains control over the course.	Decisions made by learners or jointly by the instructor and learners. Hence, joint control over the course.	12,* 21, 29, 34*
5. Evaluation	Instructor evaluates course in terms of extent to which instructor's goals are met.	Instructor evaluates course in terms of extent to which learners feel their goals are met.	7, 16,* 26, 32*
6. Methods	Relatively few teaching-learning methods used. Methods are selected by the instructor according to his preferences or ideas.	Wide variety of teaching-learning methods are selected by the learners according to their individually preferred methods and learning styles.	6, 15, 20,* 37*

7. Instructor-learner relationships	Distant, closed, formal relationship.	Close, open, personal relationships.	8, 41,* 45, 47*
8. Group	Not trusting, people relatively distant from each other.	Trusting, supportive, close, deep relationships.	2, 23,* 46,* 48
9. Instructor	Instructor is seen in role, rather than as person.	Instructor is seen as a person, rather than a role.	18, 36, 39,* 42*
10. Feelings	Generally not considered legitimate for people to express feelings about each other, the learning process, or the content of the course.	Full expression of feelings permitted and encouraged.	9,* 19, 28,* 38
11. Expository versus Discovery Approach	Expository approach to teaching. Information and ideas presented to learners by instructor.	Discovery approach to learning. Situation and resources provided for learners to generate, experience, and discover ideas for themselves.	1, 14,* 33, 44*
12. Certainty	Positivism; ideas presented as though definite, authoritative, 'the right answer.'	Relativism; emphasis on the fact that there are no right answers, that each person's opinion is valid.	4,* 17, 27,* 35

Reprinted from P. Suessmuth, Ideas for Training Managers and Supervisors, San Diego, CA: University Associates, Inc. 1978. Used by permission. Adapted from T. Boydell, Experimental Learning, Manchester, England: Manchester Monographs, Manchester University.

In the 48 item scale, each of the 12 dimensions has 4 items: two of them have a plus 3 score for learner centerd couse and two of them have negative 3 for learner centered. Thus, when scoring, the signs of half the responses are reversed. This gives a range on each dimension from negative 12 (instructor centered) to positive 12 (learner centered).
    The twelve dimensions and associated items are shown in Appendix D. (Scores on these items marked with an asterisk reversed.)

CHAPTER 7

The Instructional Designer

Objectives

After completing Chapter 7, readers should be able to

- identify and describe the role of the instructional designer in HRD.

- identify and describe the seven subroles of the instructional designer.

- distinguish among the seven subroles.

- identify and describe the activities and responsibilities of the instructional designer during each of the nine phases of the program planning, design, and evaluation process.

- identify and describe the 16 competencies for the instructional designer.

- distinguish among the 16 competencies and identify which ones are appropriate for each of the nine phases of the program planning, design, and evaluation process.

- utilize IBSTPI's "Checklist for Instructional Designers" in the analysis and critique of learning programs and training activities either designed by or evaluated by the instructional designer.

- identify the competencies listed by the Ontario Society for Training and Development.

- explain the two role cluster models that describe instructional design.

- explain the relationship of the role of the instructional designer to the other HRD roles.

The role of instructional designer is often the most misunderstood of the four fundamental roles in HRD. It is an easy one to overlook. In fact, early competency and role studies such as Nadler's (1970) and the Model for Excellence (McLagan & Bedrick, 1983) failed to identify the role of the instructional designer as separate from that of the learning specialist. In many organizations, instructional design is done by the same individual who presents and/or facilitates the training program; therefore, it is viewed by many as a part of the learning specialist's responsibilities. Regardless of the type of organization or how the role is assigned, the role of instructional designer is essential to the design, development, and evaluation of learning programs and training activities. Thus, it is important to examine it in detail. To do so we describe first the subroles of the instructional designer, followed by the activities, the competencies, and the relationship of the instructional designer to the manager of HRD, the learning specialist, and the consultant, the other fundamental roles of HRD.

SUBROLES OF THE INSTRUCTIONAL DESIGNER

There are seven subroles of instructional design: (1) evaluator, (2) instructional writer, (3) media specialist, (4) needs analyst, (5) program designer, (6) task analyst, and (7) theoretician. Each of these will be examined separately.

EVALUATOR

As an evaluator, an instructional designer must identify the correct evaluation strategy for each learning program and/or training activity. This includes the development of the appropriate instruments and the selection of correct evaluation methods. Each instrument and method must be within the framework of the overall evaluation strategy of the organization. They should also be directed at the type of information that is most useful and important to the organization.

It is essential that the instructional designer develop evaluations that will determine whether or not the learning objectives were met. They should also measure how effective the selected learning activities were in meeting the objectives. Finally, the instructional designer should create appropriate strategies and instruments for the evaluation of the learning specialist who conducted or facilitated the program or activity.

It is important to understand that, even though evaluations are conducted at the conclusion of a learning program or training activity, they must be fully considered and accounted for during the design and development phase of each program or activity. (See Chapter 10 for more information.) Therefore, it is the instructional designer who has the ultimate responsibility for identifying and creating the most appropriate evaluations. It is the learning specialist (a separate person or the original designer) who must administer and analyze them.

Donaldson and Scannell (1986) identified five steps an instructional designer should follow in the evaluation process. They include

1. data collection procedures,
2. analysis of data,
3. interpretation and drawing conclusions from the data,
4. comparison of the conclusions to the stated objectives, and
5. recording recommendations for change in the next program.

INSTRUCTIONAL WRITER

The second subrole of an instructional designer is instructional writer. This includes the development of written materials for learners as well as for the learning specialist, who will use them during the program or activity. In many cases a binder or notebook can hold stated learning objectives, articles and position papers, references, names and addresses of participants and instructors, and learning activities to be conducted. Written materials also include items not included in the notebook—handouts, modules, and other supportive materials used during learning programs and training activities.

An important task of the instructional writer is to develop a written training proposal. This is generally done after a needs analysis has been completed, assuming of course, that the analysis indicated a need for training. The proposal should describe the need for training, the objective(s) of training, the expected results if training is conducted, the type of participants, an outline of the proposed program, a detailed budget, and the type of facility required for training.

MEDIA SPECIALIST

The third subrole of an instructional designer is that of media specialist. This includes the identification and selection of the most appropriate audiovisuals used in learning programs and training activities. The principal reasons why audiovisuals are so effective are (1) they improve the involvement on the part of the learner, (2) they increase retention, and (3) they assist in the organization of the program.

There is never one best medium to use during any HRD program. However, the following criteria can assist in the selection of the most appropriate one:

1. Group size
2. Size and shape of the training facility

3. Personal preference

4. Cost involved

5. Portability

6. Session's content and learning objectives

7. Time availability (Donaldson and Scannell, 1986).

An instructional designer should measure the use of each piece of audiovisual equipment against these criteria and select the audiovisuals that are appropriate. This person does not have to be skilled in the use of audiovisual equipment, but he or she must be aware of the importance and impact of selected audiovisuals, as well as their appropriateness.

NEEDS ANALYST

One of the most important subroles of an instructional designer is that of needs analyst. This requires an awareness of the importance of needs analysis, as well as the skills and abilities to conduct one.

A needs analysis can help the instructional designer answer a number of important questions. Is training or learning needed in the first place? Who needs the training or learning? Are they aware of their needs? What are the exact needs of the organization? What form of training should be conducted? Some learning programs and training activities work best in formal classrooms, while others are better suited for on-the-job training or individual one-on-one training. A needs analysis can help determine the appropriateness of training for each situation.

An instructional designer should be able to conduct a needs analysis using a variety of methods and models. (See Chapter 9 for more information.) Each of these methods and models can improve the type of results and the accuracy of the information obtained. An instructional designer should understand which methods and models are appropriate in various situations. This is best accomplished by understanding the advantages and disadvantages outlined in Chapter 9.

PROGRAM DESIGNER

The major part of an instructional designer's responsibility is to design effective, change-oriented learning programs and training activities. Thus, the subrole of program designer is fundamental to an instructional designer.

In Chapter 10 program design is identified as an essential phase in the program planning, design, and evaluation process. It includes the identification of the learning objectives on which the program is to be centered. It also identifies the learning activities that are needed to accomplish each learning objective. In some circumstances, more than one activity is required to accomplish a single objective. In others, a single learning activity can accomplish more than one learning objective. Of course, this type of learning activity would be very complex and detailed, requiring learners to perform several different tasks.

In addition to identifying learning objectives and activities, the instructional designer must also prioritize them. If time is short, the most important objectives can be addressed first, which will help foster program results.

Sometimes, to enhance learning, experiential learning activities are necessary (see page 139). In most situations, generalizations are made based on the shared learning experiences and feelings and emotions of learners and applied to actual situations. This type of learning activity requires that special facilitation skills be developed and that the locus of control of the learning environment be shifted from the learning specialist to the learners. An experiential learning activity is very effective when properly designed and conducted. However, it should be used with care. When used inappropriately or incorrectly, it can have a distinctly adverse effect on learning.

The last part of the design phase includes the identification of the most appropriate media, materials, and training aids needed for the learning program or training activity. This is often accomplished as part of the media specialist subrole. In instructional design, several subroles often interact simultaneously.

TASK ANALYST

The sixth subrole that must be integrated into the role of instructional designer is that of task analyst. Task analysis means identifying specific components of a job in order to determine what an employee really does. Breaking a job task down into small segments provides learners with a step-by-step description of what they are expected to do on the job.

In task analysis, instructional designers describe and measure employee performance on each part of a job. It helps them focus on what should be taught in a course or learning program and how it should be measured. Conversely, it helps insure that what is taught is transferred to the job. It can often be used to make important modifications on jobs as well as demonstrate to management the contribution that the HRD department is making to the objectives of the organization. Finally, a task analysis provides needed information regarding measurable criteria of job performance, which can be used to determine the results of training.

According to Michalak and Yager (1979), a complete task analysis should contain 10 elements.

1. A statement of the task to be performed.
2. When and how often the task is to be performed.
3. The quality and quantity of the performance required.
4. The conditions under which the task is to be performed.
5. The importance of each task to the overall goals of the job.
6. Aptitudes, skills, or knowledge necessary to perform the task.
7. The type of learning needed.
8. The learning difficulty.

9. The equipment, tools, and materials needed.

10. Where the best place is to learn the task.

Each of these provides instructional designers with the information they need to design and develop effective change-oriented learning programs and training activities.

THEORETICIAN

The final subrole, theoretician, refers to the development of models and theories related to the learning process and/or to the enhancement of job performance. The instructional designer must reflect on the organization and its important operational divisions and conceptualize a "better way" to perform on a particular job. This often requires a capacity to visualize abstract concepts and ideas and to determine their relationship. As theoretician, the instructional designer, should have a futurist perspective and a willingness to approach problems from unique and different angles. In some circumstances this subrole requires advanced knowledge in adult learning theory and program design. Most importantly, it requires a commitment first to the identification of the most efficient way of bringing about change within the individual and the organization, and second to the development of dynamic and evolving learning programs and training activities.

ACTIVITIES OF INSTRUCTIONAL DESIGNERS

In Chapter 10 we outline the nine phases of the program planning, design, and evaluation process: (1) Philosophy of Teaching and Learning, (2) Needs Analysis, (3) Feedback, (4) Program Design, (5) Program Development, (6) Program Implementation, (7) Program Management, (8) Evaluation, and (9) Accountability. The activities and responsibilities of Program Design (Phase 4) are covered in detail; however, in this chapter, as a way of reviewing the role of instructional designer in program design, we will look at those responsibilities and activities in light of each phase of the program planning, design, and evaluation process.

During the *philosophy* phase, the instructional designer must identify his or her philosophical orientation to the teaching-learning process. This self discovery implies that the training style picked will be the most appropriate one for a divergent group of learners. Another implication is that the learning styles of the learners will be identified and the learning programs and training activities will be adjusted or modified to accommodate such styles. The final implication is that instructional designers must realize that the decisions they make during the remaining eight stages will be filtered through their philosophical orientation; that is, their beliefs will influence their decisions. In other words, when an instructional designer identifies a particular learning objective, he or she will do so based on a personal philosophy of the teaching-learning process. This activity should be accounted for by the instructional designer and later decisions adjusted if and when necessary.

The second activity, *needs analysis,* is one of the most important subroles of an instructional designer. During this phase, activities include identifying potential needs analysis methods and models, collecting data, analyzing and interpreting data, identifying potential areas for program development, and establishing needs-based learning programs and training activities.

Once needs have been identified, programs can be designed to address those needs. First, however, is the third activity, in which perceived needs are shared with key organizational decision makers. *Feedback* insures that both they and the instructional designer are in agreement regarding the problem they both face. The program to be designed and developed will then be supported as well as defended within the organization. Moreover, validation of need at this stage will prevent the design and development of costly underutilized programs, which would reflect on the quality of the HRD department. Finally, feedback helps build essential and powerful linkages within the organization, improving the image of the HRD department and assuring the future of learning in the company.

The fourth activity of an instructional designer is the actual design of a learning program or training activity. This subrole, program designer, was discussed in detail earlier in the chapter and is, of course, where the term "instructional designer" comes from. *Program design* is a very important phase, but it is only one of the total nine phases. Therefore, too much attention paid to program design in isolation with little regard for information gathered and/or activities in other phases will result in learning programs that do not improve performance or change behaviors. Thus, it is important to maintain a proper perspective on the value of this phase.

The next activity the instructional designer is responsible for is *program development.* During this phase, activity moves from creation to labor. In other words, after a program or activity has been designed or created, the instructional designer must produce the required components. These components consist of lesson plan(s), instructional strategies, instructional materials, and learners' materials. A lesson plan is simply a schematic which identifies the audience, topic, and content to be covered, the location of training, the time frames of training, and the learning objectives to be addressed. Figure 7.1 provides a sample of a lesson plan outline. Page 1 on the left provides a comprehensive outline of the requirements of the lesson. Page 2 provides for a minute-by-minute accounting of the instructor's time. It should be noted that a detailed lesson plan like the one in Figure 7.1 should be completed for each separate segment of a learning program or training activity.

Next, the instructional designer must develop instructional strategies appropriate for the program or activity. Methodologies are selected that will enable the learning specialist to accomplish the learning objectives. This means integrating the learning activities and the learning objectives before selecting appropriate methods of instruction. Instructional designers must consider the following criteria when developing an instructional strategy.

1. Time available
2. Group size
3. Type of learners involved and their level of expertise
4. Learning objectives
5. Learning specialist competencies and abilities
6. Type of learning (i.e., cognitive, affective, psychomotor)
7. Background of the learner
8. Level of instruction (training, development, education)
9. Purpose of learning program or training activity

Once instructional strategies have been determined, the instructional designer can develop the instructional media required for the program or activity. This might be as simple as developing an overhead or as complex as creating a film or videotape. Regardless, each should ultimately enhance learning and retention. During this subphase of program development, the instructional designer should refer to the comprehensive lesson plan that was developed and determine the type and sequence of appropriate media. Finally, media should complement a presentation, not replace it; therefore, the media selected should not prohibit or interfere with the learning process.

Lesson Plan

Organization: __________

Department: __________

Title of Lesson Plan: __________

Instructor(s): __________

Trainees: __________

Where: __________

Training Objectives:

Classroom Requirements:

Training Aids and Equipment:

Trainee Supplies:

Trainee Handouts:

References:

Page 1

Topic __________

TIME	CONTENT	NOTES	A. V.

Page 2

Figure 7.1 Lesson Plan

Reprinted from L Donaldson and E. Scannell: Human Resource Development: The New Trainers Guide, *2nd ed. Reading, MA: Addison-Wesley, 1986.*

Finally, learners' materials, including such things as handouts, notebooks, flip charts, articles or position papers, work samples, tools, and equipment, are provided. Each of these is extremely important to the development of a successful program or activity. Without them, the effectiveness of a learning specialist can be severely weakened, establishing a barrier that cannot be overcome by the learners.

The sixth phase of the program planning, design, and evaluation process is *program implementation*. It is during this phase that the learning specialist delivers or facilitates the learning program or training activity. In most circumstances, the instructional designer does not participate in the actual delivery process. However, if the person who designed the program will also be responsible for its delivery, then he or she will be performing an activity that is different from program design. Since many designers are also learning specialists responsible for delivery, it is understood that there is a close relationship between the two roles. An instructional designer must be able then to shift from one role to the next.

Phase 7, *program management,* is another area of activity instructional designers are responsible for. This includes controlling, directing, and coordinating the design, development, and implementation phases of the program planning, design, and evaluation process. This is a type of regulation device to make certain that the program or activity is properly constructed and shaped to bring about performance improvement.

The identification and development of an *evaluation* strategy is the eighth activity of an instructional designer. It is one of the most important activities to be performed because it determines the effectiveness of the program, the skill of learning specialists, the capacity of the learners, and, ultimately, the competency of the instructional designer.

The designer begins by determining which of four levels of evaluation is appropriate. The first level of evaluation is *reaction,* which determines the attitudes and beliefs of the participants toward the program. The second level is *learning* evaluation. This measures the knowledge, skills, and attitudes that were increased or changed as a result of the program. A *behavior* evaluation is third and has as its goal the measurement of the changed behaviors that resulted in improved performance. Finally, an instructional designer can select a *result* evaluation that will determine the overall effects of training in terms of improved organizational efficiency or profitability.

In addition to deciding on an appropriate evaluation level, an instructional designer has to develop an evaluation strategy that will measure the effectiveness of the overall program as well as the competencies and skills of the learning specialist. Program effectiveness and ease of operation is as important as the reaction of learners. The program should also be measured against the stated learning objectives to determine if they were obtained and to what degree. The design of a program should be examined as a way of identifying areas of weakness and strength. Finally, the type of learner evaluations should be critiqued to reflect the effectiveness of overall learning.

Instructional designers also develop evaluations for learning specialists that measure their competency and effectiveness as instructors or facilitators. The following areas should be included in a learning specialist evaluation:

1. Interpersonal skills

2. Communication patterns

3. Presentation skills

4. Development and management of learning environment

5. Instructor's credibility

6. Question-and-answer skills

7. Effective use of media

8. Appropriate use of instructional methods

9. Ability to explain complex and difficult material

10. Facilitation skills

11. Proper analysis of learners

12. Effective use of feedback and motivation techniques

The ninth and final activity of an instructional designer involves the development of appropriate *accountability* strategies related to the learning program. This refers to the establishment of a feedback process whereby the effects of the program or activity are communicated to the program designer, the learners, the learning specialists, the managers of HRD, and/or the organization at large. It is important to understand that every learning program or training activity affects one or all of these groups. Therefore, it is essential that each receive feedback regarding their performance, in order to improve and enhance future programs and activities as well as the performance of one or all of the groups.

COMPETENCIES FOR INSTRUCTIONAL DESIGNERS

In 1986 the International Board of Standards for Training, Performance and Instruction (IBSTPI) published a comprehensive list of competencies for instructional designers. They are referred to as *The Standards*. The purpose of the list is to provide instructional designers and organizations with criteria for designing learning programs. They may also be used to establish individual training plans for areas of weakness in learner performance, and to measure the current skills levels of instructional designers. They represent the most comprehensive listing of competencies yet published for instructional designers (see Table 7.1).

The 16 competencies are reflected in the nine phases of the program planning, design, and evaluation model outlined in Chapter 10 (see Table 7.2).

Table 7.1   IBSTPI's 16 Core Competencies for Instructional Designers

1. Determine projects that are appropriate for instructional design.
2. Conduct a needs assessment.
3. Assess the relevant characteristics of learners/trainees.
4. Analyze the characteristics of a setting.
5. Perform job, task and/or content analysis.
6. Write statements of performance objectives.
7. Develop the performance measurements.
8. Sequence the performance objectives.
9. Specify the instructional strategies.
10. Design the instructional materials.
11. Evaluate the instruction/training.
12. Design the instructional management system.
13. Plan and monitor instructional design projects.
14. Communicate effectively in visual, oral, and written form.
15. Interact effectively with other people.
16. Promote the use of instructional design.

©*International Board of Standards for Training, Performance, and Instruction (1986). Reprinted from* Instructional Design Competencies (1986), *pp. 3, 12, 13, by permission of International Board of Standards for Training, Performance, and Instruction.*

Table 7.2   Instructional Designers Competencies in the Program, Planning, Design, and Evaluation Process

Phase 1. Philosophy of Teaching and Learning
   Competency 1: Determine projects that are appropriate for instructional design.

Phase 2. Needs Analysis
   Competency 2: Conduct a needs assessment.
   Competency 3: Assess the relevant characteristics of learners/trainees.
   Competency 4: Analyze the characteristics of a setting.
   Competency 5: Perform a task and/or content analysis.
   Also
   Competency 14: Communicate effectively in visual, oral, and written form.
   Competency 15: Interact effectively with other people.

Phase 3. Feedback
Competency 14: Communicate effectively in visual, oral, and written form.
Competency 15: Interact effectively with other people.
Competency 16: Promote the use of instructional design.

Phase 4. Program Design
Competency 6: Write statements of performance objectives.
Competency 7: Develop the performance measurements.
Competency 8: Sequence the performance objectives.
Also
Competency 14: Communicate effectively in visual, oral, and written form.
Competency 15: Interact effectively with other people.

Phase 5. Program Development
Competency 9: Specify the instructional strategies.
Competency 10: Design the instructional material.
Competency 11: Evaluate the instruction/training.
Also
Competency 14: Communicate effectively in visual, oral, and written form.
Competency 15: Interact effectively with other people.

Phase 6. Program Implementation
Competency 14: Communicate effectively in visual, oral, and written form.
Competency 15: Interact effectively with other people.

Phase 7. Program Management
Competency 12: Design the instructional management system.
Competency 13: Plan and monitor instructional design projects.
Also
Competency 14: Communicate effectively in visual, oral, and written form.
Competency 15: Interact effectively with other people.

Phase 8. Evaluation
Competency 11: Evaluate the instruction/training.
Also
Competency 14: Communicate effectively in visual, oral, and written form.
Competency 15: Interact effectively with other people.

Phase 9. Accountability
Competency 16: Promote the use of instructional design.
Also
Competency 14: Communicate effectively in visual, oral, and written form.
Competency 15: Interact effectively with other people.

IBSTPI also developed a comprehensive checklist for evaluating learning activities and training programs (see Figure 7.2). Figure 7.2 reflects only a part of the complete checklist provided by IBSTPI. The checklist is first a reminder of things to be done during the development of programs and activities. It can also be used as a formative feedback device to inform the designer of areas of weakness, and as a summative feedback device to inform the designer whether the course meets the standards of the HRD department. The checklist includes steps to follow in its use.

Figure 7.2   Checklist for instructional designers

How To Use It

To use the checklist for evaluating training quality, follow these steps:

Step 1.   Look at the first instructional decision made in the development of the course—most probably, "Was the project an appropriate one for instructional design?"

Step 2.   Look at the criteria for making that decision provided in item 1 of the checklist.

Step 3.   If the decision made for the course matches the criteria in the checklist, you can feel confident that a quality training decision was made.

Step 4.   If the decision does not match the criteria, then, if possible, have the instructional designer re-think and/or re-do that portion of the process.

Step 5.   Repeat Steps 1, 2, 3 and 4 above, matching each aspect of the development of the course against the corresponding criteria given in the checklist.

1. Determine Projects

☐ Do problems selected for instructional design:
  __ involve a knowledge, skill or attitude deficit?
  __ conform to organizational expectations regarding problem solutions?

☐ Are the problems not solvable by more effective/efficient non-instructional design solutions?

2. Needs Assessment

☐ Does the needs assessment/analysis plan include:
  __ objective(s) of the needs assessment/analysis?
  __ identification of the target audience?
  __ procedures for sampling the target audience and organizational objectives?
  __ strategy and tactics for data collection?
  __ specifications of instruments or protocols to be used?
  __ methods of data analysis to yield results congruent with data?
  __ description of how decisions will be made based on the data?

☐ Is the needs assessment/analysis plan feasible to implement, taking into consideration at least:
  __ organizational resources and constraints (e. g., personnel, finances, time)?
  __ requirements of information needed to diagnose the presented problem?

☐ Was the needs assessment/analysis conducted so that the plan was executed as developed?

☐ Are the instructional problems identified congruent with data on:
  __ identified discrepancies between what is happening now and what should be happening?
  __ frequency of the discrepancies?
  __ criticality of the discrepancies?
  __ incidence of the discrepancies?
  __ costs of the discrepancies?
  __ reasons for the discrepancies?
  __ benefits of reducing the discrepancies?
  __ likelihood of reducing the discrepancies?

3. Learner Analysis

☐ Are the learner/trainee characteristics selected for assessment:
  __ trageted directly at the area of need?
  __ consonant with organizational policies, needs, resources and constraints?
  __ feasible to collect data about in terms of resources and logistical limitations?

__ translatable into design specifications?
__ related to the area of the problem, including consideration of physical, demographic, physiolog-
   ical, aptitude, experience, knowledge, learning style or attitudinal characteristics?

☐　Do the methods for assessing learner/trainer characteristics include:
__ procedures for sampling the target audience congruent with organizational policies, needs,
   resources, and constraints?
__ strategy and tactics for data collection?
__ specifications of instruments or protocols to be used?
__ methods of data analysis to yield results congruent with data and information requirements?

☐　Is the profile of learner/trainee characteristics:
__ congruent with the raw data?
__ complete in terms of the characteristics selected for analysis?
__ useful for making instructional design decisions to address the performance discrepancies indicated by the needs assessment/analysis results?

12. Management System

☐　Does the instructional management system provide for the following features:
__ entrance into the instruction is quick and easy?
__ entering learners are diagnosed as to their readiness for instruction?
__ learners are directed to appropriate sections with a minimum of time and effort?
__ each step, section, or experience within the instruction is provided with transitions and
   references?
__ each instructional element is easily identified in terms of both content and purpose?
__ competence is documented in such a way that both management and learners know precisely
   what is required, when, and the standards applicable?
__ exit from the instruction is well documented and diagnostic of future needs?
__ record keeping is adequate for both individual and organizational purposes?

14. Communications

☐　Do communications in visual form:
__ use cues well and consistently?
__ highlight key attributes in a visualization?
__ minimize irrelevant attributes?
__ select all concrete concepts?
__ select some abstract concepts?

☐　Do communications in oral form:
__ use correct grammar?
__ use appropriate understandability level?
__ use acceptable organization?
__ use acceptable presentation format?
__ (in response) answer question being asked?
__ use rules or standards of conduct accepted as appropriate by an authentic source?

☐　Do communications in written form:
__ use correct grammar?
__ use appropriate understandability level?
__ use acceptable organization?
__ use acceptable presentation format?
__ (in response) answer question being asked?
__ use rules or standards of conduct accepted as appropriate by an authentic source (e. g., Flesch
   or APA standards)?

Reprinted from IBSTPI, The Standards, 1986.

In 1987 the Ontario Society for Training and Development updated an earlier competency study of HRD practitioners, including instructional designers. The study revealed that five broadly identified competencies for instructional designers were required at a high proficiency level. These competency areas included

1. Communications

2. Evaluation

3. Group dynamics/process

4. Instructional techniques

5. Training equipment and materials

Three were required at a medium level of proficiency:

1. Course design

2. Learning theory

3. Person/organization interface

In 1983 the Model for Excellence Study identified nine competencies for the subrole of program designer. They include

Adult learning understanding

Competency identification skills

Computer competence

Data reduction skills

Intellectual versatility

Model building

Objectives preparation

Training and development techniques/understanding

Writing skills

Seven subroles, including program designer, were identified at the beginning of the chapter. They must all be accounted for as a means of determining the exact competencies required for instructional designers. Under the Model for Excellence approach, six of the seven subroles are clustered under a concept development model and a research model (see Figure 7.3). These two models reflect their relationship and the related competencies that must be developed. The media specialist subrole is not included. The essential competencies for media specialist are

Adult learning understanding	Intellectual versatility
Audiovisual skills	Library skills
Computer competence	Objectives preparation skills
Cost/benefit analysis skills	Presentation skills
Facilities skills	Questioning skills
Feedback skills	Training and development
Industry understanding	techniques understanding
	Writing skills

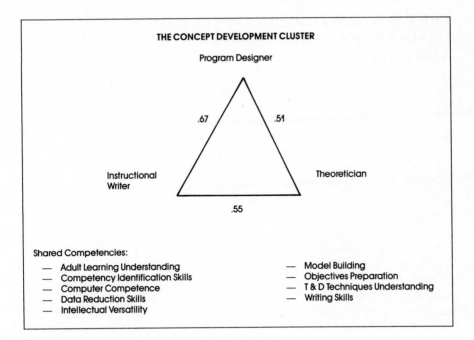

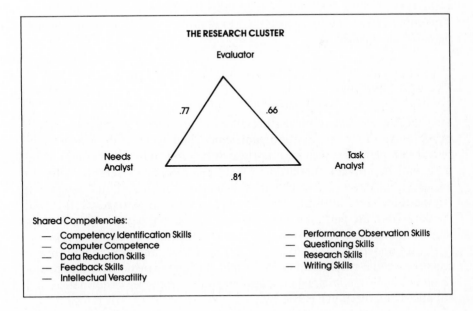

Figure 7.3   Role clusters that describe instructional design

Models for Excellence, *American Society for Training and Development. Reprinted by permission. All rights reserved.*

THE RELATIONSHIP OF INSTRUCTIONAL DESIGNER TO MANAGER, LEARNING SPECIALIST, AND CONSULTANT

The relationship among the four fundamental roles in the field of human resource development is best described as overlapping. In other words, the design of learning programs and training activities can be done by each of these practitioners, and in many situations they are. This perhaps is the primary reason why the instructional designer role does not receive the credit it deserves and is not viewed by many in the field as a separate HRD role. However, it should be understood that the performance of instructional design requires specialized skills and competencies. It is also essential if learning programs and training activities that bring about performance improvement and enhanced organizational efficiency are to be developed.

For example, without properly designed programs and activities learning specialists cannot provide the type of instruction that motivates and encourages learners. In addition, managers of HRD cannot demonstrate to the decision makers in the organization that the HRD department is improving the performance of employees, thus enhancing the organization. Third, consultants cannot advise the implementation of organizational learning programs that would reflect the importance and value of learning to the competitiveness of the organization. Each of these difficulties reflects the importance and value of instructional design and its contribution to improved performance and overall organizational efficiency.

CONCLUSION

Many organizations have turned their attention toward HRD programs as a way of improving and enhancing the organization. This has been done in an effort to remain competitive as well as competent. But "good" training, education, and development programs simply do not just happen. Someone must be skilled in the design and development of them. This person is the instructional designer. It is important to remember that the learning specialist, the manager of HRD, and the consultant are performing the role of instructional designer if and when they design and develop learning programs or training activities. Therefore, all four must understand the program planning, design, and evaluation process, and the essential activities and responsibilities of an instructional designer. The result will be better designed programs, improved employee performance, and enhanced organizational efficiency.

CHAPTER 8

The Consultant

Objectives

After completing Chapter 8, HRD readers should be able to

- identify the four trends that have contributed to the growth of consulting in HRD.

- determine why a consultant is required in an organization.

- identify the factors that should be considered in determining the usefulness and importance of a consultant.

- distinguish between internal and external consultants in HRD.

- identify the eight fundamental purposes of consulting.

- identify and distinguish among the range of consulting roles in HRD.

- determine the multiple roles of the HRD consultant.

- determine the level of consulting activity in problem solving.

- identify the types of change agents that implement change within an organization.

- identify and describe the stages of the consulting process.

- determine why HRD professionals have difficulty making the transition into consulting.

- identify the competencies of HRD consultants.

Many consultants enter the consulting profession from the ranks of the human resource development field. Of these, most have extensive experience as learning specialists and/or instructional designers. While many become competent as consultants, Bellman (1983) warns that the transition is not always easy. As learning specialists and instructional designers, they operated in an artificial environment (the classroom) where they knew the answers to all the questions, since most of them had been asked before. In classrooms they were experienced in applying selected solutions to standard problems, in a kind of "off-the-shelf" approach. In these structured environments they were able to exercise the greatest degree of control (Hudson, 1988).

As consultants in HRD, they are often surprised to find themselves in a very different world, which complicates their transition. Now they must search for problems and synthesize solutions to them. Instead of knowing all the answers to the right questions, now they must find answers to questions that cannot be answered by their classroom experience. Instead of being in control, they are in service to the organization, and must now focus on desired changes, rather than on the individuals involved (Hudson, 1988).

Consultants in HRD are on unfamiliar turf. No longer in their familiar, comfortable classroom, they may feel overwhelmed, inundated by the complexities of the problems they must solve. There may be a tendency to retreat to the classroom (avoidance) or to bring an easy classroom solution to a difficult problem (simplification). As learning specialists and/or instructional designers they had time to plan, design, evaluate, and adjust. As consultants, however, they are often asked to decide in seconds. People may not respond, or they may behave exactly the way the textbook models predict (Hudson, 1988).

However, in spite of these difficulties, HRD professionals can make the transition from the classroom to the field. To do so is necessary for them to change their perspective on the problem-solving process. Bellman (1983) offers these suggestions for accelerating this transition:

- Ask more questions.
- Provide fewer answers.
- Move away from theory and models.
- Move toward reality.
- Change one's measurement of success from "did my class flow smoothly" to "did I effect constructive change."

Because consulting is so difficult and demanding, HRD practitioners should proceed with care before they accept this role (cited in Hudson, 1988).

GROWTH IN HRD CONSULTING

Lippitt and Lippitt (1986) report that at least four trends in business and industry have contributed to growth in consulting.

1. *Technological development.* The impact of accelerated technological development has been dramatic, creating an ever-increasing need for individuals and groups to share knowledge, skills, and experiences. In many fields, because knowledge gained in college is only viable for one to two years, learning must continue throughout one's career. In the field of HRD in particular, increased technology in learning is having a profound impact on HRD programs. In either case, more and more consultants are being used to provide instruction as well as consultation and advice.

2. *Crisis in human resources.* The growing awareness of the importance and dignity of human resources has created new needs for consultation services. The value of a well-trained employee can be reflected in the increased productivity and profitability of the organization. It can also be measured in the cost of recruiting, selecting, hiring, and training employees. Thus, more and more organizations consider human resources as they develop their strategic plans. As a result, employee assistance programs, career counseling, job enrichment programs, and job engineering, to name but a few, are among the many human resource services now being provided by organizations. HRD practitioners cannot be expected to know all there is to know about all human resource services, so outside consultants are called in to assist.

3. *Underdeveloped consulting skills of managers and supervisors.* Many managers and supervisors act as part-time, internal consultants. Although they lack the skills they need to function as true consultants, they do have an aptitude for it. Organizations may develop the consulting skills of these managers and supervisors, a long and costly process, or hire an outside consultant. In some situations, they do both.

4. *Discretionary time.* Many organizations use volunteers to accomplish their goals and objectives, a trend often referred to as "discretionary time." These individuals are often not well trained, and many need greater interpersonal and other interactive skills to perform effectively. In addition, because most volunteers provide only a few hours of service a week to organizations, more are needed to accomplish the same amount of work that full-time employees accomplish. Therefore, the actual number of people requiring training will increase, and more consultants will be needed.

Each of these trends has contributed to the growth of the consulting profession, but why do businesses need consultants? In other words, "why call in a consultant?"

WHY A CONSULTANT FOR HRD PROGRAMS?

It is important to remember that retaining a consultant is a decision that should be made with care. It requires managers and supervisors to rely on another person's knowledge, skills, and abilities, qualities often unknown to them, as are the results of the person's performance. Wells (1983) provided several questions that may be helpful in deciding whether such outside assistance is required, is timely, and will be beneficial:

- Has the problem or task been clearly defined?
- Is it evident that the problem or task cannot be addressed by the staff?
- Can an outside consultant offer a dimension that is unavailable internally?
- By utilizing an outside consultant, will the professionalism of the staff be enhanced, in addition to solving the problem or improving the organization?
- Is there a commitment to change within the organization?

In answering these questions, it is important to know what professional consultants have to offer and how their qualifications may differ from the qualifications of the staff. There are a variety of factors to consider: objectivity, overcoming resistance to change, analytic skill, specialized knowledge, time, sensitivity to organizational change, and political issues.

Objectivity. A consultant can provide an impartial perspective free of the influence of internal loyalties and values, organizational culture, corporate traditions, vested interests, and closed-mindedness. This is perhaps the single greatest quality that consultants bring to organizations.

Overcoming resistance to change. Because of internal difficulties such as divergent goals, conflicting ideas, or organizational policies and politics, solutions to problems may be impossible to implement internally. However, by using an outside consultant, who can maintain an objective viewpoint, managers and supervisors are better able to overcome this resistance to change and provide a more timely and orderly solution. In addition, professional consultants will not compromise their integrity by endorsing changes that, however popular, do not adequately solve the organization's problems. This may not be the case with employees, who fear reprisals as a result of offering unpopular solutions to problems.

Analytic skill. While consultants hold no monopoly on this skill, it is their business to know how to generate information, analyze it, distinguish between a problem's symptoms and its causes, determine solutions to problems, and recommend an appropriate one(s). This is gained from experience in dealing with difficult situations in a variety of organizations.

Specialized knowledge. Today, a consultant must possess a unique set of skills and/or specialized knowledge in order to be truly useful to organizations. Too many HRD consultants entering this highly specialized area of practice know little or nothing about performance improvement through learning. As a result, the term "HRD consultant" has come to mean more of an independent entrepreneur who simply designs and delivers learning programs and workshops. This limited view of the HRD consultant is having a profoundly negative impact on the field as a whole and on professional HRD consultants in particular.

Time. Many managers and supervisors are already overloaded, which results in delay of important projects and/or solving important organizational problems. Consultants can serve as catalysts for such projects and/or problems by providing needed energy and leadership. For many projects, the cost of an outside consultant should be weighed against the cost of internal staff time, and also against the potential cost of delays or inaction. Also, how much time—and ultimately, money—will the organization save as a result of utilizing an outside consultant?

Sensitivity to organizational change. An experienced consultant can guide managers and supervisors through the change process in a way that minimizes resistance and opposition. This is because they have dealt with organizational change in a variety of situations and understand why resistance to change occurs.

Political issues. Every organization, regardless of size or composition, has a political structure. It is necessary to insure stability and continuity, and employees, managers, and supervisors must adhere to it to remain part of the organization. However, this structure is often a part of the problem, a dilemma that employees find impossible to point out to essential decision makers. It is not, however, impossible for an outside objective third party to address such sensitive issues. Under these circumstances, then, it is helpful to have a consultant to serve as the spokesperson for the members of the organization.

THE ROLE OF THE HRD CONSULTANT

Margulies and Raia (1972) separate consulting resources into task-oriented consultants and process-oriented consultants. Task-oriented consultants are technical experts, gathering data and analyzing and providing specific and concrete recommendations. Process-oriented consultants guide the process of problem resolution and leave the specific tasks up to the client. In reality, of course, these two roles represent two extremes, with the exact mode of orientation (depending on the client's specific needs and capabilities) lying somewhere along a continuum between the two. This model—and the characteristics associated with each role—is illustrated in Figure 8.1.

Lippitt and Lippitt (1986) examined the model advanced by Margulies and Raia and substituted *directive* for task oriented and *nondirective* for process oriented, as seen in Figure 8.2. In the directive role, consultants are active advocates in the problem-solving process, whereas in the nondirective role they function as objective observers, raising questions for reflection and better understanding. They warn, however, that to speak of consultant roles as separate

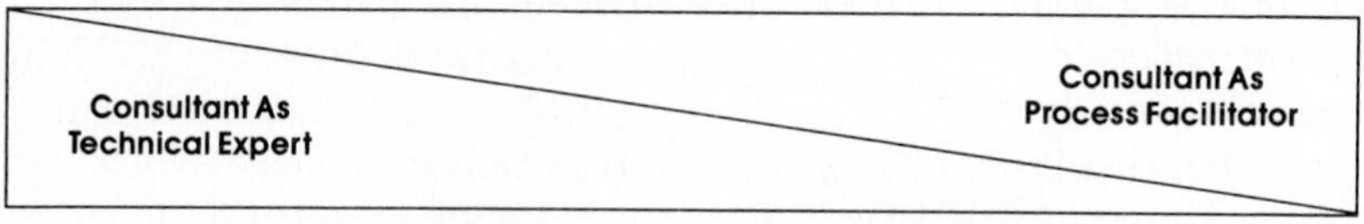

Task Orientation | Process Orientation

ROLE CHARACTERISTICS

Task	Process
1. *Problem Verification* by "expert" evaluation and collection of data.	1. *Problem Verification*: by "problem sensing" and facilitating a clear articulation that includes attitudes and feelings.
2. *Problem Solving* provides ideas and opinions, designs research for data, and develops solution for the client-system.	2. *Problem Solving*: works on the problem-solving capability of the system, improves problem-solving process, and facilitates creativity.
3. *Feedback* presents research data with "expert" interpretations.	3. *Feedback*: provides meaningful data, facilitates assimilation of data, and allows for client interpretation.
4. *Utilization of Research* makes specific and concrete recommendations based on data.	4. *Utilization of Research*: develops client use of data and facilitates action by client based on learning.
5. *Relationship to Client* is objective, detached, and task oriented. Connection is short term and problem oriented.	5. *Relationship to Client*: is personal, involved and process oriented. Connection is long term and system oriented.
6. *Involvement* is primarily with the problem to be solved.	6. *Involvement*: is primarily with people and groups in the organization.
7. *Systems Approach* concern is with implications of the problem for other parts of the organization.	7. *Systems Approach*: concern is for collaborative relationships and exchange of resources among parts of the organization.

Figure 8.1 Range of consulting roles

Reprinted from Margulies and Raia, Organization Development: Values, Process and Technology, *New York: McGraw Hill, 1972.*

and distinct is to distort reality (Hudson, 1988). The role of any consultant should and will vary from moment to moment, causing an effective expert to react to the situation at hand. Role choice, according to Lippitt and Lippitt, will depend on such criteria as the following:

- The nature of the contract
- Client goals
- Norms and standards of the client
- Personal limitations of the consultant
- What worked before
- Internal versus external consultants (cited in Hudson, 1988)

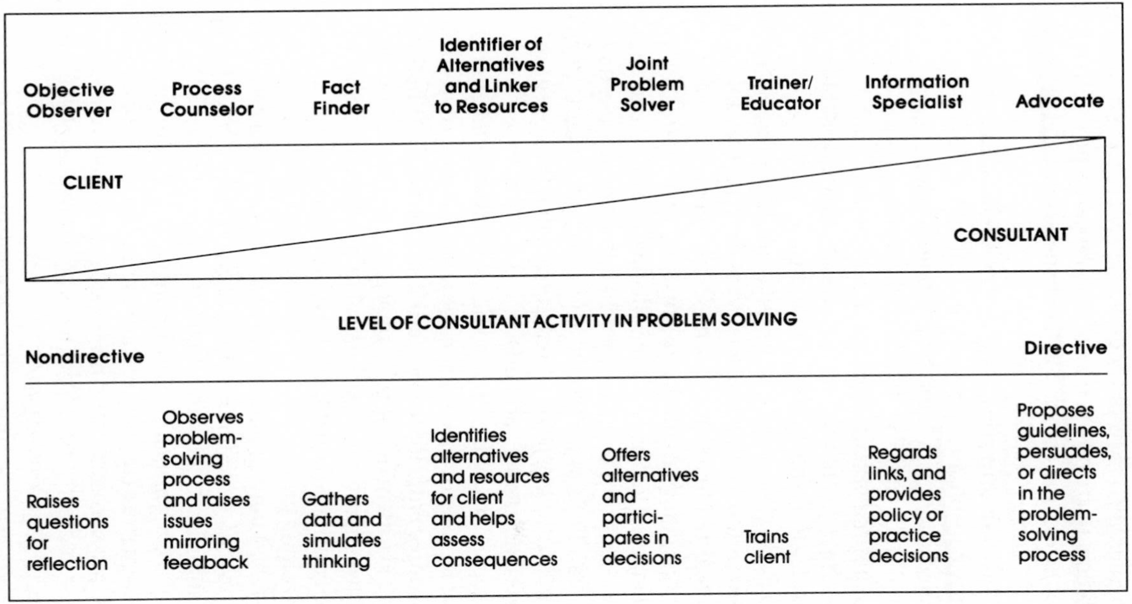

Nondirective ←——————————————————————————————→ Directive

CLIENT   CONSULTANT

LEVEL OF CONSULTANT ACTIVITY IN PROBLEM SOLVING

Objective Observer	Process Counselor	Fact Finder	Identifier of Alternatives and Linker to Resources	Joint Problem Solver	Trainer/ Educator	Information Specialist	Advocate
Raises questions for reflection	Observes problem-solving process and raises issues mirroring feedback	Gathers data and simulates thinking	Identifies alternatives and resources for client and helps assess consequences	Offers alternatives and participates in decisions	Trains client	Regards links, and provides policy or practice decisions	Proposes guidelines, persuades, or directs in the problem-solving process

Figure 8.2   Multiple roles of the consultant

Reprinted from G. Lippitt and R. Lippitt, The Consulting Practice in Action, (2nd ed.), San Diego, CA: University Associates, Inc., 1986. Used by permission.

The nature of the contract. This refers to the type of duties and/or activities a consultant must undertake during the consulting relationship. In some situations, consultants are asked to serve as experts and provide guidance and direction as clients attempt to address problems or implement change in the organization. At other times, consultants are asked to analyze a situation and provide feedback regarding their findings. Some are asked to provide potential solutions to problems while others need only advocate a position or technique. Regardless, the nature of the contract will help determine the consultant's ultimate role.

Client's goals. The goals and objectives of clients reflect their desires and aspirations; thus, many consultants approach the consulting situation with the attitude that a satisfied client is a happy client and a happy client will hire the consultant again. But, in addition, it only makes sense that the consulting process be directed at desired outcomes that will also positively affect the organization. In light of this, the nature of the client's goals and objectives is an appropriate target for the consultant's attention.

Norms and standards of the client. Successful consultants realize that they perform within an environment that impacts every decision they make. This environment is often referred to as the *organizational culture.* It is made up of value systems, rules and regulations, codes of conduct, dress codes, and organizational roles and games. It represents the collective norms and standards of the organization. It is important to remember that most employees have accepted these norms and standards as their own. Therefore, consultants must consider them during the consulting process. Often the role that the consultant will play is dictated by these norms and standards.

Personal limitations. The saying, "I don't do windows" could apply to consultants as well. That is, consultants ought to be aware of their own strengths and weaknesses before they enter into a consulting arrangement. When consultants are asked to engage in activities or roles they are not qualified for, they should refuse to accept the assignment, regardless of its potential or financial rewards. To do so would be considered unethical, as well as affect the consultant's performance in the consulting process.

What worked before. Many consultants base their choice of a role or an activity to perform on previous experience. This practice is often not appropriate or wise, but it does affect the type of role a consultant performs.

Internal versus external consultants. Consultants selected from outside the organization are free to perform in a different manner from that of consultants selected from inside the organization. This is a dilemma that we address in detail later in the chapter. It greatly affects the roles performed as well as the types of recommendations or solutions selected.

Having considered all of the above, effective consultants will choose among a number of alternative roles, which we detail in the following paragraphs.

Advocate. In this role, the consultant is most directive. He or she endeavors to influence the client in the selection of particular goals or values, and to become a more proactive problem solver.

Informational Specialist. This role also requires that the consultant be very directive, but there is some client involvement in problem solving. The client's primary responsibility is to define the problem and explain the situation to the consultant so that together they can provide the information needed by the organization. As an information expert or technical specialist, the consultant is fulfilling the most traditional role of consulting. He or she is the person who maintains the expert knowledge, skills, and/or professional experience that is so vital to the organization.

Learning Provider (Trainer/Educator). HRD professionals believe that performance improvement and organizational change can occur as a result of continuous training and education within the client system. The consultant may provide the client with training programs and learning activities that enable performance improvement or organizational change to occur; or he or she may advise which learning processes are best to use. Regardless, in order to function in this role, the consultant will need the competencies of a learning specialist and a program designer.

Joint Problem Solver. This role requires the consultant to become an active participant in the problem-solving process. He or she must provide the objectivity needed to properly define the existing problem(s), as well as to evaluate the alternatives for an effective resolution of the problem. In addition, the consultant must utilize a synergistic approach, collaborating with the client in a perceptual, cognitive, action-taking process to solve the problem (Lippitt & Lippitt, 1986).

Alternative Identifier and Linker. In this role, the consultant identifies appropriate alternative solutions to the problem facing the client. He or she must establish relevant criteria for assessing the alternatives, develop cause-effect relationships for each alternative, and establish an appropriate set of strategies. In this role the consultant is not directly involved in the decision-making process. The client is more proactive during this role-relationship than during any of the previous ones.

Fact Finder. The consultant functions primarily as a researcher in this role. The focus is on gathering, analyzing, and synthesizing information the client needs to make vital decisions. This process can be very complex, such as a formal survey utilizing several methods and techniques, or it can be as simple as listening. Fact finding, often overlooked and minimized as a part of the problem-solving and decision-making process, is perhaps actually the most critical. Again, the consultant is less proactive in this role than in any of the previous roles.

Process Counselor. This role requires the consultant to help the client focus on and develop diagnostic skills needed for addressing specific and relevant problems. Attention is paid to how things are done, rather than to what tasks are to be performed. This may include the development of interpersonal and group skills to be integrated with task-oriented activities. The goal of this role-relationship is for the client to become more effective and responsive.

Objective Observer/Reflector. The consultant functions as a philosopher and as verifier in this role. The primary responsibility is to ask reflective questions that will help the client clarify, modify, or alter a given situation. In this nondirective role, the consultant guides the client to overcome barriers that prevent appropriate performance.

Subroles of Consultants

The role of the consultant consists of several subroles. Each of these develops out of Lippitt and Lippitt's (1986) multiple roles discussed above (see Figure 8.2). The following matrix will help reflect this relationship.

Evaluator . . . . Objective Observer

Group Facilitator . . . . Joint Problem Solver

Individual Development Counselor . . . . Process Counselor

Instructor . . . . Trainer/Educator

Marketer . . . . Advocate

Needs Analyst . . . . Fact Finder

Strategist . . . . Identifier of Alternatives

Task Analyst . . . . Fact Finder

Transfer Agent . . . . Process Counselor

CONSULTANT COMPETENCIES

Organizations should be aware that there is a large number of consultants for hire, many of whom lack the expertise and competency necessary to handle the complex problems facing organizations. According to Dunn (1982), many HRD practitioners have become consultants as a result of terminations or because they failed to qualify for HRD positions. Byrne (1983) stated that the only real requirement for being a consultant is six dollars for business cards. The number of HRD consultants abounds because it is so easy to get into. Robinson and Younglove (1984) revealed that external consulting is one of the most sought after career transitions for internal HRD professionals.

Regardless of the growing nature of the consulting component of HRD, the competencies unique to this profession have not been clearly identified. In fact, it is important to understand that consultant competencies were not identified in the 1983 Model for Excellence Study sponsored by ASTD. However, consultants must maintain certain unique competencies, skills, and/or knowledge in order to function professionally. In an attempt to address this concern, the Ontario Society for Training and Development (OSTD) identified the consultant role as one of the four principal roles in HRD. In their 1976 and 1986 (revision) study, they identified the following areas of core competency for consultants:

- Communication
- Course design
- Evaluation
- Group dynamics process
- Learning theory
- Human resource planning
- Person/organization interface
- Instructional practice
- Training materials and equipment
- Training needs analysis

In addition to these, consultants should maintain (1) facilitation skills, (2) an understanding of HRD and organization theory and behavior, (3) interpersonal skills, (4) presentation skills, (5) questioning skills, (6) counseling skills, (7) data reduction skills, (8) feedback skills, (9) negotiation skills, (10) writing skills, and (11) performance observation skills.

Lippitt and Lippitt (1986) studied 32 consultants to determine the competencies needed to perform adequately.* The competencies are clustered in three categories: (1) knowledge, (2) skills, and (3) attitudes. They are as follows:

Knowledge
1. Thorough grounding in the behavioral sciences;
2. An equally thorough foundation in the administrative philosophies, policies, and practices of organizational systems and larger social systems;
3. Knowledge of educational and training methodologies, especially laboratory methods, problem-solving exercises, and role playing;
4. An understanding of the stages in the growth of individuals, groups, organizations, and communities and how social systems function at different stages;
5. Knowledge of how to design and facilitate a change process;
6. Knowledge and understanding of human personality, attitude formation, and change;
7. Knowledge of oneself: motivations, strengths, weaknesses, and biases; and

*Reprinted from G. Lippett and R. Lippett, *The Consulting Process in Action* (2nd ed.), San Diego, Calif.: University Associates, Inc., 1986. Used with permission.

8. An understanding of the leading philosophical systems as a framework for thought and a foundation for value systems (p. 170).

Skills

1. Communication skills: listening, observing, identifying, and reporting;
2. Teaching and persuasive skills; ability to effectively impart new ideas and insights and to design learning experiences that contribute to growth and change;
3. Counseling skills to help others reach meaningful decisions of their own accord;
4. Ability to form relationships based on trust and to work with a great variety of persons of different backgrounds and personalities; sensitivity to the feelings of others; ability to develop and share one's own charisma;
5. Ability to work with groups and teams in planning and implementing change; skill in using group-dynamics techniques and laboratory-training methods;
6. Ability to use a variety of intervention methods and the ability to determine which method is most appropriate at a given time;
7. Skill in designing surveys, interviewing, and using other data-collection methods;
8. Ability to diagnose problems with a client; to locate sources of help, power, and influence; to understand a client's values and culture; and to determine readiness for change;
9. Ability to be flexible in dealing with all types of situations; and
10. Skill in using problem-solving techniques and in assisting others in problem solving (p. 171).

Attitudes

1. Attitude of a professional: competence, integrity, feeling of responsibility for helping clients cope with their problems;
2. Maturity: self-confidence; courage to stand by one's views; willingness to take necessary risks; ability to cope with rejection, hostility, and suspicion;
3. Open-mindedness, honesty, intelligence;
4. Possession of a humanistic value system: belief in the importance of the individual; belief in technology and efficiency as means and not ends; trust in people and the democratic process in economic activities.

INTERNAL/EXTERNAL CONSULTANTS IN HRD

If, after evaluating a situation, advice or assistance still seems necessary, one might first look within the organization. Internal consultants offer some distinct advantages. They are already familiar with the organization and do not have to spend the time it takes to learn a new organizational system and culture. Hudson (1988) points out that internal consultants are, however, caught in a catch-22. If they are too cautious in their approach, they may be considered just another set of hands. If they are too critical or too radical, people think they are disloyal and insensitive. According to Hudson, to be most effective internal consultants must be secure within the organization. Organizational security depends on playing the role of expert, rather than being just another player on the team. Lippitt and Lippitt (1986) suggest that the internal consultant (1) behave like an independent/outside consultant, (2) be proactive and aggressive at least 25 percent of the time, (3) focus on the job to be done rather than on the political environment of the organization, and (4) maintain individuality.

In many situations it is best to utilize *external consultants,* people who have little or no organizational/political relationship with the organization. Their primary function is to identify problems and provide solutions when appropriate. Lippitt and Lippitt (1986) suggest that external consultants (1) reject an assignment if their gut reaction is to say no, (2) learn the language and symbols of the organization, (3) accept internal help from HRD practitioners and others, (4) collaborate with internal consultants, and (5) be human.

There are several similarities between internal and external consultants. First, both play multiple consulting roles and both want to be successful. Both are primarily helpers and must work with and through the organization's members. But they must also rely on them to accomplish the tasks they recommend. This is often difficult because they have no real authority over these organizational members.

There are several differences between the two as well. For example, external consultants usually have more influence on the organization because they are perceived as experts or prophets. This gives them an instantaneous power base. Another advantage they have is that they maintain a broader perspective and can be more objective than internal consultants and organizational members. Still, they are an unknown quantity, whereas internal consultants are not. Remuneration and longevity, for external consultants, are usually tied to results. Internal consultants are paid and retained as a part of the organization's support team.

Internal consultants, because of their availability, can spend more time with organizational members. They can identify important linkages within the organization because they are aware of and understand the organization. However, external consultants do not have to live down past failures and affiliations as do internal consultants. External consultants are also free to leave the situation when consultation is complete, while internal consultants are not. Finally, external consultants are free to reject consulting assignments. Internal consultants must accept them as part of their organizational responsibilities.

Another consulting resource is the *internal-external consultant,* located within the organization, usually the corporate home office, who is sent out to field units for consultant work. In this type of orientation the consultant is an insider to the overall organizational system yet functions as an outsider to the client system. This approach is very popular within large organizations because individuals can develop the required specialized knowledge, skills, and abilities and still be objective and independent of organizational politics.

IMPLEMENTING CHANGE

To implement change, an organization must first decide that change is needed and then select the appropriate change objectives. First, however, two other issues must be resolved: (1) the type of change agent that would be appropriate, and (2) the type of intervention to use.

THE TYPES OF CHANGE AGENT

A change agent is an individual (or group of individuals) reponsible for designing and introducing change. In the case of organizational change, it must be someone who possesses an independent perspective and is not bound by the culture, politics, and traditions of the organization. This could be either an outsider or an insider. According to Tichy (1975), there are four basic types of change agents: Outside Pressure (OP) type, People-Change-Technology (PCT) type, Analysis-for-the-Top (AFT) type, and Organizationl Development (OD) type (see Figure 8.3). The differences lie in personal characteristics, values relative to change, attitudes regarding what mediates change, change techniques and methods employed, and the setting in which change is carried out.

Outside Pressure Type. This type of change agent works from outside the organization. They are not members of the group or system they are trying to change. They use mass demonstrations, violence, and civil disobedience to accomplish their objectives. For obvious reasons, this type of change agent is not a positive approach for modern organizations to take. The OP type is clearly outside the management-consultant relationship.

People-Change-Technology Type. While working for management, this type of change agent focuses on improving the way people behave. They utilize various behavioral science techniques and learning methodologies. They are concerned with such things as employee motivation and morale, including absenteeism, quality and quantity of work, and employee turnover. They use methods such as job enrichment, management by objectives, the one-minute manager, and behavior modification to accomplish their objectives. This approach is based on the belief that if employees change their behavior the organization will also change.

Analysis-for-the-Top Type. The focus of this approach is on changing the organizational structure or technology in order to improve production and efficiency. This type of change agent is best suited for highly technical organizations which rely on exact procedures and processes.

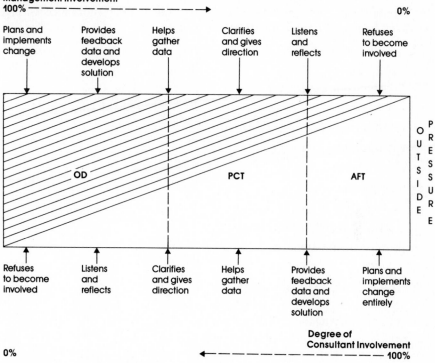

FIGURE 8.3   Types of change agents
Adapted from N. Tichy, Human Relations, 28(9) (September 1975): 771–779.

Organization Development Type. An organization development change agent focuses attention on internal processes such as interpersonal relationships, group dynamics, communications, and decision making. There is a strong emphasis on organizational culture and its change. This intervention strategy includes programs such as sensitivity training, quality circles, and team building.

Figure 8.3 reveals the relationship between management and consultants. OP type change agents are inappropriate for most if not all organizations. In addition, they are outside the organization and so managerial involvement is usually limited. AFT types are used when management does not want to be involved in the change process and would prefer that an expert plan and implement change. On the other hand, if management wants to be intimately involved in the change process, the OD change agent is the most appropriate choice. This is because of their internal orientation as well as the systemwide approach they use. A middle-of-the-road approach is the PCT type, even though this change agent is difficult to place. This type will generally design and implement the changes desired by management, but not until management has outlined the problems to be addressed and provided detailed information regarding the situation.

THE INTERVENTION

Interventions describe a method or means to manage change more successfully. Some of the most common interventions include

- Learning programs and training activities
- Job design
- Coaching and counseling
- Team building
- Conflict resolution
- Organizational mirroring
- Life planning
- Survey feedback
- Management by objectives
- Quality of work life programs
- Process consultation

HIERARCHY OF PURPOSE

One way of grouping the activities of consultants is in terms of their areas of expertise. These include needs analysis, strategic planning, career development, organizational development, human resource planning and forecasting, program design, instructional design, and evaluation. Another way to categorize consultants is to view the process they engage in as a sequence of phases: entry, contracting, examination, areas of review, details of structure, evaluation, presentation, and follow-up (see The Consulting Process, below). However, these phases are less discrete than most consultants would admit, and they are difficult to separate for comparison. Perhaps the most useful and effective approach is to consider the purposes of consulting. According to Turner (1983), eight fundamental purposes are arranged in a hierarchy according to the influence each has on organizational change. From lowest to highest influence, the purposes are

1. Providing information to the client.
2. Solving the client's problems.
3. Conducting a diagnosis that may redefine the problem.
4. Making recommendations based on the diagnosis.
5. Assisting with implementation of recommended solutions.
6. Building consensus and commitment around corrective action.
7. Facilitating client learning—that is, teaching the client how to resolve similar problems in the future.
8. Permanently improving organizational effectiveness.

Purposes 1 through 5 are the ones most requested by clients. Often referred to as the traditional purposes of consulting, they are generally considered legitimate functions. Purposes 6 through 8 are less likely to be addressed by HRD consultants because clients are less likely to request them (see Figure 8.4). They are also considered by-products or results of earlier lower-level purposes. It is difficult to focus on them unless earlier ones have been examined first. Another reason higher level purposes are less likely to be addressed is because it requires increased sophistication and skill to do so, both in the process of consulting and in the establishment and management of the consultant-client relationship. It is important to remember, external as well as internal consultants must first address the purpose that the client requests and then direct their attention to other purposes.

1. PROVIDING INFORMATION

The most common reason for retaining a consultant is to obtain information regarding a program, human resource system, instructional strategy, needs analysis technique, and/or research. The organization may desire a consultant's special expertise or the most up-to-date information regarding a special need of the organization. Also, the organization may be unable to allocate the human resources required to obtain the information because of time or financial considerations. Regardless, consultants are being utilized because they possess specialized information vital to the well-being of the organization.

2. SOLVING PROBLEMS

Organizations often give consultants difficult problems to solve. These problems vary from organization to organization and from department to department. It can be argued that organizations that can identify the roots or cause of

Figure 8.4   Hierarchy of consulting purposes

Adapted by permission of the Harvard Business Review. An exhibit from "Consulting is More Than Giving Advice" by Arthur N. Turner (September/October 1982). Copyright © 1982 by the President and Fellows of Harvard College; all rights reserved.

their problems do not need a consultant. What the consultant does is to make certain that the identified problem is indeed the one that needs to be solved. In other words, the consultant defines the real issue. They do not spend time providing solutions to undefined problems. Thus, a useful consulting process involves working with the problem, as "defined" by the client, in such a way that more useful definitions emerge (Turner, 1983).

3. CONDUCTING AN EFFECTIVE DIAGNOSIS

The third purpose of consulting is to conduct an effective diagnosis for the organization. This includes problem identification, collection of appropriate information, and analysis of the information. A complete diagnosis includes an external environmental analysis (i.e., economic conditions, political and technological status) and an internal environmental analysis (i.e., organizational structure, managerial abilities and attitudes, organizational culture). However, much of this information is confidential. Managers, fearful of uncovering difficult situations they might be blamed for, are often reluctant to provide essential information to the consultant. As a result, this process sometimes strains the consultant-client relationship. Regardless, managers and supervisors, as well as executives should become involved in the diagnosis process. This will insure that they acknowledge their role in the problem and accept the actions and recommendations provided by the consultant. In addition, they can develop the diagnostic skills they need to conduct future analyses without the assistance of a consultant. This will improve the effectiveness and efficiency of the organization, as well as reduce the capital expenditure for consultants and diagnostic experts.

4. PROVIDING RECOMMENDATIONS

The recommendations consultants provide represent the summarization of what the consultant has learned about the organization and the actions that must be taken for improvement. According to Turner (1983), the purpose of the engagement is fulfilled when the consultant presents a consistent, logical action plan comprised of steps designed to improve the diagnosed problem. In other words, the consultant recommends and the client decides how to implement. When making recommendations to organizations, HRD consultants should consider EEOC requirements, employment conditions, attitudes toward improvement through learning, importance of human resources to the organization, training facilities and budgets, and important HRM activities. If these are absent, then the recommendations may end up on the client's bookshelf next to other expensive and nonimplemented reports. It is important to remember, a written report or oral presentation should be clearly presented and convincing. It should also relate to the diagnosis on which the recommendations are based.

5. IMPLEMENTING CHANGES

In addition to making the recommendations, consultants are often asked to implement them. This purpose is a matter of considerable debate between consultants and managers. Many consultants believe that the implementation of their recommendations requires a manager or supervisor who is familiar with the organization and who has the authority to bring about change. On the other hand, implementation of a set of recommendations will often require specialized skills or knowledge that many managers and supervisors lack. It also requires an understanding of the potential outcome and impact of a recommendation, something that can only be obtained through experience in observing similar recommendations being implemented in other organizations. Many managers believe a consultant would do a better job at implementing the recommendations. Poorly implemented changes can only result in a waste of time and money and would further complicate an already difficult situation. Also, managers, supervisors, and executives should participate in the implementation of recommendations, as well as serve as linkages between important client groups. Without these key linkages, implementation and hence change will not occur, nor will people be willing to do things differently, regardless of any positive outcomes.

6. BUILDING CONSENSUS AND COMMITMENT

Any change useful to an organization will depend on the members of the organization or group working together. Each member should consider the good of the overall organization before considering personal and professional goals. In order for this to occur, consultants must provide sound and convincing recommendations and present them persuasively. More importantly, they must design and conduct a process for building consensus and commitment that will bring about lasting and needed change. Necessary steps include the identification of essential decision makers and how to involve them.

Consultants can monitor the client's readiness and commitment to change by considering the following questions:

1. How willing are the members of the organization to implement change?
2. Is upper level management willing to learn and utilize new management methods and practices?
3. What type of information do members of the organization readily accept or resist?
4. What are their attitudes toward change?
5. What are the executives' attitudes toward change?
6. To what extent will individual members of the organization regard their contribution to overall organizational effectiveness as a legitimate and desirable objective (Turner, 1983)?

Another way to gauge readiness for change is to evaluate the enthusiasm for a particular recommendation. This provides an instantaneous measure of resistance and resentment. Once the level of enthusiasm has been determined a consultant will be able to withdraw or encourage a recommendation prior to its complete implementation.

In developing consensus and commitment, it is essential that the consultant build a working relationship with each client and client group. Trust and a readiness to accept change can be developed during interviews to gather information as well as during the implementation phase. From the beginning, an effective relationship becomes a collaborative search for acceptable answers to the client's real needs and concerns (Turner, 1983). Ideally, the relationship will be mutually beneficial.

7. Facilitating Client Learning

It is important to enhance the client's ability to cope with immediate problems. But it is equally important to help clients develop the knowledge and skills they need to adjust to future conditions and address future problems. Many view this as a part of organizational development. Organizations improve when their individual members improve.

Consultants further facilitate learning by allowing clients to participate in the consulting process. Participation enables them to see problems from a different perspective and with the good of the overall organization in mind. In addition, managers, supervisors, and executives develop problem-identification skills, diagnostic skills, implementation skills, and an understanding of the importance of consensus and commitment in bringing about change. The consultant helps develop a *learning culture* within the organization, which fosters additional changes that are important to the organization and its members.

During the consultant process the learning needs of each of the many participants are discovered, which become the basis for training programs and learning activities HRD consultants can be a part of. It is important to separate "workshop" consultants from "organizational development and change" consultants. The former are primarily responsible for developing and implementing training programs and learning activities. They should know adult learning theory and have skills in the design, implementation, and evaluation of learning programs. The latter must understand organizational system and structure and be skilled in organizational design. They must also know how to gather, diagnose, and evaluate information about the organization, in order to provide recommendations for change and identify the steps needed to implement the proposed recommendations. Organizational development and change consultants must also understand the linkages of the organization and realize the importance of employee involvement in bringing about change. The primary focus of workshop consultants is training. Organizational development is the focus of OD and change consultants. However, both are referred to as HRD consultants.

8. IMPROVING ORGANIZATIONAL EFFECTIVENESS

The final purpose of the consulting process is referred to as "organizational effectiveness." Turner (1983) defined this term as the ability to adapt future strategy and behavior to environmental change and to optimize the contribution of the organization's human resources. This enables top-level management to maintain the organization's future in an ever-changing world. Organizational effectiveness implies that management is dedicated to a process of developing and maintaining the most important systems and linkages. Consultants assist the decision makers in selecting the most appropriate ones. As part of the process, the consultant focuses on the approaches, plans, and programs that are most appropriate for the organization, which needs not depend on what the consultant has to sell. Recommendations and solutions can be tailor-made to the organization's immediate and future problems. At the same time, consultants should try to overcome the barriers and obstacles that prevent change.

THE CONSULTING PROCESS

Once we understand the multiple roles consultants assume, the competencies they require, and the purposes for consulting, we can focus attention on the actual consulting process. There are two preliminary steps and four primary phases: examination, evaluation, presentation, and follow-up. Prior to examination, the consultant engages in *relationship building* and formulating the *contract*. Either the consultant or the client makes the initial contact. It is then determined if a working relationship, one that is mutually beneficial, can be established. During this first preliminary part of the process the client identifies and clarifies the need for change and potential areas of intervention. Next, the consultant needs to determine the client's readiness for change and attitudes toward change. Finally, an agreement is reached regarding the establishment of a working relationship and the necessary procedures required to begin the consulting process.

The second preliminary step involves identifying the desired outcomes, clarifying the time perspectives, establishing a division of labor, and identifying areas of accountability. This is when the contract between the consultant and client is formulated and the consulting process begins (see Figure 8.5).

PHASE 1. EXAMINATION

The consulting process begins with an examination of the organization. There are two subphases, *area of review* and *details of the study*. Each of these provides the type of information the consultant needs to conduct a complete and comprehensive organizational review.

When consultants begin the area of review, they must make some fundamental decisions regarding the focus of the consulting process. They can (1) study the entire organization, (2) study a type of managerial function (i.e., personnel management), or (3) study a unit or division within the organization. They can then determine the nature of the review as well as its complexity. It also helps in the allocation of resources and management of time.

The details of the study refer to five organizational components consultants must understand in order to become familiar with the organization: (1) plans and objectives, (2) structure, (3) policies and procedures, (4) methods of control, and (5) physical and human resources. In other words, consultants must know the organization well before they can begin phase 2, the process of evaluation.

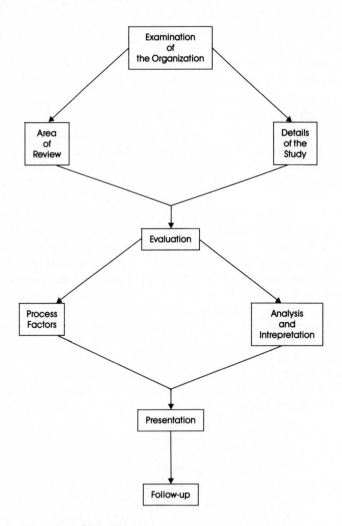

Figure 8.5   The Consulting Process
(P. Harper, Oklahoma State University, 1985)

PHASE 2. EVALUATION

The second phase of the consulting process is the evaluation of the entire organization, a type of management function, or a division within the organization. It consists of two separate subphases, *process factors* and *analysis and interpretation*. It is during the evaluation phase that the majority of the consulting activities are performed. It is also the time when consultants conduct personal interviews, design and implement questionnaires in order to collect data, and observe the performance and behavior of individual employees.

Process factors is the first part of the evaluation. Five separate analyses are carried out, each is designed to examine a particular component of the entire organization, a management function, or a division within the organization. *First,* the consultant examines the economic outlook of the organization to determine its present and future condition. This is done as a way of predicting financial stability and readiness for change. In other words, a healthy organization, or at least one that has the capacity to be healthy, will be more receptive to the implementation of new and innovative ideas, systems, and/or training programs. It will also be in a better position to take advantage of potential opportunities. *Second,* the consultant examines the adequacy of the organizational structure. This includes the design of the organization in terms of communications, lines of command, division of labor, and span of control. Each of these elements provides insight into the functionality of the organization and the potential to implement change. *Third,* the consultant examines the adequacy of control. This includes leadership patterns and the style of the organization, as well as the formal and informal communications systems within the organization. The relationship between employees and management is examined as well, to determine their willingness and desire to implement change and their confidence in each other. *Fourth,* for a proper evaluation, employees must provide individual perceptions of the organization, observations of employee-manager relationships, information regarding the operation and structure of the organization, and access to essential and vital records. Therefore, consultants must provide adequate protection for those employees who assist them in their inquiry. Failure to do so will prevent open and honest disclosure and reduce the probability of an accurate analysis and interpretation of the organization. Fifth, consultants need to determine the "method of operation" of the organization. This refers to how the organization goes about making and implementing change, communicates, integrates employees into the organization as well as into the decision-making process, and rewards employees for outstanding service and performance.

Analysis and interpretation, the second part of the evaluation, is the actual analysis of the organization and its problems. It is during this subphase that the method of analysis is determined, the analysis is actually conducted, and the information (data and perceptions collected during analysis) is interpreted. Once an interpretation has been completed, consultants can develop the recommendations that bring about change and/or the interventions that bring about performance improvement.

Phase 3. Presentation

The third phase of the consulting process is the presentation of the findings and the recommendations for change and interventions that bring about performance improvements. Presentation includes an informal presentation, a written report, and a formal/final presentation. First, the consultant provides an overview of the evaluation that was conducted and how it relates to the suggested recommendations and interventions. This information is presented off the record, so managers, supervisors, and executives can react before the findings, recommendations, and interventions become official. It is important to integrate the insights and perceptions of managers, supervisors, and executives, as well as hear their suggestions as to the most appropriate approach to take, to insure that the recommendations and interventions are adopted by organizational decision makers.

A written report formally documents the analysis and the proposed recommendations and interventions. It includes the method of analysis, supportive data and information, and the perceptions and opinions of employees as well as attitude surveys and other important findings. A written report also provides a record of the consultant's efforts and activities and is evidence of their performance.

After the written report is completed a formal presentation is in order. It is during this activity that consultants will need to present their recommendations and interventions in such a manner as to persuade organizational decision makers to adopt them. Thus, an impressive and convincing presentation should be designed, utilizing the media that complements the consultant's presentation skills and personality the best.

Phase 4. Follow-up

The final phase, often overlooked by consultants, is extremely important. Follow-up assures that the recommendations and interventions suggested are being implemented. During this phase consultants can determine the area(s) where managers and supervisors need assistance. They can also serve as mediators with power brokers within the organization who might prevent the implementation and adoption of the needed changes and interventions. In addition, consultants can tie up any loose ends in the consulting process, and use the follow-up phase to ascertain any future interventions and/or services that may be needed. Finally, this phase communicates to organizational decision makers the deep concern the consultant has regarding the utilization of the recommendations and interventions, as well as for the overall well-being of the organization.

CONCLUSION

The role of the HRD consultant must be examined very carefully—the location in the organization (i.e., internal, external, and/or internal/external); the different relationships between the consultant and members of the organization; the hierarchy of purpose for consulting; and why a consultant is needed in today's organization. Consultants must understand that the consulting role is not fixed. It consists of a process that results in changes and interventions that bring about performance improvement. Finally, examination analysis of the consultant role includes an identification of the competencies that are unique to the role. Once these analyses have been completed, one should have a good understanding of the role of consultant in HRD.

(The authors would like to acknowledge the efforts of Thomas Hudson, Doctoral student at the University of Nebraska, Lincoln, for his research and contribution in the development of this chapter.)

CHAPTER 9

Assessing the Need for HRD

Objectives

After completing Chapter 9, readers should be able to

- define needs assessment as it relates to HRD.

- cite four reasons for engaging in needs assessment.

- describe how interviews are used in needs assessment.

- develop a questionnaire that would be useful in needs assessment.

- support the rule of tests as a method of needs assessment.

- describe the situations in which group problem analyses would be superior to interviews.

- tell what records and reports are useful in needs assessment.

- list and briefly describe at least four needs assessment models.

- develop a training proposal.

In the organizational context, the distinction between "problems" and "needs" can be subtle, a nuance HRD practitioners would do well to consider. It is tempting to represent the training function as some sort of panacea, a solution to any and all problems facing the organization. That approach is laden with peril. The problem may not fall within the training realm at all, but may instead be a function of inadequate supplies, improper finance, inappropriate promotion, production glitches, or some other short-term problem or crisis. Part of the solution may rest with training, but problems like these are usually solved by departments other than HRD. Attempts to rely on training to solve them are frequently doomed to failure and are an embarrassment to the HRD department. A learning program or training activity should be developed and offered only in response to a methodically identified need for it. It should never be considered a quick, automatic, sure-fire solution to a given short-term problem.

DEFINITION OF NEEDS ASSESSMENT

A source of confusion is the lack of a generally accepted, useful, and substantive definition of *need* in the context of human resource development. Perhaps the term has survived in the field because it is vague and has so many meanings. HRD practitioners sometimes use the term loosely to suggest something essential for their clients or constituents, rather than merely self-serving. They use it in slogans and rhetoric to cultivate a supportive and committed environment; and they use it to communicate insight and specificity, while actually saying nothing. The concept of need may be popular because it appears to emerge from empirical information that obviates the necessity for value judgments.

Atwood and Ellis (1971) suggest that a need is a deficiency that detracts from a person's well-being. Archambault (1957) uses the term to describe individuals' objectively demonstrable deficiencies in relation to their environments. Walton (1969) isolates four elements in a statement of needs: (1) a factual description of some empirically verifiable characteristic of an individual, (2) a comparison of this description with some desirable characteristic defined by an external criterion, (3) a conclusion that a change is desired, and (4) a strategy for satisfying the need through education.

It is useful to think of need as a gap between a current set of circumstances and some changed or desirable set of circumstances. The circumstances can be described in terms of proficiency (knowledge, skills, attitudes), performance, or situations. Needs can deal with desires, interests, or deficiencies. They can be specified for an individual or aggregated for groups or organizations. The changed set of circumstances can be described in terms of ways of altering the current situation. It follows, then, that needs assessment, to be useful for human resource development, must be defined in terms of measuring (as scientifically as possible) and appraising that gap between the current situation and the desirable set of circumstances.

THE IMPORTANCE OF NEEDS ASSESSMENT

It is time to emphasize how imperative needs assessment is in carrying out the function of training within an HRD department. The rationale for developing objectives before embarking on a project obtains here. In general, without a clear understanding of needs, training efforts are at best randomly useful and at worst, useless.

In the literature on needs assessment, Michalak and Yager (1979) have done the best job of establishing the importance of using needs analysis techniques. They suggest four major reasons why needs analyses must be done before training programs are developed.

1. To identify specific problem areas in the organization. Both the HRD practitioner and management must know what the problems are so that the most appropriate training (if training is the answer) will be directed to those organizational problems. For example, if a manager approaches the HRD department with a request for a communications program, too often the trainer's response (eager to serve management) will be to proceed to scout around for a good communications program and conduct the training without conducting a needs assessment first. This approach almost inevitably fails. Nodding their heads appreciatively, everyone says, "That was a good program," but when they go back to their departments, business proceeds as usual because the training was not directed to the real needs of the participants. A better response would have been, "Yes, but let's start by taking a look at the situation. We will talk to a few people to find out what the problems are. Then when we develop the program, we can zero in on a specific situation, rather than just use a random approach."

2. To obtain management commitment. Management usually thinks of training as a "nice thing to do." This attitude can be laid directly at the doorstep of a poor (or nonexistent) needs assessment. The way to obtain management commitment to training is to make certain that the training directly affects what happens in that manager's department or organization. Trainers, of course, should see themselves in the same way that controllers or engineering managers do, that is, as making a direct contribution to their department's bottom line (the profit picture).

Trainers must be careful not to delude themselves into thinking that management commitment is present just because the manager approves of, supports, pays for, sends people to, or even helps teach in the training program. Real management commitment comes from the knowledge that training, because it affects departmental performance, profit, and results, will also affect the manager's own performance. At the end of the year all managers must account for themselves. If the training clearly improved their performance, they will be committed to HRD. When an HRD practitioner improves performance on the job and thereby the productivity of the manager's human resources, true management commitment will follow. Training programs will not be avoided or cut; and training budgets will not be trimmed. Taking employees off the job and putting them into a classroom will become a problem of both management and trainer, not the trainer's alone.

3. *To develop data for evaluation.* Unless data on needs are developed prior to conducting the training program, the evaluations that take place after the program is completed may not be valid. By looking at needs first, trainers can measure the effectiveness of the training program.

4. *To determine the costs and benefits of training.* Training is often looked upon as a nuisance rather than a contribution to the bottom line of the organization. This happens when trainers fail to develop a cost-benefit analysis for the training they conduct. Few managers, when faced with a problem that is costing them $100,000 a year, would balk at spending $10,000 for a solution to that problem. And yet on all sides trainers complain that management will not spend any money on training. But if they do a thorough needs assessment and identify the problems and performance deficiencies, management can in many instances put a cost factor on the training needs.

The major question that trainers need to address in cost-benefit analysis is "What is the difference between the cost of no training versus the cost of training?" This means finding out what the costs (out-of-pocket, salary, lost business, etc.) would be if the need continues without any solution being applied. Then an analysis and determination must be made of the cost of conducting the training program that can change the situation. The difference between these two factors will usually tell both trainer and manager whether or not the training should be conducted.

WHY ENGAGE IN NEEDS ASSESSMENT?

In order to have coordinated, methodical, cohesive, and accountable training programs that share symmetry with the organization's objectives, a needs assessment program must be established in the training realm. A study of the work environment and the personnel involved will identify the existing level of employee performance. This is the same as measuring the productivity of manufacturing, for example, against industry standards; or, where productivity is difficult to measure, such as in medical situations, determining other apparent areas of need. Accounting problems might surface, indicating a need for training in that area.

In addition to the obvious benefits to the organization, a sometimes serendipitous advantage shows up under the label, "People tend to support what they help to create." Because needs assessment involves employees and management, these people feel they have contributed to the design of the program, and are indeed "a part of"—not "apart from"—the program (Donaldson & Scannell, 1986).

METHODS EMPLOYED IN NEEDS ASSESSMENT

There are numerous ways, strategies, and schemes that HRD managers can use to tease out needs from the various constituencies within an organization. They are normally referred to collectively as "methods" and in the aggregate may total 20 or 30. Six of them, the ones most useful in human resource development will be highlighted here. They are interviews, questionnaires, tests, group problem analyses, records and report studies, and job analyses and performance reviews.

INTERVIEWS

It could be argued that if you want to find out what people need, the best thing to do is to ask them. It turns out that this is a method frequently used in needs assessment. People in organizations are asked what they need in the form of training. Interviews are a common way of gathering information in any situation—that is, talking to people to find out their perceptions of problems and their ideas about solutions. Sometimes the interviews are formal; sometimes they are informal. In some cases conducting individual interviews is the only technique used to determine the dimensions of a problem identified as having training implications. In other cases the interviews are just the first step. By interviewing a few people and getting an idea of what the problem is, the trainer can decide what kinds of questions need to be asked on a survey instrument in order to maximize the value of that instrument.

Michalak and Yager (1979) suggest that in order to use this technique most effectively, the interviewer must plan the interview. The first question to ask is, "At the end of this series of interviews, what information will I need so that I can conduct an effective training program?" Some examples of the kinds of information that will be needed are

- The exact nature of the problem.
- The areas affected in the organization.
- The number of people involved.
- What the performance deficiency is.
- What the employees are not doing that they should be doing.
- What the employees are doing that they should not be doing.

Once the interviewer has determined these points of information, he or she should then ask, "What questions do I need to ask in order to get this information?" For example, if one of the objectives is to determine the nature of the problem, some of the questions might be

- Have you ever not received the information you needed?
- Have you heard about other people not receiving the information they needed?
- How have you received the information you need?

Once the information and the questions are determined, the next question is how to conduct the interview. Here are a number of hints that may help improve the quality of interviews.

The *physical setting* or the environment in which the interview is conducted is as important as the interview itself. An interview aimed at getting information or at sharing ideas should be conducted in a comfortable atmosphere. The interviewer should move away from behind a desk into a more relaxed and casual setting so that no physical barriers are placed between the interviewer and the interviewee. Ideally, the interview should be conducted on neutral ground, such as in a conference room.

The best way to *record the data* from interviews differs with each individual. Most people, however, find it distracting to have the interviewer constantly writing notes. Two alternatives to this method follow.

1. The interviewer may pause occasionally to give the interviewee a thought question. For example, "Think about this for a minute. If you had a chance to change the situation that you just described, what would you do?" Then, while the interviewee is thinking about the question, the interviewer records whatever data are relevant from the previous few minutes. The value of this method is that the interviewee is less likely to be cued about what things are acceptable or unacceptable to the interviewer.

2. The interviewer can tape-record the entire interview. There are positive and negative aspects to this method. Some interviewees may be less candid when they know they are being recorded. One way to reduce this problem is by being straightforward with the interviewee; that he or she wants to tape-record the information to avoid writing notes. The interviewee should be assured that no one in management, for example, will hear the tapes. By using a tape recorder with a counter on it the interviewer can avoid having to listen to the entire tape when recording the data later. The interviewer can index the spot where the salient information was given and record the information much more quickly.

A question that is often asked is *how many people should be interviewed*. The answer to this is that it depends on the purpose of the interviews. If the interviews are going to be the entire source of data, more people will need to be interviewed than if the interviews are a preliminary step in the development of a questionnaire. When the employees are all at the same level in the organization, we have found that a minimum of four should be interviewed. It is not at all unusual to be able to obtain 95–98 percent of all the necessary information from the first four interviews. Experienced interviewers tell us that once they get past the fourth interview of a homogeneous group of employees, the information becomes redundant.

The way the interview is begun is of utmost importance. The first thing that needs to be done is to allay the fears and anxieties of the interviewee. The purpose of the interview should be explained fully. An example might be: "We have been asked by your management to develop a training program in customer relations. We said we wanted to talk to some of the people who do a good job in customer relations, and that's the reason you are here. We would like to ask you a few questions to find out what actually happens in customer relations so that the training program we develop will really be helpful."

When the interviewee is reasonably satisfied with the purpose of the interview, the first question ought to be either positive or neutral. An example of a neutral question would be: "Tell me about your job." This helps most people to talk without any problem. An example of a positive question would be: "What do you like best about your job?" Here again the interviewee feels free to talk, and this positive question serves as a good icebreaker.

After several minutes of discussing either the neutral or the positive question, the negative questions can be introduced. Some examples are

- What do you feel are some of the problems in customer relations?
- If you were allowed to make any changes that you wanted to around here, what changes would you make?
- What are some of the problems in the organization?
- What are some of the things that people do ineffectively in the organization?

The interviewer should dig deeply and *be intensive*. Often one answer to a question will not provide adequate information. For example, if an interviewee says that he or she was quite pleased about a promotion, do not assume that this is due to a desire for success (though it may well be); ask instead why the interviewee was pleased. The interviewer does not always have to ask a question formulated in a complete sentence. Sometimes a simple phrase such as "Then what?" is enough to encourage the person to continue talking. Silence can also be a question. It implies that the listener wants to hear more.

QUESTIONNAIRES

The descriptor "questionnaires" is a general name for a wide range of instruments that can be used in the assessment of needs for training. They are usually used when the number of people from whom information is to be sought is too unwieldy for the interview method.

Questionnaires can reach many people in a short period of time at relatively low cost. If carefully administered, they give people a chance to express themselves without fear of embarrassment or retribution. Another advantage is that questionnaires yield data that are easily summarized and reported.

There are also some negative aspects to the use of questionnaires in the training field. There is usually little provision for free expression or extemporaneous responses; and sometimes they are not very effective in getting at causes of problems and possible solutions. Finally, they may be difficult to construct.

Following are seven suggestions for making questionnaire construction more manageable:

1. Write explicit instructions so that the respondents will know exactly what to do. An example follows.

   > Read each of the statements below carefully. Circle SD if you strongly disagree, D if you disagree, A if you agree, and SA if you strongly agree.

2. Provide a space after each question for a comment from the respondents when appropriate. This will alleviate the first shortcoming mentioned above.

3. Be sure that the respondents can validly answer the questions. Two examples follow.

   > "Is the personnel department responsive to the needs and problems of employees?" This question calls for a judgment about others. It would be better for each respondent to comment about himself or herself: "Has the personnel department been responsive to your needs and problems?"

   > "Does your supervisor spend sufficient time developing your performance appraisal?" This question calls for an opinion that employees cannot really make. It might be better to prepare a question about the value of the appraisal.

4. Be specific. Three examples follow.

   > "Was the training relevant to your department's needs?" More information can be obtained if a question that requires more than a yes/no response is asked; such as, "Which training programs were relevant to your department's needs?"

   > "Make any general or specific comments you would like about our service program." This question is too general to obtain good feedback. It might be better to ask: "What suggestions do you have to improve our service?" "What is the longest time you had to wait for service?" "Have you ever had to return any item we serviced? Explain."

"Are the order forms beneficial to you?" In this question "beneficial" is vague. It might be better to ask how the forms are used on the job or what problems employees are having with the forms.

5. Highlight negatives to reduce the likelihood of someone misreading the question. An example follows.

"What parts of the program were not relevant to your work situation?"

6. Ask one question at a time. Two examples follow.

"Do you get the information you need to do your job or should there be more interdepartmental reports, staff meetings, and "blue letters" from the chairman?" This question could be rewritten thus:
"Do you get the information you need to do your job?"
　　　　　　　　　( ) Yes　　　　　　　　　( ) No
Put a check in the appropriate column to indicate how helpful each of the following was in getting information to you.

	Inadequate	Helpful	Very Helpful
1. Interdepartmental Reports			
2. Staff Meetings			

Explain each item you checked as "inadequate."

"Were the training materials understandable and pertinent to your job?" This question should really be broken down into two separate questions, one about "understandable" and the other about "pertinent."

7. Use descriptive terms to help participants answer questions that have a scale. An example follows.

"How much responsibility do you feel toward your new job as compared to your last job?"

　1　　　　　　　2　　　　　　　3　　　　　　　4　　　　　　　5

TESTS

Various kinds of tests are administered to employees of organizations. Many are valuable in helping to assess training needs. The kind most often used are those designed to measure performance of one kind or another. Achievement levels of individuals and groups can be assessed through testing. Entry-level skills, for example, are easily measured. After a person has been on the job for some time, periodic appraisal may show a real need for cognitive, affective, or even psychomotor updating. Commercial tests in a variety of content areas are readily available should internal sources be lacking.

There are several advantages to using tests. As diagnostic tools they help identify specific areas of deficiency. They may also be helpful in selecting from among potential trainees those people who can be trained most profitably. And the results of tests are usually easy to compare and report.

Testing may also limit the HRD practitioner. Tests that have been validated for specific situations are often not available—and tests validated elsewhere may prove to be invalid in a new situation or location. The results of testing usually give strong clues to their validity, but the tests cannot always be relied on as being conclusive. As a diagnostic device, a test is only second best when compared to specific measures of job performance.

When using tests in HRD, one should keep several cautions in mind. Be certain you know what the test measures; be sure it is worth measuring in the specific situation; and then be sure to apply the results of the test to factors or situations where the test is valid. Finally, tests should not be used to take the blame or to serve as a buffer for any difficult or unpopular decisions that management should make.

GROUP PROBLEM ANALYSES

Some suggest that "group problem analysis" only means interviews done in groups. This is probably true, but there are several advantages to this method of needs assessment. It permits synthesis of several points of view; it often promotes general understanding and agreement; it can build support for needed training; and it can in itself serve as a form of training.

On the negative side of the ledger, as a form of needs assessment group problem analysis is time consuming and initially expensive and supervisors may feel too busy to participate. They may want others to do the work for them. Sometimes the results of group activities such as this may be quite difficult to quantify and summarize.

A number of situations have been suggested in which group problem analysis is superior to interviews. They include

1. If many employees have information on a problem, it is a more efficient use of time to conduct 3 group problem analysis sessions than 10 to 20 individual interviews.

2. When the subject of the session is one that will not cause participants to feel they might get into trouble if the truth were known, group techniques work well. In situations where participants are asked about their own shortcomings, individual interviews tend to be more effective than group interviews.

3. When talking about other areas of the organization, that is, employees or bosses of the interviewees, or other departments, the group techniques are very effective because participants do not feel threatened by the information.

Group problem analysis works best when quick results are neither promised nor expected. The leader should begin with a problem that is known to be of concern to the group. Once that is done, the group should begin to make its own analyses and set its own priorities. Facilitating group communication is the key to success in group problem analysis. Just as in individual interviews, the techniques that will get the group talking must be nonthreatening. One very effective question to use in getting a group talking about their on-the-job problems is: "What gets in the way of your doing your job as well as you would like to do it?" The answers to this question tend to fall into three areas:

1. The system. The interviewees will tell about things in the system that keep them from doing their jobs as well as they would like to do it.

2. Management. The interviewees will talk readily about some of the inconsistencies and poor management practices that they have observed.

3. The interviewees themselves. Eventually, the interviewees will get around to pointing the finger at themselves, that is, their own skill deficiencies and motivational problems, which are related to the problem being discussed.

RECORDS AND REPORT STUDIES

The study of secondary data can prove to be quite fruitful in the assessment of an organization's needs. Many times these data are easily accessible in the form of records and reports that already exist within the company, most often supervisors' reports on employees and employee performance records. Requests for data may come from an individual's immediate superior. Some requests come from officials of the organization and, of course, require prompt action, but remember that the request may not represent a bona fide training need. Again, an honest inquiry may articulate the real problem or dispose of an artificial one.

Supervisors are becoming increasingly people oriented and can be a sincere and continuing source of information regarding areas where training is needed. People don't always know what they need or may mistakenly cite an incorrect need. Employee efficiency and production records are a good source of review. A quick check with the personnel department will determine which records may be available. Since privacy laws are becoming more stringent, be certain that you do not ask to see information considered to be privileged data. Assuming, however, that these records are approved for perusal, several areas of need may come to light. Productivity, sales, and operating ratios are but a few of the items that may be compared to pinpoint an individual need.

Records and reports provide excellent clues to trouble spots. They are also the best objective evidence of the results of problems. They are usually of concern to and understood by operating officials. But they have some limitations as well. They normally do not show causes of problems or possible solutions. They may not provide enough cases to be meaningful. Records and reports, because they are historical in nature, may not reflect the *current* situation or recent changes. In general, they should only be used as checks and clues in combination with other methods of needs assessment.

JOB ANALYSES AND PERFORMANCE REVIEWS

Lengthy books have been written on the subject of job analysis and performance review. Here we present simply the fundamentals. In general, the classic job analysis develops precise information about an actual job; on-the-job performance is covered in the performance review. Jobs can be easily broken down into manageable segments for the purposes of both training and appraisal.

On the negative side, these techniques are time consuming and difficult for people who are not trained in job analysis techniques. Many supervisors dislike reviewing their employees' inadequacies with them personally. The individual training needs that come to light are sometimes difficult to translate into organizational needs. Trainers who choose this technique should develop the special job analysis techniques they need. They should also arrange training sessions for others who are to do it. The analyses should be of the current job and current job performance and, once completed, should be reviewed with the employees.

In the foregoing sections we have covered some of the methods used in the general effort of needs assessment in the organization. These are the more frequently used ones, but there are several others as well, such as observation, consultation, print media, work samples, force field analysis, critical incident techniques, behavioral scales, management requests, assessment centers, and formal research. HRD managers who want to use any of these needs assessment techniques only has to learn how to use them and add them to their repertoire.

A CHECKLIST FOR METHOD SELECTION

Some ask what is the best procedure for selecting a needs assessment method. Stephen Steadham's (1980) checklist for selection criteria is one of the best responses to that question. Once they complete the checklist, trainers find that the job of selecting a needs assessment method becomes a great deal easier.

A Checklist for Needs Assessment Method Selection Criteria

What resources are required and available for the needs assessment?

1. Time involved for both client system and the consultant in the needs assessment effort:
   a. in developing the data collection process
   b. in administering or implementing the process

2. Money needed for the effort:
   a. direct costs for processing a computerized survey
   b. indirect costs for excusing staff from regular duties for interviews

To what degree will the needs assessment consultant and the client system be involved in the design and administration of the data collection effort?

1. In terms of increased awareness?
2. In terms of immediate problem solving simply as a result of surfacing the needs data?
3. In terms of commitment to take action or basic findings?

How "healthy" is the client system? Are there massive communication blocks that would preclude using certain collection methods such as group discussion? For example:

> It would be inappropriate to use a method that could produce a mountain of needs data if there was already a low limit on budget expenditures for a program response.

Who is to be involved in the data collection?
    What are the reasons certain people were excluded or included?

What does the client system intend to do with the assessment?
    What are the limits or plans for using the assessment results?

Do the client system's decision makers have a preference for one data collection method over another?

To what extent does the client system already *know* the needs?
    How clearly is the need already being articulated?

How much time lag can there be between collecting the data and taking action?

What types of "needs" are to be uncovered:

1. Needs felt by the actual or potential program participant?
2. Needs which others (staff, for example) either observe or presume the program participant has or should have?

What degree of reliability or validity is needed by the client system to act on the data?
    To what extent must program participants agree with or accept the results of the data collection effort?

How confidential or anonymous are the data to be?

What is the level of trust between the client system and the consultant in the needs assessment effort?

How good is the relationship?

How comfortable is the needs assessment consultant with a particular method?

MODELS USEFUL FOR NEEDS ASSESSMENT

Once the strategies of needs assessment have been developed, they can be configured into models. These models are sometimes quite complex and vary in purpose, scope, and magnitude. Six general clusters of needs assessment models have been identified in the literature. McKinley (1973) identified three: individual self-fulfillment models, individual appraisal models, and system discrepancy models. Three additional clusters have been described by others: diagnostic models, analytic models, and democratic models. The brief descriptions that follow indicate generally the approaches trainers can use. It is a useful way to locate the relevant studies on needs assessment strategies.

1. *Individual self-fulfillment models* include random appeal and selective appeal models. Random appeals aim at discovering the individual needs (usually defined as interests or wants) of a large segment of the population that are potent enough to attract the individuals to training activities and make a program financially self-supporting. They do not appeal to organizational needs. Selective appeals focus on the presumed individual needs of a known segment of the organization. Programs based on this model generally use formats that have already been tested with the specialized population. There are problems with these approaches—lack of measurement precision, trainer and organizational bias in analyzing results, and a tendency toward creating and maintaining a market rather than focusing on training needs.

2. *Individual appraisal models* include the collaborative and noncollaborative participation of individuals in determining their own training needs. In the collaborative model learners have the assistance of others in clarifying their own training needs. In the noncollaborative or self-appraisal model they assess their own training needs using assessment techniques. The problems with these models are that learners usually cannot recognize and do not understand essential learning needs. Biases are built into measurement instruments that may not be related to individuals' actual circumstances; and individual initiative must be depended on for specification and follow-up.

3. *System discrepancy models* seek to identify the gap between "what is" and "what ought to be" in a given situation. They include two types of approaches to developing training programs. Problem-need approaches attempt to define deficiencies and then develop remedial programs. Training needs and objectives are directly related to diagnosed difficulties in the system. Goal-identification approaches have a general improvement thrust rather than a

specific remedial focus. They assume that objectives that are carefully derived from the goals of the organization will reflect desired learning outcomes that some trainers would term needs.

4. *Diagnostic models* view need as something whose absence or deficiency proves harmful. This approach, also called the medical model, searches for both met and unmet needs and uses available knowledge and logic to decide which deficiencies would be harmful. In the simplest case, the trainer identifies a need by observing what happens when adults are deprived of a resource and then projects what would happen if they had that resource. Needs specified using the diagnostic model can be more precisely described in terms of a performance deficit than in terms of a treatment deficit. The former is illustrated by the assertion, "Physicians need to achieve mastery of cardiopulmonary resuscitation before they receive their license to participate in continuing medical education programs." Treatment needs that are broadly described are poorly related to feasible actions, while performance-deficit needs statements give no intrinsic guidance to what treatment is needed.

5. *Analytic models* define a direction in which improvement would occur, given information about the status of a person or a program. It places a premium on informed judgment and systematic problem solving. It seeks full description of the thing or person whose needs are being assessed. It focuses on improvement rather than remediation and does not require advance statements of standards or success criteria. Two problems with this approach are that it is an abstraction that may be difficult to apply and requires skilled problem solvers.

6. *Democratic models* involve interactive and collaborative efforts at specifying needs using nomination and voting techniques. Nominal group processes and delphi techniques (Delberq et al., 1975) exemplify this approach. The problems with this model are the possibility that the required consensus may discourage dealing with critical issues and that progress in reducing dissonance in the population may be impeded by waiting for majority approval.

DEVELOPING A TRAINING PROPOSAL

Once needs have been assessed, those that can be met by training are identified. It is usually incumbent, then, on the HRD practitioner to develop a proposal for management that describes what training is to be done. Some have suggested that the best way to approach management is through a phenomenon that was first described as *data confrontation* (Michalak & Yager, 1979). The HRD practitioner does not have to confront the manager personally, but rather shares the data received and lets the manager confront the data. There is no need for the trainer to say, "Your people are unhappy" if the results of the questionnaire point out that 87 percent of the people would transfer if it were not for the poor economic situation. The data speak for themselves and are powerful; they are objective, measurable, and, in many cases, irrefutable.

In addition to avoiding a personal confrontation with management, there are several other things HRD practitioners can do in order to be more effective in this phase of the job. *First,* when getting the approval of the manager to conduct the needs analysis, the trainer must make it clear that after the data have been put together, the trainer and manager both share the data. *Second,* the HRD practitioner should meet first with the top manager of the department to share the data and then let the manager share the information with subordinate managers, with the trainer working as a process attendant. This is especially important when some of the data are sensitive. It would be politically foolhardy to have the top manager in the organization be surprised by the data. By meeting with the trainer in advance and by getting some recommendations for solutions, the manager can go into a meeting with subordinate managers from a position of strength. The support received from the subordinate managers will be enhanced tremendously through this technique.

Third, training jargon should be avoided. Actions taken should be stated simply and directly. For example, instead of saying, "We conducted a needs analysis," the HRD practitioner can say, "We talked with some of your people in groups of eight or nine and here's what they told us." *Finally,* the HRD practitioner should have recommendations ready. Most managers, after reviewing the data, will ask the question, "What can we do about it?" Have alternative responses available to share with management.

Once needs have been analyzed and identified and data confrontation has occurred, the final step is to develop the training proposal itself. It should spell out the need for training, the expected results, the people to be trained, and the expected consequences if training is not conducted. It should include an outline of the proposed program. The following sample is illustrative.

Sample Proposal

INTERCOMPANY MEMO
FROM: Garrison Engleman, HRD Manager
TO: Diana Conforth, Vice-President Operations
SUBJECT: Training Proposal

Objective
Reduce costs of "widget" stampings by 10 percent

The Need for Training
A needs analysis was conducted in the production department to determine if training could improve performance and lower production costs. Our analysis indicated that two major problems can be reduced by training. One is the abnormally high waste factor, found to be 14 percent of stamping stock, and the second is the improper handling procedures being followed by the stock feeders.

Sheet steel stock is being damaged in the warehouse and on the line. This damage due to improper handling is a major cause of the high waste factor. Waste is also occurring due to improper alignment procedures by the stock feeder.

Expected Results

Proper handling and feeding procedures should result in the waste factor being lowered to approximately 4 percent. About 7 percent of the reduction will accrue from improved handling procedures and 3 percent from improved stock feeding procedures.

Prospects for Training

All lift-truck operators and stock clerks in the sheet steel warehouse and all stamping machine operators, fourteen feeders, six lift-truck operators, and two stock clerks. The thirty-six prospective trainees should be trained concurrently to gain the support of all those involved.

Outline of the Program

Waste Reduction Training Program

I. Orientation
   a) Explain problem and training objective to participants.
   b) Establish minimum level of proficiency trainees must achieve.
   c) Explain rewards or benefits participants will receive by reaching required proficiency level.

II. Concurrent training sessions in warehouse and in production department
   a) Demonstration
   b) Practice session
   c) On-the-job test

III. Discussion
   a) Problems encountered
   b) Suggested solutions

IV. Second session
   a) Demonstration
   b) Practice session
   c) On-the-job test

V. Evaluation
   a) Waste factor results
   b) Performance results
   c) Attitude results

Expected Conditions Without Training

Without training, the waste factor is expected to continue at the current 14 percent waste level. This level may even increase as the cumulative effect of poor attitudes and improper work habits reinforce each other over time.

Recommendations

A training program is recommended to begin immediately and is expected to last approximately three months, with follow-up tests and evaluation to continue for one year.

CONCLUSION

The trainer will only be successful (and perceived as such) to the extent that needs are carefully assessed and programs developed and carried out that meet those needs. Following the suggestions in this chapter will carry the trainer a good deal of the way.

CHAPTER 10

Program Planning, Design, and Evaluation

Objectives

After completing Chapter 10, readers should be able to

- identify the nine phases of the program planning, design, and evaluation process.

- describe the differences between the activity strategy and the impact strategy.

- identify the seven perceptual modalities.

- describe why learning styles are important when designing learning programs.

- identify the five purposes of needs analysis.

- describe the feedback process and explain why it is important.

- identify the five outcomes of the design phase and their respective importance.

- identify the four outcomes of the development phase.

- list the components of the implementation phase.

- describe the management phase and how it interrelates with the design, development, and implementation phases.

- describe the importance of evaluation in learning.

- differentiate among validity, reliability, and usability.

- identify the components of evaluation.

- describe the process of evaluation.

- identify the levels of evaluation and their respective importance.

- describe and explain accountability as it relates to program design.

HRD practitioners concerned with assessing needs, establishing learning objectives, designing or selecting learning activities, choosing and implementing training strategies, and evaluating learning outcomes are engaged in a process known as *programming*. Programming consists of nine interrelated subprocesses referred to as phases. These nine phases are often referred to as the program planning, design, and evaluation process. In this chapter we examine each of these subprocesses and determine their relationship to one another.

Each phase of the program planning, design, and evaluation process serves as a foundation for the others. The activities conducted in each phase are based upon this relationship. The nine phases are

Phase 1. Philosophy of Teaching and Learning

Phase 2. Needs Analysis

Phase 3. Feedback

Phase 4. Program Design

Phase 5. Program Development

Phase 6. Program Implementation

Phase 7. Program Management

Phase 8. Evaluation

Phase 9. Accountability

THE GENESIS OF LEARNING PROGRAMS WITHIN ORGANIZATIONS

Most HRD programs include hundreds of learning activities and training programs. Most begin because of one of two reasons: (1) a request for training by managers and/or supervisors, or (2) some symptoms of performance deficiency.

As a way of addressing these, HRD practitioners can choose between two training strategies: (1) an activity strategy and (2) an impact strategy. These implementation strategies differ in their focus, how they are measured, and how they are viewed within the organization (Robinson, 1987).

An *activity strategy* is an approach practitioners use to design and develop learning programs when little or no impact on organizational change is desired or expected. Programs are offered as an "activity" for employees. Often referred to as a fringe benefit approach, the focus is on the delivery of the programs. HRD practitioners who embrace this approach report on the number of courses they offer and the number of people attending them as a way of measuring and validating their value. HRD programs that adopt this approach are viewed by organizational decision makers as something HRD professionals do. This strategy is often used as an answer to managers' and supervisors' requests for training.

An *impact strategy* is an approach practitioners use to develop and deliver programs when organizational change is not only expected but, as much as possible, can be assured. The focus is on obtaining organizational results through learning and skill transfer. HRD practitioners who use this approach report on outcomes as a means of validating their programs. Within the organization, decision makers view training as something management does, but with the support of the HRD department. Frequently, HRD practitioners utilize this strategy as a way of improving performance deficiencies. As more and more organizations begin to expect greater results from training, the impact strategy appears to be the favored view. It is increasing in popularity but unfortunately is not the predominant choice.

PHASE 1. PHILOSOPHY OF TEACHING AND LEARNING

The program planning, design, and evaluation process begins with the program designer identifying a philosophical orientation to the teaching-learning process (see Chapter 7). This includes the personal orientation or training style examined in detail in Chapter 6. It also includes the establishment and utilization of the learning styles of the learners who will be involved in the program.

Scholars generally agree that every individual has a unique approach to learning; however, they do not agree on how to define or explain a person's learning style. One approach suggests that a person's learning style is composed of different modalities that together make up his or her unique style (French, 1975). These modalities include, but are not limited to, the perceptual, cognitive, emotional, and social modes. The perceptual mode is the only one dealt with in this chapter. It refers to the means through which an individual extracts information from the environment through the senses. It is comprised of seven elements: (1) aural, (2) haptic, (3) interactive, (4) kinesthetic, (5) olfactory, (6) print, and (7) visual. (James & Galbraith, 1984)

1. *Aural* individuals learn best through listening.
2. *Haptic* individuals learn best through the sense of touch.

3. *Interactive* individuals learn best through verbalization.

4. *Kinesthetic* individuals learn best while moving.

5. *Olfactory* individuals learn best through the senses of smell and taste.

6. *Print* individuals learn best through reading and writing.

7. *Visual* individuals learn best through observations.

James & Galbraith (1984) suggested that several questions should be addressed by HRD practitioners and program designers when planning and designing learning programs. The answers to these questions may have some practical implications for HRD practitioners involved with the design of programs for adult learners.

1. Why is it important for HRD practitioners and program designers to be knowledgeable about perceptual learning styles? First, prior to the development of learning programs, program designers should take into account the diversity of learners in order to identify the most appropriate learning activities, materials, procedures, methods of instruction, and strategies for the learning group (Smith, 1982). For example, placing individuals in learning activities that enable them to utilize their dominant learning style can facilitate learning. This also helps highly motivated learners to accomplish their educational goals. During the program implementation phase, this information can provide program designers with the bases for the selection of materials, methods, procedures for grouping learners, and ways to provide individualized instruction (James & Galbraith, 1984).

2. What impact does learning styles information have on program planning, design, and evaluation? Utilizing learning styles allows the program designer to be flexible in meeting individual learning needs. This requires creativity on the part of the program designer who must develop a variety of ways to meet learners' diverse needs. The learning environment can become more of a learning center, with a variety of activities occurring at the same time; the learning specialist functions as a manager of learning (James & Galbraith, 1984).

3. How can learners utilize perceptual learning styles information to their best advantage? In addressing this question, James and Galbraith (1984) state that "understanding the learning style concept is essential to the individual, because the utilization of one's most effective learning style will enhance learning. Also, knowledge of learning style allows individual learners to pursue their personal learning projects in a more effective and efficient manner. Learning styles knowledge can also assist adult learners in recognizing why some past learning activities were more worthwhile or useful than others, and why some learning activities were less meaningful to them" (p. 21).

Because most people are not aware of their own personal learning style(s), they are unable to select the method of learning that is best suited for them. Program designers and HRD practitioners can assist learners in identifying their dominant learning style. To help create an awareness of learning styles and to enhance the identification of individual styles, James and Galbraith (1984) designed the "Perceptual Learning Style Inventory" (see Figure 10.1).

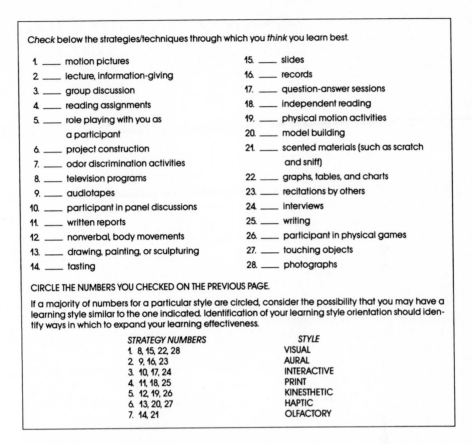

Check below the strategies/techniques through which you *think* you learn best.

1. ___ motion pictures
2. ___ lecture, information-giving
3. ___ group discussion
4. ___ reading assignments
5. ___ role playing with you as
    a participant
6. ___ project construction
7. ___ odor discrimination activities
8. ___ television programs
9. ___ audiotapes
10. ___ participant in panel discussions
11. ___ written reports
12. ___ nonverbal, body movements
13. ___ drawing, painting, or sculpturing
14. ___ tasting

15. ___ slides
16. ___ records
17. ___ question-answer sessions
18. ___ independent reading
19. ___ physical motion activities
20. ___ model building
21. ___ scented materials (such as scratch
    and sniff)
22. ___ graphs, tables, and charts
23. ___ recitations by others
24. ___ interviews
25. ___ writing
26. ___ participant in physical games
27. ___ touching objects
28. ___ photographs

CIRCLE THE NUMBERS YOU CHECKED ON THE PREVIOUS PAGE.

If a majority of numbers for a particular style are circled, consider the possibility that you may have a learning style similar to the one indicated. Identification of your learning style orientation should identify ways in which to expand your learning effectiveness.

STRATEGY NUMBERS	STYLE
1. 8, 15, 22, 28	VISUAL
2. 9, 16, 23	AURAL
3. 10, 17, 24	INTERACTIVE
4. 11, 18, 25	PRINT
5. 12, 19, 26	KINESTHETIC
6. 13, 20, 27	HAPTIC
7. 14, 21	OLFACTORY

Figure 10.1   Perceptual learning style inventory

Reprinted from W. James and M. W. Galbraith, Lifelong Learning: An Omnibus for Research and Practice. *Copyright 1984 American Association for Adult and Continuing Education. Washington, D.C. Reprinted with permission.*

According to James & Galbraith (1984), "this inventory provides learners with a means of identifying strategies and techniques through which they think they learn best. Comparing the pattern of responses to the learning style, an immediate picture of the perceived most dominant learning modes may emerge" (p. 22). Program designers can utilize this inventory to identify the learning styles for the target group. Every learner can be reached, and the instructional learning process becomes more effective and efficient.

Once the program designer's philosophical orientation to the teaching-learning process and the learning styles of the targeted group have been identified, these can be used as a filter for each of the next eight phases of program design. This also provides program designers with a framework for decision making as well as for materials and methods selection. This filter should be used as a guide when designing needs assessments, identifying learning objectives and activities, and matching media with activities. Both the philosophical orientation of the program designers and the identified learning styles of the targeted learning group should be used as a reference while a program is being planned, designed, developed, and implemented.

PHASE 2. NEEDS ANALYSIS

As we saw in Chapter 9, one source of confusion regarding needs analysis is the lack of a generally accepted, useful, and substantive definition of need. It is useful to think of a need as a gap between a current set of circumstances and some changed or desirable set of circumstances. In other words, a need is the difference between "what is" and "what should be." Thus, the gap between these two is considered the need of the individual, group, and/or organization. In an HRD setting, these circumstances can be described in terms of proficiency (knowledge, skills, attitudes), performance, or situations. Need can also deal with desires, interests, or deficiencies. The "changed or desired" set of circumstances can be described in terms of ways of altering the current situation. The most common forms of alteration are training/learning programs that are planned, designed, and developed by HRD practitioners and/or program designers (Figure 10.2).

Needs analysis is a term that has been used to describe a process with at least five purposes. They are (1) clientele analysis, (2) identification of an area of demand for training/learning programs, (3) identification of area of need, (4) causal analysis, and (5) task analysis.

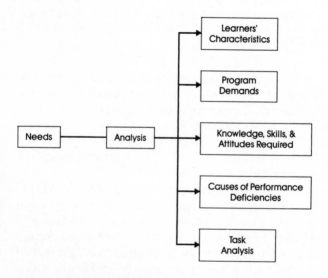

Figure 10.2   Needs analysis phase

A *clientele analysis* is the process of comparing the characteristics of the participants in the training/learning program with those of the general population of individuals who could be served. This will provide the type of descriptive information program designers need to tailor a program for a selective audience. This also insures that the program is consistent for both groups.

The second purpose of a needs analysis is to identify the *areas of demand* for training/learning programs in order to offer programs of significant interest to encourage participation. It also provides program designers with information regarding the size of the potential audience and their level of interest in a specific type of training.

The third purpose consists of *identifying discrepancies between a current and a desired set of circumstances.* This includes techniques of identifying and understanding problem areas. In addition, it includes the collection and analysis of data, which reveals the difference between the current and desired set of circumstances. The magnitude and intensity of the difference is also determined.

The fourth purpose of needs analysis is to determine the *cause(s) of performance deficiencies.* Program designers should begin by examining the learners to determine their current level of knowledge and skill and to measure their attitudes. This information should then be compared to the required level. The difference between the two will become the basis for future training programs and learning activities. Program designers should examine the managers and supervisors to ascertain their effects on performance deficiencies. Finally, program designers should examine the organizational culture, climate, and structure to determine their effects upon performance deficiencies.

The final step in a needs analysis is to conduct a *task analysis.* This analysis is based on the job requirements of employees. The tasks to be performed by employees are listed and those for which training is required are selected. These tasks are then analyzed in detail to determine the knowledge, skills, and attitudes required for acceptable performance. Learning programs can then be designed accordingly.

Program designers should conduct needs assessments in order to meet each of these five purposes. The information collected should be analyzed and interpreted and the conclusions should become the basis for each program which is planned, designed, developed, and implemented. Various models and techniques can be used to meet these purposes and/or gather information regarding needs. These are addressed in detail in Chapter 9.

PHASE 3. FEEDBACK

Once a needs analysis has been conducted it is tempting for the program designer to immediately use the information gathered and interpreted to design new learning programs. Under this approach, the program designer becomes absolutely responsible for the outcomes of the programs. First, this isolates HRD practitioners from other organizational members. It also prevents managers and supervisors from sharing in the performance improvement process. This approach also prohibits managers and supervisors from addressing the needs of employees once they have been identified.

To make certain that vital decision makers within the organization have the opportunity to share in the design and development of learning programs that foster growth and/or an increase in knowledge, skills, and improved attitudes, a four-step process should be followed. This process will insure that managers and supervisors support and defend the actions of HRD practitioners regarding the programs they design and develop because it guarantees their involvement in the decision-making process. In other words, people support what they create.

First, program designers should present the data collected and the respective interpretations to a group of essential managers and supervisors who maintain the authority to fund and implement new training programs. Second, an agreement or conclusion regarding the data should be obtained by the group. Third, HRD practitioners should seek agreement regarding the implications of training. Fourth, the group should decide on the action that should be taken.

This approach insures that the new program(s) designed, developed, and implemented will be supported and thus promoted by others in the organization. It also provides a second validation step prior to the costly design and development phases. Finally, it allows program designers to reach agreement with decision makers on the "problems" facing the organization and their potential "solutions." This is necessary before the HRD manager authorizes the expenditure of human and financial resources to design, develop, and implement training/learning programs that do not improve performance or meet individual needs.

PHASE 4. PROGRAM DESIGN

Once an agreement has been reached regarding the identification of the current performance problems and the individual needs within the organization, the program designer can begin the task of designing programs that improve performance and address individual needs. The design phase is based on the information discovered in the needs analysis phase. This should include trainee characteristics, program demands, knowledge, skills, and attitude requirements, causes of performance deficiencies, and task analysis (see Figure 10.3).

Based on the information collected during needs analysis, program designers should develop (1) learning objectives, (2) learning activities, (3) a structure and sequence for the learning objectives and activities, (4) experiential learning activities, and (5) instructional media, materials, and methods of instruction that are most appropriate.

LEARNING OBJECTIVES

Regardless of its type and length, every training program and learning activity has a set of desired outcomes. These outcomes are statements of what the learner should know, be able to do, or how the learner should behave as a

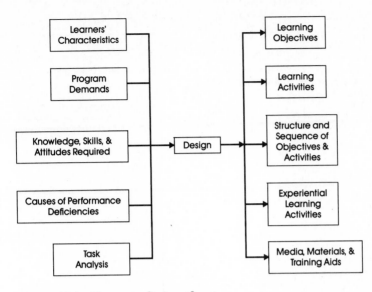

Figure 10.3   Program design phase

result of the program. These outcomes, known as learning objectives, serve four primary functions: (1) they define the desired outcomes of the program, (2) they serve as a guide to the selection of strategies and methods of instruction, (3) they serve as criteria for the development and/or selection of learning activities, and (4) they provide criteria for the evaluation of learning (Lutterodt, 1983). Thus, learning objectives play a critical role in the planning and implementation of instruction.

Learning objectives, however, focus on results rather than on the methods of instruction used. In other words, learning objectives are statements of what should result from instruction. They serve the learning specialist as a standard for which he or she will guide and direct learners. For the learner, they serve as a goal for their effort. Thus, they serve as a way for learners to monitor their own progress.

In addition, learning objectives should be used in the selection of methods of instruction alongside the different media by which content and information are conveyed. Learning objectives also provide criteria for constructing tests and performance examinations used in the evaluation of learners.

A well-written learning objective describes the behavior that must be observed in order to verify that the intended learning has taken place. In order for this to take place an objective should contain three components (see Figure 10.4). First, the desired performance or learning must be identified. Second, the conditions under which the task must be performed or learning duplicated should be identified. Third, the minimal, acceptable level of performance or knowledge must be identified. This is often referred to as a standard of performance or knowledge. A standard may relate to the speed, accuracy, specifications of performance, and/or consequences which may result from the performance or knowledge.

Learning Objective _____

_____

Identify the following related to the above objective.

Performance	Conditions	Standards

Figure 10.4   Criteria for learning objectives

Once the performance or knowledge, conditions, and standards have been identified, learning objectives can be written more clearly and precisely. In Chapter 6, a list of action verbs were identified. These enable HRD practitioners to write measurable objectives that are clear and precise.

LEARNING ACTIVITIES

During the design phase it is essential that various learning activities be developed that will provide learners with an opportunity to develop the knowledge, skills, and behavior desired. These activities must also be based on the identified learning objectives as well as the information collected and analyzed during the needs analysis phase.

Learning activities may include games, group projects, panel discussions, debates, readings, presentations, reports and papers, and on-the-job observations and/or performance. Each should be selected based upon the unique opportunities they provide the learner, in other words, on the maximization of the understanding of an idea, truth, skill, and/or attitude. For example, each activity listed above provides a different way of deepening the understanding of an idea, truth, skill, or attitude. The selection of the most appropriate learning activity is based on the characteristics of the activity that will produce the greatest level of understanding. Thus, the learning objective asks the question, "Where am I going?" The learning activities selected answer the question, "How will I get there?"

STRUCTURING AND SEQUENCING LEARNING OBJECTIVES

Structuring and sequencing learning objectives is less critical than developing learning objectives and identifying learning activities. However, it is important to rank order learning objectives in order to maximize the effectiveness of learning programs. Also included in this subphase is the management of various learning activities to meet the needs of learners and to meet program demands.

EXPERIENTIAL LEARNING ACTIVITIES

It is important during program design to determine if experiential learning activities are appropriate for meeting the learning objectives as well as for addressing the five input components that influence the design phase. If experiential exercises are appropriate, then they should be developed according to the criteria for experiential learning presented in Chapter 6.

MEDIA, MATERIALS, AND TRAINING AIDS

Descriptors such as media, materials, and training aids are often used by HRD practitioners, but their meaning sometimes is not clear. Each of these terms does have a distinct meaning. The term *media* refers to means of conveying something. When used in an instructional context, it means to transmit instruction. Examples of instructional media include films, print, and audio tapes. The term *materials* refers to printed matter such as texts, tests, and handouts. Materials contain messages while media transmit messages. Transparencies, photographs, and handouts are examples of materials. *Training aids* is used to refer to both instructional media and materials. Training aids assist the learning specialist in the training process (Lutterodt, 1983).

It is important during the design phase to identify the media, materials, and training aids that are most appropriate to accomplish the learning objectives. It is also necessary to identify those that will be used in learning activities and experiential exercises. It is, however, not appropriate to select, develop, or perfect these at this time. During this phase, the task confronting the program designer is the identification of media, materials, and training aids. Their development is reserved for the next phase, program development.

PHASE 5. PROGRAM DEVELOPMENT

In the development phase, the designed program is translated into actual training materials and strategies. In addition, each lesson is developed and supporting media are selected. It is important to remember that the inputs for the development phase are the outputs from the design phase (see Figure 10.5). The outputs for the development phase include, among others, lesson plans, instructional strategies, instructional media, and learner materials. During this phase the testing and validation of media and materials should also be included.

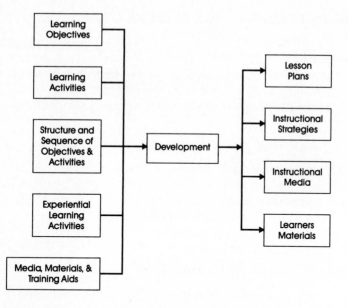

Figure 10.5　Program development phase

LESSON PLANS

During this first part of the program development phase, it is essential that the lesson plan document be completed. Lesson development requires complete decisions in a number of areas. The types of decisions include

- Content to be covered
- Sequencing of activities
- Selection or design of training media
- Selection and/or development of experiential exercises
- Timing and planning of each activity
- Selection of methods of instruction to be used
- Number and type of evaluation items

These are generally communicated to the learning specialist in the form of a lesson plan. A lesson plan is a document that identifies the audience (who), the topic or content (what), the location (where), the time frame (when), and the objectives (why) (Donaldson & Scannell, 1986).

INSTRUCTIONAL STRATEGIES

Detailed decisions regarding methods of instruction and the ways in which they will be used are known as instructional strategies. This includes the choice of methods and media appropriate for each instructional event and the structure and timing of instructional events within a lesson (Lutterodt, 1983). For each lesson there are five distinct instructional events for which instructional strategies are required. They include (1) introduction, (2) presentation, (3) application, (4) practice, and (5) review.

During the introduction, the learning specialist communicates the learning objectives to the learners, identifies the rationale for the lesson, and reviews any previous information and/or learning that is required prior to the introduction of new material and information. Presentation includes the organized presentation of content, information, ideas, materials, and facts. This could also include question-and-answer and group discussion approaches. Application is the transfer of knowledge and information into personal action. Practice enables the learner to rehearse until the information becomes internalized. Review includes feedback as well as review of the content, information, ideas, and facts received earlier.

Each of these instructional events indicates a different method of instruction. The classification of learning objectives is helpful in selecting the most appropriate methods and techniques. For example, demonstrations are necessary for the presentation of skill objectives. A psychomotor skill usually calls for a practical demonstration, whereas a cognitive skill may require a paper/pen demonstration. In addition, the nature of the practice component (part 4 of an instructional event) of a lesson depends in part on the learning objectives. It will also depend in part on the learner's characteristics and available facilities and equipment.

Structure and Timing. When program designers consider how various instructional events and lessons should be structured, sequenced, and timed, they should (according to Lutterodt, 1983) consider the following:

1. How much time is required to accomplish the learning objectives?

2. How much time is required for instructional presentations, application, practice, and review, respectively?

3. How many objectives can be covered in each instructional period?

4. How many aspects of a topic can be grouped for practice?

Remember, the amount of time spent in presentation and practice will depend on the topic and on the importance of the knowledge, skill, and/or behavior to the organization and to improved performance. Figure 10.6 reveals various possible structures of a lesson.

When considering the timing and lesson structure, program designers should consider the attention span of learners and the nature of the learning objectives prior to choosing the methods of instruction and media to be used. Each of these will provide insight into the development of the most appropriate instructional strategy.

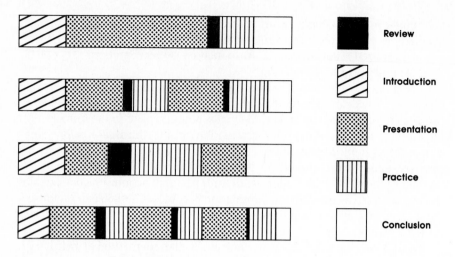

Figure 10.6 Possible structure of a lesson

INSTRUCTIONAL MEDIA

The third output of the program development phase is the identification of appropriate media. To be useful, the media should be appropriate to and reinforce the instructional content being presented by the learning specialist.

In selecting the most appropriate media for an instructional event, program designers must consider the nature of the task, the learning environment, and the characteristics of the learners. At the same time, they need to consider the learning styles of the learners as well as their own training style orientation in order to select the media that fit best and that will maximize learning.

Nature of the Task. When considering the nature of the task, an important criterion to examine is the type of learning objectives being addressed by the program. For example, some types of media are excellent for teaching psychomotor skills but not cognitive skills. The nature of the task is also affected by the size of the group participating in learning and the content of the lesson. An overhead projector is often used during workshops and conferences because it is convenient and considered the proper mode of operation. Other types of media might be more appropriate for a large group, such as individual handouts and films.

Learning Environment. The size and shape of the learning environment should be considered at this point. For example, training sessions are often conducted in hotel and motel meeting rooms which were not designed to accommodate or support learning. As a result, the presentation and placement of visuals can be very troublesome and often ineffective. Meeting rooms with too many windows may prevent films, VCR presentations, and the overhead projector from being used effectively. Very few HRD departments maintain a total inventory of media to be used. Thus, a single presentation that requires a large expenditure for media may have to be substituted for another medium considered more reasonable and useful. Finally, the lack of portability of equipment may prevent the use of certain types of media.

Characteristics of Learners. The experience of the learners, their education, age, and learning styles, all affect the type of media selected. The experiences of learners affect the selection of media because more experienced learners may need less visual support, such as diagrams and models, than inexperienced learners. All too often, an instructional event will include learners with different levels of experience, and it will be necessary to decide which groups need which type of support. This, of course, greatly complicates the process of media selection. Education and age will affect the selection of media in much the same way as experience, in that diversity of learners' educational level and age will require different combinations of media. Of course, each instructional event is also different, which complicates the process. Other practical considerations, for example, availability of hardware and software and its respective cost, also provide constraints on media selection. The time available for a presentation, its application, and practice can also dictate the type of media selected and used.

LEARNER MATERIALS

The final output of the development phase consists of the materials the learners use, the most common being the handout. The purpose of this form of material is to provide information pertinent to the learner as well as a quick reference for future study and review.

Handouts can include several important types of information useful to learners: (1) objectives, (2) exercises, (3) references, (4) outlines, (5) tables and figures, and (6) basic content related to the lesson. Since each lesson is based on a set of learning objectives, it is important to report them to the learner in order to make clear what is expected and how they will be measured. Exercises should be included to allow learners to practice necessary skills and deepen personal awareness. References assist learners in future inquiries. They also provide self-directed learning and individualized study. Outlines are used as a way of structuring and prioritizing information that is important. They also help in discussion, since learners can concentrate on listening, taking notes, and questioning during the instructional event without having to mentally organize the material at the same time. Also, outlines help learning specialists focus on the important ideas, facts, and concepts and remain on task, instead of concentrating on minor points or facts. Finally, tables and figures can be used when large amounts of information need to be presented in a concise manner, or when a graphic representation is required. Visual learners also prefer this type of presentation because it allows them to better understand the information and/or concept (Lutterodt, 1983).

PHASE 6. PROGRAM IMPLEMENTATION

Up to this point in the program planning, design, and evaluation process, the program designer has been the principal architect. Implementation, however, is the learning specialist's primary responsibility. The materials developed by the program designer during the development phase, such as the lesson plans, instructional materials, and learners materials, are important input to the implementation phase and should be used extensively by the learning specialist.

The outputs of this phase include the learning environment, the utilization of appropriate methods of instruction, the matching and utilization of appropriate materials and media with learning activities, the identification of instructional objectives, and conducting the instructional event (see Figure 10.7). Each of these has been addressed in detail in Chapter 6 and should be referred to for a complete understanding of the program implementation phase.

PHASE 7. PROGRAM MANAGEMENT

This phase actually overlaps the last three (design, development, and implementation), because every learning program requires a structure by which to sequence, manage, and record each instructional event and lesson. For example, a program that consists of several instructional events must be organized to maximize learning. This requires the program designer to make critical decisions regarding the importance of each instructional event and arrange them in the most appropriate order. It is also important to maintain complete and accurate records regarding the performance of each learner during each instructional event. They should keep records of the attendance of each learner and

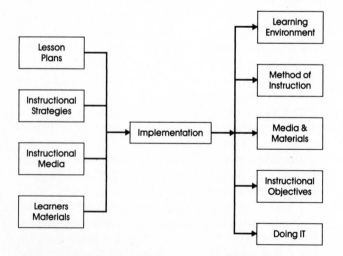

Figure 10.7   Program implementation phase

identify learning difficulties. This type of maintenance is known as program management. Figure 10.8 reveals how program management overlaps each of the three previous phases.

Again, the primary purpose of program management is to maintain accurate information regarding the learner and his or her performance. This phase is often not viewed as a systematic part of the program design process and is not accounted for in many of common program design approaches. However, as more and more organizations demand financial accounting for the dollars spent on learning activities and training programs, it becomes an increasingly important dimension of the process. It also provides excellent documentation when an HRD practitioner needs to justify the worth, effects, and effectiveness of a particular program. It is the type of quantitative evidence of success that is often missing in HRD programs.

PHASE 8. EVALUATION

Successful training programs must meet specific learning objectives. They must also measure the effectiveness of learning specialists and the competencies of program designers. Another purpose of an evaluation is to determine the impact that learning had on a person and whether or not a change in behavior occurred. Finally, program evaluations should measure the impact that learning had upon the organization and its employees in order to determine its benefits.

There are many reasons why evaluation of training programs is necessary. The principal reason for an evaluation is to determine if the program accomplished its assigned objectives. In other words, did the training program enable the learner to develop adequate knowledge, skills, and attitudes in order to close the gap between "what is" and "what should be"?

Another reason for evaluating training programs is to determine the strengths and weaknesses of programs. Each program should be evaluated to validate that the proper design was employed, the program designer developed the program correctly, the program was implemented correctly, and the appropriate controls were used.

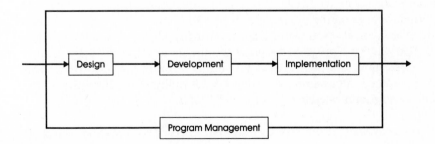

Figure 10.8   Program management phase

Finally, training programs should be evaluated to determine the cost/benefit ratio so that management can assess the value of a program. This is often referred to as the *justification phase* of program evaluation.

The final reason training programs should be evaluated is to establish a data base that can be used to demonstrate the productivity and effectiveness of an HRD department. This is referred to as the *marketing phase* of program evaluation. Many HRD departments are not viewed as being responsible for productivity improvements or organizational effectiveness. Thus, it is vital that HRD practitioners collect and maintain data regarding their programs in order to promote their department.

It is important to remember that a program evaluation should be accurate. Therefore, three criteria should be used to measure the effectiveness of an evaluation, validity, reliability, and utility. Each of these will be examined separately.

Validity

Validity is concerned with the extent to which the assessment procedure measures what it is supposed to measure. Evaluations developed with this in mind will be more objective because they attempt to isolate the effects of training. Three types of validity are relevant to program design situations: content, predictive, and concurrent validity.

Content Validity.   Content validity is determined by constructing an analysis that identifies the performance behaviors required. The knowledge, skills, and/or attitudes identified as essential are used as the foundation for crucial questions used to assess the applicant's performance and/or level of competence. Therefore, content validity is demonstrated when the questions and problems used during evaluation are representative of the specific competencies that reflect actual practice (Shimberg, 1981).

Predictive Validity.   Predictive validity refers to an evaluation's ability to predict future performance. To determine the predictive validity of an evaluation, two types of data are required: (1) results of the evaluation, and (2) individual performance later on the job (Lutterodt, 1983). If individuals who score high on the evaluation also perform at a high level on the job, the evaluation has high predictive validity. If program designers account for this type of validity in their evaluations, they can then predict the future performance of learners. This becomes valued information that supports the utility of the department and should be communicated to organizational leaders.

Concurrent Validity.   Concurrent validity is concerned with whether or not the evaluation results provide an adequate estimate of the present performance of the knowledge, skills, and/or behaviors that are being tested. As with predictive validity, concurrent validity involves the relationship between the evaluation and some other measure. For example, comparing the results of a written test with that of a supervisor's formal observation. If there is a strong correlation between the results, the simpler and/or most cost efficient approach might be used to replace the more complex and costly evaluation (Shimberg, 1981).

RELIABILITY

Reliability refers to the consistency and stability of a measurement. In other words, an evaluation is reliable if the results are consistent. An evaluation is considered reliable if the scores do not change over time. This is referred to as test-retest reliability. It is also considered reliable if the scores do not change if different forms of the same evaluation are used. For example, if the order of questions is different from evaluation to evaluation, but each evaluation includes the exact same questions and the results are similar, then the evaluation is considered reliable. This is referred to as equivalent-form reliability. Evaluations are considered reliable if the scores do not change regardless of who determines the results. This is referred to as inter-rater reliability.

UTILITY

The methodology used in an evaluation not only must be valid and reliable but also must be easily used (Michalak & Yager, 1979). The program designer must consider the ease of scoring, administering, and interpreting various evaluations prior to selecting the most appropriate one to assess the program. This includes the subjectivity of an evaluation as well as the comparability of scores and performances. The program designer must also consider the cost of an evaluation in terms of the time it takes to administer and the number of HRD practitioners needed to adequately conduct the evaluation. Both of these considerations are reflected in the cost-effectiveness of an evaluation.

COMPONENTS OF EVALUATION

As indicated in Chapter 6, effective and useful evaluations must be accomplished for every component in the program. This begins with the program itself. Next, the learning specialist should be evaluated to determine effectiveness, abilities, attitudes, and interpersonal skills. The learners should be evaluated to determine if the program helped them increase their knowledge and skills and/or improve their behavior. Increases in these areas often result in improved performance, which is reflected in on-the-job results and/or organizational impact.

Evaluating the Program. The primary question to be answered when evaluating the program should be, "Was the purpose of the program accomplished?" In order to answer this question program designers must turn their attention to the learning objectives and measure the program design against them. It is also important to measure the value and usefulness of the program content (Donaldson & Scannell, 1986).

It is designed to determine whether a learning program or training activity might make a difference. It also helps identify the type of activity that is most worthwhile. It seeks to predict if on-the-job behavior can or should be changed and whether changes in specific knowledge skills and attitudes would be sufficient to alter behavior. Finally, it seeks to determine if an HRD intervention can achieve such behavioral changes.

Another purpose of program evaluation is to determine the appropriateness of the design in terms of its practical, theoretical soundness and responsiveness. Brinkerhoff (1987) refers to this as the second stage of evaluation. If the program is determined to be properly designed it can then be moved from the design phase to development and implementation.

The final purpose of program evaluation, according to Brinkerhoff, is to determine if the program was implemented in accordance with its design. Special attention is given to unplanned departures from the design and whether they were necessary. If they were necessary, the program will need to be redesigned to account for such changes. This type of program evaluation is designed to monitor beginning programs and training activities, gathering feedback about the concerns and attitudes of learners and others in order to improve the program. The findings are recycled back to the design phase and adjustments are made accordingly.

Evaluating the Learning Specialist. When evaluating the learning specialist, the learners' perceptions should be utilized. In addition, it is important to use critical observers as evaluators. Learning specialists should be measured on their ability to

1. hold the learners' interest.
2. assist the learner.
3. summarize clearly.
4. identify clear learning objectives.
5. communicate ideas, facts, and emotions.
6. organize the learning environment.
7. relate to the learner.
8. establish a comfortable and supportive learning environment.
9. select appropriate methods of instruction.
10. select appropriate learning activities.
11. know the material being presented (Donaldson/Scannell, 1986).

It is important to remember that the program designer is often the person responsible for the identification and selection of many of the above. It is, therefore, vital that learning specialists be held accountable only for those that they are directly responsible for.

Evaluating Program Results and/or Impacts. Finally, the principal objective of a training program or learning activity is to improve performance, which results in increased organizational efficiency. In order to accomplish this, an evaluation of the organization's behavioral environment is required prior to designing the learning program. After the training program has been offered, and learners have had significant time to implement the new knowledge and skills provided through the program, another organization's behavioral environment analysis is conducted. The results are compared and conclusions drawn regarding the impact of the program on the environment. Another approach for determining the results of a training program is to measure the productivity changes that have occurred as a result of the training program. They include: absenteeism, accident rates, work quality, direct cost reductions, sales volume, supervisory ratings, and profits. It is important to measure these prior to training and compare them with the results after training. In addition, trained employees should be compared to untrained employees to obtain an accurate measure of program results.

THE PROCESS OF EVALUATION

The process of evaluation consists of five steps. Each step is essential and must be based on the previous step. In simplest terms, the evaluation process is one of comparing results against objectives (Donaldson & Scannell, 1986). The five steps include

1. Collection of data

2. Arranging and analyzing the data

3. Interpreting and drawing conclusions from the data

4. Comparing the conclusions to the stated objectives

5. Recording the recommendations for changes in the next program

During the first step, six basic data collection techniques can be used. They are (1) pre-tests and post-tests, (2) work reports and records, (3) questionnaires, (4) interviews, (5) observations, and (6) management's perceptions of change. Each of these can be used to collect the necessary data from which conclusions are drawn and recommendations made. (See Chapter 9, Assessing the Need for HRD, for more detailed information.)

LEVELS OF EVALUATION

As identified earlier, evaluation should account for every component in the program. These represent the levels of evaluation, each for a different purpose. For example, it is sometimes useful to obtain the opinions, feelings, and perspectives of learners regarding a learning program for the purpose of improving it. While this is indeed important and serves a useful purpose, it does not determine if the learners increased their knowledge or skills as a result of the program. In addition, it does not indicate that behavior changed or improved as a result of the program. Finally, this approach does not determine if the organization benefited because of the program.

Reaction.   Obtaining the opinions, feelings, and perspectives of learners regarding a training program simply identifies their reaction to the program. This *evaluation* is known as a *reaction* evaluation and is the first level of evaluation (Kirkpatrick, 1976). It is also the easiest to develop and administer and is the most widely used by HRD departments. According to Robinson (1987), over 75 percent of HRD departments utilize this approach at least 81–100 percent of the time.

Learning.   The second level of evaluation is known as *learning.* The purpose of this type is to measure learners' achievement of the learning objectives. It demonstrates which principles, facts, skills, and attitudes were obtained from the training effort. A learning evaluation is much more difficult to develop and administer because it requires the program designer to develop evaluation questions that are directly linked to the learning objectives. This approach generally includes a pre-test prior to training and a post-test after training, to determine if learning occurred and at what level. Because learning evaluations are more difficult to develop and administer, only 22 percent of HRD departments use this approach at least 81–100 percent of the time (Robinson, 1987).

Behavior.   The third level of evaluation is referred to as a *behavior* evaluation. Its purpose is the identification of any behavioral change that occurred as a result of training. According to Robinson (1987), more than 30 percent of HRD departments do not conduct this type of evaluation because it requires that HRD practitioners measure the effects of training several months after it occurs. This is done in order to allow the learner time to internalize the information and/or ideas obtained during training. Behavior is difficult to measure because there must be an established data baseline to determine if a behavioral change has resulted. The primary difference between learning and behavior is that behavior is an outward manifestation of learning. In other words, when learning occurs it changes one's behavior.

Result or Impact.   The final level of evaluation, known as a *result* or *impact* evaluation, is designed to determine the effects of learning on the organization. Over 60 percent of HRD departments fail to conduct this type of evaluation. They are the most difficult to develop and administer because so many variables must be controlled in order to obtain evidence that the organization improved as a result of training. For example, many organizations conduct sales training programs for their employees. If sales increased during the fiscal year, was it because of training or was it because of other factors? Perhaps a major competitor experienced delivery problems and customers began using alternative products, including the ones sold by this organization. Under this circumstance it would be difficult to determine the exact "cause" of the sales increase. The only way to isolate such variables is for program designers and HRD practitioners to employ exacting research methodologies and conduct statistical analyses to determine the effects of various variables including training. This is not always necessarily cost effective, and many practitioners lack the skills needed to obtain the results.

When determining whether or not a result or impact evaluation is needed, program designers should address the following questions.

1. What are the desired outcomes in behavioral terms?

2. How will program designers and learners know the outcomes have occurred?

3. What is a reasonable time period for skill transfer to occur?

4. What are the effects of the work environment on skill transfer?

The answer to each of these diagnostic questions will help program designers and HRD practitioners determine the appropriateness of a result or impact evaluation.

In the result or impact evaluation, program designers should identify discrete, specific behaviors to be measured. For example, as a behavioral outcome, "skillful selling" would be inappropriate. Rather, "to describe a product to customers noting its benefits and features" is a specific behavior which could be measured. If a set of similar behavioral outcomes could be identified, all of which occur because of a specific learning program, then a result or impact evaluation could be designed. However, it is important to determine the way such a behavior is to be measured before a result evaluation is developed. One way to determine if this behavior occurred is to ask the customer. Another approach would be for the salesperson's manager or supervisor to observe the sales demonstration. This would help validate that this behavioral outcome is measurable.

In addressing the third question, it is important to allow learners time for new knowledge, skills, and attitudes to be transferred into improved behavior which results in organizational efficiency. But how much time is the major question. According to Rockham (1979), the performance of learners decreases immediately after training occurs because the learner is attempting to incorporate a new skill which is often uncomfortable and difficult. It is not until the skill has been practiced many times that the learner is comfortable with it and is able to perform at a higher level of productivity (see Figure 10.9). Therefore, a result or impact evaluation should not be conducted for at least six months after training. Rockham (1979) also indicated that a behavior evaluation should not be conducted for three to six months after training.

Finally, program designers should not design or develop a result or impact evaluation before determining the impact and influence that the work environment has on training results. For example, if the work environment is nonsupportive of training and learning, then the training and/or learning results will

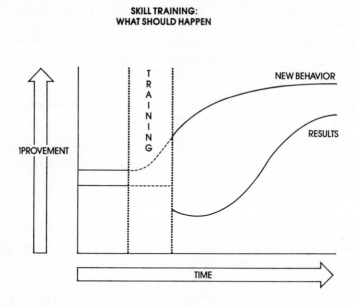

Figure 10.9 Rockham model (results/impact)
Reprinted from N. Rockham, Training and Development Journal, American Society for Training and Development, 1979. Reprinted with permission. All rights reserved.

most likely reflect this condition. In other words, training results are a function of the learning experience × work environment. Therefore, a work environment that measures zero (0) will reflect a zero (0) training result. In this case, the HRD department could be designing and implementing excellent training/learning programs, but it could not support this claim because productivity and efficiency have not resulted. This is because the work environment has failed to reinforce the learning. Under these conditions, it is important to correct the environment before additional training programs are designed. It is also important to report such evidence to organizational decision makers, not only to correct the situation but also to identify why behavioral change did not occur as a result of training.

As a way of helping determine the feasibility of a result or impact evaluation, program designers would want to answer the following questions:

Do learners
- value the knowledge, skills, and attitudes being taught?
- feel confident to use the knowledge and/or skills?

Do managers of learners
- coach, reinforce, and model the skills being taught?

Does the organization

- reward the use of the knowledge, skills, or attitudes?
- eliminate task interferences?
- provide organizational feedback?

Behavior and result evaluations are most appropriate for training programs that are designed to build skills. They are also appropriate for those programs where cost to the organization is high and/or the potential impact is large. In addition, they are appropriate for training programs that are designed to resolve an identified problem or maximize a business opportunity. Finally, they are appropriate when there is an organizational decision maker who is depending on program results.

PHASE 9. ACCOUNTABILITY

The final phase of the program planning, design, and evaluation process is accountability. During this phase, program designers and HRD practitioners should utilize the information gathered in the evaluation phase and implement the necessary changes. It is also during this phase that the learner, the organization, the program designer, and the learning specialist are held responsible for their actions. In other words, they are held accountable for the results of the training program. Unless this occurs, newly acquired behaviors that result in organizational proficiency may not occur or will be extinguished. Rockham (1979) pointed this out in his study. All too often behavior improves for a short period of time after training but is not reinforced or encouraged by managers and supervisors and begins to decline, as reflected in Figure 10.10.

Learners should be accountable for the information, knowledge, skills, and/or attitudes presented during training. They should be evaluated after training to assure that these were acquired. They should be evaluated some months later to determine whether or not they have internalized the knowledge, skills, and/or attitudes and how it affected their behavior on the job. In other words, did the training change their mode of operation and is it overt?

The *organization* should be held accountable for improved learning and desired behavioral change because it is the ultimate benefactor. But more importantly, the organization has the power to encourage change and to provide the assistance and support needed to bring about improvements. It is also ultimately responsible for establishing the environment needed for change to occur. The organization should not expect the program designer and the HRD practitioners to be totally responsible for learning within the organization. The learners, while accountable for their performance and improvement, cannot be held totally responsible either. The organization must provide leadership in order that learning occurs and performance improves.

Program designers should be held accountable for the design and development of training/learning programs that result in improved performance. They

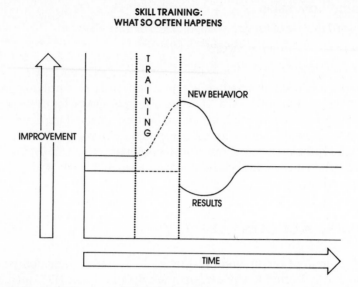

Figure 10.10   Rockham model (behavior)

Reprinted from N. Rockham, Training and Development Journal, American Society for Training and Development, 1979. Reprinted with permission. All rights reserved.

should be responsible for the identification of appropriate learning needs; the establishment of learning objectives that address the identified learning needs; the selection of learning activities that enable the learning objectives to be accomplished; the development of materials, the identification of the most appropriate learning methods and media to be used; and the development of appropriate evaluation instruments that are valid, reliable, and useful and measure whether or not the learning objectives have been reached.

Learning specialists should be held accountable for the implementation phase of the program planning, design, and evaluation process. This includes the proper utilization of media, materials, and methods. They are also responsible for the dissemination of information and the facilitation of learning. This includes the establishment of a supportive and comfortable learning environment as well as providing interesting learning activities designed to foster improvement. In addition, they should have mastered the material being presented prior to the beginning of the learning program and be prepared to provide insight as to its application.

CONCLUSION

Program planning, design, and evaluation is a process that consists of nine interrelated phases. Each phase is dependent upon the other (see Figure 10.11). The process begins with the identification of the program designer's philosophy

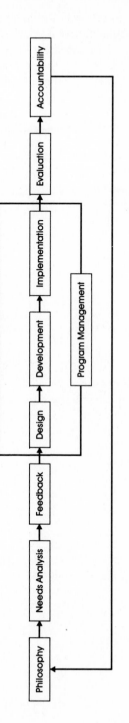

Figure 10.11   The program planning, design, and evaluation process

of teaching-learning. This serves as a filter for the remaining eight phases. The process continues with the identification of needs, feedback, and the design, development, implementation, and management of the program, with management overlapping the other three. Finally, the program, the learning specialist, and the training results are evaluated, and the participants are held accountable for their responsibilities and actions.

Marketing and Positioning the HRD Program Within the Organization

Objectives

After completing Chapter 11, readers should be able to

- tell why marketing is appropriate for HRD programs and practitioners.

- explain three exchange processes, as well as the tenets of the marketing concept.

- design a mission statement for their HRD program and be able to critique it.

- conduct an external and internal environmental analysis and identify for each the fundamental implications for their HRD program.

- select the most appropriate target market and construct a target market matrix.

- develop and evaluate a product, place, promotion, and pricing strategy for their HRD program.

- create a concept life cycle and portfolio analysis of their existing HRD courses and determine the most appropriate strategy related to each.

- select the most appropriate marketing strategy for their HRD program.

- produce a comprehensive marketing plan for their HRD program.

- summarize the implications of marketing for HRD programs and practitioners.

When an organization is growing and expanding, HRD is important and necessary in the eyes of top management. In fact, they sometimes see it as part of the reason why the organization is so prosperous. During financially difficult periods, however, it becomes a burden, and commitment to the training function is eliminated or at least severely reduced. This communicates to executives, mid-management, and supervisors a lack of faith on the part of the organization, and diminishes the importance of the HRD department.

This is a common occurrence. As a result, to keep their programs viable and relevant, HRD managers are taking a hard look at marketing to see what this discipline might have to offer. But what does the term "marketing" mean? To many, marketing is simply a process of selling, promoting, or advertising a product or service for the purpose of improving its acceptance or image. For example, to some, developing a brochure on the HRD program and courses and learning activities offered is *their* marketing activity. Some HRD practitioners even develop themes and logos. These functions are an important part of any promotion strategy; when applied, however, they are far too simplistic.

In this chapter we show how complex and complicated a process marketing is. We also make the point that marketing is adaptable to most, if not all, HRD situations. Marketing begins with the development of a service-oriented attitude, focused at meeting the needs of the customers who are served. This is often referred to as the "marketing concept" and, simply stated, means that HRD practitioners will aim all their efforts at satisfying their clients. From this orientation, HRD practitioners do not use marketing to manipulate clients to do what serves the interest of HRD; rather, they find effective and efficient means of serving and meeting the needs and interests of the client.

Based on an express interest of the client, new courses and learning activities are designed and developed to assure that the HRD program is centered around real, or at least perceived, needs. Thus, during difficult economic periods, training becomes vital, and will be supported as well as defended by users.

Next, HRD practitioners must understand that "exchange" is the central concept, the offering of value to another party in exchange for value. In other words, the training offered by HRD practitioners must be viewed as equal in value to the time, energy, effort, and personal commitment devoted to the training session, as well as to the dollars paid out. If the training received is equal to or exceeds the time/dollars offered by management/employers, then exchange will take place. If not, then the exchange will not transpire. This simple concept is often overlooked as HRD practitioners strive to develop HRD programs. It is important to remember, the more exchanges that occur between the HRD program and others within the organization, the better the image of the HRD program.

To become professional marketers, HRD practitioners must become skilled at understanding, planning, and managing exchanges. This includes developing skills in how to research and understand the needs of others; how to design a valued offering to meet those needs; how to communicate the offering effectively; and how to present it at the right place and time. Marketing for HRD can then be defined as the analysis, planning, implementation, and control of programs designed to bring about voluntary exchanges of values with target markets for the purpose of achieving organization objectives.

In this chapter we outline a seven-step process HRD practitioners can follow in developing a strategic marketing plan for their programs (see Figure 11.1). The goal is to provide them with a vehicle for maximizing exchanges within an organization. An indirect effect of increased exchanges should be a greater appreciation of training, and thus, greater respect and an improved image for the HRD department.

THE MISSION

HRD practitioners begin the development of a strategic marketing plan by examining the "mission" of their HRD program. In establishing a mission statement, HRD practitioners should answer the following questions: "What is our purpose?" "Who are our customers?" "What is of value to our customers?" "What should our purpose be?" and "What will our purpose be in the future?" This is a soul-searching and time-consuming-process. Each member of the HRD department will have a different view of what the program is about and what it should be about. It is, however, essential that each member ultimately agree with the mission of the program and support it. A well worked-out mission statement gives everyone a sense of purpose, direction, significance, and achievement. As Kotler (1987) reported, a mission statement acts as an "invisible hand" which guides widely scattered practitioners to work independently and yet collectively toward the realization of the department's goals.

A helpful approach is to establish the program's scope along three dimensions: first, the user group, namely, who is to be served and satisfied; second, users' needs, namely, what is to be satisfied; third, technologies, namely, how are users' needs to be satisfied. For example, consider an HRD program that serves only blue-collar employees who just want specialty training for their present job and prefer on-the-job training. This HRD program's mission is represented by a small cube in Figure 11.2(a). Now consider the mission of another HRD program that services many user groups, for a variety of reasons and utilizing a number of technologies, as shown in Figure 11.2(b).

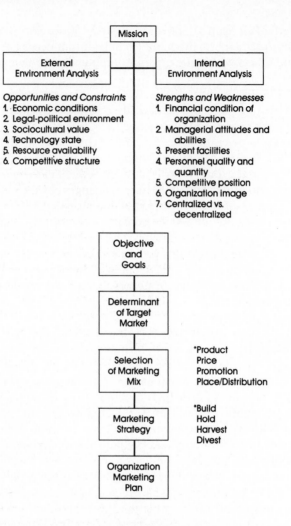

Figure 11.1   Strategic marketing planning process
Reprinted from J. W. Gilley and S. A. Eggland, Training and Development Journal, American Society for Training and Development, 1987 Reprinted with permission. All rights reserved.

It becomes apparent that the missions of these two HRD programs are not the same. Therefore, when departmental goals and objectives are established, the strategic marketing plan for each program should reflect and account for their respective differences.

A final word with respect to the mission of an HRD program: it should be feasible, motivating, and distinctive. In other words, a mission should be obtainable while it is viewed by HRD members as worthwhile and unique.

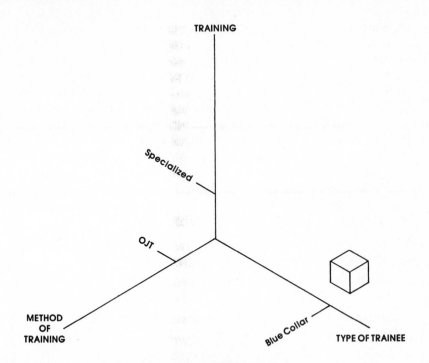

Figure 11.2(a)   Mission focus of two HRD programs
Adapted from Kotler, P. Marketing of Nonprofit Organizations, 2nd edition, Prentice-Hall, 1986.

EXTERNAL AND INTERNAL ENVIRONMENTAL ANALYSIS

The second step in establishing a strategic marketing plan for HRD programs is an external and internal environmental analysis. This will help the HRD department determine their opportunities and constraints (external) as well as examine their strengths and weaknesses (internal). Another purpose is to determine which contingency will aid and/or prevent the accomplishment of the department's mission. From this analysis, adjustment would be made to compensate for constraints and weaknesses while building on opportunities and strengths.

OBJECTIVES AND GOALS

Once an internal and external analysis has been conducted, HRD practitioners will be ready to turn their attention to the establishment of the program's "objectives and goals." These differ from the program's "mission," in that the mission suggests where the program "is coming from" whereas objectives and goals suggest where it "is going to" (Gilley & Eggland, 1987).

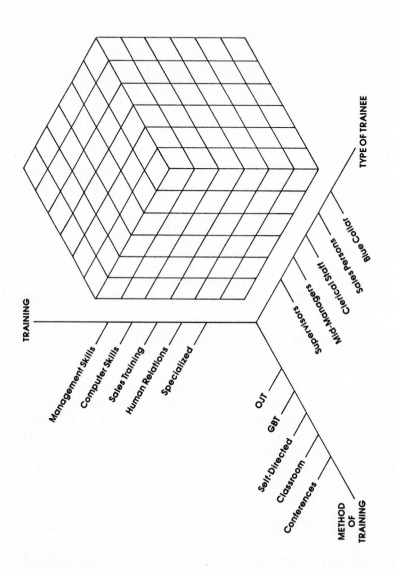

Figure 11.2(b)   Mission Focus

Adapted from Kotler, P. Marketing of Nonprofit Organizations, 2nd edition, Prentice-Hall, 1986.

HRD program objectives can vary from year to year, depending on the perception of the major problems that the program must address at the time. However, the purpose of each objective should be to accomplish the broader mission of the program. HRD practitioners who fail to filter their objectives through their mission will discover themselves off-course and will awaken to the realization that they are engaging in activities they were not intended nor qualified to accomplish.

The chosen objectives must be restated in an operational, quantifiable, and measurable form. These are the goals. For example, an objective "to increase enrollment" must be converted into a goal, such as "a 20 percent enrollment increase among first-line supervisors during the first quarter." A goal statement allows HRD practitioners to prepare, plan, control, and allocate financial and human resources as a means of accomplishing the program's objectives. By establishing goals, HRD practitioners are determining if the objectives are feasible, as well as determining who is responsible and accountable for accomplishing the objectives, and what strategies and activities should be used. Each of these questions must be addressed when deciding whether to adopt a proposed goal. Once a set of goals is agreed upon, HRD practitioners are ready to examine and determine the most appropriate market for the program.

TARGET MARKETING AND MARKET SEGMENTATION

The first step in determining the most appropriate market, that is, the target market, is to understand the term "market." A market is a set of all people who have an actual or potential interest in a product or service and the ability to pay for that product or service. When examined more closely, every market is heterogeneous, that is, it is made up of quite different types of consumers, or market segments. For example, in a large insurance company, administrative personnel, insurance agents, underwriters, regional sales managers, and corporate executives, taken together, would be the target market for the HRD department in the company. Taken individually, each of these job classifications is a market segment, each with a different degree of interest in the organization as well as the profession. The HRD practitioners within this organization would benefit by constructing a market segmentation scheme that would reveal the characteristics of each of these groups. From this they can decide whether to try to serve all of the segments (mass marketing) or concentrate on a few of the more promising ones (target marketing).

In addition to interest in the product or service, a market could also be segmented by variables such as age, sex, educational level, geographical location, and life-style. To continue our example, suppose the HRD practitioners decided to examine an HRD market segmentation scheme for the insurance company. There are five job classifications (market segments): administrative personnel, insurance agents, underwriters, regional sales managers, and corporate executives; and there are also five types of training (products): human relations,

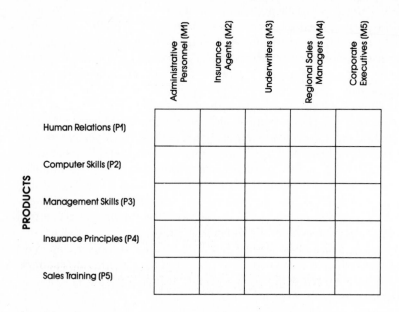

Figure 11.3   HRD product/market segmentation of an insurance company

training, computer skills, management skills development, principles of insurance, and sales training. These segmentations are illustrated in Figure 11.3. In addition, there are also five basic patterns of market coverage. Figure 11.4 illustrates the patterns, along with five alternative approaches to marketing HRD in the insurance company.

Product/market concentration: The HRD program concentrates on only one segment *(computer skills* for *administrative personnel)*.

Product specialization: The HRD program decides to offer only one product to all of the markets *(management skills)*.

Market specialization: The HRD program decides to service only one of the market segments *(underwriters)* with all of the training products.

Selective specialization: The HRD program tailors its product offerings in such a way as to meet the specialized needs of each market segment.

Full coverage. The HRD program offers all products to all market segments.

These patterns of coverage, together with the product (HRD training courses) and market segments (job classifications) comprise the segmentation scheme. HRD practitioners use the scheme to decide which approach to take.

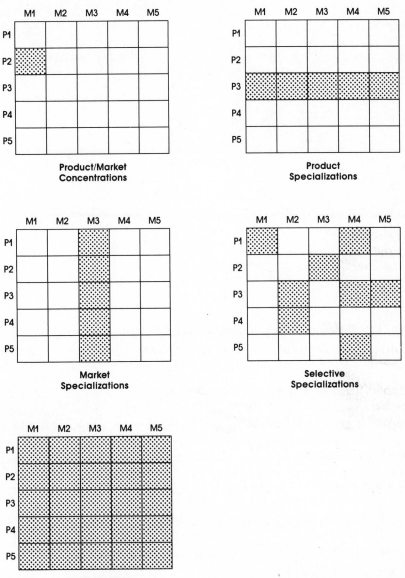

Figure 11.4   Five patterns of market coverage

After examining each of the five alternatives, the HRD practitioners in the insurance company must decide which will best accomplish the objectives and goals of the program and remain consistent with the program's overall mission. In some circumstances a combination of equally attractive alternatives might be selected if that appears to be the most appropriate approach.

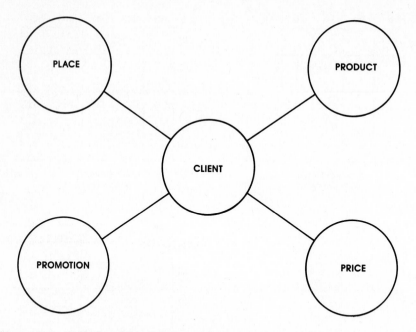

Figure 11.5   Relationship of the marketing mix and the customer

THE MARKETING MIX

Having selected its target market approach, the insurance company will now have to select a marketing mix. "Marketing mix" is defined as a particular blend of controllable marketing variables that are used by an organization to achieve its objective in the market. While there are a number of variables that comprise the marketing mix, it is useful to reduce the number to four basic ones:

Product—training courses and learning activities

Price—cost of course to department or cost of lost productivity

Promotions—advertising, sales promotion, publicity, and direct selling

Place—course location and facilities

These four major parts of the marketing mix are often referred to as the "Four Ps" (McCarthy & Perreault, 1984). Figure 11.5 illustrates their relationship and their focus on the client—"C" and demonstrates that customers and their needs are at the center of the marketing mix, which is consistent with the marketing concept.

PRODUCT STRATEGY

The product area of human resource development is concerned with the development of the most appropriate learning programs and training activities for the target market. One important thing to remember is that products/services should satisfy the needs of the target market.

Returning to our example, if the HRD practitioners in the insurance company are to improve the overall image of the HRD program, then they must discover, design, and develop appropriate and needed training courses and learning activities. These courses and activities must also be directed at the present and/or future needs of the organization. If for any reason this does not occur, the courses and activities may not be accepted by a significant number of employers, managers, and supervisors, which may severely impact the image of the HRD program. Failure of the HRD practitioners to focus on the marketing concept will prevent even the best designed strategic marketing plan from improving the image of the HRD program.

CONCEPT LIFE CYCLE

Every training course and learning activity, regardless of the type it is, goes through a life cycle. This cycle, known as the Concept Life Cycle (Gilley, 1987), consists of four stages: exposure, acceptance, maturity, and decline (see Figure 11.6). Some training activities, such as sensitivity training, move through the life cycle at a very rapid rate. Other activities, such as management skills development, require much more time to pass through all four stages. The rapidity with which a course or learning activity will move through this cycle depends on its importance to the organization sponsoring or adopting it and its practical application (Gilley, 1987).

By understanding the concept life cycle and its assumptions, the HRD practitioners in the insurance company can better manage their financial and human resources. This is accomplished through the proper allocation of financial revenue for course development and the appointment of human resources during periods of high demand for the course or learning activity.

The *exposure stage* is a critical period for new training programs. The training program has just been developed and the number of individuals adopting or utilizing it is small. Thus, it is important to communicate, through promotional activities, the advantages, benefits, usages, and purposes of the training program. Another characteristic of the exposure stage is this: In order to pay the high initial research and development costs, the cost of the training program will be higher than normal in this stage. Because only a few individuals are participating, expensive research and development is paid for by fewer people, which forces the price of the course to get even higher. As a result, many training programs are not adopted by enough individuals and departments, or fail to progress into the growth or acceptance stage.

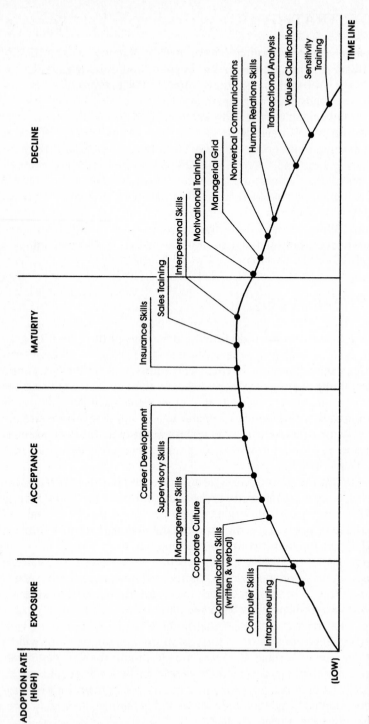

Figure 11.6   Concept Life Cycle

Reprinted from J. W. Gilley, Lifelong Learning: An Omnibus for Research and Practice. Copyright 1987 American Society for Adult and Continuing Education, Washington, DC. Reprinted with permission.

Intrapreneuring and computer skills are examples of training programs that are presently identified as being in the exposure stage of the concept life cycle. Both of these recently introduced programs are being adopted by many organizations and maintain their steady interest. Computer skills training, being further into the exposure stage, has a greater number of participants.

As training programs begin to be adopted by more and more individuals and departments, they enter a period of growth or *acceptance*. During this period it becomes more apparent that people are aware of the program's benefits. It is also during this period that other program providers begin to offer similar training programs. Thus, because they want to differentiate their training programs from others, original providers will point out its benefits by emphasizing the respective differences. This helps develop a competitive niche over other training programs (Gilley, 1987).

Because more individuals and departments take a course during the growth stage, more revenue is generated. Because more revenue is being generated, the original development costs are often eliminated and HRD practitioners can concentrate on generating revenue to cover the operational costs of the training program. It is important to remember that, as a percentage of the overall price of the program, operational costs are generally less than developmental costs. This, combined with increased participation, reduces the overall price of the training program and in turn reduces the cost of the program to the participants. Thus, the benefits received are higher in relationship to the cost incurred, encouraging even greater participation in the program. In sum, greater awareness plus lower costs results in higher acceptance, and the longer the growth stage lasts, the greater the probability that the program will be successful.

Communications skills, corporate culture, management skills, supervisory skills, and career development programs are all examples of programs presently in the growth stage of the concept life cycle. Each has existed for a long time and has enjoyed steady adoption and acceptance by organizations and individuals. One important characteristic of all of these programs is that they are perceived to be important to the organization and continue to gain acceptance and recognition (Gilley, 1987).

When acceptance begins to level off, the training program is reaching the *maturity stage*. This stage is characterized by severe competition as many program providers enter the market. During this period, program providers emphasize differences in their version of the training program. As a result, weaker programs are forced out of the market and those that remain make fresh promotional efforts to capture the interests of remaining individuals and organizations. During the latter stages of this period, interest begins to decline, which forces the program provider to consider alternatives for the program, such as new markets and new approaches (Gilley, 1987).

Insurance skills, interpersonal skills, motivational training, sales training, and the managerial grid have one thing in common: they all declined in popularity and acceptance during the past few years. Still, each remains an important form of training in many organizations. This is the principal characteristic of the maturity stage.

The *decline stage* is reached when interest in the program begins to drop off rapidly. This normally occurs because a new training program has been introduced and substituted for the original one and program providers consider eliminating the unpopular or unneeded program. They may cut off promotion efforts and make plans for phasing out the program (Gilley, 1987).

Human relations skills, transactional analysis, values clarification, and sensitivity training are examples of programs that have reached the extreme end of the concept life cycle (see Figure 11.6). In most organizations, programs of this type have been eliminated as a form of training because they are no longer perceived as essential for performance improvement.

IDENTIFICATION AND APPLICATION
OF THE CONCEPT LIFE CYCLE

It is very important that HRD practitioners use the concept life cycle to make critical decisions regarding the overall HRD program. They need to identify which stage a particular training program presently occupies. They need to decide on spending, because the financial and human resources needed to support different programs differ from stage to stage. The concept life cycle also helps them understand that change is unavoidable and that preparing for change is essential, something that is consistent with nature.

HRD practitioners can identify the position a particular course or activity occupies on the concept life cycle by considering a number of factors:

1. How important is the training program, and what impact will it have on individuals and/or organizational development?

2. How many research or topical articles on the program have appeared in professional journals in recent years?

3. How many consultants, program providers, book publishers, and academics are currently offering the training program?

4. Is the training program a topic of discussion at professional meetings and conferences?

5. Is conference time allocated to help practitioners better understand the purposes and benefits of the program?

6. Are advertisements and promotional brochures on the program being made available through professional journals and magazines or by direct mail?

7. Are new and improved versions of the training program now surfacing? (Gilley, 1987)

The HRD practitioners in our example insurance company can utilize the concept life cycle in several ways. First, they can identify which stage the training courses are presently occupying. This will help them project the future growth and popularity of their various courses and learning activities, adjust the number of participants, as well as increase or decrease the financial and human resource allocations. They can use the concept life cycle to establish organizational training and learning policies, since it provides information on the potential of each training course and learning activity. Finally, they can see that the concept life cycle is consistent with nature in that all living things have a beginning, a period of growth and maturity, and a decline, and that a training program or learning activity will naturally follow a similar course (Gilley, 1987). They will realize that change is unavoidable and that preparing for it is essential. The concept life cycle is an important tool, but it does not show the relationship between the importance of and the practical application of a particular training program. A portfolio analysis of these two factors is the tool they need to more effectively critique training programs.

PORTFOLIO ANALYSIS OF IMPORTANCE AND APPLICATION

An analysis of a training program can be based either on its importance relative to other programs or on its practical application. In this context, an "important" training program is seen as being vital and essential to the accomplishment of the overall mission of the organization. Failure to provide it could result in failure to reach organizational objectives. A training program having "practical application" is viewed as being presented in a logical "how-to" manner for the purpose of improving the performance of employees. This dichotomy can be plotted along a continuum anchored by the two extremes. However, a realistic evaluation of a training program includes both relative importance and practical application as equal partners in the analysis process. Rather than arrange importance and application along a single continuum, it is appropriate instead to reflect their working relationship. The fundamental assumptions of this relationship can be illustrated by constructing two continuums, one horizontal and one vertical. The horizontal continuum reveals the degree of practical application of the training program, while the vertical continuum reveals its relative importance (see Figure 11.7). By thus analyzing importance and application, various training programs and learning activities can be plotted within the model. Moreover, four primary positions can be identified: Super Stars, Wandering Stars, Constant Stars, and No Stars (Gilley, 1987, based on the Boston Consulting Group's matrix).

Super Stars are training programs perceived to be very important and applicable (high–high). They are a vital focus of the organization and/or training department and should be given tremendous attention and financial support. They may be considered "hot" nationally, and are used in a number of professional environments. However, it is important to remember that the identification of program importance and applicability is an individual evaluation; therefore, training programs may be identified differently in various settings (Gilley, 1987). Supervising skills, management skill development, and communication skills are examples.

PRACTICAL APPLICATION

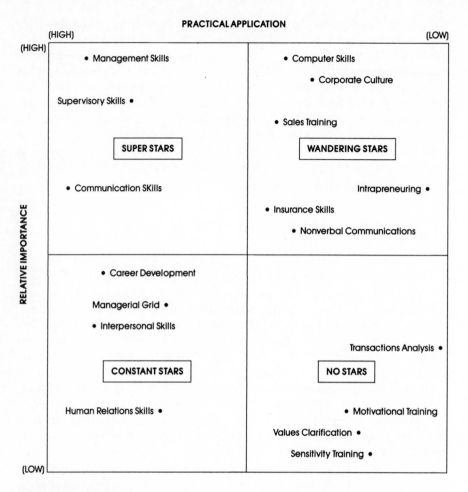

FIGURE 11.7   Portfolio analysis

Reprinted from J. W. Gilley, Lifelong Learning: An Omnibus for Research and Practice. Copyright 1987 American Association for Adult and Continuing Education, Washington DC. Reprinted with permission.

Wandering Stars are training programs perceived to be very important but not very applicable (high–low). The principal focus of improvement, then, is applicability. If HRD practitioners can improve the applicability of this type of program, it can be quickly moved to the Super Star category. Sales training, insurance skills, computer skills, intrapreneuring, and corporate culture programs are often identified in this group. This is because it is difficult to apply learning concepts and measure accurately the amount of learning that has transpired (Gilley, 1987).

Constant Stars are training programs perceived to be only moderately important but highly applicable (low–high). Since their applicability is high, they often exist in large numbers. In fact, this category represents the largest number of training programs, and adult educators often rely on it for their overall training program. Career development and human relations skills are often grouped in this section, since they have received mixed reviews regarding their effectiveness and importance (Gilley, 1987).

No Stars are training programs perceived to be low in both relative importance and practical application (low–high). These types of training programs receive little if any attention or financial support but will occasionally be offered, often to fill in the gaps on a training calendar. Sensitivity training, transactional analysis, motivational training, and values clarification programs are examples of this type.

APPLICATIONS OF THE MODEL

HRD practitioners can utilize this portfolio analysis of importance and application to examine training programs. The model can also be used to aid HRD practitioners in the allocation of training revenues, by identifying programs that will require additional support and that are diminishing in importance. Finally, by using this model, practitioners can prioritize their training programs, to increase their effectiveness and efficiency. Based on these three assertions, the portfolio analysis model can be perceived as an effective program analysis tool for HRD practitioners (Gilley, 1987).

By providing a comprehensive approach (comparing of the relationship between relative importance and practical application for each training program), the model also aids HRD practitioners in time management. Each program is analyzed in an organized and systematic manner, reducing errors in judgment and duplication of effort.

TRAINING STRATEGIES

Once training programs have been prioritized, HRD practitioners can establish training strategies for each training program. The strategy can be viewed as the master plan to formulate training policies and decisions. There are four fundamental strategic decisions that apply to each training program: To Build, To Hold, To Harvest, and To Divest.

To Build. The objective of this decision is to enhance the importance of applicability of the training program. It is very appropriate for Wandering Stars, but is often adopted for Super Stars and Constant Stars. Training programs that have the potential of improving their current position or ranking are subject to this strategy. This decision often requires committing additional financial and human resources to the development or improvement of the program. The strategy is often risky and costly and requires conviction regarding the potential of the program (Gilley, 1987).

To Hold. The objective of this decision is to preserve the current position and/ or rank of a training program. It is appropriate for Super Stars and strong Constant Stars to insure their continued strength. Also, this strategy is used when HRD practitioners believe it is not the proper time to institute a Build strategy. The primary focus of this strategy is on long-term results, and it is the most conservative of the four decisions. Finally, this strategy is appropriate for No Stars that serve to fill in the gap (Gilley, 1987).

To Harvest. This strategy focuses on short-term results and attempts to maximize the benefits of training programs. Programs perceived to have a limited future but that are presently considered either important and/or applicable to an organization are candidates for this strategy. Weak Constant Stars, Wandering Stars with limited potential, and No Stars are most appropriate here.

To Divest. This strategy involves divesting the resources (financial and human) assigned to a training program because they can be better invested elsewhere. It is very appropriate for No Stars and very weak Constant Stars since both have little relative importance. In addition, this strategy is often used for Wandering Stars when an organization cannot afford to finance the development of additional training programs. As training revenues shrink, this approach is used to improve the efficiency of existing courses and gives HRD practitioners a chance to reduce the number of training programs offered.

PUTTING IT ALL TOGETHER

As a training program moves through the concept life cycle, its portfolio position may also change. As this occurs, the strategy will also change. Therefore, HRD practitioners should use the concept life cycle and portfolio analysis in combination to establish the most appropriate training strategy (Gilley, 1987) (see Figure 11.8).

At any stage of the concept life cycle a training program can be identified in any of the four primary positions of the portfolio analysis model. Therefore, the strategy selected for the training program will be based on two factors: first, the stage the training program is in; and second, the position it holds in the portfolio analysis model. As these combinations change, different strategies will become more appropriate. For example, the strategy selected for a training program in the exposure stage and identified as a Super Star would be a Build approach. However, if the same Super Star program has entered the maturity stage, then a Hold–Build strategy, hold as a first strategy, build as a second strategy, would be more appropriate. The implication of this would be that "new" financial and/ or human resources would not *automatically* be allocated for the further development of the program. As this program moves into the decline stage, a Hold-Harvest strategy would become appropriate—which means that the

Concept Life Cycle Stage	Importance/Applicability Position	Strategy
Exposure	Super Star	Build
	Wandering Star	Hold
	Constant Star	Hold-Harvest
	No Star	No Involvement*
Acceptance	Super Star	Build
	Wandering Star	Hold-Build
	Constant Star	Hold-Hold-Build
	No Star	Harvest-Divest
Maturity	Super Star	Hold-Build
	Wandering Star	Hold-Harvest
	Constant Star	Hold-Harvest-Build
	No Star	Harvest-Divest
Decline	Super Star	Hold-Harvest
	Wandering Star	Harvest-Hold
	Constant Star	Divest-Harvest-Hold
	No Star	Divest

*During exposure, no involvement means a wait-and-see approach.

Figure 11.8   Putting it all together

Reprinted from J. W. Gilley, Lifelong Learning: An Omnibus for Research and Practice. *Copyright 1987 American Association for Adult and Continuing Education, Washington, DC. Reprinted with permission.*

organization is positioning the program to be phased out or deemphasized. Thus, the financial and human resources used to maintain this program will begin to be allocated to other more important areas (Gilley, 1987).

In addition, a training program can change its position in the portfolio analysis model as it moves through the concept life cycle. For example, a program that begins (exposure) as a Super Star may remain in this category until the maturity stage, where it becomes a Constant Star. As a result of this change, the relative importance of the program has declined and HRD practitioners will want to reconsider the strategy in order to reflect the program's present strength. If the program were to move into the No Star category during the decline stage, a divest strategy would appear most appropriate.

Figure 11.8 accounts for many, but not all, possible combinations when the two models are used together and can be used as an outline, or strategic planning guide, for adult education. The strategy selected should be based on the stage and position of a program. These two models (concept life cycle and portfolio analysis) can provide HRD practitioners with an approach for systematically evaluating HRD programs (Gilley, 1987).

PLACE STRATEGY

Once training programs have been prioritized, HRD practitioners can then turn their attention to establishing a place strategy for their program.

A place strategy involves getting the right product to the target market at the right time. A product is not much good to a client if it is not available when and where it is wanted and needed. In the case of HRD programs, place includes the location of training: on-the-job, in formal classroom settings, off-the-job, and/or independent/self-directed study, as well as the facilities used where the training takes place. Adult learning research supports the view that a comfortable and supportive environment is conducive for learning and should be considered when training programs are designed and developed as well as delivered.

Another important consideration is the time of day. Again, users should be consulted prior to the scheduling of a training program. For example, the HRD practitioners in the insurance company might prefer afternoon training sessions; however, their customers, let's say the insurance agents, might prefer early morning training sessions, since afternoons and evenings are their optimal selling period. Failure to adjust to the user's preferred time may establish resistance, which could ultimately affect the outcomes of training, as well as the attitude of the employee toward the training program (Gilley & Eggland, 1987).

Another part of the place strategy is the method of instruction selected. Several types of training approaches will probably need to be developed, since there is a myriad of human resources to serve in the insurance company. In addition, the insurance agents and regional sales managers will most likely be scattered throughout the state, region, or country, while administrative personnel, underwriters, and corporate executives will be located at the corporate offices. As a result, the HRD practitioners must develop a delivery system that accounts for geographical as well as professional differences.

Another overlooked part of the place strategy is the location of training programs. All too often, training sessions are scheduled at the training offices or classroom (i.e., on the fifth floor of the corporate office building). While this is convenient for the HRD staff, it might be more convenient, as well as more appropriate, to conduct training in the customer's office or work station. This would save precious minutes of valuable production time. More importantly, it would communicate to the customers that the HRD practitioners respect them and their time. In addition, customers (trainees) are more comfortable in an environment they know. If utilized, this could become an important advantage to the HRD practitioners.

PROMOTION STRATEGY

The promotion strategy is concerned with communicating to the target market the advantages and benefits of the product or service. Promotion includes personal selling, mass selling, public relations, and sales promotion. It will become the HRD practitioners' responsibility to identify the most appropriate methods to use, as well as to blend them into a workable combination.

Personal selling involves direct face-to-face communication between HRD practitioners and potential users, who might be executives, mid-management, supervisors, or support personnel. The primary advantage is that the benefits of the program can be personalized and adapted to each situation. However, this individual attention comes at a price. Personal selling is very time-consuming and costly and is difficult to do well. The HRD practitioners in the insurance company may select to use this mode of promotion as a way of building important personal relationships and contacts with key decision makers within the organization, while simultaneously taking the opportunity to discover the needs of various departments and the future directions of the company.

Mass selling is communicating with a large number of users at the same time in an indirect and nonpersonal manner. Two forms of mass selling are advertising and public relations. Advertising is any paid form of nonpersonal presentation of the products and services offered by the HRD program. This includes brochures, printed materials, posters, journal and, when appropriate, magazine advertising. For HRD programs within organizations, the most common form of advertising is brochures and posters, which communicate the purposes of the program, its offerings, and the advantages and benefits of training. The HRD department in our example insurance company would greatly benefit from these types of promotions, since it serves a large number of market segments with a variety of training programs and it is difficult to communicate directly to each market effectively. Therefore, a more indirect approach, one that will reach each market while still communicating the benefits of the program, is appropriate.

Public relations is any unpaid form of nonpersonal presentation of the products and services offered by the HRD program. The company's newsletter and local newspapers are excellent ways to tell the organization's members about the HRD program and its benefits. Another form of public relations is "up-close-and-personal" articles about individuals who have developed special skills and competencies as a direct result of training that improved performance. For example, sales training could have helped increase the number of sales calls, reduce lapse rates, and increase sales and closing ratios for a new insurance agent. This type of success story is an excellent example for demonstrating that training makes a difference. HRD practitioners should utilize this type of evidence in promoting their program to key decision makers within their organizations.

A final form of public relations is for HRD practitioners to publish articles in professional journals about their programs or about aspects of their programs that are unique, different, and successful. This communicates to upper management that the HRD practitioners are competent and respected within their profession. It also allows practitioners to think through an idea or segment of their program that could ultimately improve it. Finally, published articles are a source of pride for corporate executives. It demonstrates that their organization is indeed on the cutting edge of excellence (Gilley & Eggland, 1987).

Sales promotion refers to promotional activities—other than personal selling and mass selling—that stimulate interest, trial, or involvement by users. Logos, themes, catalogs, and novelties are examples. The insurance company's HRD practitioners could develop a departmental logo or theme to be included on certificates and other inexpensive rewards given each participant in their training program. This could help the participants remember their training experience, as well as differentiate the HRD program from other organizational activities and programs.

PRICE STRATEGY

Price is one of the most important and complex variables used by HRD practitioners in accomplishing the goals and objectives of the program. It is often, however, the most misunderstood and abused element of the marketing mix. Many HRD practitioners make the mistake of discounting the importance of price when developing training courses and activities. Since HRD is an internal operation, they often charge no fee for their programs (other programs are only reimbursed through administrative adjustment in budgets between departments). But make no mistake about it, an HRD program is a product, and each participant is giving up something of value in order to attend a training session. Time, energy, effort, and personal commitment are the most common things that are exchanged for the training received (Gilley & Eggland, 1987).

Price can also be used as an important positioning tool for HRD practitioners. The most important courses and activities should require the most time, energy, effort, and commitment in return for the greater amount of knowledge and skill development. The insurance company's HRD practitioners should analyze and prioritize their training program, determine which of the courses are the most important, and design them according to the principles of the exchange process.

Price can also be a reflection of the quality of the product. Too low a price may suggest a poorly designed and developed training program. A price set too high may miss the users who perceive the training program as just average, therefore, not justifying a high price. Indirectly, then, price can determine the success or failure of an HRD program and its survival in the long run.

All four Ps—product, place, promotion, and price—are needed in a marketing mix. In fact, they should all be tied together, since none of the Ps is more important than the other and all contribute to one whole. That is why the four Ps are arranged around the customer (C) in a circle (Figure 11.5)—to demonstrate that they are all equally important.

HRD practitioners, therefore, must make certain that they develop products that will satisfy the target market *(product)*; design systems where the right product is at the right place at the right time *(place)*; tell their target users about the availability of the courses they have designed, as well as communicate to upper management the benefits of the program *(promotion)*; and analyze and prioritize their course offerings, as well as adjust the expectations and outcomes to reflect fair exchange of value *(price)*. However, the needs of the target market is what virtually determines the nature of the most appropriate marketing mix. Thus, HRD practitioners need to analyze their potential target markets with great care and skill.

As the term indicates, a marketing mix is a blend of the four variables. It should be understood that each organization is different and requires a different emphasis in the marketing mix.

MARKETING STRATEGY FOR THE OVERALL HRD PROGRAM

Having determined the marketing mix, the next step is the formation of an overall marketing strategy for the HRD program. There are four strategies that can

	Existing Programs	New Programs
Existing Markets	Market Penetration	Product Development
New Markets	Market Development	Diversification

Figure 11.9   Marketing strategies for HRD departments

be endorsed by HRD practitioners: market penetration, market development, product development, and diversification (see Figure 11.9). Each of these strategies has as its goal the maximization of growth; however, their approaches are quite different. HRD practitioners should examine each strategy carefully and determine which is most appropriate in order to improve the position of HRD within the organization.

Product development requires committing additional financial and human resources to the development or improvement of training programs and/or markets. The HRD department uses a *Market penetration* strategy to increase acceptance of its current programs in its current market (see Figure 11.3) through a more aggressive marketing effort. This is most appropriate when the organizational leadership has endorsed the current training program but middle management and employees have not. Also, this approach is appropriate when there is growth potential in current markets.

A *market development* strategy is employed when the HRD department seeks to increase acceptance of existing programs by offering them to new markets. Other divisions may need existing training programs previously denied them because of organizational policy or current leadership. This could also occur as a result of new acquisitions or organizational restructuring. HRD practitioners may be limiting wider acceptance of their programs by assuming that nonusers are simply not interested in their training program or are too busy. Market development is designed to prevent this.

Alternatively, the HRD department may develop new or improved products for its current market, as a way to increase acceptance of their programs. This strategy is perhaps the most widely used by HRD practitioners. It can be even more effective when viewed as a "strategy," rather than an expectation of HRD practitioners.

A *diversification* strategy is based on the belief that growth can result from offering new programs to new markets. This approach should be the result of a comprehensive needs assessment, as well as sound marketing judgment centered around the market concept. It makes sense when the present approach is not showing much additional opportunity for growth, or when the opportunities outside of the present orientation are superior. Diversification can be risky because it exposes the HRD department to areas outside its existing area of expertise.

Regardless of which marketing strategy is selected, HRD practitioners should reexamine their current mission to determine if their new approach falls within it. If not, then a decision to alter or update the HRD department's mission statement is in order. However, it should be understood that a mission statement is designed to direct and focus the program and should be altered only after careful consideration.

The HRD practitioners in the insurance company, for example, must decide which of the strategic decisions is most appropriate for them as they implement their marketing strategy. In addition, the opportunities and constraints as well as the strengths and weaknesses of the company should be reviewed prior to the incorporation of any marketing strategy. Finally, a review of the goals and objectives and mission statement should be conducted before a marketing strategy is agreed upon, in order to determine if the strategy is consistent with them.

MARKETING PLAN FOR HRD PROGRAMS

The final outcome of the marketing process is the development of a marketing plan for HRD programs. A marketing plan should consist of a mission statement, internal and external environment analysis, goals and objectives, an identified target market or markets, an appropriate marketing mix, and an overall marketing strategy centered around the marketing concept and based on the belief that the exchange process is the key to increased usage. Once these six steps have been conducted, the marketing plan is complete. The purpose of the steps is to help HRD practitioners formulate policies and decisions as a means of improving the image and acceptance of their program.

There are several implications for HRD programs and practitioners. *First,* the development of a strategic marketing plan can benefit an HRD program by focusing on the needs of the ultimate user. This forces HRD practitioners to consider the needs of users prior to developing and implementing training programs. Therefore, a strategic marketing plan can be viewed as a micro-needs assessment technique, since it is directed at the discovery of needs that serve as the foundation for future activities.

Second, a strategic marketing plan is beneficial because it increases HRD practitioners' awareness of the importance of the exchange process. In addition, this realization helps them understand that the improvement of their program's image is directly linked to improvement of its perceived value. As a result, image enhancement becomes possible only through increasing the value of training programs in the eyes of ultimate users.

Third, a strategic marketing plan forces HRD practitioners through a systematic "re-think" process. This includes their mission statement, an internal and external environmental analysis, and their goals and objectives. The "re-think" process will help HRD practitioners plan for future contingencies and changes while reestablishing the focus and direction of the program.

Fourth, a strategic marketing plan will force HRD practitioners to analyze their user groups to determine the most appropriate markets. From this analysis, financial and human resources can be better allocated. Training programs can also be tailored for the groups with the greatest interest and need.

Fifth, a strategic marketing plan will help HRD practitioners determine the most appropriate blend of marketing variables needed in order to enhance their programs. This will enable them to develop products that are needed at a price perceived as fair. In addition, it will help HRD practitioners determine the most appropriate facilities, locations, and times for training, as well as identify the best delivery system possible. Finally, it will help them determine the best approach for promoting the training programs and the HRD department to users and key organizational decision makers.

Sixth, the establishment of a marketing plan is a means for bringing together both the target market and the marketing mix in such a way as to establish an overall strategic approach for the HRD program. This will enable the HRD practitioners to realize the direction the program is going.

Seventh, a strategic marketing plan is a holistic process, designed to improve the image of the HRD program through increasing the HRD practitioners' awareness of the importance of the exchange process. The ultimate goal of a marketing plan is to increase the number of exchanges that can only occur by tailoring the HRD program around the needs of the users. A greater respect for the HRD program should result as more and more individuals satisfy their needs through training. An indirect but equally important result of a strategic marketing plan is an improved image for HRD programs within the organization.

CONCLUSION

Marketing is not a substitute for quality and competence. It is a method of communicating the value of HRD to others within the organization. To that end, a seven-step strategic-marketing planning process tailored to enhance the image of HRD has been provided.

First, the strategic-marketing planning process can benefit HRD by focusing on the needs of the ultimate user. Second, the strategic-marketing planning process is beneficial because it measures HRD practitioners' awareness of the importance of the exchange process. Third, the strategic-planning process is helpful because it forces HRD practitioners through a systematic "re-think" process designed to help refocus the HRD program. Fourth, it forces HRD practitioners to analyze their user groups to select the most appropriate markets for learning programs and training activities. Fifth, it helps HRD managers and practitioners determine the most appropriate blend of marketing variables needed in order to enhance the image of HRD. Sixth, the establishment of a marketing strategy can bring together both the target market and marketing mix in such a way as to establish an overall strategic approach for the HRD program. Seventh, the strategic-marketing planning process is a holistic approach to improve the image of the HRD program throughout the organization.

CHAPTER 12

The Benefits and Costs of HRD

Objectives

After completing Chapter 12, readers should be able to

- define cost-benefit analysis.

- list and describe at least 10 "costs of training."

- demonstrate an understanding of benefits that accrue from training.

- describe the cost-effectiveness model.

- tell about the developmental opportunity approach to cost-benefit analysis.

- explain why several agree that the multi-criterion approach to cost-benefit analysis is most useful.

- develop a critique of human resources accounting.

Human resource development activities and programs normally occur in an environment that is highly aware of both the benefits derived and the costs associated with those benefits. Unlike many public sector educational institutions, human resource development in nonpublic school agencies and institutions must demonstrate the benefits accruing to the institution and its personnel. HRD departments are also usually obliged to associate specific costs with these benefits. It is the purpose of this chapter to examine the notion of cost-benefit analysis as a function of the human resource development department.

Cost-benefit analysis shows program costs and evaluates them against the benefits. The increasing cost consciousness has put pressure on the HRD department to find ways to demonstrate the value training has for an organization. In order to describe that value, it is necessary to clearly understand the costs associated with training.

THE COSTS OF TRAINING

It is not easy to derive costs in the field of human resource development. Many HRD managers were formerly associated with a public education system that all too often was not attuned to the cost side of the ledger. This problem is confounded by the notion of nonquantifiable costs, a nightmare for the HRD manager who must respond to a supervisor schooled in the theory and practice of cost-benefit analysis.

What are some of the categories of training costs? Among the most obvious is the *salary of trainees*. This is a straightforward cost that is readily apparent to even the most inexperienced cost-benefit analyst. It is the dollar amount due the employee-trainee associated with the time that is spent in training.

A slightly less obvious cost in this genre is *organization benefits*. These are, of course, real costs and include in a cumulative fashion such items as paid holidays, vacation and sick leave, Social Security, unemployment insurance, and organization retirement plans, health insurance, and educational benefits. This is a short, average list of benefits. Many organizations have more—several of which would be difficult to quantify. Items such as employee lounges, discounts on goods and services, and company cars head the list. In general, however, most organizations and their personnel departments know what these costs are and add them to salary when discussing employee compensation. They cover a wide range of percentages of salary but tend to average about 30 percent.

Replacement cost occurs when people are engaged in training. This is a cost of training that is frequently overlooked. But it is a real cost, even if a replacement is not officially made. For example, if a cashier is sent to a training program, a replacement is secured to run the check-out station during the cashier's absence. Often, however, the check-out stand is left vacant with other cashiers expected to "take up the slack." This may result in longer check-out lines, reduced sales, reduced employee morale, and, perhaps, loss of customer goodwill. These outcomes most certainly result, however quantifiable to the organization.

When an employee is involved in a training activity there is *lost production*. In the case of an industrial organization, fewer widgets or no widgets are manufactured. In a service-providing agency, fewer or lower quality contacts with clients, constituents, or customers are developed. In the latter case the costs are harder to measure but are no less real.

For many, *overhead* is among the most difficult cost concepts to understand. Many trainees are seemingly unaware of overhead and/or don't feel it is a valid cost to be charged against their efforts. It is also usually the case that few in an organization are able to accurately calculate per-employee overhead costs. This circumstance, however, does not justify excluding overhead from the list of cost factors.

Overhead includes fixed organizational costs that will not change materially as activities are varied. It can include the cost of a building or rent, facilities, desks, equipment, janitorial services, telephone and other communication services, stationery, office supplies, staff personnel such as legal staff, accounting staff, personnel departments, and so on. The factor for overhead (as a function of salary) varies widely—from .075 to 6 times salary.

Among the easiest costs to understand and calculate are the specific and direct costs of training. They include *instructor costs, course materials costs, cost of classrooms,* and *course design costs.* In each case, these costs may be incurred as purchases from external vendors. When that happens the cost of any or all of these items is very straightforward and apparent. A great deal of training is developed, secured, and delivered in this fashion—that is, purchased from outside vendors. One has only to look at membership directories of training organizations to appreciate the amount of brokered training that occurs.

On the other hand, calculating the costs associated with training that is developed and delivered "in-house" is somewhat more difficult. Some of the factors mentioned earlier (benefits, overhead, etc.) complicate the cost calculations. In general, however, a cost-conscious human resource development or training department should have only limited difficulty arriving at a cost figure for delivering training.

It is left to the cost accountant to determine the cost of the instructor delivering the training, including salary and benefits for separation time, travel time, and other training program-related efforts.

Costs directly related to the training program are also measurable but sometimes difficult to calculate. They include all of the costs of designing and preparing course materials, including handouts, transparencies, video productions, slides, tests, and so on. This figure can include actual raw materials, production costs, overhead, and a myriad of other cost categories.

Classrooms are a cost item as well. They are usually either rented or owned. In the case of a rented classroom, determining the cost is simple. If it is owned, an appropriate portion of overhead should be ascribed to the training cost amount.

Woven through the previous discussion is the assumption that there are *administrative costs* associated specifically with training that must be acknowledged when accounting for the costs of training. They include the cost of the HRD manager's and secretarial or clerical salaries, the costs of screening and selecting learners, equipment, and training room costs, audiovisual supplies, and costs of in-company promotion or announcement of courses.

Finally and simply, there are often travel and living costs included in training. Trainees frequently travel to remote sites, and there are real and simply calculated costs associated with these trips to plan, deliver, and evaluate training.

THE BENEFITS OF TRAINING

If the costs of training are elusive and difficult to quantify, the benefits accruing from training efforts are even more problematic to measure. Stated in an elementary fashion, benefits can be defined as the performance value resulting from training.

The ramifications of identifying and measuring benefits are enormous, and a comprehensive discussion is somewhat beyond our scope. It may be possible to start with a simple example—say a "gizmo" assembler—and measure productivity before and after exposure to training. The assumption here is that an increase in the productive assembly of "gizmos" could be attributed to any associated training. But already those schooled in the techniques of research will be quick to point out that several intervening and confounding variables may be at work to help change production results. There is the time of day, plant morale, pay raises, and the well-known "Hawthorne effect" that may have had a part in changing the level of production.

If this example is not complex enough for the reader, consider the case of training the salesperson in a way that is designed to improve sales. Think of the factors (in addition to training) that could affect the level and quality of sales! Then consider the difficulty in controlling for these factors when attempting to measure for any benefits associated with sales training. This is mentioned not to discourage the neophyte cost-benefit analyst but to develop a sense of respect for the enormity of doing the job of cost-benefit analysis carefully and properly. This is a subject for several volumes of writing and certainly a developing science. For the purposes of this book, our treatment of cost-benefit analysis should be considered to be introductory.

MODELS FOR COST-BENEFIT ANALYSIS OF TRAINING

To suggest that the reader will find a definitive working model here is inappropriate. Rather, several approaches (models) to measuring costs and benefits will be presented. They will range from the simple to the only slightly complex. It is left to the reader to select from what is offered with an eye toward his or her own organizational utility.

To scientifically measure behavioral changes (benefits), three general rules should be followed: (1) There must be an experimental group which is to be trained and a control group which is not to be trained. (2) Behavior must be measured in terms of specific actions that can be seen or counted in both groups before and after training of the experimental groups. (3) The measured changes must be compared and results inferred following statistical analyses.

Many HRD practitioners do not have the expertise or the time or money to conduct such measures. It would behoove them, however, to acquire the resources to develop an entre into this important area. Most employees will want to know about the specific *dollar* returns they and their companies are realizing from the expenditure of time and efforts on training initiatives. Several models for examining costs and benefits of training are presented below.

COST-EFFECTIVENESS ANALYSIS

This variation on the cost-benefit analysis technique is among the simplest that will be discussed. It has been suggested by Shipp (1980) who describes it as one way to quickly and simply estimate the cost effectiveness of training programs already underway. He suggests this approach because emphasis on cost effectiveness has been troublesome. HRD managers are not accountants and are usually so busy with training responsibilities they have little time to reconstruct the accounting data demonstrating the money-saving value of past training programs. Plans to accumulate data on future programs are now being developed by most training directors, but what is needed in the meantime is a quick, reasonably accurate method of estimating the value of training programs currently underway and of programs planned for the immediate future. Shipp says simply and classically that the costs must be computed first, the effectiveness "estimated and then the two must be compared." Following is a condensation of his suggested procedure (Shipp, 1980, p. 23):

COMPUTING THE COST

In computing the cost, the first task is to determine the total contact hours: how many courses will be offered during the budget year, the number of scheduled training hours for all courses offered during the budget year, and how many trainees will be taking the courses.

Multiply: total courses offered
× total training hours
_____
result
× total trainees
_____
Total Contact Hours

For example, an examination of the training schedule reveals that next year 36 courses may be offered. The courses will vary in length. The average length is 40 hours and the average number of trainees is 10 per course.

Multiply: 36 courses
× 40 hours/course
_____
1440 course hours
× 10 trainees/course
_____
14,400 Contact Hours

The actual training costs start with the training department budget, less any costs for services performed in other functional areas. The actual training costs would be:

$215,000   training department budget
− 15,000   (half of $30,000 salary for work in personnel)
_____
$200,000   Actual Training Costs

Next, the standard cost for a contact hour must be computed by dividing the total contact hours into the actual training costs:

$$\frac{\text{actual training cost}}{\text{total contact hours}} = \text{Cost per Contact Hour}$$

In our example:

$$\frac{\$200,000}{14,400} = \$13.88 \text{ per Contact Hour}$$

To compute the standard cost for each individual course, the number of contact hours must be multiplied by cost per contact hour. (Remember, the number of contact hours is the length of the courses in hours multiplied by the number of trainees.)

The course in our example will be scheduled for 40 hours and will be attended by 25 trainees. The standard cost of the course is:

1000 contact hours (40 course hours × 25 trainees)
<u>× $13.88 cost per contact hour</u>
$13,880 Standard Cost

Finally, any additional costs associated with a particular course must be added to the total standard cost for the course. For instance, if the training department must pay either the wages of trainees or the wages of other workers to replace the trainees on the job, those wage costs would also become part of the cost of the course. Other expenses such as the cost of an outside instructor, additional room rental, or materials purchased specifically for the course would also be added at this point.

Let's say the course is held in a local motel conference room at a cost of $750. A guest speaker is invited and paid $250. Trainees average $25,000 per year in salary and benefits, or $12.02 per hour. That hourly wage of $12.02 is multiplied by 40 (the length of the course in hours) and that result is multiplied by 25 (the number of trainees) for a total of $12,020 in trainee costs. The total cost of the course is the standard cost plus the additional room rents, fee for the speaker, and trainee costs.

$13,880	standard cost
750	rent for motel room
250	speaker's pay
12,020	trainee costs
$26,900	Total Cost

ESTIMATING EFFECTIVENESS

Once the costs of the course have been estimated, the benefits or savings associated with the course must also be determined. One easy method is to estimate savings potential and/or increased revenues. A panel of HRD practitioners, supervisors, and employees rates the potential of the course by examining the job descriptions and the training objectives to determine the potential for change that may be accomplished by training. The panel determines the potential for recovery of training costs by estimating the value of any resultant change in job performance over the next year.

Assume that an HRD department instructor, three sales managers, who have taken a sales management course, and three of their supervisors are asked to rate the value of job changes for a participant in the course. In examining the training objectives and the job descriptions, they isolate three potential areas of improvement. Each rater estimates the value of the improvement in efficiency or savings to the company. The raters are not told the costs of the training program, but they are told how savings or changes in costs may be calculated. Their estimates are listed in tabular form:

Rater	Area 1	Area 2	Area 3
1	$650	($150)	$350
2	(800)	250	400
3	(400)	350	350
4	550	300	350
5	600	350	(150)
6	500	(400)	300
7	600	300	(450)
Modified mean =	$580	$310	$350

The potential value of the sales management course is calculated by discarding both the highest and lowest scores in each job area (circled) and using only the remaining scores in order to determine a modified mean. This method controls for any individual bias toward the course, gross math errors, and other variables, and levels the scores so that one widely deviating figure does not exert an undue influence. The total of the modified means is the total estimate of the potential value of the course.

$$
\begin{array}{ll}
\$\ 1{,}240 & \text{sum of modified means} \\
\times\quad 25 & \text{number of trainees} \\
\hline
\$31{,}000 &
\end{array}
$$

An alternative method for determining potential savings that provides even better estimates of the effectiveness of training programs is the use of historical accounting and other department records to document actual changes in performance owing to participation in a training program. If the data are available, they provide more precise information than the estimate method. This precludes the necessity to use a rating panel. Unfortunately, usable data is seldom available at the beginning of a cost-effectiveness program. Every effort should be made, however, to begin accumulating hard data so that reliance on estimates can be reduced.

COMPARING COST AND EFFECTIVENESS

The costs of a course and the estimates of effectiveness can now be compared to see if the course is cost effective. If the estimates of the potential savings (or increased revenues) exceed the costs, the course may be said to be cost effective. If costs exceed estimated value, then the course is not cost effective and must be analyzed further. The cost of the course in our example was $26,900; the estimated potential value was $31,000. A comparison of the two indicates that the course, when considered independently of other factors, is cost effective.

Of course, other factors must be considered before allocating funds. The cost effectiveness of other courses must be compared. If a choice must be made about allocating training department resources, even a cost effective course may be dropped from the schedule in favor of other courses or alternative uses of resources that promise a higher return. Conversely, a course that is not cost effective may remain in the schedule if it is mandated and must be conducted without regard to the returns on the training dollar, or if it provides a necessary service at less real cost (cost minus any savings or revenue increases) than an alternative source of training.

Estimates of cost effectiveness are adequate interim techniques for determining the relative value of training courses. But estimates cannot take the place of hard data planned for and specifically collected for cost-effectiveness analysis.

Although this method relies on those in the organization who are in a position to exercise good judgment, the accuracy of the estimates depends largely on the precision of the instructions the raters are given for determining potential savings or revenue increases. The modified mean technique helps to overcome some errors caused by guessing or personal bias, but it will not eliminate problems created by inadequate instruction or imprecise methods of estimating potential values. For programs where hard data are not available, the estimate technique as described here can provide reliably sound analysis of the value of training and can substantiate the training director's contention that training is an investment rather than an expense.

DEVELOPMENTAL OPPORTUNITY AND THE PROFIT AND LOSS STATEMENT

Human resource development professionals have sometimes been criticized as having little concern for the "bottom line." It has been said that they know and care little for the notion of profit and loss. Coupled with this phenomenon is the knowledge that many companies are encouraging in-house entrepreneurish behavior sometimes called "intrapreneuring." It is hoped by proponents of this camp that employees will grow out of their narrow specialties and develop general business acumen.

This approach set forth by Rice (1981) first requires familiarity with the fundamental business formula:

$$\frac{\begin{array}{r} \text{Revenue} \\ - \text{ (Costs + Expenses)} \end{array}}{\text{Profit}}$$

(The formula works for a nonprofit organization if the word "profit" is changed to "reserve" or a similar term.)

Expanded somewhat to apply to a manufacturing—sales organization, which serves as a convenient example, the formula looks like this:

$$
\begin{array}{r}
\text{Net Sales} \\
- \text{ (Cost of Sales)} \\
\hline
\text{Gross Profit} \\
- \text{ (Expenses)} \\
\hline
\text{Profit}
\end{array}
$$

Switched vertically with numbers inserted, the formula begins to resemble an income statement:

Net Sales	1,000
Cost of Sales	− 200
Gross Profit	800
Expenses	− 700
Before-tax Profit	100

In order to serve management purposes, the above exhibit can be slightly expanded and itemized:

Net Sales Units	100
Average Net Sales Price	× 10
Net Sales	1,000
Cost of Sales:	
Raw Materials	− 100
Labor	− 100
Gross Profit	800
Expenses:	
Sales Salaries	− 200
Advertising	− 200
General:	
Office Salaries	− 200
Office Supplies	− 100
Net Profit	100

The foregoing are, of course, the very simplest of income and expense reports. Most departments in an organization have access to much more detailed income and expense reports—probably broken down by division or profit center. Every item on such a report directly affects the bottom line—either by producing dollars or using dollars through costs and expenses.

It is important to remember that these items of income and expense are not absolutely fixed. They are controlled by the actions of employees. Productivity per hour worked or dollar spent is usually dependent on the skills and knowledge with which the action takers are equipped. Such a report, therefore, can be a convenient device for surveying the categories and topics of training and education the organization might require. But more important, it can be adapted to the topics of potential training to the line functions through which they contribute to the profit goal. For example, the revenue-gathering portion of the condensed report can be set up to identify training topics with the exactly relevant line functions:

$$\frac{\begin{array}{c}\text{Net Sales Units}\\ -\text{ Selling Costs}\\ -\text{ Market Research}\\ \times\text{ Average Net Sales Price}\\ -\text{ Pricing}\end{array}}{\text{Net Sales}}$$

Note that there are three potential training topics associated with unit net sales in an organization. Some obvious ones have been selected to make the point. But in applying this technique, one can be as exhaustive as one likes.

In Figure 12.1, notice there are listed a few of the most common training topics under the various items on the report to illustrate the technique described here. Notice also the rating columns in this listing of training topics.

	Priority	Present Competence	Developmental Opportunity
Net Sales Units			
SELLING COSTS	8	7	3
MARKET RESEARCH	5	2	8
Average net sales price			
PRICING	4	8	2
Net Sales			
Cost of Sales			
Raw materials			
QUALITY CONTROL	2	6	4
Labor			
SAFETY	1	9	1
NEGOTIATING	6	3	7
Gross Profit			
Expense			
Sales Salaries			
COMPENSATION	1	9	1
Advertising			
MEDIA BUYING	3	5	5
General			
Office Salaries			
SALARY			
ADMINISTRATION	1	7	3
Office Supplies			
PURCHASING	1	8	2
Net profit			

Figure 12.1   Training priority, competence, and opportunity rating chart

Reprinted from O. Rice, Looking at T&D in Light of Profit and Loss. Copyright 1981, Training Magazine. Reprinted by permission.

Under "Priority," questions are asked that profit-center managers live by: On a scale of 1 to 10, how significant is the effect on the bottom line of each given topic? How many dollars might increased skill or knowledge save? How much might productivity be improved? In other words, just how critical is the function in terms of profit control? Token numbers have been inserted to show how these measures might be ranked.

If there is a cooperative climate in the organization one may be able to engage line colleagues and possibly the CEO in arriving at these estimates. The HRD manager may even be invited to participate in modeling or simulation exercises on which critical profitability decisions are based. If the climate is not encouraging, one can make a start on one's own. Later, if they're true to their commitments, colleagues will recognize the important contribution the training director is trying to make.

Next, notice the column, "Present Competence." It is filled with rankings that estimate the present average competence of employees in each of the skill knowledge areas listed—whether from prior training, experience, or native ability.

Obviously, these will be highly subjective evaluations, and possibly controversial if certain line colleagues are sensitive about their domains. But if there are facts to back up the assessment that a function is sagging, anyone who is honestly concerned about the success of the organization should go along with the ratings.

Help can be acquired from various quarters in making these estimates. Employees usually know how well they're doing. Managers are supposed to know. The HRD manager can make conjectures about where the opportunities for profit improvements are.

VARIANCE REPORTS

You may wish to apply some of the conventional techniques of needs and competency assessment here. Usually the reports on which this technique is based tell their own story. Most organizations prepare monthly and/or quarterly "variance reports"—comparisons of the forecast dollars-and-cents performance with what has actually happened. These reports often reveal dramatically where the organization is lacking and where help may be needed.

As line colleagues are approached for assistance in developing these measurements and/or as research conclusions are shared, one may want to emphasize that these are strictly working estimates, that they are merely approximate and subject to adjustment.

Finally, note the column, "Developmental Opportunity." Quite simply, these numbers are the complements of the numbers in the previous column; that is, they bring the total for "competence" and "opportunity" to 10. Wherever competence is low, opportunity is high, and vice versa.

What HRD managers should be looking for, in an attitude of practical entrepreneurship, are topics that have both a high "priority" and a high "opportunity" rating—areas in which you can document the most clear-cut, dollar-conscious opportunities for the vital concerns of the organization. In the chart, "Market Research" and "Negotiating" are prime examples. With the insight gained during research, and with discretion, there will be subtle back-up evidence of the need for training intervention.

The point is, there will be basic, profit-oriented talking points with which to negotiate the contribution the HRD department can make to the organization. This is a tool that will permit movement closer to leadership in allying training and education with the profitability of the organization. There will be actual operations problems to which training solutions can be applied. Line employees will welcome the creative contribution and collaborate with HRD as a peer.

THE MULTI-CRITERION APPROACH TO EVALUATION OF BENEFITS

Thomas F. Urban and his co-authors (1985) have suggested that rigorous, systematic efforts have generally been neglected. A recent study of 20 corporations regarded as leaders in corporate training concluded that to the extent that evaluation efforts have been undertaken, they seem to have been focused on technical training. Even when evaluation took place, there was no consensus on the best type of evaluation criteria. Recently, top management is agreeing that if training programs do not show quantifiable gains, the programs should be discontinued.

More and more writers are agreeing that a multi-method approach to assessing effectiveness is useful. Campbell (1970), for example, recommends that subjective evaluations by participants (internal criteria) be combined with measures assessing behavioral change on the job (external criteria) in order to evaluate fully the effectiveness of training programs.

Urban's research outlines a multi-criterion approach to evaluating a large-scale supervisory training program in a major U.S. oil company (Urban, 1985, p. 68). In addition to the internal criteria of participants' reactions to the program, longitudinal measures were taken in regard to subsequent attrition and career progressions of participants, or external criteria. They also developed measures of participants' organizational investment and conducted a cost-benefit analysis. While some evaluation approaches build on existing notions, comprehensive multi-evaluation criteria go beyond these in scope, permitting the convergence of both internal and external criteria to be examined.

THE SUPERVISORY TRAINING PROGRAM

The supervisory training program (STP) was designed for employees newly promoted into first-level supervisory positions and supervisors who had not attended a supervisory training program in the last five years. Program participants were nominated by their managers for a specific program based on the manager's assessment and discussions of the supervisor's training needs.

The content of the programs included communication, group dynamics, problem solving, decision making, and other supervisory skills. Conducted six to ten times per year, each program contained the same generic content and was conducted by three members of the training staff at an off-site location. Participants were selected from diverse functional areas and geographic locations.

The average age of the 533 participants was 30 years, approximately 90 percent earned between $25,000 and $63,000, and approximately 22 percent were female and minority group members. The majority of participants came from Texas, Alaska, and Louisiana.

CONCEPTUAL MODEL

An understanding and cost justification of the STP effectiveness was developed through use of multiple methods and criteria. Evaluation criteria were developed from a conceptual model outlining the multi-criterion approach to evaluation. The STP project was evaluated relative to participant reactions concerning content and context, as well as promotions, grade increases, and attrition performance effects. At the end of each program, participants evaluated their interest in the program, perceived relevance of the program content, the trainers, and the overall course.

Participant interest in the course material was determined to be a necessary, but not sufficient condition for implementation on the job. For the 15 programs, overall interest received an average of 5.04 on a 6-point Likert scale, and perceived applicability of the course material an average of 5.02 on a similar scale. The overall course rating averaged as 3.46 on a 4-point scale, with the trainers' ratings averaging 3.63. Participant reactions suggested that the STP rated high in terms of interest, perceived applicability, course, and trainers. Participants' narrative comments, which were content analyzed, were also favorable. While participant reactions are useful, additional criteria were used to determine program effectiveness and to provide a basis for comparison across methods.

ATTRITION

Training programs may not change observable behavior on the job, but they may have value in reducing attrition. Perhaps the most important effect of a development activity is the positive feelings resulting from participants' perceptions of corporate interest in their personal and career development. Participants elected for organizational rewards, such as developmental experiences, may reciprocate through increased loyalty and commitment and longer tenure with an organization. Training is costly, but so is turnover. Replacement costs for managers are equal approximately to their annual salary. Therefore, a central question in measuring training effectiveness is whether the participants remain with the organization providing the training.

During 1980–1981, the attrition of experienced personnel was of vital importance to the energy industry. Smaller independent oil firms were raiding the major firms to secure experienced engineers, geologists, geophysicists, and managers. Retaining these professionals was of paramount importance for the exploration and production of energy resources by the major oil companies. Of the 533 supervisors participating in 15 programs between 1979 and 1981, 20 subsequently left the organization. This is an annualized average attrition rate of 2.2 percent, compared to an overall 6.4 percent for all employees in this category.

The attrition rate for all critical-skill categories, except geologists, was significantly lower for participants. The low or nonexistent availability of experienced critical-skills employees magnified the significance of the low attrition rate.

CAREER PROGRESSION

Enhancing performance on the job is a central focus of any developmental activity. Since observing performance changes was not possible, the outcomes of the organizations reward process served as a substitute measure. Participants' grade increases and title changes gauged organizational rewards. A longitudinal analysis determined organizational reward and career progression of participants in the three programs offered in 1979.

The participants received more grade increases and title changes than those in the nonparticipant sample. The 105 participants received a total of 105 grade increases—more than twice as many as the nonparticipants.

COST-BENEFIT ANALYSIS

A systematic and informed evaluation effort should provide an indication of program investment or costs to use as a benchmark against which to evaluate benefits. In one study, the costs of a single program appear below.

Participant salaries (1 week at average salary):	$21,500
Trainers salaries (3 trainers for 1 week at average salary):	2,200
Transportation, lodging and meals (participants and trainers):	36,000
Program expenses (materials, conference rooms, etc.):	5,000
Approximate total cost:	$64,700

A single program costs approximately $65,000, and nearly 4.0 percent of the participants' annual average salary. If HRD efforts are viewed as investments in human resources, then a long-range investment perspective seems desirable. Comparing the $65,000 program cost with the total tenure of the program participants, the investment per year was $218.86. If the cost of the program was amortized over the projected organizational tenure of the participants, the amortization per year would be $77.20. This expense is minimal related to projected returns from a supervisory career.

Another analysis was conducted on October 1981 participants. Information on the resources that they had under their control was collected from participants. A comparison between these resources and the total amount expended for the 15 programs conducted between September 1979 and October 1981 was made. The total expenses for programs would be recovered if participants in one program subsequently increased their resource utilization (e.g., through better management skills) by only 0.1 percent. In addition, if the supervisors could get their 253 direct reports to increase resources an average of $256.92 per direct report, the program expense would be covered.

The Urban study reports a program evaluation effort of a large-scale management training and development program in a major company. The evaluation approach employs multiple criteria, rather than relying on a single dimension which typically is of questionable validity. Using several different methods allows the examination of convergence in the results from the different criteria, thus permitting more confident conclusions concerning the program's effectiveness. In this study, positive participant reactions, post-program promotion, and pay grade increases, reduced turnover rates, and effective cost measures converged in supporting the effectiveness of the program.

There are dozens more models that are useful to the cost-benefit analyst in an organization. It is only left to the resourcefulness of the reader to glean them from the literature. They may be more or less useful than the sampling of these approaches to the topic presented here. The point is to select one (or more) approach and employ it in an attempt to measure results of the HRD effort.

HUMAN RESOURCES ACCOUNTING—A CRITIQUE

While the previously cited models have an element of neatness and symmetry associated with them, there are those who would urge caution with the assignment of mere numbers to human resources. They say that the variables are too diverse and discrepant and are in a realm that is not amenable to comparison with, say, other resources required for manufacturing. The reader would do well to heed these cautions and use results of cost-benefit analyses with discretion. Anthony Jurkus (1979) suggests that typically, criticism of human resources accounting concerns the problems of usefulness, methodology, consensus among proponents, and timeliness.

Questions related to the problem of usefulness involve the extent of management's interest in, and understanding of, human resources accounting and its importance to managerial plans and decisions. If a manager knows how human resources accounting may be used in planning, then such data are of course useful. But if he or she does not view the data as critical to planning, there is obviously little value in assembling it.

The problem of methodology in human resources accounting arises from a lack of symmetry with traditional accounting procedures, as critics are quick to point out. That is, the accepted accounting definitions of assets specify or imply ownership by the organization. Since human resources are of course not owned, theoretically they cannot be accounted for in the way of traditional assets—so the whole methodology of human resources accounting breaks down, according to these critics.

There are also those who argue that the time for human resources accounting in the cost-benefit analysis arena has not come. Their position is that neither accounting nor behavioral science has progressed so far that either researchers or managers can obtain precise human resources accounting data with which to accurately describe, predict, or control organizational conditions.

CONCLUSION

Finally, it is important to remember that in order to achieve equal status with other cost/profit centers in an organization, HRD practitioners must strive to achieve some accountable status. The most promising method to traverse this route is to select and honestly employ a cost-benefit model in the training department. The results, whether positive or negative, will lend credibility to the HRD function.

CHAPTER 13

Professional Certification and Development

Objectives

After completing Chapter 13, readers should be able to

- differentiate among the three principal credentialing processes.

- identify the genesis of professional certification.

- summarize the importance and purposes of professional certification.

- identify and critique the certification activities of HRD-related societies.

- identify the qualification criteria unique to each of three certification programs within HRD-related societies.

- describe the certification activities of ASTD.

- summarize the three comprehensive studies relating to support for professional certification in the field of HRD.

- identify the element of the Professionalization Cube and its implications for the field of HRD.

Society expects practitioners of all disciplines to be professional and competent. There are many ways to identify and determine competence today. One approach, professional certification, is often misunderstood or confused with other credentialing processes such as accreditation and licensure. One should be cognizant of the fact that professional certification is a homogeneous process, that is, it follows a uniform structure, and the various certification programs contain similar characteristics (Galbraith & Gilley, 1986).

WHAT IS PROFESSIONAL CERTIFICATION?

During the past several decades *professional certification* has been used to describe a process that is said to separate individuals who are competent from those who are not. It seems, however, that it is often used as a catch-all term to describe a variety of credentialing processes. The two most popular professionalization processes, *accreditation* and *licensure* are often confused with professional certification.

The Bratton and Hildebrand model (1980) suggests that clearer discriminations can be made if we look at these three processes in terms of (1) the recipient of the credential, (2) the certifying body, and (3) the degree of volunteerism required for each (see Table 13.1). Accreditation regulates instructional programs. It is voluntary and generally administered by an association or agency. Licensure is a required process, administered by a political body or governing group. Professional certification can be defined as a voluntary process by which a professional association or organization measures and reports on the degree of competence of individual practitioners (Galbraith & Gilley, 1985).

The fact that professional certification, accreditation, and licensure are sometimes used interchangeably presents other problems. HRD practitioners may view them as one and the same because they do not understand the purpose, nature, and delivery system of each, causing misunderstanding, confusion, and frustration on the part of those concerned with the topic of professional certification. Further, this lack of knowledge and information impedes communication and diminishes enthusiasm, which hampers the implementation process of professional certification programs (Gilley & Galbraith, 1986).

This definitional dilemma has become a staggering problem for practitioners in HRD, and continues to restrict the free exchange of ideas regarding the primary purposes of professional certification. The term must be defined before

Table 13.1   Comparison of Professional Certification, Accreditation, and Licensure

Type of Credential	Recipient of Credential	Credentialing Body	Required or Voluntary
Professional Certification	Individuals	Association/Agency	Voluntary
Accreditation	Programs	Association/Agency	Voluntary
Licensure	Individuals	Political Body	Required

Adapted by permission of the publisher from B. Bratton & M. Hildebrand, Plain talk about professional certification, Instructional Innovator, 25, (9) (December 1980): 22–24, 29.

the subject of professional certification can be thoroughly examined and understood.

Professional certification is used in a variety of occupational disciplines, including HRD. It is viewed as a vital part of the evolutionary process of professionalization because it focuses attention on the competencies that constitute an occupation. Competencies are used to define an emerging field. HRD practitioners use these identified competencies for self-assessment. They also provide information for academic and professional preparation programs for HRD program development, and can aid employers in identifying qualified practitioners. In this chapter we demonstrate the relationship between professionalization and professional certification. Both the developmental process of a profession (professionalization) and the characteristics that constitute it require professional certification, or the establishment of entry-level requirements. Lawrence (1981) believes that limiting entry into a profession will increase the demand for qualified professionals and improve the quality of the profession. Credentialing is not a phenomenon of the twentieth century. It has a long and rich heritage.

HISTORY OF CREDENTIALING

The earliest record of credentialing can be traced back to ancient Athens. In the thirteenth century Roman emperor Frederick II developed the first—medical—credentialing practice.

In the United States, credentialing has evolved from two orientations, the medical and legal professions and teaching. The first medical licensing was instituted by the State of Virginia in 1639. The legal profession did not maintain a credentialing program until the 1730s when the Supreme Court of the State of New York imposed an apprenticeship on lawyers before allowing them to argue their cases. During this period credentialing was not used extensively. It was not until the turn of this century that the medical profession became heavily engrossed in the credentialing process and the famous Flexner report was published by the American Medical Association in 1910. This report resulted in the permanent interlocking of accreditation and licensure.

As a result of the Flexner report, more than 40 percent of the medical schools closed down within a five-year period. In 1918 the dental profession followed the AMA's lead by establishing their own credentialing program. The Bar Association established their first credentialing program in 1923, and the pharmacy profession established theirs in 1940. By 1970, the health occupations field alone licensed more than 30 different occupations. As a direct result, a national health credentialing agency was established dedicated to the improvement of credentialing.

The second focus and development of credentialing in the United States was in the teaching profession. During the Colonial Period credentialing of "task masters" was common in order to guarantee and maintain orthodox religious beliefs. However, as the country began to expand and become more complex, local communities were forced to establish individual criteria for instructors, and not necessarily along religious lines.

By the end of World War II, there were a variety of credentialing processes for teachers in the United States. Consequently, the National Education Association instituted a professional standards movement to improve and standardize existing credentialing programs. Still, different levels and types of credentialing processes exist today. It has been only during the past three decades that certification in the teachers' movement has become a more uniform and established part of the professional development process.

Today, according to a recent report by the American Society of Association Executives, more than 450 associations offer certification programs. The medical, legal, and teacher certification models are *licensing* mechanisms, regulated by local bodies, and thus are different from today's professional certification credentialing process. The professional certification model, in contrast, arose in response to the recognized need to promote professional competence of association members. Rapid expansion of knowledge and technology has placed additional pressure on individuals and occupational groups to achieve and maintain professional competencies. The professional certification process has been viewed by some as an essential element in the acquisition of those competencies.

SUPPORT FOR PROFESSIONAL CERTIFICATION

In May, 1982, when asked whether they would choose to apply for certification if a voluntary certification process were to be developed under the sponsorship of an independent professional association, 76 percent of HRD professionals responded "yes." Of those interviewed, 67 percent (1,760) believed that a certification process for trainers would provide direction and guidance to newcomers in training; 49 percent thought it would improve the average level of performance in the field of HRD (Should trainers be certified?, 1982). In 1985, ASTD's Professional Standards Task Force surveyed 2,000 of its members to determine the need for certification. Among the HRD practitioners surveyed, 58 percent indicated they agreed that such a program was warranted.

Finally, in November 1986, *Training* magazine surveyed 7,500 subscribers and reported that 59 percent were in favor of formal certification (Lee, 1986). Within that study, only 39 percent thought certification would be unworkable for the field of HRD; 81 percent thought HRD practitioners should be required to demonstrate mastery of a certain set of skills; and 77 percent indicated HRD practitioners should be required to demonstrate mastery of a certain body of knowledge. Finally, 62 percent believed certification would do a lot for the professional image of HRD practitioners. All three studies clearly indicate support for professional certification, but none outline the process of professionalization—something we attempt to do at the end of the chapter.

SIGNIFICANCE AND PURPOSE OF PROFESSIONAL CERTIFICATION

By identifying competencies, professional certification can improve the performance of HRD practitioners. As a result, practitioners have greater confidence and self-satisfaction in the tasks they perform. Participants in a professional certification program must continuously analyze and reevaluate their level of competence against the endorsed competence level established by the profession in order to determine deficiencies and strengths. Thus, practitioners can develop a self-improvement plan of action to overcome any deficiencies and further improve their skills. "Finally, perhaps the most important aspect of professional certification is that it communicates clearly to practitioners the expectations of the profession, enabling them to perform their roles and tasks within the profession more effectively" (Galbraith & Gilley, 1987, p. 9).

Gailbraith & Gilley (1986) added that professional certification provides structure and continuity to the field of HRD. Because of the dedication to quality, professional certification further enhances its image. Thus the profession can better maintain the quality of practitioners through professional certification programs that regulate and restrict entry into the profession. In the final analysis, professional certification allows HRD to present to the general public the valid and reliable approach it needs to the dissemination of qualified practitioners.

According to unpublished manuscripts by Miller (1976) and Gilley (1985), the identification and advancement of professional competencies is the primary purpose for professional certification. Secondary purposes include (1) avoiding external regulation, (2) enhancing prestige of the field, (3) stabilizing individual job security, (4) increasing the influence of societies and associations on the profession, (5) protecting the public, clients, and employers, and (6) improving academic programs.

Unlike licensure, professional certification is often seen primarily as an impetus to professional development. It encourages practitioners to achieve high standards and it encourages the field of HRD to focus the use of resources in order to assist them in doing so. Other possible benefits (and drawbacks) will be discussed in the following sections.

In the process of certification, standards of practice are determined. The converse is not true, however; that is, a profession may establish standards without developing a certification system. For example, an association may merely offer an explicit "code of practice." In the long run, some may see this as a rather weak movement in the direction of quality control. But even though setting standards need not lead to certification in the sequence of events, in practice their existence may add impetus to a move to certification.

BENEFITS AND DRAWBACKS

Regardless of the express purpose of certification, its significance lies in the fact that individuals, in preparation for certification, are required to increase their knowledge and ability, and that, rather than the designation itself, is its greatest benefit. Self-improvement is satisfying to the individual and increases one's sense of self-worth, which is a benefit to employers. Ultimately it increases the quality of the products and services in HRD.

Enhancement of the Profession. The HRD practitioners must meet a set of criteria before they are identified as being competent. The establishment of the set of criteria enhances the field of HRD. Among the fundamental characteristics of a profession, there is one that is critical: The regulatory mechanism by which individuals are screened in order to determine their level of competence. This mechanism, a stage in the process of professionalization, is not fully developed for the field of HRD or its practitioners.

Identification and Improvement of Competencies. The identification of competencies unique to the HRD field sets it off from others in the eyes of the public. It also aids HRD practitioners in focusing on, studying, and improving those competencies, which may lead to the development of variations or more sophisticated practices.

Bratton (1984) reported that identified competencies are helpful to HRD practitioners and the field in six different ways:

1. They will provide experienced professionals with a tool for self-assessment and professional growth.

2. They will provide a common set of concepts and vocabulary that will improve communication among professionals and other professional groups.

3. They will provide the academic and professional preparation programs with information for program development.

4. They will provide a basis for a potential certification program.

5. They will aid employers in identifying qualified applicants.

6. They will provide a basis for defining an emerging field of study (pp. 1–2).

According to Galbraith & Gilley (1986), "The identified competencies should reflect the skill of a professional in HRD regardless of the position, title, or academic degree held. Competencies should be performance oriented rather than academic oriented, as well as reflect the skills of experienced practitioners as opposed to entry-level individuals" (p. 28).

Academic Curricular Design. Certification programs may serve as an academic curricular feedback mechanism to assist in the development of HRD programs for those seeking to go into a given profession. Certification can assist HRD professors in their curricular development and design. This will assure that the appropriate skills and competencies are attained by those individuals aspiring to practice in the HRD area. As a result, the identified competencies can be used to develop guidelines, appropriate course work, internships, practicums, and independent projects.

Recognition for Practitioners. Public perception of HRD may be more positive when the field is seen as having a credentialing process. Thus, clients may have a higher regard for a profession (and the individuals in it) if there is evidence that the profession evaluates its own members. Not only does certification provide protection for clients/consumers, it may also stabilize the job for HRD practitioners (job security). Certification can provide recognition of individuals who have attained a certain level of competence. Increased earnings may result from certification designations such as CPA and CPU.

Governmental Concerns. Government groups may value the field of HRD more when it is self-evaluating (and therefore looks more like other established professions). With increased government spending in training and retraining, there may be increased requirements that the training materials and processes be carried out by certified HRD practitioners. Several bills before Congress in the past few years have contained such a caveat (Webster & Herold, 1983).

Standardization of the Profession. As a result of setting criteria, the field of HRD should see its practitioners move toward greater competence. In other words, the number of qualified practitioners should increase. This can come about through selection, better training programs, and better focused self-improvement efforts of practitioners. Hence, the process of credentialing may have the effect of internally increasing quality. Finally, standardization also provides assurance to the field that its practitioners will maintain a level of competence that is consistent throughout the profession.

Assist In Hiring Practices. Certification may provide some information to organizations planning to hire HRD practitioners. Instead of buying a pig in a poke, they can be assured that anyone so certified can demonstrate the competencies they are looking for. (This, of course, assumes that the certification system is valid and that it addresses those matters that are valued by the client.)

Divisiveness. There are, however, a number of negative implications for the field of HRD. The first and most obvious one is the divisiveness that a proposal for (and implementation of) certification can cause. Early in discussions, battle-lines can be drawn between HRD practitioners. Many may feel threatened (often properly so, because the procedures and implications of certification have not been made explicit). It is difficult, therefore, to remain objective and conduct reasonable discussions and investigations. Sometimes the mere appearance of an item on the agenda will lead to a schism among practitioners. When that happens, options and variations are not likely to be examined.

Division Among Professionals. Implementation may be virtually precluded by the nature of the field itself. In other words, HRD is very diversified, inter-disciplinary to such a degree that it becomes almost impossible to identify a common core of competencies. The diversity of competencies makes their identification a demanding task. The reality of identifying, defining, and measuring competencies for each role or job held by HRD practitioners seems questionable. Developing an appropriate level for each identified competency further confuses the issue (Warzynski & Noble, 1976).

Applicant Evaluation. A third drawback may be the expenditure of resources and energy necessary to develop a fair and acceptable certification process for the field. It is very difficult to establish a set of criteria that will be inexpensive to develop and at the same time thorough enough and comprehensive enough to separate the competent individuals from the less competent. The establishment of qualification criteria that measure competency level can be a very stringent and nearly impossible task. In some cases, pencil-and-paper tests are given to individuals to determine their knowledge level when some other form of assessment technique would serve better; a performance evaluation, perhaps, which tells whether the individual can perform the duties in question. At the same time, it becomes very difficult to validate, as well as determine the reliability of such assessment instruments without an expensive validation process. As a result, many times the instruments designed and developed to separate competent from incompetent practitioners are wholly inadequate. It may be that opponents of certification do not object to certification so much as to the drain on the profession.

Financial and Human Costs. Conversely, some might argue that, since astronomical expenditures are necessary to develop a valid program, the certification process for HRD may end up being "the best we can do with the limited resources allotted to us." This, opponents would say, is not good enough. The sponsoring professional association is usually responsible for the total cost and financing of the professional certification program. Failure to provide adequate funds could indeed impede the process for the field of HRD.

Membership Restrictions. Another proposed disadvantage is that certification may be discriminatory, exclusive, and normative. The consequences of this may be negative for HRD practitioners, the associations, and the field. For example, an association that seeks and depends on a wide membership may suffer dramatic losses if it implements restrictions. A somewhat amorphously defined profession in its early stages of growth such as HRD may find its boundaries and content not well defined and professional certification presently inappropriate.

Regulation of the Profession. The objection is also raised that certification may place the field of HRD in the role of gatekeeper, when that is not a role the practitioners want or a desirable perception of the profession. Another assumption concerning professional certification is that the "sponsoring association is in a position to regulate and control the profession; however, because of the diversity of HRD, this may not be feasible" (Galbraith & Gilley, 1986, p. 31).

PROFESSIONAL CERTIFICATION ACTIVITIES IN HRD-RELATED SOCIETIES

Several HRD-related associations and societies have committed themselves to the implementation of professional certification procedures for their memberships as a means of enhancing professionalization. Each of these programs was established for the purpose of advancing and/or increasing the competency of practitioners within the field of HRD and, in particular, their area of specialization. The objectives of this section of the chapter are to provide an overview of the certification programs provided by HRD-related societies and to identify the certification criteria commonly used in HRD-related societies and the specific criteria of each of the certification programs.

Five HRD-related societies have developed and implemented professional certification programs for their memberships. They include the American Society for Personnel Administrators (ASPA), the American Compensation Association (ACA), the American Association for Counseling and Development (AACD), the Institute of Management Consultants (IMC), the Ontario Society for Training and Development (OSTD), and the National Career Counseling Association (NCCA). Two other societies, the American Society for Training and Development (ASTD) and the National Society for Performance and Instruction/Division of Instructional Development within the Association for Educational Communications and Technology (NSPI/DID-AECT), have not developed or implemented a certification program at this time, but both maintain an interest in this form of competency development and have studied the concept. In addition, the International Board of Standards for Training, Performance and Instruction (IBSTPI) was formed for the purpose of defining and identifying competencies for the field of HRD and ultimately developing certification programs for the primary HRD roles (managers, instructors, instructional designers, and consultants). Each of these professional societies specializes in a variety of functional areas, including instructional designs (ASTD, NSPI, OSTD), human resource management (ASPA), career counseling and development (NCCA, AACD, ASTD, OSTD), needs assessment (ASTD, NSPI, OSTD), program planning and evaluation (ASTD, NSPI, OSTD), computer training (ASTD, NSPI, ASPA), employee assistance (AACD), employee compensation and benefits (ACA, ASPA), and HRD consulting (ASTD, ASPA, IMC, OSTD).

AMERICAN SOCIETY FOR PERSONNEL ADMINISTRATORS

ASPA has maintained a professional certification program since 1975. According to Galbraith & Gilley (1986), the purposes are

- to recognize individuals who have demonstrated expertise in particular fields;
- to raise and maintain professional standards in the field;
- to identify the body of knowledge as a guide to practitioners, consultants, educators, and researchers;
- to aid employers in identifying qualified practitioners; and
- to provide an overview of the field as a guide to self-development (p. 20).

The primary focus of this association is human resource management, but HRD is viewed as a part of their overall mission.

They sponsor three levels of "accreditation" (a misnomer for what is actually certification) through the Personnel Accreditation Institute (PAI). These levels are Professional in Human Resources (PHR) and Senior Professional in Human Resources-Specialist (SPHR-S) and Generalist (SPHR-G). Within senior specialist accreditation there are six functional areas:

1. Employment, placement, and personnel planning
2. Training and development
3. Compensation and benefits
4. Health, safety, and security
5. Employee and labor relations
6. Personnel research

Galbraith & Gilley (1986) added that applicants are required to meet various criteria, which include a written examination, professional references, evidence of ethical behavior, applicable professional experience, and current employment in the respective field. An academic degree in personnel management may be substituted for much of the work experience requirement.

AMERICAN COMPENSATION ASSOCIATION

ACA maintains an emphasis in human resource development through their certification program aimed at compensation professionals. This program consists of 14 courses designed for those seeking to develop competencies in the functional areas that comprise the compensation and employee benefits profession. Each course in the program deals with specific information associated with compensation practice and theory. In addition, applicants are required to successfully pass a written examination at the end of the course (Galbraith & Gilley, 1986). Over 5,000 individuals attend an ACA seminar each year, and ACA currently maintains a faculty of about 130.

AACD AND NCCA

The National Board for Certified Counselors (NBCC) has certified more than 9,000 members of the American Association for Counseling and Development (AACD) in general counseling since March 1983. Another highly specialized HRD society, National Career Counselor Association (NCCA), a division of AACD, initiated certification activities in career counseling in late 1984 through the National Council for the Credentialing of Career Counselors (NCCCC). This certification program requires a professional degree, a comprehensive written examination, an internship, professional work experience, professional references, evidence of ethical behavior, and proof of current employment in the field. This specialized type of certification is an example of the different types of certification programs that are available within the HRD field. Galbraith & Gilley (1986) stated that "neither AACD nor the NCCA programs are comprehensive enough to be endorsed by the entire field of HRD" (p. 21). It should be noted that some scholars do not view these two associations as a part of the HRD family (Nadler, in conversation, 1986).

INSTITUTE OF MANAGEMENT CONSULTANTS

The IMC, also maintains a professional certification program. According to Galbraith & Gilley (1986), "Their primary focus is the advancement of professional competence in the consulting field. To be certified, candidates must submit a list of six personal and professional references, an application that details the description of their consulting practice, and written summaries of five clients. They must also sit for an oral examination by a panel of three Certified Management Consultants, to certify their technical and professional competence. The category of membership depends on the educational degree held and the number of years of professional experience. To remain certified, continuing education is required, including completion of various seminars, workshops, and courses" (p. 21).

ONTARIO SOCIETY FOR TRAINING AND DEVELOPMENT

In March 1976, a subcommittee of the Ontario Society for Training and Development (OSTD) was established to investigate the core competencies of a trainer. The resulting report and recommendations were adopted by the OSTD executive board, and, in December of the same year, the first version of the document was published under the title, "Core Competencies of a Trainer." The document's contents included an extensive list of skills, demonstrable of abilities, and area of knowledge and/or understanding within 11 distinct categories of competence. As such, it was essentially a checklist, or reference source, training and development practitioners could use to compare their own performance qualifications and development plans.

While this document was not designed to serve as a certification process, it is dedicated to the identification of current proficiency levels and is a vehicle for enhancing one's competencies as a trainer. OSTD suggests four ways that this document could be utilized by trainers and HRD practitioners.

- As a job appraisal tool that emphasizes strengths and weaknesses.

- As a way or organizing one's strengths, which can enhance one's career development activities.

- As a way of recognizing the major strengths that one could most likely use to bridge one's transition from one position to another of greater responsibility and scope.

- As a resume-writing tool, designed to emphasize one's assets—that is, the areas of knowledge, skills, and competencies in which one can demonstrate one's proficiency during interviews.

In addition, the OSTD developed a "Weighted Bibliography" designed around each of the four identified roles of HRD practitioners (instructor, designer, manager, consultant). Utilizing factor analysis, the OSTD weighed each of the publications according to their importance. Categories included: Must Know, Really Should Know, Should Know, Possibly Should Know, Nice to Know, and Unrelated. In the final analysis, the "Core Competencies of a Trainer" and the "Weighted Bibliography" are self-directed learning tools designed to improve and enhance the competencies of trainers and HRD practitioners while establishing standards for the field.

ASTD AND NSPI STUDY CERTIFICATION

ASTD and NSPI have not developed or implemented nor endorsed the concept of certification as a means of advancing or increasing individual competency. However, these societies have studied the concept and its impacts on their respective areas but have not elected to develop a certification program. Their efforts and activities are worth reporting and serve as a reference for other HRD-related societies.

AMERICAN SOCIETY FOR TRAINING AND DEVELOPMENT

Galbraith & Gilley (1986) reported that "In 1972, the membership of ASTD voted against certification as a process through which professional development could be obtained. As an alternative, the Professional Standards Committee was asked to examine and concentrate its efforts on acquiring the basic competencies for the HRD professional (Hatcher, 1974). Again, in 1978, HRD professionals indicated that the lack of professional development was still perceived to be a major concern (Clements, Pinto, & Walker, 1978).

Since professional development was of paramount importance to the members of ASTD, they engaged in several research activities designed to identify HRD roles and competencies. In 1978, Pinto and Walker identified 14 different activities that HRD practitioners performed. This study served as a foundation for future research conducted by ASTD" (p. 19).

The most recent competency study was the Model for Excellence (1983), which identified 15 roles and 31 competencies for training and development practitioners. The study is a landmark in the field and opened the door to the consideration of certification. In fact, Mac McCullough, former vice-president for professional development at ASTD, reported during an interview published in the *Training and Development Journal,* "With the results of the competency study, ASTD was now ready to reexamine certification."

According to Galbraith & Gilley (1984), the Board of Directors of ASTD commissioned the Professional Standards Task Force (1984) to study the perceptions of its members regarding professional standards and certification. The task force was to investigate the issue of professional standards and certification using appropriate research processes, and to make recommendations to the Board of Directors regarding the development of professional standards and/or certification programs. Six fundamental research processes were employed and five recommendations were presented to the ASTD Board of Directors in November 1985. (See Chapter 14 for related information.)

NATIONAL SOCIETY FOR PERFORMANCE AND INSTRUCTION

In 1982, the National Society for Performance and Instruction (NSPI) and the Division of Instructional Development (DID) within the Association for Educational Communication and Technology (AECT) established a joint certification task force in order to consider professional certification for instructional designers. During the past seven years, this task force has identified 16 performance-based instructional-training competencies, performed a major literature search that cross-references published materials and competencies, met with attorneys, accountants, researchers, and representatives currently administering successful professional certification programs, and developed an assessment center type of performance examination (Galbraith & Gilley, 1986).

INTERNATIONAL BOARD OF STANDARDS FOR TRAINING, PERFORMANCE AND INSTRUCTION (IBSTPI)

In 1985, a nonprofit organization, the International Board of Standards for Training, Performance and Instruction was created for the purpose of continuing certification research, competency development and validation, and consultation service. While a final decision has not been reached regarding professional certification, IBSTPI efforts have provided leadership and direction for the field of HRD related to the issue of professional certification.

QUALIFICATION CRITERIA UTILIZED BY HRD-RELATED SOCIETIES

In a recent study of 70 associations and societies that maintain professional certification programs, 10 qualification criteria were identified as the most important when evaluating applicants for certification (Gilley, 1985).

1. Professional experience
2. Successful completion of written examination
3. Completion of a program of study
4. Current employment in the respective industry trade field
5. Successful completion of performance examination
6. Membership in a professional association or society
7. Completion of additional training and/or continuing education
8. Evidence of ethical behavior
9. Personal and professional references
10. Successful completion of an oral evaluation and/or interview

Although some professional associations do not use all of these criteria, they are commonly used by HRD-related societies in their certification programs. The qualification criteria in six HRD-related society certification programs are presented for the purpose of comparison in Table 13.2.

The professional experience requirement is two years for AACD (general counseling), five years for NCCA (career counseling), one to four years for ASPA's basic accreditation and five to eight years for their senior level accreditation. A written examination is required in AACD, ASPA, ACA, NCCA not in (OSTD) and IMC. AACD and NCCA require a master's or doctorate in counseling or a closely related field. ASPA does not require adegree, but an undergraduate degree in personnel management or the social sciences reduces the requirement for work experience. Each of the societies maintain that applicants for certification must be currently employed in the respective field. A performance examination is not required in AACD, ASPA, ACA, or NCCA, but IMC does require an analysis of current consulting

Table 13.2   Certification Criteria for HRD-Related Societies

	PHR	ASPA		AACD	NCCA	IMC	ACA	OSTD
		SPHR-S	SPHR-G	General	Career	HRD	COM	HRD
1. Professional Experience	1–4 yr	5–8 yr	5–8 yr	2 yr	5 yr	5 yr	none	3 yr
2. Successful Completion of Written Examination	yes	yes	yes	yes	yes	yes	yes	no
3. Education	no	no	no	MA	MA	no	no	no
4. Currently Employed in the Respective Field	yes	yes	yes	yes	yes	yes	yes	yes
5. Successful Completion of Performance Examination	no	no	no	no	no	yes	yes	no
6. Required Membership of Sponsoring Society	no	no	no	no	no	yes	no	no
7. Completion of Additional Training/Continuing Education	yes	yes	yes	yes	yes	yes	no	yes
8. Evidence of Ethical Behavior	yes	yes	yes	yes	yes	yes	yes	yes
9. Personal and Professional References	yes	yes	yes	yes	yes	yes	no	yes
10. Internship	no	no	no	yes	yes	no	no	no

activities, while OSTD utilizes a self-assessment examination.

Only NCCA requires an applicant for certification to become a member of their association prior to being allowed to obtain certification status. Additional training and/or continuing education is a requirement of all the societies except ACA, and they are currently reconsidering this criteria. Evidence of ethical behavior is a requirement of all the societies, while ACA is the only society that does not require personal and professional references from its applicants. AACD and NCCA require a supervised counseling experience, but the other HRD-related societies do not require this type of criteria.

By way of comparison, Table 13.3 reports five other important provisions of the seven HRD-related societies' certification programs. All of the certification programs are competency-based and the expiration time for certification is three years in ASPA, NCCA, and OSTD and five years in AACD and IMC. ACA is presently evaluating the importance of recertification. Recertification requirements vary considerably, but continuous successful practice and evidence of continuing professional education often eliminate the need to retake the qualifying examination.

All seven societies reserve the right to revoke an individual's certification status for illegal or unethical behavior. Also, they each maintain a written code of ethics to which certified individuals must adhere. Certification fees range from $50 to $250.

The relationship between the institutes, boards, and councils that carry out certification procedures and the societies that provide the candidates is unclear. Brochures distributed by the certifying boards emphasize their own independence and make only passing reference, or none at all, to the related society, even though the institutes were each established by their respective societies. The amount and kind of influence which the society can exert over the certifying board has serious implications for its control over the process of certification.

Presently ASPA's certification program is administered through the Personnel Accreditation Institute. AACD's certification program is administered through the National Board for Certified Counselors and the National Council for the Credentialing of Career Counselors is the certifying board for NVGA. ACA does not maintain an independent certifying body while IMC certifies individuals through their parent group.

THE PROFESSIONALIZATION CUBE

According to Gilley & Galbraith (1987), "professionalization and professional certification processes have three components in common: level of knowledge/competency enhancement, level of importance of the occupation to society, and level of control by members of the occupation. To obtain professional status, each of these components must be evident. For example, the legal

Table 13.3   Provisions of HRD-Related Certification Programs

| | ASPA | | AACD | NCCA | IMC | ACA | OSTD |
| | SPHR-S | SPHR-G | General | Career | HRD | COM | HRD |
	PHR						
1. Competency Based	yes	yes	yes	yes	yes	yes	yes
2. Expiration Time	3 yr	3 yr	5 yr	3 yr	none*	5 yr	3 yr
3. Revocability	yes	yes	yes	yes	yes	no	yes
4. Fee Charged	$110	$250	$120	$50	$250	$70 (per)	$75
5. Certifying Board	PAI	PAI	NBCC	NCCCC	IMC	ACA	OSTD

profession requires that potential candidates complete an academic program that insures that a high degree of knowledge has been acquired. In addition, the legal profession has established a regulatory mechanism, the bar exam, which each potential member must successfully complete prior to initiation into the legal community. By endorsing and encouraging the specificity of the legal profession, society recognizes the social significance and importance of the profession. While not all occupational groups have reached the level of professional status, each can utilize the three components of professionalization and determine their present status.

The 'Professionalization Cube' consists of the three components of professionalization, which reflects the operational relationship of the various occupational status levels. Each of the occupational levels is represented by a series of three numbers. The first number represents the level of knowledge/competency required of each member in order to participate in an occupation. The second number represents the level of importance that society places on the occupation. The third number reflects the level of control members of the occupation place on others prior to entering and practicing the vocation (see Figure 13.1).

The relationship of professional certification to the three components of the professionalization process is evident and congruent with the purposes for the development and maintenance of certification programs. The three major purposes of professional certification are to increase the competency level of practitioners, to control or restrict the number of qualified persons entering the occupation, and to increase the importance of the occupation to society" (pp. 99–100). Professional certification is the only process that can simultaneously enhance all three of these elements.

Gilley & Galbraith (1987) added that "The implications for the field of HRD lie within the integration of the three common components of professionalization. Therefore, the field of HRD must address its present status in relationship to the level of knowledge and competence required of practitioners, the level of importance as viewed by society, and the level of control by the profession regarding entry and practice of their membership. Once status is determined, HRD should consider what action, if any, is appropriate in order to move the field to a more professionalized status. One appropriate action would be the endorsement of professional certification as a means of enhancing and improving the professional status of the field. Based upon the fact that a strong relationship exists regarding the principal tenets of professionalization and professional certification processes, the development of a long-range strategic plan, which includes a professional certification program, seems warranted if the field of HRD is to obtain profession status" (p. 100).

While it is evident that the field of HRD has not obtained profession status, it is also clear that it has evolved. Presently, the field of HRD can prescribe to a body of knowledge and a set of competencies regardless of their lack of endorsement by many in the field. HRD has also grown in importance during the past 20 years, and entering the field becomes more demanding and rigorous each day.

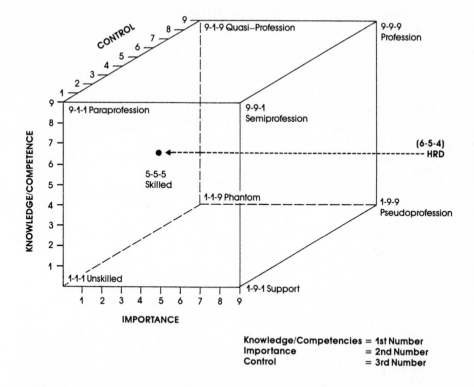

Figure 13.1   Professionalization grid

Adapted from J. W. Gilley and M. W. Galbraith, Professionalism and Professional Certification: A Relationship, Proceeding of the Twenty-Eighth Annual Adult Education Research Conference, *1987.*

Based on these three elements, a case can be made that the field of HRD currently can be perceived as a (6-5-4), which is reflected as being midway between a semi- and quasi-profession (see Figure 13.1). Efforts to move the field to profession status could be greatly improved if a professional certification program was implemented.

CONCLUSION

Obtaining professional status is a goal of most HRD practitioners. Clearly, there are advantages and disadvantages to the implementation of a comprehensive and standardized certification program. The characteristics that constitute a profession and the developmental process of a profession demand it. But if the field of HRD is to progress beyond its present status, a decision to accept or reject certification needs to be examined by all the representative associations and by each HRD practitioner.

Therefore, the field of HRD must determine if the financial and human costs exceed the benefits derived from implementing professional certification programs. If the benefits are greater than the costs, then professional certification should be implemented. If, however, the cost exceeds the benefits of such programs, an alternative solution must be developed to advance the profession.

According to Galbraith & Gilley (1986), "the advantages and benefits of professional certification can only be achieved once an open and honest dialogue has been conducted by practitioners in the field" (p. 39). It is hoped that this chapter has provided HRD practitioners with the information and answers they need in order to reach an appropriate decision regarding professional certification."

CHAPTER 14

Professionalization of the Field of HRD

Objectives

After completing Chapter 14, readers should be able to

- define the terms "profession" and "professionalization."

- describe the professionalization process from the philosophical, developmental, characteristics, and nontraditional orientations.

- describe the evaluation of professionalization in HRD.

- identify, describe, and distinguish among the following competency and research studies:
  1. Nadler Model
  2. Civil Service Commission Study
  3. Ontario Society for Training and Development Study
  4. Association of Education, Communication, and Technology Study
  5. American Society for Personnel Administration Study
  6. Pinto-Walker Study
  7. NSPI/DID (AECT) Joint Study
  8. ASTD Model for Excellence Study
  9. IBSTPI Study

Occupations have been measured on the basis of their importance and on the difficulty of the tasks that are associated with them. Today, occupational classifications include professions, semiprofessions, paraprofessions, quasi–professions, skilled and unskilled. Within each of these kinds of professions is an element of service to others, since few if any individuals possess the knowledge and skills needed to be self-sufficient in meeting their own needs. Therefore, the difference between classifications of occupations is not the service itself, it is in the nature of the service (Gilley & Galbraith, 1987).

By determining the nature of an occupation's service, society can classify that occupation. This helps develop an orientation to the occupation and enables society to separate one occupation from another. It is, however, difficult to obtain an agreed-upon definition of a professional and what constitutes a profession. Bullett (1981) defined a profession as a "field of human endeavor with a well-defined body of knowledge, containing basic principles common to all applications and techniques unique to the field, with practitioners skilled and experienced in applying these techniques, dedicated to the public interest (p. 5)." This definition includes several elements that are consistent with other definitions of a profession (Gilley, 1986). They include (1) a specialized body of knowledge, (2) application of developed competencies, (3) common principles, and (4) a dedication to the public interest. These elements have been used as a standard by which many occupational fields have been measured, including HRD.

It should be pointed out that much attention has been given to the enhancement of the HRD field and its practitioners. In fact, each of the HRD-related societies discussed in Chapter 13 has addressed this issue, and most employ some course of action aimed at improved professionalization (see Chapter 13 and the section on competency studies and research later in this chapter). However, the field of HRD is still in its infancy. Only recently has the professionalization process become the focus of research conducted by academics, practitioners, industry leaders, and consultants, as well as by HRD-related societies. We examine many of these studies later in this chapter. First, the four orientations of the professionalization process will be reviewed, along with an examination of them and their applicability to HRD.

THE PROFESSIONALIZATION PROCESS

Vollmer and Mills (1966) defined professionalization as an evolutionary process that introduces an organized and systematic approach to the development of an occupational field as it moves toward professional status. Professionalization was also defined by Farmer (1974) as "the dynamic process whereby an occupation can be observed to change in certain crucial characteristics in the direction of a profession" (p. 58). Both of these definitions stress development to a higher level of status. Within HRD, the professionalization process has been going on since the early seventies. Today, several professional associations and societies related to HRD are actively engaged in the advancement of the field to a more professionalized status (see the section on evaluation of professionalization later in this chapter).

According to Gilley and Galbraith (1987), "professionalization can be approached from four perspectives: a philosophical orientation, a developmental orientation comprised of various stages, a characteristics orientation, and a nontraditional orientation. Each provides insight into the evolutionary process of HRD as a profession" (p. 97).

THE PHILOSOPHICAL ORIENTATION

There are several different philosophical approaches to the professionalization of a discipline. Each has important implications for the field of HRD and its practitioners.

Many believe that the professionalization process consists of formal activities such as certification, accreditation, and licensure. This is often referred to as the *traditional* approach. For the field of HRD, this is less than acceptable, because it implies a formal regulatory approach to professionalization, which most practitioners do not desire (Gilley, 1986). According to Carlson (1977), a less formal approach would be more appropriate, one that emphasizes individual freedom and a democratic peer review, not a systematic process whereby each member of an occupation must acquire the "official body of knowledge." The less formal philosophical approach would not view professional certification and licensure as viable processes for improving a profession because of their controlling and restrictive nature (Gilley & Galbraith, 1987).

Another philosophical orientation to professionalization is the *attitudinal* approach, based on the construct that individual attitudes of professionalization, sense of calling, personal freedom, public service, and self-regulation will determine the level of professionalization. Thus, individuals can evaluate the status and prestige of various occupational groups, independent of governmental or societal influence. According to Gilley & Galbraith (1987), "this approach accepts the tenets of self-regulation and control, which can include professional certification as well as other forms of diagnostic evaluation" (p. 98). Again, HRD practitioners could select this approach to increase professionalization. Professional certification, if it appears appropriate and useful, may be required.

Still another philosophical orientation to professionalization is referred to as *eclecticism.* This approach uses procedures, techniques, methods, and concepts from a variety of sources, systems, and schools of thought. "Eclecticism accepts the belief that a single orientation is limiting and that the use of numerous procedures and concepts can better serve the individual and the profession. From this philosophical base, professional certification and licensure would be alternatives, depending on whether HRD practitioners believed them to be advantageous" (Galbraith & Gilley, 1986, p. 12).

Because of the diverse nature of the field, many believe that it is impossible to establish a single process by which HRD practitioners can achieve ideal professionalized status. However, the advent of an agreed-upon set of competencies, outputs, and standards could provide the foundation for such a process (Gilley & Galbraith, 1987). The focus of the 1987–88 Competency and Standards Study sponsored by ASTD and directed by Patricia McLagan has enabled the field to develop such a set of competencies, outputs, and standards.

DEVELOPMENTAL ORIENTATION

According to this perspective, a profession must evolve through a series of stages to achieve optimal status. A professional field would also have to have specific characteristics that could serve as a framework to differentiate occupations within the field. These two components constitute the basis of the developmental orientation (Gilley & Galbraith, 1987).

After studying the development of a number of professions, Whyte (1977) established six stages of development. *First,* professional development begins with an informal association of individuals who maintain a common occupational interest. *Second,* identification and adoption of a distinct body of knowledge takes place. *Third,* practitioners are formally organized into an institute or society. *Fourth,* entry requirements, based on experience alone or on a combination of experience and qualification, are established. *Fifth,* ethical and disciplinary codes are determined. *Sixth,* the final stage of professionalization, is the revision of the entry requirements, through which academic qualification and a specific period of experience become mandatory for practitioners within a field.

The field of HRD has failed to progress systematically through all six developmental stages. It has not identified a standardized body of knowledge or established entry requirements for HRD practitioners, which prevents its evolution to the final stage of a profession. In May 1988, however, the HRD Professors Network of ASTD held a conference to examine the feasibility of establishing and adopting a common body of knowledge for the field of HRD. This conference provided the framework for further exploration into the vital issue of professionalization.

CHARACTERISTICS ORIENTATION

Professionalization can also be viewed from a perspective that identifys the characteristics of a vocation in order to assist in its progress toward professional status (Vollmer & Mills, 1966). According to this orientation, each of the characteristics must be in place and fully developed before a discipline is considered a profession. Professional certification and licensure are viewed as appropriate and acceptable strategies for HRD and its practitioners.

Furthermore, Scheer (1964) maintained that a profession contains eight essential interrelated characteristics vital to its development. Of course, the degree of importance of the different characteristics varies from occupation to occupation. The eight characteristics include

1. A code of ethics

2. An organized and accepted body of knowledge

3. Specialized skills or identified competencies

4. Minimum education requirement for members

5. Certification of proficiency provided for, before members can achieve professional status

6. An orderly process in the fulfillment of responsibilities

7. Opportunities for the promulgation and interchange of ideas among members

8. Demands acceptance of the disciplines of the profession, realizing that the price of failure or malpractice is to be "out" of the profession

Looking at the field of HRD in light of these eight characteristics, only two clearly apply: a code of ethics and interchange of ideas among members. Both are provided through membership in HRD professional societies—for example, the American Society for Personnel Administration (ASPA), the American Society for Training and Development (ASTD), and the National Society of Performance and Instruction (NSPI).

Two other characteristics, the establishment of an accepted body of knowledge and the identification of specialized skills or competencies, have received considerable attention during the past several years within HRD-related societies. In the 1983 Model for Excellence Study, a comprehensive list of 31 competencies (see Figure 14.3) and 15 roles of training and development (see Figure 14.1) were identified. Although this was not the first list of competencies identified for the field of HRD, it has received much more attention. Recently (1989), a revised version of the study was published. The focus was expanded to cover the roles and competencies of HRD practitioners, allowing one additional area to be included, career development. The expansion also allowed for the identification of outputs and standards for each of the HRD roles. (This study identifies eleven roles for the field of HRD.)

In addition, a nonprofit organization, the International Board of Standards for Training, Performance and Instruction (IBSTPI) was created for the purpose of conducting and publishing competency research as well as other forms of professional development materials and information. To date, this organization has published two competency studies, one for instructional designers (Table 7.1 in Chapter 7) and one for learning specialists (Table 2.1 in Chapter 2). A third and fourth study are currently being conducted for HRD managers and performance technologists, respectively. ASPA sponsors two levels of "accreditation" (actually certification) but there is no minimum educational level set for applicants (the fourth characteristic). Except for this, it can serve as a good example for the field of HRD.

The field of HRD human resource development has no certifying body that tests the proficiency of its members, the fifth characteristic listed above. ASPA does maintain the Personnel Accreditation Institute, which offers certification on two levels: Professional in Human Resources (PHR) and Senior Professional in Human Resources (SPHR). The American Compensation Association offers certification upon completion of a number of courses of study, but is not represented or sponsored by a recognized HRD professional association.

NSPI has been studying certification for instructional designers during the past several years. In fact, IBSTPI was established as a direct result of NSPI's effort. NSPI has not established a certification program, but IBSTPI continues to research the concept. ASTD has been actively studying certification for the past several years but has failed to take action regarding its implementation. Although the field of HRD has recognized the importance of enhancing the competencies of its practitioners, it has failed to endorse a standardized approach. Thus, it fails to meet the fifth characteristic of a profession.

Finally, the field of HRD does not currently maintain an orderly process for the fulfillment of responsibilities (the sixth characteristic), nor does it demand an acceptance of the disciplines of the profession (the eighth characteristic). However, ASTD and NSPI have paid considerable attention to these characteristics in recent years.

NONTRADITIONAL ORIENTATION

The fourth philosophical perspective challenges the traditional model by advocating that the individuals who comprise an occupational group should determine the tenets of their profession (Cervero, 1985). According to Galbraith and Gilley (1986), "The nontraditional perspective maintains that the members of a discipline are able to discern the unique characteristics and needs of the occupation. Because of this awareness, they are better able to identify the essential elements that constitute what they believe to be a profession. This approach to professionalization seriously questions the importance of professional certification because neither it nor any other credentialing process can adequately measure the diverse dimensions of a specific occupation. Given the wide diversity of the field of HRD, many believe this approach has merit. In addition, it may or may not embrace the tenets of the philosophical, developmental, and characteristics orientations, depending on whether HRD practitioners see these as being essential to the development of their professional identity" (p. 17).

Each of the four philosophical orientations toward professionalization maintains that professionalized status can be obtained. They differ only in their approach and measurement techniques. To understand the professionalization process as it relates to the field of HRD, historical events and research studies need to be examined and put into proper context.

The evaluation of professionalization began in 1944 when the American Society for Training Directors (ASTD), now known as the American Society for Training and Development, was founded. However, it was not until the early fifties that the practitioners began examining their respective roles and ways of improving the professionalized status of the field. As recounted in a "Professional Standards Committee Report of Activity" (ASTD, 1953), the issue of professional certification was being examined as a means of advancing the field. The committee reported, "After considering the matter at some length the conclusion was reached that this is not the appropriate time to deal with the question of certification . . . . Since considerations cannot be delayed indefinitely if training is to establish itself as a real profession, it may be desirable to make a thorough study of the entire matter as a basis for future action by the American Society for Training Directors" (p. 35). So began the process of examining the field of HRD to determine a way of increasing its professionalized status.

COMPETENCY STUDIES AND RESEARCH IN HRD

During the past two decades, a number of competency studies and research projects have been designed to identify the knowledge and skills required of HRD practitioners. The studies have provided the additional information that is needed to describe the field, which increases practitioners' awareness of HRD. They are also one way students and entry-level employees can determine whether or not HRD would be a rewarding and challenging career area for them. To date, nine major studies have shaped the field of HRD.

1. Nadler Model (1970)
2. Civil Service Commission Study (1976)
3. Ontario Society for Training and Development Study (1976, 1986)
4. Association of Education, Communication, and Technology Study (1977)
5. American Society for Personnel Administration Study (1979)
6. Pinto-Walker Study (1978)
7. NSPI/DID (AECT) Joint Study (1981)
8. The New Models for HRD Practice (1983, 1989)
9. IBSTPI Study (1985, 1988)

Each of these studies will be examined separately, including the implications and impacts of each on the field of HRD.

NADLER MODEL (1970)

In 1967, Lippitt and Nadler published an article that many view as a ground-breaking piece of literature in HRD. The article, entitled "The Emerging Roles of the Training Director," later became the foundation for Nadler's model of HRD, published in his book, *Developing Human Resources,* in 1970.

Nadler's model reported that the field of HRD consisted of three major roles: administrator, consultant, and learning specialist. The model also reported that each of the primary roles consisted of several subroles, as follows:

Administrator
- Developer of personnel
- Supervisor of ongoing programs
- Maintainer of relations
- Arranger: facilities, finance

Consultant
- Advocate
- Expert
- Stimulator
- Change Agent

Learning Specialist
- Facilitator of learning
- Curriculum builder
- Instructional strategist

This model has been instrumental in stimulating research as well as in the development of other models. In addition, Nadler's model stresses the importance of identifying the components of HRD in order to advance and enhance the field. Finally, this model provided the first structure for performance appraisal and development of HRD specialists.

CIVIL SERVICE COMMISSION STUDY (1976)

In 1973, the Civil Service Commission began a study to determine the barriers to effective employee development in the federal government. According to Chalofsky (1983), this study revealed that the employee development (HRD) specialists provided limited consulting and career counseling support to their organizations. This finding led research teams to further examine the tasks that HRD specialists actually do perform. In 1976, the Civil Service Commission reported that there were five fundamental roles of federal HRD specialists, and provided a list of the competencies required for each role. The roles included

career counselor, consultant, learning specialist, program manager, and training administrator. This model served a dual purpose: It provided a structure for
the federal government (roles, competencies, and tasks), and it provided a standard of performance for HRD specialists.

The Nadler model was used as a basis for this study and the similarities are
evident. One significant change was the addition of the role of career counselor.
This becomes even more significant, since the 1983 Model for Excellence Study
also failed to identify the career counselor role. However, the study was updated
in 1989, and the role of career counselor was added. This was part of the expansion to include the entire field of HRD, rather than just training and development, the focus of the earlier 1983 study. This addition ended 20 years of debate
among HRD practitioners over the role of career counselor.

ONTARIO SOCIETY FOR TRAINING AND DEVELOPMENT STUDY (1976)

In December 1976, OSTD published the "Core Competencies of a Trainer." It
listed the competencies identified as being unique to HRD. It also identified four
fundamental roles of HRD practitioners: instructor, designer, manager, and
consultant. The document's contents included an extensive list of skills, abilities, and knowledge within each distinct category of competency. Also included
were the 11 activities areas each of the four roles participated in. They included:

- Administration
- Communication
- Course design
- Evaluation
- Group dynamic process
- Learning theory
- Human resource planning
- Person/organization interface
- Instruction
- Materials and equipment management
- Needs analysis

This document was designed as a personal evaluation tool used to identify
one's current proficiency level as a vehicle for enhancing one's competencies as
a trainer. To this end a "Weighted Bibliography" was designed around each of
the four identified roles of HRD practitioners, to be used as a self-directed learning resource. In 1986, this model was updated and, with the cooperation of
three major universities, a personal certification program was offered to students and practicing HRD specialists as a means of enhancing professional
proficiency.

Association of Education, Communication and Technology Study (1977)

In 1977, the AECT created a special Certification Task Force to study professional certification and to develop a set of recommendations. This task force, composed of representatives of the association's major divisions, state and national affiliates, worked closely for three years to produce a final report. In 1979, the Board of Directors adopted the following two recommendations: (1) that AECT accept the responsibility for encouraging and developing a professional certification program for educational technologists, and (2) that AECT divisions—Instructional Development, Media Design and Production, and Media Management, be responsible for delineating competencies and specifying assessment procedures (Bratton & Hildebrand, 1980).

The AECT's Division of Instructional Development (DID) began the project of defining competencies of instructional designers for the purpose of credentialing industrial trainers, media specialists, and other HRD practitioners. AECT-DID produced a set of 16 proposed competencies for instructional designers in 1980. These are listed in Table 14.1.

In 1980 it was reported that a certification program would be established. Designed to improve and enhance the professionalized status of instructional designers and media specialists, it would have three focuses: instructional development, media management, and media design and production. It was

Table 14.1   AECT-DID's 16 Core Competencies for Instructional Designers

---

1. Determine project appropriate for instructional development.
2. Conduct needs assessment.
3. Assess learner characteristics.
4. Analyze the structural characteristics of jobs, tasks, and content.
5. Write statements of learner outcomes.
6. Analyze the characteristics of the learning environment.
7. Sequence learner outcomes.
8. Specify instructional strategies.
9. Sequence learner activities.
10. Determine instructional resources (media) appropriate to instructional objectives.
11. Evaluate instruction/training.
12. Create course, training package, and workshop management systems.
13. Plan and monitor instructional development projects.
14. Communicate effectively in visual, oral, and written form.
15. Demonstrate appropriate interpersonal, group process, and consulting behaviors.
16. Promote the diffusion and adoption of the instructional development process.

Reprinted from B. Bratton, Instructional Training Design Competencies and Sources of Information About Them, Iowa City, IA.

hoped that a certification qualification examination could be developed and field-tested by 1981 and be available for general administration by 1983; however, this did not materialize. Instead, AECT-DID joined the NSPI certification effort. This merger will be examined in detail later in this chapter. To date, AECT has not designed or developed a certification program. However, the 16 competencies listed in Table 14.1 have been validated and published by a nonprofit organization for the purpose of advancing the knowledge and competencies of HRD practitioners focusing on instructional design (see IBSTPI Study).

AMERICAN SOCIETY FOR PERSONNEL ADMINISTRATION STUDY (1979)

ASPA established an "Accreditation Institute" on January 1, 1976. The program offered by the institute seeks to identify persons who have mastered the various foundations and levels of personnel and labor relations. The original program featured four areas of accreditation (actually certification), a specialist and a generalist category consisting of two levels each. The institute provided examinations in seven functional areas, including training and development.

Today (1989), the institute is known as the Personnel Accreditation Institute (PAI). It is an independent, nonprofit organization formed for the purpose of accrediting professionals in the field (Palomba, 1981). Presently, PAI offers two levels of certification: Professional in Human Resources (PHR) and Senior Professional in Human Resources (SPHR). Both specialty and generalist exams are still given, and training and development remains one of the specialty areas in which senior exams can be taken.

Palomba (1981) reported that a good certification procedure can achieve three goals. *First,* the development of the body of knowledge required for successful practice in the various areas of personnel will provide valuable assistance in designing efficient human resource management/development curriculums at the college and university level. *Second,* young practitioners will have sound guidelines as they develop into HRM/HRD professionals. *Third,* senior practitioners will be encouraged to update their knowledge. PAI maintains each of these purposes and can be viewed as a professionalization vehicle for the field.

PINTO-WALKER STUDY (1978)

In 1976, ASTD charged its Professional Development Committee with the responsibility of developing a role model for HRD practitioners. This committee elected to adopt the findings of the Pinto-Walker Study, an empirical research study of 3,000 HRD professionals nationwide, rather than publish another theoretically based role model. This study focused on what HRD practitioners "actually do," and resulted in a 14-item factor analysis. In other words, the study developed a list of 14 activities that training and development practitioners actually perform, rather than a role model. The 14 activities are

1. Needs analysis and diagnosis
2. Determining appropriate training approaches
3. Program design and development
4. Developing material resources
5. Managing internal resources
6. Managing external resources
7. Individual development, planning, and counseling
8. Job/performance-related training
9. Conducting classroom training
10. Group and organization development
11. Training research
12. Manage working relationships with managers and clients
13. Managing the training and development function
14. Professional self-development

The model consisted of 104 separate microactivities listed under the 14 macroactivities and was the first empirically based study for the HRD field. It is used extensively in designing professional development activities and evaluating the performance of HRD practitioners. The study focused, however, on what practitioners actually do, not what they should be doing, and in the present, not in the future. This limits its usefulness as a professionalization vehicle for the field of HRD, but it remains an important and essential study focused on the responsibilities and activities of HRD practitioners.

NSPI/DID (AECT) JOINT STUDY (1981)

In 1980, NSPI formed a task force to investigate standards for the instructional design field. The activities of this group duplicated the efforts of the AECT's Division of Design (DID) Certification Task Force. It appeared that the two associations could benefit from a joint effort regarding the professionalization of the field. Therefore, in 1981, under the direction of Barry Bratton, the AECT's Division of Design (DID) Certification Committee and the NSPI's Standards Committee joined forces to investigate the desirability and feasibility of professional certification for persons in the instructional/training design field. In 1981 Bratton and Colemen presented a draft list (AECT's competencies) of instructional designer competencies at the NSPI national conference and discussed the possibilities of professional certification as a means of enhancing the profession.

The combined task force continued to meet to examine the issue of professional certification and/or other professionalization activities. Throughout the years of work, the task force members adhered to the following precepts with regard to the competencies:

- The competencies should reflect the skills of a professional instructional/ training designer regardless of his/her current job, position, title, academic degree.

- The competencies should be performance oriented rather than academic oriented.

- A professionally competent designer should be able to perform most (if not all) of the competencies when given the opportunity to do so.

- The competencies should reflect the skills of experienced, professional designers—as opposed to students, trainers, or entry-level designers.

Developing a professional certification program became difficult because the task force could not resolve the issue of competency assessment, which is the basis of most professional certification programs. It became apparent that, unless it was satisfactorily addressed, this issue would prevent the development of a certification program, so it became the focus of the group during the remaining years of operation. Finally, an assessment center method was explored as a means for assessing competencies, but divergent results prevented its adoption. The task force continued to examine the issue of assessment but failed to adopt an acceptable process. In 1985, the Joint Certification Task Force dissolved when a nonprofit organization, the International Board of Standards for Training, Performance and Instruction (see below), was founded. The purpose of IBSTPI was to promote high standards of professional practice in training, performance, and instruction; for the benefit of individual and organizational consumers; through research, definition of competencies, measurement of competencies, education, and certification (Bratton, 1985).

ASTD MODEL FOR EXCELLENCE STUDY (1983, 1988)

The first ASTD national conference was held in Chicago in September, 1945. The meeting included the five founders of the organization and 51 other training and development practitioners (Hatcher, 1974). Since this humble beginning, the society has grown to over 23,000 members representing more than 8,000 organizations.

The earliest training activities were conducted by learning specialists recruited out of the classroom by industry during World War II (Lippitt & Nadler, 1967). After the war, many of these learning specialists returned to the classroom, but many remained in industry and moved gradually into administrative roles. In time, management found itself with good administrators but weak learning specialists. It was during this period that the first professionalization efforts began. As reported earlier, the issue of professional certification as a means of enhancing the field was first discussed as early as 1953. The issue continued to be of concern throughout the fifties and sixties.

According to Hatcher (1974), in 1970, there were two ASTD committees concerned with the question of professionalism. The first, the Professional Standards and Ethics Committee, proposed a Code of Ethics and a set of Professional Standards. The Code of Ethics was adopted by the Board of Directors. The Professional Standards were based on designed levels of membership determined by (1) the type of college degree already held, and (2) years of experience based on length of service in training. The second committee, the Long-Range Planning Committee, proposed establishing a task force to investigate the development of a professional certification program for training and development practitioners based on examination of knowledge and competence. It was concluded by this task force that, in order to qualify as a profession, the field must meet certain criteria. They were

1. The profession has a specialized body of knowledge.
2. The needed body of specialized knowledge is communicable.
3. The profession has a strong professional organization.
4. The profession sets its own standards.

At that time it was clear that several of the criteria had not yet been met. Specifically, numbers 1, 2, and 4.

The membership of ASTD considered the issue of professional certification once again in 1972 at the National Conference in Houston, Texas. The concept was "overwhelmingly voted down" because the members were less concerned with being certified as professionals and more concerned with how to acquire basic knowledge and skills to perform competently (Hatcher, 1974). As a direct result of the consensus of ASTD members, the Professional Standards Task Force established a three-phase professional development program: (1) developing a training manual for professional development of trainers, (2) developing an external degree program in training and development to be offered nationally, and (3) adopting professional certification if and when appropriate.

The manual was not designed to tell practitioners how to be better trainers but rather as a guide in self-discovery and development. The objective of the manual was

- to provide a guide for professional development experiences to both new and experienced trainers.

- to encourage professional development experiences on a local basis, allowing maximum participation at the least cost.

- to stimulate academic offerings in the area of training and development on the college and university level.

The manual was completed in the fall of 1973 and was made available to the membership at a nominal charge. Many believe that *The Handbook of Training and Development,* edited by Roger Craig, was the direct result of this manual.

During 1973 this task force began exploring the feasibility of offering a national degree program in training. Originally the program (an external master's degree in training) was to be offered through the New York Institute of Technology. It was anticipated that the degree would consist of 27 credit hours in the core program, 6 hours of electives, and possibly the option of taking a total of 42 credit hours in lieu of a thesis. This program was designed to utilize the local chapters of ASTD as clusters, with participation from local and regional leaders. The program was to be launched in 1974. However, the external degree program was not developed, because many academic programs specializing in HRD were beginning to emerge, and they provided a better alternative for practicing professionals (Gilley, 1985).

The task force hoped that these two efforts, a manual and an external degree program, would fulfill the first two criteria listed above. Unfortunately, neither of these efforts was a great success. All that was left was for the field to set its own standards (Criterion 4). This was to be accomplished through the establishment of a professional certification program. The purpose of the program was to enhance the field by identifying entry requirements and levels of acceptable practice.

In 1974 Hatcher was seeking assistance from individual members of ASTD by requesting feedback concerning the direction of the newly proposed certification program. It is important to remember, certification was voted down in 1972, but in 1974 was being reconsidered. The program was never developed because the competencies on which certification was to be based had not been identified. In fact, the identification of the competencies unique to the field of HRD would become the focus of each of ASTD's research efforts for the next 14 years.

Because of an awareness of the need for and interest in professional development, ASTD commissioned the Professional Development Committee in 1976 to study the competencies required for effective performance in training and development (Clements, Pinto, & Walker, 1978). In addition to identifying the competencies needed by training and development practitioners, the committee focused on identifying personal strengths and weaknesses related to job requirements and resources and opportunities to increase job effectiveness. In a study of 1,000 practitioners, the committee cited that "the lack of professional development" was the primary form of "unethical behavior" among training and development practitioners. In fact, this behavior was identified 5 percent more often than any other behavior. This committee also produced the "Pinto-Walker Study" described earlier.

In 1981 the Professional Development Committee commissioned the ASTD Training and Development Competency Study, presently referred to as the Model for Excellence. The committee believed that "it is only after its work on competencies has been completed, that the issue of certification can be raised" (McCullough & McLagan, 1984, p. 24). Patricia McLagan was appointed director of the study and her study team was charged with developing a prescriptive model for the training and development field, specifically, "to produce a detailed and updated definition of excellence in the training and development field in a form that will be useful to and used as a standard of professional performance and development . . ."

The Model for Excellence Study (1983) defined the training and development field as (1) one of nine human resource specialty areas (this book includes a tenth—career development. See Figure 1.7 in Chapter 1); (2) focusing on helping individuals change through learning; (3) consisting of 15 functions or roles (see Figure 14.2); (4) producing 102 outputs (see Figure 14.2); and (5) requiring a body of knowledge that supports 31 competency (knowledge/skill) areas (see Figure 14.3). The study distinguished training and development from other human resource functions that training and development is often confused with. It also identified the impact of probable future conditions on competency requirements and defined training and development work in terms of results and outputs rather than tasks and activities, which was the focus of many of the other studies. Another product of this study was that it identified and described the competencies required to perform the key roles of the field.

— EVALUATOR . . . The role of identifying the extent of a program, service or product's impact.

— GROUP FACILITATOR . . . The role of managing group discussions and group process so that individuals learn and group members feel the experience is positive.

— INDIVIDUAL DEVELOPMENT COUNSELOR . . . The role of helping an individual assess personal competencies, values, goals and identify and plan development and career actions.

— INSTRUCTIONAL WRITER . . . The role of preparing written learning and instructional materials.

— INSTRUCTOR . . . The role of presenting information and directing structured learning experiences so that individuals learn.

— MANAGER OF TRAINING AND DEVELOPMENT . . . The role of planning, organizing, staffing, controlling training and development operations or training and development projects and of linking training and development operations with other organization units.

— MARKETER . . . The role of selling Training and Development viewpoints, learning packages, programs and services to target audiences outside one's own work unit.

— MEDIA SPECIALIST . . . The role of producing software for and using audio, visual, computer and other hardware-based technologies for training and development.

— NEEDS ANALYST . . . The role of defining gaps between ideal and actual performance and specifying the cause of the gaps.

— PROGRAM ADMINISTRATOR . . . The role of ensuring that the facilities, equipment, materials, participants and other components of a learning event are present and that program logistics run smoothly.

— PROGRAM DESIGNER . . . The role of preparing objectives, defining content, selecting and sequencing activities for a specific program.

— STRATEGIST . . . The role of developing long-range plans for what the training and development structure, organization, direction, policies, programs, services, and practices will be in order to accomplish the training and development mission.

— TASK ANALYST . . . Identifying activities, tasks, sub-tasks, human resource and support requirements necessary to accomplish specific results in a job or organization.

— THEORETICIAN . . . The role of developing and testing theories of learning, training and development.

— TRANSFER AGENT . . . The role of helping individuals apply learning after the learning experience.

Figure 14.1   15 key training and development roles

Models for Excellence, *American Society for Training and Development. Reprinted by permission. All rights reserved.*

Evaluator:

1. Instruments to assess individual change in knowledge, skill, attitude, behavior, results.
2. Instruments to assess program and instructional quality.
3. Reports (written and oral) of program impact on individuals.
4. Reports (written and oral) of program impact on an organization.
5. Evaluation and validation designs and plans (written and oral).
6. Written instruments to collect and interpret data.

Group Facilitator:

7. Group discussions in which issues and needs are constructively assessed.
8. Group decisions where individuals all feel committed to action.
9. Cohesive teams.
10. Enhanced awareness of group process, self and others.

Individual Development Counselor:

11. Individual career development plans.
12. Enhanced skills on the part of an individual to identify and carry out his/her own department needs/goals.
13. Referrals to professional counseling.
14. Increased knowledge by the individual about where to get development support.
15. Tools, resources needed in career development.
16. Tools for managers to facilitate employees' career development.
17. An individual who initiates feedback, monitors and manages career plans.

Instructional Writer:

18. Exercises, workbooks, worksheets.
19. Teaching guides.
20. Scripts (for video, film, audio).

21. Manuals and job aids.
22. Computer software.
23. Tests and evaluation forms.
24. Written role plays, simulations, games.
25. Written case studies.

Instructor:

26. Video tapes, films, audio tapes, computer-aided instruction and other AV materials facilitated.
27. Case studies, role plays, games, tests and other structured learning events directed.
28. Lectures, presentations, stories delivered.
29. Examinations administered and feedback given.
30. Students' needs addressed.
31. An individual with new knowledge, skills, attitudes or behavior in his/her repertoire.

Manager of Training and Development:

32. T&D department or project operating objectives.
33. T&D budgets developed and monitored.
34. Positive work climate in the T&D function or project group.
35. Department/project staffed.
36. T&D standards, policies and procedures.
37. Outside supplies/consultants selected.
38. Solutions to department/project problems.
39. T&D actions congruent with other HR and organization actions.
40. Relevant information exchanged with clients/departments (internal and external).
41. Staff evaluated.
42. Staff developed.

Marketer:

43. Promotional materials for T&D programs and curricula.
44. Sales presentations.
45. Program overviews.
46. Leads.

47. Contracts with T&D clients (internal and external) negotiated.
48. Marketing plan (developed and implemented).
49. T&D programs/services visible to target markets.

Media Specialist:

50. T&D computer software.
51. Lists (written and oral) of recommended instructional hardware.
52. Graphics.
53. Video based material.
54. Audio tapes.
55. Computer hardware in working order.
56. AV equipment in working order.
57. Media users advised/counseled.
58. Production plans.
59. Purchasing specifications/recommendations for instructional/training software.
60. Purchasing specifications/recommendations for instructional/training hardware.

Needs Analyst:

61. Performance problems and discrepancies identified and reported (written/oral).
62. Knowledge, skill, attitude problems and discrepancies identified and reported (written/oral).
63. Tools to assess the knowledge, skill attitude and performance level of individuals and organizations.
64. Needs analysis strategies.
65. Causes of discrepancies inferred.

Program Administrator:

66. Facilities and equipment selected and scheduled.
67. Participant attendance secured, recorded.
68. Hotel/conference center staff managed.
69. Faculty scheduled.
70. Course material distributed (on-site, pre-course, post-course).
71. Contingency plans for back ups, emergencies.
72. Physical environment maintained.
73. Program follow-up accomplished.

(Figure 14.2 continued)

Program Designer:
74. Lists of learning objectives.
75. Written program plans/designs.
76. Specifications and priorities of training content, activities, materials and methods.
77. Sequencing plans for training content, activities, materials and methods.
78. Instructional contingency plans and implementation strategies.

Strategist:
79. T&D long range plans included in the broad human resource strategy of the client organization.
80. Identification (written/oral) of long range T&D strengths, weaknesses, opportunities, threats.
81. Descriptions of the T&D function and its outputs in the future.
82. Identification of forces/trends (technical, social, economic, etc.) impacting T&D.
83. Guidelines/plans for implementing long-range goals.
84. Alternative directions for T&D.
85. Cost/benefit analyses of the impact of T&D on the organization

Task Analyst:
86. Lists of key job/unit outputs.
87. Lists of key job/unit tasks.
88. Lists of knowledge/skill/attitude requirements of a job/unit.
89. Descriptions of the performance levels required in a job/unit.
90. Job design, enlargement, enrichment implications/alternatives identified.
91. Sub-tasks, tasks, and jobs clustered.
92. Conditions described under which jobs/tasks are performed.

Theoretician:
93. New concepts and theories of learning and behavior change.
94. Articles on T&D issues/theories for scientific journals and trade publications.
95. Research designs.
96. Research reports.
97. Training models and applications of theory.
98. Existing learning/training theories and concepts evaluated.

Transfer Agent:
99. Individual action plans for on-the-job/real world application.
100. Plans (written/oral) for the support of transfer of learning in and around the application environment.
101. Job aids to support performance and learning.
102. On the job environment modified to support learning.

Figure 14.2   The critical outputs for the training and development field

Models for Excellence, American Society for Training and Development. Reprinted by permission. All rights reserved.

1. *Adult Learning Understanding* ... Knowing how adults acquire and use knowledge, skills, attitudes. Understanding individual differences in learning.
2. *A/V Skill* ... Selecting and using audio/visual hardware and software.
3. *Career Development Knowledge* ... Understanding the personal and organizational issues and practices relevant to individual careers.
4. *Competency Identification Skill* ... Identifying the knowledge and skill requirements of jobs, tasks, roles.
5. *Computer Competence* ... Understanding and being able to use computers.
6. *Cost-Benefit Analysis Skill* ... Assessing alternatives in terms of their financial, psychological, and strategic advantages and disadvantages.
7. *Counseling Skill* ... Helping individuals recognize and understand personal needs, values, problems, alternatives and goals.
8. *Data Reduction Skill* ... Scanning, synthesizing, and drawing conclusions from data.
9. *Delegation Skill* ... Assigning task responsibility and authority to others.
10. *Facilities Skill* ... Planning and coordinating logistics in an efficient and cost-effective manner.
11. *Feedback Skill* ... Communicating opinions, observations and conclusions such that they are understood.
12. *Futuring Skill* ... Projecting trends and visualizing possible and probable futures and their implications.
13. *Group Process Skill* ... Influencing groups to both accomplish tasks and fulfill the needs of their members.
14. *Industry Understanding* ... Knowing the key concepts and variables that define an industry or sector (e.g., critical issues, economic vulnerabilities, measurements, distribution channels, inputs, outputs, information sources).
15. *Intellectual Versatility* ... Recognizing, exploring and using a broad range of ideas and practices. Thinking logically and creatively without undue influence from personal biases.
16. *Library Skills* ... Gathering information from printed and other recorded sources. Identifying and using information specialists and reference services and aids.
17. *Model Building Skill* ... Developing theoretical and practical frameworks which describe complex ideas in understandable, usable ways.
18. *Negotiation Skill* ... Securing win-win agreements while successfully representing a special interest in a decision situation.
19. *Objectives Preparation Skill* ... Preparing clear statements which describe desired outputs.
20. *Organization Behavior Understanding* ... Seeing organizations as dynamic, political, economic, and social systems which have multiple goals; using this larger perspective as a framework for understanding and influencing events and change.
21. *Organization Understanding* ... Knowing the strategy, structure, power networks, financial position, systems of a SPECIFIC organization.
22. *Performance Observation Skills* ... Tracking and describing behaviors and their effects.
23. *Personnel/HR Field Understanding* ... Understanding issues and practices in other HR areas (Organization Development, Organization Job Design, Human Resource Planning, Selection and Staffing, Personnel Research and Information Systems, Compensation and Benefits, Employee Assistance, Union/Labor Relations).
24. *Presentation Skills* ... Verbally presenting information such that the intended purpose is achieved.
25. *Questioning Skill* ... Gathering information from and stimulating insight in individuals and groups through the use of interviews, questionnaires and other probing methods.
26. *Records Management Skill* ... Storing data in easily retrievable form.
27. *Relationship Versatility* ... Adjusting behavior in order to establish relationships across a broad range of people and groups.
28. *Research Skills* ... Selecting, developing and using methodologies, statistical and data collection techniques for a formal inquiry.
29. *Training and Development Field Understanding* ... Knowing the technological, social, economic, professional, and regulatory issues in the field; understanding the role T&D plays in helping individuals learn for current and future jobs.
30. *Training and Development Techniques Understanding* ... Knowing the techniques and methods used in training; understanding their appropriate uses.
31. *Writing Skills* ... Preparing written material which follows generally accepted rules of style and form, is appropriate for the audience, creative, and accomplishes its intended purposes.

Figure 14.3   31 competencies for training and development practitioners

Models for Excellence, *American Society for Training and Development. Reprinted by permission. All rights reserved.*

With the identification of a set of competencies, the Professional Development Committee again turned its attention toward the issue of professional standards and certification. In April 1984, Julie O'Mara was selected to chair a task force to investigate the issue of professional standards and make recommendations to the Board of Directors of ASTD regarding the implementation of a professional standards program. The Professional Standards Task Force (PSTF) accomplished a number of things: (1) a literature search on credentialing and activities of other training-related societies; (2) an association survey to determine the procedures established, issues addressed, and qualification criteria used by other associations maintaining certification programs; (3) a membership survey (2,000) to determine the desirability of the establishing professional standards and certification procedures; (4) an HRD executive survey (1,000) to determine their perception of professional standards and certification; (5) testimony at the National ASTD conference in Dallas; and (6) a search of related legislation (Galbraith & Gilley, 1986). The PSTF recommended that (1) the HRD field have professional standards by which one can evaluate the quality of its critical outputs (102 identified in the Model for Excellence); (2) ASTD must establish, implement, and communicate such professional standards; (3) there not be certification at the present time; (4) ASTD annually review the status of certification in the field of HRD and related legislation and determine its role; and (5) initiate an ongoing process to educate HRD practitioners regarding standards, ethics, and certification.

Based upon these recommendations, ASTD commissioned the updating of the Model for Excellence in 1987. Again under the direction of McLagan, the 1987/88 ASTD Competencies and Standards Study was begun. The purpose of this study (known as "New Models for HRD Practice") was

- to review, revise, and update the 1983 study's training competencies and outputs to reflect the changing competitive forces and impacts on American business and industry.

- to identify "standards of excellence for each of the 102 outputs.

- to produce an updated model and job aids for use in the field by line managers and training practitioners as well as the academic community.

- to design a strategy for the continuing development of products that meet the needs of users in business, industry, government, and education.

To date, the competency study has been expanded to include the entire HRD field instead of only the training and development area, which was the focus of the 1983 study. This includes the addition of career development to the Human Resource Wheel (Figure 1.7). Standards were developed for each of the 102 outputs. Several new roles and competencies were identified while others were eliminated (see Figure 14.4).

NEW MODELS FOR HRD PRACTICE, 1989

NEW ROLES (1989)	OLD ROLES (1983) ELIMINATED
Administrator	Group Facilitator
Individual Career Counselor	Individual Development Counselor
Instructor/Facilitator	Instructional Writer
HRD Material Developer	Media Specialist
Organizational Change Agent	Program Administrator
Researcher	Strategist
	Theoretician
	Transfer Agent

NEW COMPETENCIES (1989)	OLD COMPETENCIES ELIMINATED
Business understanding	A/V skill
Coaching skills	Counseling
Electronic systems skills	Library skill
Information search skills	Relationship versatility
Observing skills	T & D Field understanding
OD theories and techniques understandings	
Project management skills	
Program authority	
Language skills	
Relationship building	
Self knowledge	
Subject matter understanding	
Visionary skills	

Figure 14.4   Differences in the 1989 ASTD New Models in HRD Practice and 1983 ASTD Models for Excellence Competency Study

IBSTPI STUDY (1984, 1988)

In December 1984, a nonprofit organization was formed to promote the high standards of professional practice in training, performance, and instruction. The purpose of this 15-member board is to conduct research that leads to the development of competencies for the primary HRD and performance technologist roles. In 1986, IBSTPI published its first competency study, entitled *Instructional Design Competencies: The Standards*. This study was based on the research conducted by the NSPI/DID(AECT) Joint Certification Task Force. In fact, many of the members of the original IBSTPI Board of Directors were members of this task force. In 1988 IBSTPI published its second competency study entitled *Instructor Competencies*, which is directed at the role of learning specialist in HRD. The board also published a set of ethical statements for the field in the summer of 1988. Currently, IBSTPI is engaged in research regarding (1) HRD manager competencies and (2) performance technologist competencies. The goal of this organization is to research and publish competency studies for each of the principal roles by 1995.

CONCLUSION

During the past 40 years the field of HRD has grown from a small post-war discipline into a 210-billion-dollar annual industry. This growth may be attributed to the increased professionalization efforts of the major HRD-related professional associations and societies, as well as to the importance placed on human resources within organizations.

There are four perspectives from which one can approach professionalization: philosophical, developmental, characteristics, and nontraditional. Three of these four emphasize the importance of professional development through professional certification. It is important to remember that all four orientations maintain the need for and importance of a body of knowledge and set of professional competencies. This is evident in each of the nine major studies reviewed. It is, therefore, not surprising that much attention has been paid to the issue of professional certification and competencies that are unique to HRD. In fact, over 98 percent of all professional certification programs are based on the competencies unique to their occupational fields (Gilley, 1985: Gilley & Galbraith, 1988). HRD is no exception.

CHAPTER 15

Careers in Human Resource Development

Objectives

After completing Chapter 15, readers should be able to

- describe the scope of human resource development activities in terms of employment.

- list several employment opportunities available in HRD.

- name several rewards associated with work in HRD.

- complete a self-assessment in preparation for employment in HRD.

- describe several possible career paths in HRD.

- tell of the future prognosis for employment in HRD.

Many readers of this book will not be currently employed in HRD settings and so will be curious about the field. They will have questions about the scope of HRD activities and employment opportunities, including available jobs and salary figures. They will also need help in planning for a career in HRD, as well as in exploring initial employment and career paths. Finally, they will need information about future employment projections and about sources of additional information about HRD careers. This chapter will supply a great deal of information in response to many needs and questions like these.

WHAT IS THE SCOPE OF HUMAN RESOURCE DEVELOPMENT ACTIVITIES?

This book is filled with answers to the question, "What is human resource development?" There will certainly be no attempt to recount them all in these paragraphs. Rather, an attempt will be made to review some of the basics of the field to the extent that they are relevant to careers.

In 1981, the American Society for Training and Development began work on the identification of the roles and competencies required of practitioners in training and development, which is, of course, a major part of the HRD field. The Human Resource Wheel was developed to give some order to a modest amount of confusion regarding its scope and roles (see Figure 1.7 in Chapter 1).

The term "human resource development" in this context includes the broad spectrum of activities within an organization that relates to the development of people in the organization and that has implications for employment. These include training and development, organization development, and career development. The Human Resource Wheel also includes most of the functions traditionally associated with corporate personnel and human resource planning departments. The concentration in this chapter will be on the careers most closely associated with the HRD segment of the wheel.

ROLES AND COMPETENCIES

The career-oriented person within HRD will be interested in examining assorted roles that might be carried out. McLagan and Bedrick, in their Model for Excellence Study, have identified and described several roles. The list of these roles in Chapter 1 (Figure 1.8) will provide some clue to the myriad of positions and specialties available in the realm of HRD. Each of them, of course, can become the focus of a career in HRD.

It is not enough simply to identify an appealing career area in HRD and then expect to enter it. One must be qualified for entry to and progression through an assortment of careers. Discussion about attributes required of persons in HRD seems to be settling around the word *competency*. Competencies are abilities that people possess that enable them to complete a role. They have been defined more formally as the knowledges and skills that are key to producing the critical outputs of the training and development field as well as its roles. Many readers will already possess many of the competencies needed for employment in HRD, acquired through preparation in colleges and universities, and in training for other employment, or as an employee in an organization. It is probable that a perusal of the list of competencies in Figure 14.3 will reveal several they already possess. Thirty-one general competency areas have been identified as useful to people working in training and development.

The career explorer in HRD might use this list in relation to his or her work experience. A positive relationship between work experience and the competency or competencies required will uncover important clues in the career search. But if there is neither experience with nor interest in any of the competencies, one might want to reconsider the challenges and opportunities of an HRD career.

OPPORTUNITIES IN HUMAN RESOURCE DEVELOPMENT

The wise career explorer in any area will put a great deal of energy into studying the opportunities that are available—both in terms of available jobs and salaries. It is with this information that the career seeker is most likely to achieve success.

What are the available jobs in HRD? And how available are they? For answers to these questions, we consulted a recent HRD industry report published by *Training* magazine. The report gleaned a wide variety of information from over 2,400 respondents, and prominent among the information gathered are clues to current employment levels in HRD. Table 15.1 indicates the numbers and percentages of HRD employees in various industrial classifications. Figure 15.1 suggests the geographical distribution of HRD activities by region, indicating a heavy concentration in the central and eastern parts of the United States.

Finally, it is useful to know about types of training. In looking at the destination of HRD dollars, Gordon (1988) developed a table that describes 15 general types of training (see Table 15.2). This again provides valuable information for exploring HRD careers. The task is to match types of training done to skills and interests possessed. This activity will certainly help to make any job search more efficient and rewarding.

Table 15.1   Industrial Classifications

Industry	Number	% of Sample
Manufacturing	344	23.0
Transportation/Communications/Utilities	127	8.5
Wholesale/Retail Trade	118	7.9
Finance/Insurance/Banking	243	16.2
Business Services	151	10.1
Health Services	138	9.2
Educational Services	115	7.7
Public Administration	196	13.1
Other (Mining, Construction, Agriculture)	64	4.3
Total	1,456	100.0

Reprinted from D. Feuer, Training Magazine Industry Report, copyright 1988 Training Magazine. Reprinted by permission.

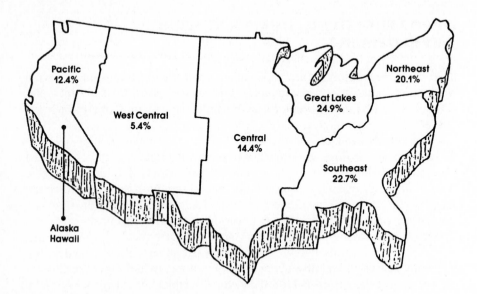

Figure 15.1   Distribution of respondents by region

Reprinted from D. Feuer, 1988 Training Magazine Industry Report, copyright 1988 Training Magazine. Reprinted by permission.

Table 15.2   General Types of Training

Types of Training	% Providing[1]	In-House Only (%)[2]	Outside Only (%)[3]	Both (%)[4]
Management Skills/ Development	81.3	11.3	14.7	55.3
Supervisory Skills	78.9	15.4	13.4	50.1
Technical Skills/ Knowledge	76.4	26.4	5.8	44.2
Communication Skills	72.1	15.0	12.4	44.7
Customer Relations/ Services	63.6	18.3	8.0	37.3
Clerical/Secretarial Skills	59.7	15.6	14.9	29.2
Basic Computer Skills	59.2	15.6	14.5	29.1
New Methods/Procedures	58.6	30.2	2.1	26.3
Personal Growth	56.0	11.2	13.4	31.4
Executive Development	55.8	5.4	20.5	29.9
Sales Skills	47.8	11.5	8.0	28.3
Wellness	45.5	13.3	13.0	19.2
Employee/Labor Relations	45.3	15.3	10.2	19.8
Customer Education	38.3	20.1	2.1	16.1
Remedial Basic Education	24.3	6.2	9.5	8.6

Of All Organizations With 50 or More Employees . . .
[1]*Percent that provide each type of training.*
[2]*Percent that say all training of this type is designed and delivered by in-house staff.*
[3]*Percent that say all training of this type is designed and delivered by outside consultants or vendors.*
[4]*Percent that say training of this type is designed and delivered by a combination of in-house staff and outside vendors.*

Reprinted from J. Gordon, "Who is being Trained to do What?," copyright 1988 Training Magazine. *Reprinted by permission.*

THE REWARDS OF WORKING IN HRD

Most professionals working in the realm of human resource development find many of the rewards to be intrinsic. They know they are appreciated and they get a great deal of satisfaction from the knowledge that they do excellent and important work. All of that is a very pleasant result of satisfying employment. Most job seekers, however, are also interested in remuneration. How *much* is the salary?

Training magazine does an annual survey of salaries paid to people working in HRD. The figures in the November 1988 issue will likely become dated relatively soon, but they are useful in the comparisons they make possible. The most recent survey shows the average salary to be $39,744. Table 15.3, a comprehensive view of their survey, provides a great deal of information about one's salary potential.

Most of the information is self-explanatory; however, some of the categories deserve mention. It is interesting to note that the largest salaries are paid on the Pacific Coast. This goes against conventional wisdom that suggests higher pay is available in the East. As one might expect, the largest salaries are paid in the largest organizations. A casual study of the industry categories suggests that the largest salaries are paid to trainees in the private sector. Educational level, years of experience, and age all follow the axiom that "more is better"—at least in terms of salary.

Most disturbing among the results is the discrepant nature of salaries paid to men and women. Men, for no apparent reason (other than sex bias), earn almost 30 percent more than women in HRD. Even more distressing is the observation that this gap is tending to get wider rather than narrower.

Finally, in the salary area, *Training* magazine has also provided a method for determining salary worth. To walk through these calculations, start with the base figure of $18,612 (regardless of actual salary), then add or subtract the dollar amount indicated after each variable. For example, an HRD manager who manages five or more full-time employees would add $6,974; a classroom trainer is an "other" and would add nothing (figure 15.2).

Table 15.3   Summary of Findings of *Training's* 1988 Salary Survey

Factor	% of Sample	Average Salary
Location		
Pacific	14.1	$40,377
West Central	6.2	37,014
Central	14.4	38,504
Great Lakes	23.2	40,272
Northeast	22.4	40,630
Southeast	19.7	39,448
Employee Size		
Less than 500	42.2	38,557
500 to 2,499	26.8	38,248
2,500 or more	31.0	43,117

Gross Sales/Assets

$19.9 million or less	35.6	38,859
$20 to $499.9 million	38.9	39,573
$500 million or more	25.5	43,770

Industry

Manufacturing	19.9	42,056
Transportation/ Communications/Utilities	9.4	46,037
Wholesale/Retail Trade	9.6	40,355
Finance/Insurance/Banking	15.6	35,169
Business Services	14.0	41,191
Health Services	9.0	37,857
Educational Services	10.4	38,878
Public Administration	11.9	35,927

Sex

Male	52.4	44,582
Female	47.6	33,920

Educational Level

No college degree	19.1	35,189
Bachelor's	19.2	35,780
Bachelor's +	19.7	39,481
Master's	35.0	42,084
Ph.D.	7.0	51,921

Years of Experience

3 or less	35.9	34,037
4 to 7	27.4	41,076
8 to 12	21.4	41,665
13 or more	15.2	47,508

Age

Under 30	12.7	28,510
30 to 35	22.3	34,733
36 to 44	37.5	40,807
45 or older	27.9	46,436

Reprinted from B. Geber, Training's 1988 Salary Survey, copyright 1988 Training *Magazine. Reprinted by permission.*

SELF-ASSESSMENT IN PREPARATION FOR EMPLOYMENT

Completion of the Salary Work Sheet in Figure 15.2 will provide entree to a more comprehensive process designed to lend some reality to individual career exploration. The reader will get a better understanding of the employment environments that are most consistent with interests. The process centers around an assessment of oneself, with the objective of identifying one's values, interests,

You've pored over all the charts that preceded this one, but still you're just not sure how your salary compares to your peers'. In the interest of resolving the mystery, we offer this work sheet, which you can use to figure out whether your salary is in line with that of other HRD professionals who have similar qualifications.

Start with the base salary (no matter what your salary actually is), and work through all the calculations to reach a final figure. For instance, if you're a training manager who oversees up to four full-time trainers, add $2,799 to the base salary. If you're an instructional designer, you fall within the "other" category. Add nothing to the base amount.

This work sheet was developed using a multiple regression analysis on information provided by 1,093 respondents to TRAINING's Readership Survey. —B.G.

Salary Work Sheet		
Base Salary	+ $18,612	$18,612
Specific Job Description		
Executive-level training/HRD manager (other training managers report to me)	+ $17,416	_____
Training manager (five or more full-time trainers report to me)	+ $ 6,974	_____
Training manager (one to four full-time trainers report to me)	+ $ 2,799	_____
Personnel or line staff manager	+ $ 7,892	_____
Other	-0-	_____
Education		
B.A. or some postbaccalaureate	+ $ 3,342	_____
M.A. or M.B.A.	+ $ 6,314	_____
Ph.D.	+ $11,005	_____
Gross Sales		
$500 million or more	+ $ 4,458	_____
Less than $500 million	-0-	_____
Age		
Your age × $550	+ $_____	_____
Gender		
Male	-0-	_____
Female	− $ 5,422	_____
Primary Training Activity		
Technical	− $ 2,515	_____
Other	-0-	_____
Industrial Classification		
Public Administration	− $ 8,728	_____
Finance/Insurance/Banking	− $ 6,404	_____
Health or Education Services	− $ 7,309	_____
Manufacturing	− $ 3,049	_____
Other	-0-	_____
Location		
Pacific	+ $ 3,786	_____
Central or West Central	− $ 4,950	_____
Other	-0-	_____
TOTAL		$_____

Figure 15.2   How much are you worth as an HRD employee?

Reprinted from B. Geber, 1988 Training Magazine Salary Survey, copyright 1988 Training Magazine. Reprinted by permission.

skills, and so on with an eye toward creating the best match between employee and employment.

The first step in any self-assessment leading toward career choice within HRD is an examination of one's interests, values, preferences, and so forth in relation to human resource development. Normally, job satisfaction is predicated on a satisfactory career environment in HRD. The factors are usually grouped into five areas—geography; goals, purposes, and values; social environment; working conditions; and money, time, and level of responsibility.

1. Geography. Among the first—though probably not most important—variables people often consider is where they want to work. They look at such geographic variables as

- Average temperature, rainfall, humidity
- Recreation facilities available
- Amount of time spent commuting to and from work
- How I want to commute—(car, public, carpool)
- Change of seasons or constant weather
- Flat or hilly, colorful or monochrome
- Urban or rural
- Crime level and safety of person and property
- Risk index (flood, earthquake, nuclear war, tornadoes)
- Amount/quality of cultural events
- Fine/performing arts
- Available schooling for children
- Close/far from neighbors
- Quality of public services and government

Answering questions related to these factors should give the HRD career explorer a good notion of the part of the world that would provide the most pleasant surroundings.

2. Goals, purposes, and values. The honest identification of employment goals, purposes, and values, although not easy, is very rewarding.

- Making money
- Solving social problems
- Creating innovative technology
- Being influential
- Improving the quality of life
- Proving something to oneself
- Helping others learn
- Being a lifelong learner
- Travel

- Raising a family
- Enjoying oneself
- Self-improvement and development
- Being seen as an expert will be very helpful
- Meeting challenges

Employment can be found in HRD that will emphasize or deemphasize any of these variables.

3. Social environment. To many, who they work with is the most important aspect of employment. "Life is too short," they say, "to spend it with people who aren't compatible." Considering some of the following characteristics of potential fellow employees will be very important.

- Organized
- Disorganized
- Thinkers and watchers
- Doers
- Individual entrepreneurs
- Team members
- Tolerant of others
- Roles clearly defined
- Mostly one age/gender/education level
- Optimists
- Friendly/quiet/nosey
- Devoted to organization's goals
- Single leader/shared leadership
- Gather outside work hours
- Honest
- Open communications/secrecy
- Quality of health
- "Games" players
- Like to work with/for other people
- Leaders
- Persuaders
- Detail and people checkers
- Good with numbers

4. Working conditions. Closely related to several of the foregoing variables are the working conditions in HRD that one is expected to enjoy or at least tolerate. The wise career explorer will decide, for example, whether he or she likes

- Lots of people around
- Flexible schedules
- A chance to walk around during day
- Time pressures
- Needed supplies/machines readily available
- To have one's own boss
- Windows
- A formal dress code
- Good lighting
- Personal space neat/cluttered
- To be able to close door to own space
- Business travel
- Fixed standards of excellence
- Fixed hours per day/per week
- Subsidized coffee, tea, cafeteria
- Free use of a phone
- Smokers separated
- Lots of color/wall decorations
- Background music
- Access to employer
- Open communications
- Group decision making

Answers to questions associated with these factors are easily acquired during a job interview.

5. Money, time, and level of responsibility. This is a catch-all category that covers many of the aspects of compensation, duties, and so on associated with employment in HRD. One should consider each of the aspects listed below and be ready to ask questions about them during a job interview.

- Salary or commission
- 60-weeks
- Authority over others
- Direct staff work
- Outcomes used to judge performance
- Having the buck stop with you
- Fringe benefits to match needs
- How much money do you need to live your lifestyle?
- How much do you want to make in five years?

- Time for family and friends
- High risk/high gain
- Produce products
- Deliver services
- Follow orders
- Work in one's field
- Continue to do what one does well
- Do new things
- Upward mobility

Finally, HRD self-assessment involves examining the competence that can be brought to the HRD employment setting. There is probably no better way to do this than to reference it to the ASTD competency study. To help with this process, we have relied on an ASTD-produced questionnaire (Figure 15.3) that asks the respondent first to select three training and development roles and then to evaluate skill level in 31 competency areas. Next, the chart in Figure 15.4 provides a scoring mechanism to determine strengths and weaknesses.

Directions: Complete the questionnaire which follows. Use it to asssess your HRD strengths and weaknesses and as a guide for preparing for a job in the field. Compare your answers to the competencies associated with different roles in Figure 5.6.

ASTD COMPETENCY STUDY

A. From the list of 15 possible Training and Development Roles below, select the three roles that are *most important to you* by "X"ing the box to the left of those roles. The roles may be important for your present job or for a future job. They will be the roles that you want to emphasize in your self-development planning.

☐ 1. EVALUATOR... The role of identifying the extent of a program, service or product's impact. Key outputs: *reports* (written and oral) of program impact on organization and individuals, *evaluation designs* and plans, *instruments* to assess program and instructional quality, and individual change.

☐ 2. GROUP FACILITATOR... The role of managing group discussions and group process so that individuals learn and group members feel the experience is positive. Key outputs: *group decisions* where individuals all feel committed to action; enhanced *awareness* of group *process*, self and other, *discussions* in which issues and needs are constructively assessed; *cohesive* teams.

☐ 3. INDIVIDUAL DEVELOPMENT COUNSELOR... The role of helping an individual assess personal competencies, values and goals, and identify and plan development and career actions. Key outputs: enhanced *skills of individuals* in identifying and carrying out development needs/goals, *tools* and resources for career development, individual career development *plans, knowledge of* where to get development support.

☐ 4. INSTRUCTIONAL WRITER ... The role of preparing written learning and instructional materials. Key outputs: teaching guides, manuals and job aids, exercises, workbooks, worksheets, role plays, simulations, games, case studies, tests, evaluation forms, scripts.

☐ 5. INSTRUCTOR... The role of presenting information and directing structured learning experiences so that individuals learn. Key outputs: students' *needs* addressed, individuals with *new knowledge, skill, attitudes or behavior* in their repertoires; lectures, *presentations*, stories delivered; structured learning events directed.

☐ 6. MANAGER OF TRAINING AND DEVELOPMENT... The role of planning, organizing staffing, controlling training and development operations or training and developent projects, and of linking training and development operations with other organization units. Key outputs: department or project *objectives; budgets; staff* selected, developed and evaluated; T&D actions *congruent* with other HR and organization actions; positive work *climate; information* exchanged; problem *solutions;* T&D *standards, policies and procedures.*

☐ 7. MARKETER ... The role of selling Training and Development viewpoints, learning packages, programs and services to target audiences outside one's own work unit. Key outputs; *marketing plans* developed and implemented, sales *presentations, leads, promotional* materials, *contracts.*

☐ 8. MEDIA SPECIALIST... The role of producing software for and using audio, visual, computer and other hardware-based technologies for training and development. Key outputs: *advice* and counsel to media users, video-based *material, graphics, lists* of recommended instructional hardware. AV *equipment* in working order, production *plans*, software and hardware *recommendations*.

☐ 9. NEEDS ANALYST... The role of defining gaps between ideal and actual performance and specifying the cause of the gaps. Key outputs: written and oral *reports* on performance problems, and on knowledge, skill and attitude discrepancies; inferences of *causes* of discrepancies; needs analysis *strategies and tools*.

☐ 10. PROGRAM ADMINISTRATOR... The role of ensuring that the facilities, equipment, materials, participants and other components of a learning event are present and that program logistics run smoothly. Key outputs: *contingency* plans for emergencies; selection and scheduling of *facilities, equipment and faculty; course material* distributed; participant *attendance* secured and recorded.

☐ 11. PROGRAM DESIGNER... The role of preparing objectives, defining content, selecting and sequencing activities for a specific program. Key outputs: *specifications, sequencing* plans and *priorities* for training content, activities, materials and methods; lists of learning *objectives;* written program *plans* and designs; contingency plans and *implementation* strategies.

☐ 12. STRATEGIST... The role of developing long-range plans for what the training and development structure, organizaton, direction, policies, programs, services and practices will be in order to accomplish the training and development misson. Key outputs: identification of *long-range* T&D strengths, weaknesses, opportunities, threats; long-range *plans* included in the broad human resource strategy of the organization; identification of *forces and trends* affecting T&D; *alternative directions* for T&D.

☐ 13. TASK ANALYST... Identifying activities, tasks, sub-tasks, human resources and support requirements necessary to accomplish specific results in a job or organization. Key outputs: *lists* of key job/unit *tasks and outputs;* lists of knowledge/skill/attitude *requirements* of job/units; *descriptions* of performance levels, sub-tasks, tasks and job clusters; descriptions of *conditions* for job performance.

☐ 14. THEORETICIAN... The role of developing and testing theories of learning, training, and development. Key outputs: new *concepts and theories* of learning and behavior change; training *models* and applications of theory; *articles* on T&D issues; research *designs* and reports.

☐ 15. TRANSFER AGENT... The role of helping individuals apply learning after the learning experience. Key outputs: plans for support of transfer of learning; individual action plans for on-the-job/real world application.

B. Evaluate your present level of competency on each of the 31 competencies listed below using the following scale:

   1. *Low or beginning* level of competency. Probably not familiar with some of the key principles; not especially confident about demonstrating this competency in relatively simple situations.

   2. *Intermediate* level of competency. Having a deep understanding and skills; able to function in a broad range of moderately difficult situations.

   3. *Advanced* level of competency. Having a broad and deep understanding and skills; able to function in complex, varied situations and be a model of subject matter mastery and skills.

	ADVANCED	INTERMEDIATE	BEGINNING
1. *Adult-Learning Understanding*... Knowing how adults acquire and use knowledge, skills, attitudes. Understanding individual differences in learning.	( )	( )	( )
2. *A/V Skill*... Selecting and using audio/visual hardware and software	( )	( )	( )
3. *Career-Development Knowledge*... Understanding the personal and organizational issues and practices relevant to individual careers.	( )	( )	( )
4. *Competency-Identification Skill*... Identifying the knowledge and skill requirements of jobs, tasks, roles.	( )	( )	( )
5. *Computer Competence*... Understanding and being able to use computers.	( )	( )	( )
6. *Cost/Benefit-Analysis Skill*... Assessing alternatives in terms of their financial, psychological, and strategic advantages or disadvantages.	( )	( )	( )
7. *Counseling Skill*... Helping individuals recognize and understand personal needs, values, problems, alternatives and goals.	( )	( )	( )
8. *Data-Reduction Skill*... Scanning, synthesizing, and drawing conclusions from data.	( )	( )	( )
9. *Delegating Skill*... Assigning task responsibility and authority to others.	( )	( )	( )

(Figure 15.3 continued)

10. *Facilities Skill* ... Planning and coordinating logistics in an efficient and cost-effective manner .... ( ) ( ) ( )

11. *Feedback Skill* ... Communicating opinions, observations and conclusions so that they are understood. .... ( ) ( ) ( )

12. *Futuring Skill* ... Projecting trends and visualizing possible and probable futures and their implications .... ( ) ( ) ( )

13. *Group-Process Skill* ... Influencing groups to both accomplish tasks and fulfill the needs of their members. .... ( ) ( ) ( )

14. *Industry Understanding* ... Knowing the key concepts and variables that define an industry or sector (i.e., critical issues, economic vulnerabilities, measurements, distribution channels, inputs, outputs, information sources) . ( ) ( ) ( )

15. *Intellectual Versatility* ... Recognizing, exploring and using a broad range of ideas and practices. Thinking logically and creatively without undue influence from personal biases. .... ( ) ( ) ( )

16. *Library Skill* ... Gathering information from printed and other recorded sources. Identifying and using information specialists and reference services and aids. .... ( ) ( ) ( )

17. *Model-Building Skill* ... Developing theoretical and practical frameworks which describe complex ideas in understandable, usable ways. .... ( ) ( ) ( )

18. *Negotiation Skill* ... Securing win-win agreements while successfully representing a special interest in a decision situation. .... ( ) ( ) ( )

19. *Objectives-Preparation Skill* ... Preparing clear statements which describe desired outputs .... ( ) ( ) ( )

20. *Organization-Behavior Understanding* ... Seeing organizations as dynamic, political, economic and social systems which have multiple goals; using this larger perspective as a framework for understanding and influencing events and change .... ( ) ( ) ( )

21. *Organization Understanding* ... Knowing the strategy, structure, power networks, financial position, systems of a SPECIFIC organization .... ( ) ( ) ( )

22. *Performance-Observation Skill* ... Tracking and describing behaviors and their effects. .... ( ) ( ) ( )

23. *Personal/HR-Field Understanding* ... Understanding issues and practices in other HR areas (Organization Development, Organization Job Design, Human Resource Planning, Selection and Staffing, Personnel Research and Information Systems, Compensation and Benefits, Employee Assistance, Union/Labor Relations) .... ( ) ( ) ( )

24. *Presentation Skill* ... Verbally presenting information so that the intended purpose is achieved. .... ( ) ( ) ( )

25. *Questioning Skill* ... Gathering information from and stimulating insight in individuals and groups through the use of interviews, questionnaires and other probing methods. .... ( ) ( ) ( )

26. *Records-Management Skill* ... Storing data in easily retrievable form ...... ( ) ( ) ( )

27. *Relationship Versatility* ... Adjusting behavior in order to establish relationships across a broad range of people and groups. .... ( ) ( ) ( )

28. *Research Skill* ... Selecting, developing and using methodologies, statistical and data collection techniques for a formal inquiry .... ( ) ( ) ( )

29. *Training-and-Development-Field Understanding* ... Knowing the technological, social, economic, professional and regulatory issues in the field; understanding the role T&D plays in helping individuals learn for current and future jobs .... ( ) ( ) ( )

30. *Training-and-Development Techniques Understanding* ... Knowing the techniques and methods used in training; understanding their appropriate uses. .... ( ) ( ) ( )

31. *Writing Skill* ... Preparing written material which follows generally accepted rules of style and form, is appropriate for the audience, creative, and accomplishes its intended purposes. .... ( ) ( ) ( )

Figure 15.3   ASTD self-assessment questionnaire

Reprinted from ASTD's Model for Excellence Self-Assessment Questionnaire, 1983. Reprinted by permission. All rights reserved.

DIRECTIONS: Compare your answers on the questionnaire in Figure 15.3 to the competencies listed in this figure. Use a blank sheet of paper to list differences between actual and desirable skill levels for the roles in which you wish to be proficient.

THE ROLES/COMPETENCIES MATRIX

This chart illustrates the level of expertise required in each competency area. Competencies and roles are both listed from most to least frequently occurring.

- ● = Advanced requirement.
- ○ = Intermediate requirement.

Requirements are only listed for competencies which sixty percent (60%) or more role respondents said are critical now and/or in five years for the role.

	Manager	Marketer	Instructional Writer	Media Specialist	Needs Analyst	Group Facilitator	Strategist	Evaluator
15. Intellectual Vers.	●	○	●	●	●	●	●	
11. Feedback Skill	●	○	●	●	●	●*		
1. Adult Lrng. Und.	○		●	●		●		
25. Questioning Skill		●	●	○	●	●		●*
5. Computer Comp.	○	○	○	●*	○			○
8. Data reduction Skill	●		●		●		●	●*
20. Org. Behavior Und.	●*	○			●	●	●	
31. Writing Skills		●	●*	●				○
4. Competency ID.			○		●			○
19. Object Prep.		●	●	○				
24. Presentation Skill	●	●*	●	●				○
27. Relationship Vers.	●	●				●*		
30. T&D Techniques Und.			●	○		○		
14. Industry Und.	●	●*	●	○			●	
21. Organization Und.	●	●			○		●*	
6. Cost/Benefit Analysis	●*	○		○			●	
12. Futuring Skill	●	●					●*	
13. Group Process Skill	●	●				●*		
17. Model Building Skill			●				●	
22. Perf. Observ. Skill					●	●		●
18. Negotiation Skill	●	●*				○		
28. Research Skills					○			●*
2. AV Skill				●*				
3. Career Dvlp. Know.	○							
7. Counseling Skill		○						
10. Facilities Skill				○				
15. Library Skills			●*	○				
23. Pers./HR Field Und.	○						●*	
26. Records Mgnt. Skill								
29. T&D Field Und.	●						●*	
9. Delegation Skill	●*							
TOTALS	18	16	14	14	10	10	10	8

* Indicates the highest expertise level for the competency.

Figure 15.4   Scoring the questionnaire

Reprinted from Models for Excellence, *American Society for Training and Development. Reprinted by permission. All rights reserved.*

People employed in HRD are identified in three different contexts. There are those who are professionally identified, those who are organizationally identified, and those who are collaterally identified. These labels are described and discussed in Chapter 1.

INITIAL EMPLOYMENT IN HRD

Once the self-assessment is finished and (presumably) indicates some degree of potential satisfaction with a career in human resource development, the potential career seeker is faced with entering that first job. How is that done? This question is difficult to answer because a number of considerations are involved. Some organizations want trainers who have worked elsewhere in the organization and who know the organization. Other organizations want to recruit specialists from outside. To get into HRD, one must have what some organizations wants, and what organizations want differ.

Many HRD practitioners begin with an organization in a technical or managerial capacity, then move into HRD, not because they planned it that way, but because some organizations tend to recruit for training positions from within. Human resource positions are highly visible, and recruiting from within has two advantages. Organizations get people they know and trust. They also get people who are already oriented to the organization and can focus immediately on the training job to be done rather than first having to learn the organization. If technical background and organizational skills are heavily weighted in the selection process, trainers are likely to be teaching others to do jobs that they themselves had performed previously. Salespeople become trainers of salespeople; engineers train new engineers; experienced managers train younger ones.

If someone is outside the field and wants to get in, that individual must figure out what he or she can do that is a training activity and sell him or herself on that basis. For example, if one is in education, one may already be a skilled presenter or competent in designing and producing programs. If in sales, one has product knowledge in a specific area, and knows the techniques that have worked.

Another way to enter is through part-time or volunteer work. It may be possible to develop a seminar or workshop that is in demand, do it for various organizations part-time while working in another position, and eventually discover an organization that wants your services full-time. If you are still in school, an internship or special project or special assignment may provide this opportunity.

As an example, we know of an HRD manager who began working life as a secondary-school marketing teacher. He later played some professional basketball, planned and supervised fast-food establishment construction, and worked as a cooperative education coordinator. Finally, after the acquisition of a second college degree, he entered the field as a trainer and is now an HRD manager in a prominent defense industry business. This scenario demonstrates the uniqueness and variety among HRD career paths.

DEVELOPING A CAREER PATH IN HRD

Once an initial job in HRD is acquired it is no time to cease thinking about career development. That job is only the first step on a career path, or the first rung on a career ladder. Effectively managing a career in HRD requires that a great deal of time, effort, and energy be invested. The kinds of efforts that must be expended include the following:

Set clear and specific goals. Contrary to the myth that goal setting limits or restricts HRD career options, carefully worked out goals move you toward those choices that best suit individual values, desires, and skills. Set goals that describe wants and where they might be achieved in the HRD field.

Spend time determining strategies that can move you toward goals. Identify the next step. It may be a new assignment in the same job, a different job in the organization, moving to a different organization, or some skill-building activity done on a volunteer basis for a professional or community group interested in HRD.

Be flexible. When determining goals and strategies for achieving them, try to determine a number of alternatives for reaching the same goal. Evaluate opportunities as they come along, based on the likelihood each has for progress toward the goal. Over time, goals may lose their appeal. Be flexible here, too. Rethink goals if they no longer seem to "fit."

Know yourself. Self-assessment, using HRD competencies in part as criteria, cannot be overemphasized in career management. Always be willing to accept and examine information about skills, interests, values, and so forth.

Work continuously at a personal development plan. Whether working at building technical skills for HRD, personal relationships, or anything else, you should work at growing. First, set personal development goals to meet requirements for the next step in the career plan. Ask others to help identify these needs. This will help get realistic information to work with and may help cement relationships for a career network.

Learn to analyze the organization. It is commonplace to be so involved with function within an organization that one forgets to step back and analyze it from a broad perspective. Being able to identify emerging sources of power within the company, trends in management style or emphasis, future HRD needs of the company, career paths, work styles, or processes that have been effective for others gives powerful information on which to base approaches to career management.

Take some risks. Create new roles, functions, and structures that meet HRD needs. Be creative. Test the system to see if these innovations will be accepted. Risk using nontraditional, as well as traditional, career strategies. Invent opportunities. Don't just wait for them to happen.

Be patient. Although it is probably not true that "all things come to those who wait," it is true that it takes time and work to build a career in HRD. For those who think this sounds like drudgery, it does not have to be. Work is fun! There are always rewards. Look for those that are already there. Invent others in HRD when more are needed.

Where one goes in HRD depends largely upon whether one wants to remain in HRD or move on to other occupations and to what degree of specification or generalization one wants to pursue. The answers to these questions will help you to choose from many available career paths.

Getting into HRD as a stepping-stone to other positions can be a wise choice. High visibility, the opportunity to increase interpersonal skill levels, and direct contact with high-level decision makers in the organization can come with many HRD positions.

If one chooses to stay in the HRD field, there are many career choices still to make. Remaining in a single organization is one option. Career growth within a single company or agency comes as expertise is recognized, with more challenging risks, and with heightened organizational influence. More often HRD managers move either to successively larger organizations or to increasingly higher level positions in similar-sized organizations.

An increasing number of HRD managers work as external consultants. Many work alone or in small consulting organizations. Others work in larger consulting companies. The consultants' work is done in a variety of organizational settings, where they are brought in on a contract basis because of their special expertise. A few move from more traditional human resource development jobs to enter the academic world and become professors in programs designed to produce more HRD managers.

Some HRD managers become human resource generalists as their careers progress. They move from more specialized writing, media, or instructional jobs to management or administrative positions. Of these, some move vertically in the organization. Others move into higher levels. Their duties include HRD as well as related functions with equal employment opportunity, personnel, and manpower planning. Others who choose to become generalists remain in the HRD unit of the organization, functioning largely in planning and administrative capacities.

Other HRD professionals choose to become more specialized, concentrating on one content or skill area. Media specialists, organization development consultants, sales training experts, and career development counselors are examples of specialists within the field. It must be evident that career paths are as varied as pieces of art—as varied as the individuals creating them.

THE FUTURE OF HRD

What does the future hold for HRD professionals? We have no crystal ball, but some prognostic generalizations can be made. Chapter 16 is dedicated to discussing many of the issues confronting HRD and its practitioners. In terms of industries with greater opportunities for HRD specialists, communications, health services, banking/finance, and manufacturing seem to have a growing commitment to HRD and will employ large numbers of people. The joint impact of deregulation and technological advances in these industries makes HRD a strategic necessity. The industries that seem the worst in this regard include mining and oil, construction, and retail trade. All indications point to growth in numbers of positions available and in budgets allocated to perform the HRD functions.

LEARNING MORE ABOUT CAREERS IN HRD

There are literally hundreds of sources of information available to HRD career explorers. Several of the more widely available ones are listed below.

Albrecht, K., and Zemke, R. *Service America! Doing Business in the New Economy.* Homewood, IL: Dow Jones-Irwin, 1985.

Archer, E. Human resource professionalism: An Unexpected Source of Conflict. *Personnel Administrator, vol. 31* (1986): 97–98, 100, 102–104.

Bear, J. *How to Get the Degree You Want: Bear's Guide to Non-Traditional College Degrees,* 8th ed. Berkeley, CA: Ten Speed Press, 1982.

Bell, C. Training and Development in the 1980s. *Personnel Administrator* (August 1980).

Bolles, R. N. *Tea Leaves.* La Jolla, CA: Ten Speed Press, 1976.

Bolles, R. N. *What Color Is Your Parachute?* La Jolla, CA: Ten Speed Press, 1980.

Brinkerhoff, D., and Smith, A. Write a Resumé, Not an Obituary. *Training, 23* (1986): 37–39.

Carnevale, A., and Goldstein, H. *Employee Training: Its Changing Role and an Analysis of New Data.* Alexandria, VA: ASTD Press, 1983.

Chalofsky, N. E., and Cerio, J. A. Professional Development Program for Federal Government Trainers. *Training and Development Journal* (December 1975): 18–20.

Chalofsky, N. E., and Lincoln, C. I. *Up the HRD Ladder: A Guide for Professional Growth.* Reading, MA: Addison-Wesley, 1983.

Connor, R. A., Jr., and Davidson, J. P. *Marketing Your Consulting and Professional Services.* New York: Wiley, 1985.

Dalton, G. W., and Thompson, P. H. *Novations: Strategies for Career Management.* Glenview, IL: Scott, Foresman, 1986.

Drucker, P. *Managing in Turbulent Times.* New York: Harper & Row, 1980.

Hansen, G. Professional Education for Careers in Human Resource Administration. *Personnel Administrator, 29* (1) (1984): 69–70, 72–73, 75–76, 78–80, 95.

Haponski, W., and Haponski, S. eds. *Directory of External Degrees from Accredited Colleges and Universities.* Clayville, NY: ETC Associates, 1985.

Hatakeyama, Y. *Manager Revolution: A Guide to Survival in Today's Changing Workplace.* Cambridge, MA: Productivity Press, 1985.

Houze, W. C. *Career Veer.* New York: McGraw-Hill, 1985.

Hoyt, D. R., and Lewis, J. D. Planning for a Career in Human Resource Management. *Personnel Administrator* (October, 1980): 53–54, 67–68.

International Directory of Executive Recruiters. Fitzwilliam, NH: Consultants News, 1984.

Jackson, T. *Guerilla Tactics in the Job Market.* New York: Bantam Books, 1978.

Lippitt, G. L. Integrating Personal and Professional Development. *Training and Development Journal* (May 1980): 34–41.

Lobb, C. *Exploring Careers Through Volunteerism.* New York: Richards Rosen Press, 1976.

Loden, M. *Feminine Leadership or How to Succeed in Business Without Being One of the Boys.* Alexandria, VA: ASTD Press, 1987.

McCaskey, M. Goals and Directions in Personnel Planning. *The Academy of Management Review* (July 1977): 454–463.

McCullough, R. C. *Planning Your Professional Development in Human Resource Development.* Alexandria, VA: ASTD Press, 1987.

McLaughlin, J. E., and Merman, S. K. *Sound Advice for Job and Career Strategists.* Denver: Portland Management Group, 1977.

McLaughlin, J. E., and Merman, S. K. *Writing a Job-Winning Resumé.* Englewood Cliffs, N.J.: Prentice-Hall, 1980.

Miller, D. B. *Personal Vitality.* Reading, MA: Addison Wesley, 1977.

Morgan, B. S., and Schiemann, W. A. *Supervision in the '80s: Trends in Corporate America.* Princeton, NJ: Opinion Research Corp., 1984.

Nadler, L. A Model for Professional Development. *Training and Development Journal* (May 1980): 14–22.

Nadler, L. *The Handbook of Human Resource Development.* New York: Wiley, 1984.

Naisbitt, J. *The Year Ahead: These Ten Trends Will Shape the Way You Live, Work & Make Money in 1985.* Washington, DC: The Naisbitt Group, 1985.

Peterfreund, S. Education in Industry—Today and in the Future. *Training and Development Journal* (May 1976): 30–32.

Piercy, N., ed. *The Management Implications of the New Information Technology.* Beckenham Kent, England: Croom Helm Ltd., 1984.

Pinto, P. R., and Walker, J. W. *A Study of Professional Training and Development Roles and Competencies.* Alexandria, VA: ASTD Press, 1978.

Recruitment Services Directory. *Personnel Journal, 65* (8) (1986): 80–104.

Rukeysen, L. *What's Ahead for the Economy?* New York: Simon and Schuster, 1983.

Robinson, D.G., and Younglove, B. *Making Your Career Transition into External HRD Consulting.* Alexandria, VA: ASTD Press, 1986.

Schuman, N., and Lewis, W. *Revising Your Resumé.* New York: Wiley, 1986.

Skiervelm, T. Training: Evolution of a Profession. *Personnel Administrator* (October 1977): 13–16, 22.

Smart, J. *Guide to 5000 Home Study Diploma-Certificate Programs.* Rocheport, MO: Smartoo, 1984.

Smith, A. P. How to Make Sure Your Next Resumé Isn't an Obituary. *Training Management Review* (November 1977): 54–60.

Stump, R. W., and the HRD Careers Committee. *Your Career in Human Resource Development: A Guide to Information and Decision Making.* Alexandria, VA: ASTD Press, 1985.

Sullivan, E., ed. *Guide to External Degree Programs in the US.* Washington, DC: ACE, 1983.

Toffler, A. *The Adaptive Corporation.* New York: McGraw-Hill, 1985.

Wasserman, P., et al. *Learning Independently: A Directory of Self-Instruction Resources,* 2nd ed. Detroit: Gale Research, 1982.

Weiler, N. W. *Reality and Career Planning.* Reading, MA: Addison-Wesley, 1977.

Weiss, A. J. HRD in the Information Age. *Training* (October, 1981).

Zemke, R. Delayed Effects of Corporate Downsizing. *Training* (November 1986).

CHAPTER 16

The Future of Human Resource Development

Objectives

After completing Chapter 16, readers should be able to

- identify the factors (economic, political, sociological, and organizational) that will impact HRD in the future.

- describe each of these factors and their respective impacts.

- identify and describe the implications these factors will have on HRD and its practitioners.

- describe the role of the HRD practitioner in the future.

- describe the new role requirements of HRD practitioners.

- identify and describe the recommendations for HRD practitioners related to specific actions that must be taken by them.

Human resource development is one of the fastest-growing professions in the United States. Business spent $40 billion on HRD programs in 1988. Figure 16.1 shows how these expenditures are allocated for U.S. organizations

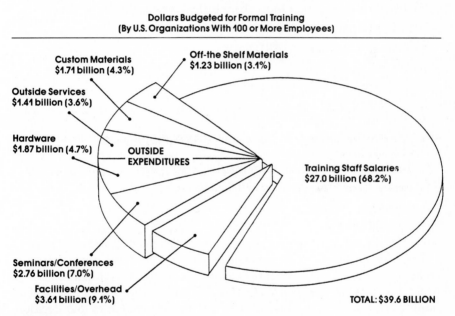

Dollars Budgeted for Formal Training
(By U.S. Organizations With 100 or More Employees)

Custom Materials
$1.71 billion (4.3%)

Off-the Shelf Materials
$1.23 billion (3.1%)

Outside Services
$1.41 billion (3.6%)

Hardware
$1.87 billion (4.7%)

OUTSIDE
EXPENDITURES

Training Staff Salaries
$27.0 billion (68.2%)

Seminars/Conferences
$2.76 billion (7.0%)

Facilities/Overhead
$3.61 billion (9.1%)

TOTAL: $39.6 BILLION

Definitions

Facilities/ Overhead—charges to the training department for buildings, classrooms or other space to be used, remodeled or built during 1988, and for utilities, administrative support from other departments, etc.

Outside Expenditures—dollar budgeted for the following five categories:

Seminars/Conferences—training by outside providers conducted either at the respondent's location or off-site, including public seminars but *not* trainee travel and per diem costs.

Hardware—audiovisual and video equipment, computers, teleconferencing equipment, etc.

Outside Services—consultants (not acting as seminar leaders), printing, material production costs, etc.

Custom Materials—audiovisual, video, printed material, computer courseware, etc., tailored to meet respondent's needs or designed specifically for respondent's organization.

Off-the-Shelf Materials—prepackaged in any format: books, films, computer courseware, structured classroom packages, etc.

Figure 16.1   Private-training expenditures

Reprinted from C. Lee, "Training Budgets: Neither Boom nor Bust," copyright 1988 Training Magazine. *Reprinted by permission.*

with 50 or more employees (Lee, 1988). During this same period, the government spent $60 billion. In addition, an estimated $180 billion was spent for formal and informal on-the-job training (ASTD, 1987). This amount of money now equals or exceeds what the nation spends for elementary, secondary, and higher education. The American Society for Training and Development (ASTD) estimated the investment by employers in employee education and training will increase by 25 to 30 percent by 1990 (Hale, 1987).

ECONOMIC, POLITICAL, SOCIOLOGICAL, AND ORGANIZATIONAL FACTORS

Economic, political, sociological, and organizational factors are expected to influence HRD during the 1990s. The principal *economic factors* will be

- Slow economic growth continues.
- Greater competition for HRD dollars.

Political factors will include

- Increased governmental regulation.
- Union activities.
- Professionalization of HRD practitioners.

The *sociological factors* that are expected to impact and affect HRD include

- Changes in the work force.
- Decline of the public school system.

And finally, *organizational factors* will include

- Changes in business structure and goods.
- Great advances in technology.

Each of these four categories of factors will affect the role of the HRD practitioner, prohibit the use of appropriate delivery systems, and impact program content, developers and deliverers, and learners in America's corporations. As a result, HRD practitioners will need to become more aware of their responsibilities for helping increase world human resource competencies and decision-making, and problem-solving capabilities. In addition, they must develop an understanding of cross-cultural values and beliefs. The shift from an industrial to a service-based economy will also affect the field of HRD.

ECONOMIC FACTORS

The Economy. The nation's economy will continue to grow at a slow pace, with the service industries increasing at the most rapid rate. As a result, HRD programs will increasingly be asked to assist managers in identifying service opportunities, to train customer service employees, and to train managers in intrapreneurial skills. Increased globalization of organizations and industries will continue, with the emphasis on international trade and marketing. HRD practitioners will need to develop skills in marketing and communication.

Competition for the HRD Dollar. Since the mid-sixties, hundreds of organizations have sprung up to compete for the ever-increasing HRD dollars, particularly the data processing industry, where technological change has meant constant training and retraining (Hale, 1987). In addition, consumers' habits affect HRD. Influenced by less product loyalty, fads, a desire to save, and demands for higher quality, HRD programs must adjust their learning programs to enable organizations to make their necessary adjustments. In addition, producers of HRD programs will have to be sensitive to packaging and marketing principles and strategies. They will have to weigh new delivery methods against industrial integrity. A shift from only productivity improvement training toward personal growth training will require a philosophical adjustment on the part of many HRD practitioners, plus increased competencies and skills.

Implications for HRD. All of the economic factors combine to provide important implications for the future of HRD. Hale (1987) identified three implications for HRD. *First,* HRD is shifting more and more to the workplace. *Second,* the ability of HRD practitioners to deliver knowledge and skills quickly to specifications is critical for success. *Third,* if HRD is to be effective, it must appeal to the learners' values, as well as satisfy personal and professional needs. In addition, HRD practitioners must make use of technology where appropriate to aid learning. Finally, HRD practitioners should encourage organizations to offer in-house retraining, outplacement services, and job redesign.

POLITICAL FACTORS

Governmental Regulation. It is difficult to predict, but increased government enforcement of current laws involving safety, comparable worth, EEO, and compliance with regulations will probably continue (Odiorne, 1985). Government emphasis on enforcement could force learning programs to include topics such as

- Why compliance is important
- What procedures are needed for compliance
- Procedures for documentary compliance
- How to conduct compliance audits (Hale, 1987, p. 24)

In the past, HRD specialists failed to prepare management for the economic effects of EEO and Affirmative Action. In the future, HRD is expected to be on the top of trends of this type. HRD practitioners must become better prepared to help management in these kinds of ways (Gentilman & Nelson, 1983).

According to Hale (1987), another area of concern is management's utilization of HRD programs for personnel decisions (recruiting, selection, promotion, etc.). HRD programs that claim to increase knowledge and skills will need valid and reliable tests. As a result, instructional programs will have to

be competency and/or performance based or they will jeopardize the organization.

HRD practitioners must also become aware of political/governmental trends
that may affect human resources. Also, HRD practices and procedures must be
in compliance with applicable laws and regulations.

Union Activities. According to Olson (1986), unions will also affect HRD in the
future. He points out that narrow craft categories have been considered as in-
hibitors to HRD. However, he identifies a trend of "cross-functional" training in
response to automation and competition from nonunion firms. He further
states that unions help determine training needs. They are also providers of
training.

> To date, they [unions] have generally pushed for more rather than
> less training . . . . Thus, many unions run skill-training programs paid
> for by companies or government programs, and they often negotiate
> for training as a cost of new corporate automation schemes. Recently
> unions have been working to enlarge the scope of company training
> programs in such areas as tuition reimbursement for blue-collar
> workers, high school equivalency and basic literacy, and training dis-
> placed or laid-off workers, under both corporate and government
> sponsorship. (Olson, 1986)

Hale (1987) stated, "As unions seek increased representation of low-skill,
low-pay jobs, they can be expected to demand more training by employers and
government. Unions are also working to organize white-collar workers, such
as secretarial and highly skilled professional and technical staff. Because
of the rapid introduction of technology and the obsolescence of this work
force, unions will play an increasingly more active role in bargaining for retraining and cross-functional training". (p. 26) HRD programs must adjust to this
trend in order to be in a position to serve unionized personnel as well as the
organization.

Professionalization in HRD. Several trends are emerging which affect the professionalization of HRD practitioners. "One trend is that managers are becoming more aware of the differences between good, adequate, and poor training.
They are beginning to discriminate between programs that increase productivity and those that do not. For example, many managers now know the difference between "mastery learning" and "normed learning" and are insisting their
learning specialists use the former" (Hale, 1987, p. 26). There is a greater reliance on performance and instructional technology to provide better training.

Another trend points to the increasing professionalization of HRD practitioners. There has been an increased interest in certification of learning specialists, instructional designers, and HRD managers. In response, ASTD has
established a set of standards for the field in their 1989 version of the Model
for Excellence. In addition, IBSTPI was initiated as a nonprofit research and

education corporation specifically to investigate and recommend certification standards for the field of HRD. Their products, *Instructional Design Competencies: The Standards* and *Instructors' Competencies, Vol. 1: The Standards* provide unique competencies for the instructional designer and learning specialist roles and are the most authoritative in the field. IBSTPI is also engaging in major research efforts to develop competencies with evaluative criteria for evaluators, training managers, and performance technologists.

Professionalization of HRD has grown rapidly for several years. At present, more than 250 universities offer master's and doctorate degrees in the field. Several others are focused at the undergraduate level. Most are dedicated to enhancement of the competencies, skills, and knowledge required for HRD practitioners.

The results of the emergence of the field of HRD have been profoundly positive. The HRD function has not changed during the last few years, but the kind of person in it has changed drastically (Lusterman, 1985). HRD practitioners hold graduate degrees in areas like curriculum design, organizational behavior, adult education, and adult psychology. Many are specialists in interactive video disc programming, instructional systems, and instructional quality assurance (Hale, 1987).

In addition, HRD departments are now being asked to become "profit centers." Many practitioners operate as internal consultants to the organization by responding to requests for services and work to be done as well as billing the receiving departments.

According to Hale (1987) "There has been increased demand by top management to evaluate the effect of HRD in terms of business goals, cost effectiveness, and responsiveness. Such demands have caused HRD managers and departments to develop cost/benefit analyses before embarking upon projects. The future will present HRD operations with the mandate to show results in terms of the bottom line" (p. 28).

Educational Diversity. Two additional areas affecting HRD are the increase in the number of illiterate adults and the number of college-educated persons seeking employment commensurate with their education. This will force HRD practitioners to develop programs that address these extreme levels of preparation. In addition, HRD practitioners must provide basic adult education within organizations, rather than rely on traditional adult education agencies to deliver such programs.

Implications for HRD Practitioners. HRD practitioners need to increase their human resource planning and futuring skills, interact with top management on a regular basis, and become actively involved in strategic organizational decisions. They should become more familiar with existing federal HRD legislation and help draft future legislation. Finally, they should help develop a common body of knowledge, skills, and attitudes for the field and encourage graduate study and training for new HRD practitioners in the basics of HRD.

SOCIOLOGICAL FACTORS

Changes in the Work Force. The continuing evolution of the work force is perhaps the most significant factor in the future of HRD. The work force is not only
the receiver of learning programs, it is also the developer and deliverer of such
programs. It will also be more diverse, as more minorities and females enter the
labor pool. More than 80 percent of women ages 25–44 are expected to participate in the labor force in 1995. In addition, over 17 percent of the growth will be
the result of the increasing number of blacks entering the labor force. Foreign
laborers (with green cards) will also increase and account for 20 percent of the
labor force in 1990 (Zemke, 1987).

The increasing number of persons in the labor force with felony records is another trend which will add complexity and diversity to the work force profile.
The FBI's crime statistics reveal approximately 30 percent of the labor pool
could have a felony history by 1995. Forty-two percent of the crimes now being
committed are committed by persons under the age of 21 (Zemke, 1987).
Felons will be a large part of the work force for many years to come.

Many of the changes taking place in the work force include the following:

- Slower rate of expansion
- Educational attainment
- Illiteracy
- Aging
- Value orientation (Hale, 1987, p. 5).

The labor force will experience a slower *rate of expansion* while competition
for motivated competent employees will increase (Bureau of Labor Statistics,
1987). Schwendiman (1987) states:

> Companies that create the most nourishing environments for
> personal growth will attract the most talented people. This takes on
> special significance when we consider the fact that we will have labor
> shortages for the rest of the century. . . . (p. 3)

Change in *educational attainment* can be seen in the number of college gradu-
ates that is expected to exceed the number of positions requiring college degrees. In addition, the number of qualified candidates for middle-management
positions is expected to be 30:1 by 1990 (Zemke, 1987). According to Hale
(1987), "a very large group of potential workers is overqualified for entry-level
work. This is particularly true of people with graduate degrees. People are
finding it more and more difficult to justify continued formal education, due to
increased opportunity in the marketplace" (p. 7).

She adds "The trend toward more and more formal education has put executive managers in a double bind. . . . they feel responsible for encouraging employees to "improve themselves" through added learning. Many organizations
offer incentives such as tuition reimbursement and released time for class attendance and study. On the other hand, it is becoming apparent that while the

bachelor's degree is almost a prerequisite for some organizations, advanced degrees are, for the most part, not wanted. People with advanced degrees demand more in salary and perks for doing the same work performed by others with bachelor's degrees or no degrees at all"(p. 7).

It is predicted that *illiteracy* will reach 18 percent by 1990. Today, 26 million adult Americans are "functionally illiterate," with another 46 million marginally literate—functioning at about fifth-grade level. ASTD predicts there will be 23 million functionally illiterate adults in the 1990s. Experts predict the number to grow at about 2.5 million people per year (Hale, 1987).

Many managers falsely believe that employed individuals are literate and unemployed ones are not. According to Bennett and Olson (1987), organizations are finding retraining of nonmanagement employees only minimally effective because of the low literacy level. If an employee cannot read or write, it is very difficult to train and retrain for new jobs requiring new competencies and skills. Bennett and Olson (1987) further report several benefits to increasing the literacy of employees:

- Increased feasibility of retraining

- Greater confidence in written communications

- Increased feelings of personal worth

- Security, enhanced feelings of loyalty and commitment to the organization

Gordon (1986b) reports that only 14.6 percent of companies surveyed offer remedial training. However, basic literacy is only part of the problem. New technologies, computer networks, and teleconferencing are changing communication strategies significantly (Hale, 1987).

The work force is *aging*. By 1995, three quarters of the labor force will be within the prime working ages (25–54), compared to two thirds in 1984. This age group will increase by 21 million, compared to an increase of 15 million in other areas of the labor force. Zemke (1987), summarizing the situation, states that it will be the oldest work force in history. The age of the labor force affects how HRD programs will be designed and delivered. Most of today's learning programs rely on lecture and printed materials. Because an older work force has poorer visual and learning acuity, HRD practitioners will have to develop different instructional methods (Zemke, 1987).

During the same period, the share of the work force who are 16–24 will drastically decline while the number of older workers eligible for pension and/or who elect early retirement increases. Many organizations have elected to actively recruit workers in upper age brackets to take jobs traditionally handled by high school and college students (Hale, 1987).

The *value orientation*, that is, the interests, priorities, and values of the work force, is also changing. One concern of organizations is that an aging work force creates a trend toward less company loyalty and less inclination of (older) employees to seek leadership roles at the expense of family responsibilities. According to Hale (1987), "some workers are not interested in relocating to less desirable locales, despite significant increases in salary and responsibility.

In some ways this trend is a paradox for HRD practitioners. Fewer workers seek leadership roles, yet management needs good leaders". While many workers are unwilling to move at all, a new type of migrant worker is emerging. They are "mostly well educated professionals and high paid blue-collar types who move around the country following the economic sun" (Hale, 1987, p. 10). David Lewin, professor at Columbia Business School, predicts, because of labor shortages, that within five years there will be an increasing demand for people willing to move (Hale, 1987).

Zemke (1986) cites a University of Michigan study which found that values are indeed changing. Seventy-seven percent of people polled believed you get ahead on personality rather than work ethic values. This is supported by studies of parents of American school-age children who believe personality is more important than hard work (Rubenstein, 1986).

The implication is that management may look to instill traditional work ethics through HRD. As a result, HRD practitioners will have to prepare managers and supervisors to work with these employees. According to Zemke (1987), the managers interviewed in the University of Michigan Study projected increased use of training to develop team building, communications, and motivation skills.

In addition, there is a movement to change corporate cultures—for more participation, more sharing, more openness, more flexibility, more risk taking, and improved quality. HRD programs should play a key role in implementing such a sweeping change (Lusterman, 1985).

In HRD, the trend is to move away from "nice-to-know" subjects toward subjects that support business goals (Hale, 1987). However, in response to changing values in the work force, these will be reexamined. According to Bell (1981), there is a need for HRD programs relating to employees' lives outside the work environment. For example, employees want to know how to deal with complex situations like aging parents, consumerism, and coping skills needed to adjust to constantly changing home environments.

Implications for HRD Practitioners. Sredl and Rothwell (1987) identified several implications for HRD and its practitioners as a result of the sociological changes that will occur in the next few decades. They include

1. HRD practitioners need to understand the learning problems of older workers and the elderly.

2. HRD practitioners should help develop alternatives for older workers regarding retirement, internal job transfers, and declining career opportunities.

3. HRD practitioners should create new ways to use older workers in entry-level positions.

4. HRD practitioners should help develop support services for dual-career couples.

5. HRD practitioners must develop an understanding of career develop-ment and its importance in human resource planning and forecasting.

6. HRD practitioners should increase efforts to improve cultural under-standing and sensitivity.

7. HRD practitioners should support improved educational programs for minorities.

8. HRD practitioners should encourage bilingual and multicultural training programs for workers and managers.

9. HRD practitioners should help develop creative, realistic workplace child care options.

10. HRD practitioners should understand and support individual differences and learning styles.

11. HRD practitioners should help develop wellness programs of all types.

12. HRD practitioners should help educate management about wellness is-sues and developments.

13. HRD practitioners should work to increase training and retraining op-tions and opportunities of all workers.

14. HRD practitioners should work more closely with unions to upgrade workers' skills.

15. HRD practitioners should work to improve ties between HRD and local economic development efforts.

16. HRD practitioners should encourage organizations to provide more training, development, and education programs for disadvantaged youths.

17. HRD practitioners should encourage organizations to provide more learning and training programs in work attitudes and ethics.

18. HRD practitioners should educate management about the importance of employee attitude and its relationship to productivity.

Decline of the Public School. Many believe that public schools are getting worse. The message is becoming clear to industry: If people are to be trained ade-quately, reliance on public schools could be a mistake.

Implications for HRD Practitioners: Sredl and Rothwell (1987) identified sev-eral implications for HRD practitioners regarding improved linkage with the public school system. They include

1. HRD practitioners should work to improve links between business and secondary schools and between business and the post-secondary educa-tion system.

2. HRD practitioners should support school programs in career develop-ment.

3. HRD practitioners should support work/service learning opportunities for all secondary and post-secondary students.

4. HRD practitioners should help in the revision of secondary school curricula to include skills in interaction and employability.

5. HRD practitioners should support bilingual and multicultural programs at the secondary and post-secondary levels.

6. HRD practitioners should develop one-on-one programs for disadvantaged youths.

ORGANIZATIONAL FACTORS

Corporate Structures and Goals. Corporate structures are changing significantly after years of relatively little change. One of these changes is the downsizing of organizations. Hale (1987) reported that "Between 1981 and 1983, half of the nation's 1,000 largest organizations eliminated at least one layer of management" (p. 11). Because of the downsizing and flattening of organizations, there will be less opportunity for advancement; therefore, management will need to find new ways to motivate employees. She adds, fewer levels of management will also increase the scope of responsibility of managers, as well as the number of skills required to perform work assignments. Figure 16.2 constructs the traditional and downsized structures of organizations.

Flattened organizations means more people in each layer. The net effect will be a reduction of as much as 50 percent in the total number of managers. In many organizations, a parallel increase in the number of staff positions will occur. This, too, could cause problems, since traditionally only line officers can aspire to positions of power (Hale, 1987).

Another problem is that HRD programs must reflect corporate strategies. If, for example, the organization is short-term oriented, so will be the HRD program. However, much of the recent criticism of U.S. corporations concerns their lack of productivity, which results from a quarterly orientation rather than a long-term orientation. As more and more organizations address their need for long-term planning, HRD programs will become more long-term focused. Long-term planning and goal setting generally falls into four categories:

1. Productivity

2. Competitiveness

3. Technical superiority

4. Building new business strategies (ASTD, 1986)

According to Hale (1987), for example, if the goal is productivity, HRD programs should focus on quality training and employee involvement. If the goal is to be competitive, HRD programs should focus on, sales, customer relations, and service training. If, however, the goal is technical superiority, HRD programs will be asked to build technical competence. If the goal is to build a new

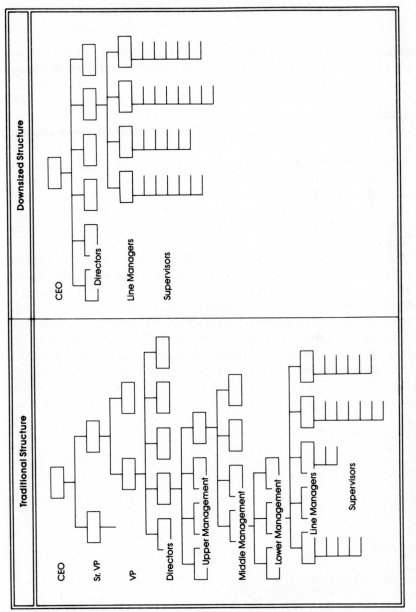

Figure 16.2 Organizational structures
Developed by Odin Westgaard, 1987.

business strategy, learning programs will have to be developed to increase management skills. She adds, with the increased interest in intrapreneurial skills, HRD programs will be expected "to train managers in how to turn their units into profit centers and manufacturing and production into service units" (p. 13).

Implications for HRD Practitioners. As a result of changing organizational conditions, HRD practitioners must develop learning programs and training activities that support the organization strategy. In addition, these programs and activities must help the organization become more efficient, productive, and quality oriented. These programs must also measure against their respective costs and produce a positive benefit in order to be considered appropriate and viable.

HRD practitioners must also develop skills and abilities that foster change and organizational improvement. Among these is the ability to work with unions and their leaders in the development of learning programs and training activities which improve the skills of workers. Also, HRD practitioners must develop negotiation and conflict-resolution skills in order to foster a working relationship with union personnel.

HRD practitioners act as facilitators and problem-solving specialists. In many organizations, HRD practitioners must begin to act as internal consultants responsible for organizational change.

HRD practitioners must be able to serve a broader range of groups as organizations downsize and become more decentralized. HRD practitioners must also train line managers and supervisors to function as learning specialists in this type of environment. Finally, HRD practitioners must be able to support participative management approaches and help develop environments that foster cooperation and mutual respect. This includes developing teams as well as individuals.

TECHNOLOGY

Figure 16.3 reflect the rapid growth of technology, a trend, according to Gordon (1985) and ASTD (1987), that will continue into the twenty-first century.

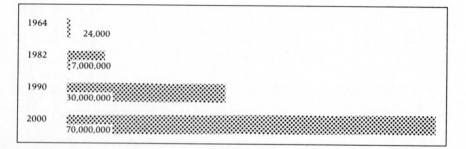

Figure 16.3   Computers in use worldwide, developed by Odin WestgAARD, 1987

Obsolescence. Because computers become obsolete at an alarming rate, several problems result for organizations as well as for HRD. For example, when should the organization upgrade its products and processes? Who must be trained and retrained to adapt to this ever-increasing problem? What's the return in investment for changes? (Hale, 1987) Lusterman (1985) states that

> Technologies are changing so fast that adapting to them is taking a bigger portion of the training dollar. Technological changes calls for attitudinal changes as well as for new skills and knowledge. There's a strong stress on the development of competencies that are new ways of thinking . . . no group . . . is immune from the new learning requirements imposed by technological change.

Updating Skills and Competencies. Like machines and computers, people also become obsolete. ASTD (1987) reports that a 25-year-old graduate will have to be reeducated eight times in the course of a 40-year career. HRD programs are expected to upgrade employees' competencies and skills in the face of technological advancement, to enable them to remain current in their field.

Technology as a Training Tool. Many organizations are utilizing a combination of instructor-led training and technology-based learning systems. Figure 16.4 provides percentages of American corporations with 100 or more employees who use computers in each of four applications. This reveals how persuasive this aspect of instructional technology is.

Computers in Training Of all U. S. organizations with 100 or more employees...								
Organizations (By Number of Employees)	% Using Computers in Training[1]		% Doing Computer-Based Training		% Using Computers for Data Management		% Using Computers for Word Processing/ Graphics	% Not Using Computers Now, but Will by 1989
	1988	1987	1988	1987	1988	1987	1988	1986	1988
100-499	59.6	56.5	37.9	32.1	49.7	44.6	53.4	48.3	10.6
500-999	57.4	63.1	31.0	39.5	47.3	54.1	52.7	57.3	14.7
1,000-2,499	67.1	65.6	45.1	39.8	57.2	56.4	59.0	57.1	9.2
2,500-9,999	77.6	73.0	56.5	50.5	71.4	65.3	72.0	67.1	5.0
10,000 or more	82.9	89.4	58.3	65.9	76.6	78.2	79.4	82.4	5.1
All Sizes	60.8	58.7	38.6	34.3	51.0	47.4	54.6	50.8	10.6

[1]Refers to organizations reporting that they use computers in some way in connection with their training efforts.

Figure 16.4   Use of computers in training

Reprinted from J. Gordon, "Computers in Training," copyright 1988 Training Magazine. Reprinted by permission.

Workshops and Technology. The most common form of delivery in HRD is the workshop using the lecture method. Hale (1987) noted that "there is increasing pressure on HRD to improve organizational performance while meeting workers' need for new skills" (p. 19). According to Ladd (1986), HRD practitioners need to rethink the use of the workshop becasue they are

- very expensive, especially due to travel, lodging, and meal costs.

- take people away from the work site, resulting in lost productivity or incurred extra costs due to reassignment of staff.

- lecture-or presentation-driven, resulting in inadequate time for practice, interaction, and activities that build skills.

- rarely designed so that the skills and knowledge presented can be supported on the job.

Ladd suggests that workshops be combined with instructional media, computer technology, and telecommunications technology. Hale (1987) recommends that workshops be supported by computer-based assessments, computer-based training, interactive video, and teletraining.

Hale (1987) stated that "Combining workshops with technology-based delivery systems can increase HRD practitioners' ability to assess individual learner's needs, screen candidates for specific training programs, give learners better and more timely feedback, provide practice on the job, test learner's proficiency, and provide more realistic simulations of situations" (p. 19).

The Society for Applied Learning Technology (in its report on the Greenbrier Conference held in December 1986) supports the assumption that technology-based delivery systems would improve the effectiveness and efficiency of training efforts.

> Despite the expenditures and the admitted deficiencies in the quality and degree of training and education, applications of technology-based learning systems are minimal in relation to potential benefits, which include reduced costs, increased learning and enhanced productivity. In contrast, it is clear that significant application of technology would result in corresponding gains in human resource development. (SALT, 1986)

Structured On-the-Job Training. On-the-job training is another principal method of delivery. The goal is to make training realistic and life like. However, there are some concerns about " . . . its inefficient use of time, unpredictable and inconsistent performance outcomes, and over-dependence on the communications skills of the supervisor" (Jacobs & McGiffen, 1987).

According to Hale (1987), "Structured OJT is designed according to proved instructional design principles" (p. 22). This approval should be combined with technology-based learning systems such as CBT and interactive video. Several advantages of structured OJT include

- Greater efficiency since training occurs in the work setting where the job performance will occur, thus increasing the relevance of the information.

- Clearer connection between information and application since job knowledge and skills can be demonstrated, practiced, and used immediately in the work setting.

- More relevant feedback since learners receive feedback and coaching directly from the person who will assess their performance.

- Greater potential for enhanced communication and respect between the learner and supervisor.

- An opportunity to improve supervisor's interpersonal and coaching skills through the use of structured assignments and tools designed to help the supervisor give constructive performance based feedback. (Jacobs & McGiffen, 1987)

Hale (1987) reported that "Even though delivery of the instruction is dependent on the skills and motives of the supervisor, the HRD practitioners will still play a key role in the structured OJT process" (p. 22). For example,

> Conduct needs and job analyses, prepare trainee materials, construct performance checklists and knowledge tests, prepare OJT trainers, and monitor and revise system performance. (Jacobs & McGiffen, 1987)

Deliverers and Technology. Another way technology will affect retraining is in the selection and use of deliverers. One example is that corporations are starting their own Corporate Colleges as well as entering into joint ventures with colleges and universities to develop and deliver training (Hale, 1987).

Implications for HRD Practitioners. HRD practitioners should increase their technological and computer skills as well as encourage increased research on technology-oriented adult learning issues. They should also use technology-based software and design learning programs and training activities that utilize computers for learning experiences. This will familiarize learners with the types of technology available, and they will become more comfortable with it, perhaps greatly increasing the computer-technology literacy of employees.

Sredl and Rothwell (1987) encourage the development of an HRD-computerized conference/bulletin board/reference service, one available for on-line inquiry by HRD practitioners via terminals or personal computers. This would enable them to use and evaluate new techniques and methods quickly, rather than postpone them.

THE HRD PRACTITIONERS OF THE FUTURE

To successfully fulfill their roles, HRD practitioners need to develop several skills and participate in a number of new organizational activities; for example,

1. Increase understanding of adult learning theories.

2. Participate in strategic planning activities.

3. Become proficient in business principles and practices.

4. Develop futuring and forecasting skills.

5. Develop needs assessment and performance analysis skills (Hale, 1987).

For too long a time HRD practitioners have been selected from among the ranks of line managers and supervisors with little or no experience in instruction, program design, evaluation, or learning theory. Because of the serious nature of corporate learning and the consequences of failing to develop adequate knowledge, skills, competencies, and attitudes, a new "professionally identified" HRD practitioner has emerged—one who understands adult learning, instruction, program design, and evaluation. Other HRD practitioners who lack this knowledge, skill, and ability are reevaluating themselves, developing plans for self-improvement.

The professionally identified HRD practitioner also understands organizational culture, business practices, and operations. As a result, he or she participates in strategic planning and other organizational management activities once reserved for middle management. This also changes how HRD is viewed in organizations and puts pressure on HRD practitioners and those aspiring to the role to develop the ability to participate in regular organizational management activities.

Professionally identified HRD practitioners develop futuring and forecasting skills to project future business trends, human resource allocations, human resource planning, and decision making. These are the kinds of skills that will be required of all HRD practitioners in the next few decades.

The trend in today's organization is toward performance management and organizational efficiency. As a result, HRD practitioners must develop a knowledge of job design and analysis, performance appraisal, and needs identification and an ability to develop learning programs and training activities that foster performance improvement and personal growth.

The HRD practitioner should, of course, be a good instructor and a competent program designer and planner. In addition to these traditional expectations, Hale (1987) reported that the role requires the HRD practitioner to be

1. A *Futurist*, so management is not caught off guard, again due to changes in environment that will/could affect business viability (Odiorne, 1985).

2. A *Participant* in strategic planning, to better link training to business goals.

3. A *Consultant* to line management, to be in the best position to advise managers on the implications of training, coaching, and counseling.

4. A *Resource,* with new, more sophisticated skills in

   • adult learning theory, to more effectively service an assertive and aging work force.

   • business, to better understand and respond to business goals.

   • performance analysis, to determine when training is a viable solution.

   • training technology, to assure training efficiency and effectiveness (p. 33).

HRD must also accomplish other elements in the future.

1. Support organizational strategic goals.

2. Re-competency and/or performance formula.

3. Appeal to the affective domain.

4. Address higher level problem-solving skills.

5. Account for societal implications (Hale, 1987).

Summary and recommendations. Several factors have surfaced as important to the future of HRD in Corporate America. According to Hale (1987), seven of these prompt specific actions:

1. HRD practitioners should establish systems to better link their efforts to organizational goals. Further, evaluation of the value of their efforts should be tied to their accomplishment of those goals.

2. HRD practitioners should examine their training efforts and materials to discover legal exposure and the effect on long-term social needs.

3. Future development efforts should be performance based; they should follow a valid instructional development process and be based on job, task, and learner analyses.

4. HRD practitioners should evaluate and select delivery systems that support affective and higher level cognitive objectives such as socialization, problem solving, and team building.

5. HRD practitioners should examine delivery systems and "smart systems" for use for on-line, real time training, to ease updating responses to rapid changes in content and technology.

6. HRD practitioners should emphasize performance and/or competency-based training supported by valid and reliable tests, since they will be needed in personnel decisions such as recruitment, promotions, and so on.

7. HRD practitioners should continue to study the use of programs and delivery systems that develop basic language and word skills (p. 35–36).

CONCLUSION

The ultimate success of HRD in the future will be limited to HRD practitioners' ability to adjust to economic, political, sociological, and organizational factors. This requires the acquisition of additional knowledge skills and competencies and the development of appropriate attitudes.

The criticality of human resources within organizations places enormous pressure on HRD programs and practitioners. The enhancement of HRD practitioners and the professionalization of the field of HRD are seen as important trends in the future.

In the future, HRD practitioners will be faced with a greater opportunity to affect the efficiency, quality, competitiveness, productivity, and profitability of most organizations. HRD practitioners must accept this opportunity as a challenge and perform accordingly. It is our hope that this book has served as a first step.

Evolution of Human Resource Development

1944 American Society for Training Directors (now known as American Society for Training and Development) created

1953 Issue of professional certification first discussed within ASTD

1970 Nadler Model of HRD introduced

1972 Professional certification voted down by ASTD

1973 Feasibility study for national external degree program in training and development begun

The Handbook for Training and Development written

1974 Birth of the competency and standards movement

1976 Civil Service Commission Study

Ontario Society for Training and Development Competency Study

1977 Association of Education, Communication and Technology (Division of Instructional Development) Competency Study begun

1978 Pinto-Walker Study (Fourteen activities of training and development practitioners)

1979 American Society for Personnel Administration establishes the Personal Accreditation Institute

1980 National Society for Performance and Instruction establishes Certification Task Force

1981 AECT[DID](NSPI) Joint Certification Task Force formed

1983 Model for Excellence (ASTD) published

1984 ASTD's Professional Standards Task Force (PSTF) formed

International Board of Standards for Training, Performance and Istruction (IBSTPI) formed

1985 PSTF recommends the development of professional standards for the field of training and development

1986 IBSTPI publishes Instructional Design Competencies: The Standards

1987   ASTD establishes the Competencies and Standards Task Force (*Models for Excellence* expanded to include HRD)

   Training Magazine reports positive support for professional certification

1988   IBSTPI publishes *Instructors Competencies: The Standards, Vol. 1*

1989   *Models for Excellence II: Standards* for the field of HRD is published

References

Chapter 1

American Society for Training and Development. *Serving the New Corporation.* Alexandria, VA: ASTD Press, 1986.

Beer, M. What is Organizational Development? *Training and Development Sourcebook.* Baird, L. S., Schneier, C. E., & Laird, D., eds. Amherst, MA: HRD Press, 1983.

Dervarics, C. Corporate classrooms: A new trend in career training. *Vocational Training Views, 16* (36)(1985): 1–10.

Gilley, J. W. "Career Development: The linkage between training and OD." *Performance Improvement Quarterly. 2* (1) (January 1989.): 6–10.

Gilley, J. W. Two myths and managerial theories. *Quality Circle Digest, 5* (8) (August 1986): 57–60.

Gilley, J. W. Adult learners and the classroom. *Data Training, 6* (4) (April 1987): 58–60.

Lawrie, J. Revitalizing the HRD function. *Personnel, 63* (6) (June 1986): 20–25.

McLagan, P., & Bedrick, R. *Model for Excellence.* Alexandria, VA: ASTD Press, 1983.

Nadler, L., ed. *Handbook of Human Resource Development.* New York: Wiley, 1986.

Nadler, L., & Wiggs, G. D. *Managing Human Resource Development.* San Francisco, CA: Jossey-Bass, 1986.

Chapter 2

Argyris, C. *Reasoning, Learning and Action.* San Francisco, CA: Jossey-Bass, 1982.

Carnevale, A. P., & Goldstein, H. *Employee Training: Its Changing Role and an Analysis of New Data.* Alexandria, VA: ASTD Press, 1983.

Gregory, J. M. *The Seven Laws of Teaching,* 21st ed. Grand Rapids, MI: Baker Book House, 1978.

International Board of Standards for Training, Performance and Instruction. *Instructor Competencies: The Standards.* Iowa City, IA: IBSTPI, 1988.

Knowles, M. S. Organizations as learning systems. *Training and Development Journal, 40* (1) (January 1986): 5–8.

Marsick, V., & Watkins, K. Learning and development in the workplace. Paper presented to the ASTD Professor Conference, St. Louis, 1986.

McLagan, P., & Bedrick, R. *Model for Excellence.* Alexandria, VA: ASTD Press, 1983.

Mezirow, J. A critical theory of adult learning and education. *Adult Education Quarterly, 32* (1)(Autumn 1981): 3–24.

Mezirow, J. A critical theory of self-directed learning. *Self-Directed Learning: From Theory to Practice.* S. Brookfield, ed. San Francisco: Jossey-Bass, 1985.

Morgan, G. & Ramirez, R., Action learning: A holographic metaphor for guiding social change. *Human Relations, 37*(1) (January 1983): 1–28.

Pinto, P. R., & Walker, J. W. *A Study of Professional Training and Development Roles and Competencies.* Alexandria, VA: ASTD Press, 1978.

Chapter 3

Cross, L. Career management development: A system that gets results. *Training and Development Journal, 37*(2) (February 1983): 54–63.

Gilley, J. W., "Guides, lists, and directories: Stocking the career resource center." *Training News, 7*(3) (March 1985): 16–17.

Gilley, J. W. & Moore, H. A. Managers as career enhancers: An overlooked resource. *Personnel Administrator, 31*(3) (March 1986): 51–60.

Gilley, J. W., "Career development as a partnership." *Personnel Administrator, 33* (4) (April 1988): 62–68.

Grote, R., & Stine, S. Mentors seen as key allies in career growth. *Training/HRD, 17*(8) (August 1980): 107–108.

Gutteridge, T. G., & Otte, F. L. Organization career development: What's going on out there? *Training and Development Journal, 37*(2) (February 1983): 22–26.

Hanson, M. C. Implementing a career development program. *Training and Development Journal, 35*(7) (July 1981): 80–84.

Hanson, M. C. Career life planning workshops as career services in organizations—Are they working. *Training and Development Journal, 36*(2) (February 1982): 58–63.

Jones, P. R., Kaye, B. & Taylor, H. R. You want me to do what? *Training and Development Journal, 35*(7) (July 1981): 56–62.

Kahnweiler, J. B. Back to the campus career development in an academic setting. *Training and Development Journal, 38*(8) (August 1984): 54–56.

Kaye, B. Whose career is it anyway? *Training and Development Journal, 38*(5) (May 1984): 112–118.

Kirkpatrick, D. L. *Evaluating Training Programs.* Washington, DC: Associated Press, 1975.

Leibowitz, Z. B., & Schlossberg, N. K. Training managers for their role in a career development system. *Training and Development Journal, 40*(7) (July 1986): 72–79.

Moir, E. Career resource center in business and industry. *Training and Development Journal, 35*(2) (February 1981): 54–57.

Otte, F. L. Creating successful career development programs. *Training and Development Journal, 36*(2) (February 1982): 39–37.

Phillips-Jones, L. Establishing a formalized inventory program. *Training and Development Journal, 37*(2) (February 1983): 38, 40–42.

Reynierse, J. H. A goal model of human resource planning. *Human Resource Planning, 14*(3) (March 1982): 29–34.

Walker, J. W. *Human Resource Planning.* New York: McGraw-Hill, 1980.

Zenger, J. H. Career planning: Coming in from the cold. *Training and Development Journal, 35*(7) (July 1981): 47–52.

Chapter 4

Beer, M. What is organizational development? *Training and Development Sourcebook.* Baird, L. S., Schneier, C. E., & Laird, D., eds. Amherst, MA: HRD Press, 1983.

Bowers, D. G., & Franklin, J. L. *Survey-Guided Development I: Data-Based Organizational Change.* San Diego, CA: University Associates, 1977.

Cummings, T. G., *System Theory for OD.* New York: Wiley, 1980.

French, W. L., & Bell, C. H., Jr. *Organizational Development: Behavioral Science Interventions for Organization Improvement.* San Francisco: Jossey-Bass, 1978.

Gilley, J. W. Seeking the common pattern. *Association Management, 37*(8) (August 1985): 125–127.

Gilley, J. W. Two myths and management theories. *Quality Circles Digest, 5*(7) (July 1986): 60–64.

Gilley, J. W. Career development a partnership. *Personnel Administrator, 33*(4) (April 1988): 62–68.

Gilley, J. W. Career development: The linkage between training and organizational development. *Performance Improvement Quarterly, 2*(1) (January 1989): 6–10.

Gutteridge, T. G., & Otte, F. L. *Organizational Career Development: State of the Practice.* Alexandria, VA: ASTD Press, 1983.

Laird, D. *Approaches to Training and Development,* 2nd ed. Reading, MA: Addison-Wesley, 1986.

Lippitt, G., & Lippitt, R. *The Consulting Process in Action,* 2nd ed. San Diego, CA: University Associates, 1986.

Margulies, N., and Raia, A., Conceptual Foundations of OD. New York: McGraw-Hill, 1978.

McLean, A. J. *OD in Transition: Evidence of an Evoluting Profession.* New York: Wiley, 1982.

McGill, M. E. *OD for Operating Manager.* New York: AMACOM, 1977.

Neilsen, E. H. *Becoming an OD Practitioner.* Englewood Cliffs, NJ: Prentice-Hall, 1984.

Phelps, M., "Organizational Development." Unpublished manuscript, University of Nebraska, Lincoln, 1988.

White, L. P., & Wooten, K. C. *Professional Ethics and Practice in OD: A Systematic Analysis of Issues, Alternatives and Approaches.* New York: Wiley, 1987.

Chapter 5

Brim-Donohoe, L. R. A case for human resource development. *Public Personnel Management Journal, 10*(4) (April 1981): 365–370.

Johnson, R. The organization and management of training. *Training and Development Handbook,* 2nd ed., R. Craig, ed. New York: McGraw-Hill, 1976.

Lawrie, J. Revitalizing the HRD function. *Personnel, 63*(6) (June 1986): 20–25.

McLagan, P., & Bedrick, R. *Model for Excellence.* Alexandria, VA: ASTD Press, 1983.

Nadler, L., & Wiggs, G. D. *Managing Human Resource Development.* San Francisco, CA: Jossey-Bass, 1986.

Newman, K. Guideline on developing program policy. *Training and Development Journal, 34*(7) (July 1980): 20–23.

Sredl, H. J., & Rothwell, W. J. *The ASTD Reference Guide to Professional Training Roles and Competencies.* Amherst, MA: HRD Press, Inc., 1987.

Suessmuth, P. *Ideas for Training Managers and Supervisors.* San Diego, CA: University Associates, 1978.

Yeomans, W. N. How to get top management support. *Training and Development Journal, 36*(6) (June 1982): 22–25.

Chapter 6

Boydell, T. *Experimental Learning.* Manchester, England. Manchester Monographs, Manchester University, 1976: 78–81.

Brostrom, R. *Training Style Inventory: Facilitator Handbook.* San Diego, CA: University Associates, 1979.

Chadwick, R. P. *Teaching and Learning.* Old Tappens, NJ: Flemming Revelle, 1982.

Cross, P. *Adults as Learners.* San Francisco, CA: Jossey-Bass, 1982.

Davis, L. N. *Planning, Conducting and Evaluating Workshops.* San Diego, CA: University Associates, 1984.

Dean, R. L., & Gilley, J. W. A production model for experimental learning. *Performance and Instruction Journal, 25*(3) (April 1986): 26–28.

Donaldson, L., & Scannell, E. E. *Human Resource Development: The New Trainers Guide,* 2nd ed. Reading, MA: Addison-Wesley, 1986.

Gilley, J. W. Adult learners and the classroom. *Data Training, 6*(4) (April 1987): 58–60.

Gilley, J. W., & Dean, R. L. Instructional design utilizing content and experience: A model. *Performance and Instruction Journal, 24*(10) (December 1985): 20–24.

Gilley, J. W., & Moore, H. A. Managers or career enhancers. *Personnel Administrator, 31*(3) (March 1986): 51–59.

Goodstein, L. D., & Pfeiffer, J. W. *The 1983 Annual for Facilitators, Trainers and Consultants.* San Diego, University Associates, 1983.

James, W. B., & Galbraith, M. W. Perceptional learning styles: Implications and techniques for practitioners. *Lifelong Learning, 7*(10) (June 1984): 20–23.

Kaye, B. L. The management of learning. *Academy of Management Review, 16*(4) (April 1977): 167–172.

Kirkpatrick, D. L. *Technique for Evaluating Training Programs.* Alexandria, VA: ASTD Press, 1976.

Knowles, M. S. *Andragogy in Action.* San Francisco, CA: Jossey-Bass, 1985.

Laird, D. *Approaches to Training and Development,* 2nd ed. Reading, MA: Addison-Wesley, 1986.

Lindeman, E. C. *The Measuring of Adult Education.* New York: McGraw-Hill, 1926.

Mouton, J. S., & Blake, R. R. *Synergogy: A New Strategy for Education, Training and Development.* San Francisco, CA: Jossey-Bass, 1984.

Nadler, L., ed. *Handbook of Human Resource Development.* New York: Wiley, 1986.

Randall, J. S. Methods of teaching. *Training and Development Journal, 32*(3) (March, 1978): 31–36.

Steinaker, N. W., & Bell, M. R. *The Experimental Taxonomy.* New York: Academic Press, 1979.

Suessmuth, P. *Ideas for Training Managers and Supervisors.* San Diego, CA: University Associates, 1978.

Thiagarajan, A. J. *Experimental Learning Packages.* Englewood Cliffs, NJ: Educational Technology, 1980.

This, L. E., & Lippitt, G. L. Learning theories and training. *Training and Development Sourcebook,* Baird, L. S., Schneier, C. E., & Laird, D. eds. Amherst, MA: HRD Press, 1983.

Zemke, R., & Zemke, S. 30 things we know for sure about adult learning. *Training, 18*(6) (June 1981): 45–50.

Chapter 7
Donaldson, L., & Scannell, E. E. *Human Resource Development: The New Trainers Guide,* 2nd ed. Reading, MA: Addison-Wesley, 1986.

International Board of Standards for Training, Performance and Instruction. *Instructional Designer Competencies: The Standards.* IBSTPI: Iowa City, IA., 1986.

Michalak, D. F., & Yager, E. G. *Making the Training Process Work.* New York: Harper & Row, 1979.

McLagan, P., & Bedrick, R. *Model for Excellence*. Alexandria, VA: ASTD Press, 1983.

Nadler, L. *Developing Human Resources*. Houston, TX: Gulf Press, 1970.

Chapter 8

Bellman, G. Untraining the trainer: Steps toward consulting. *Training and Development Journal, 37*(1) (January 1983): 70–73.

Byrne, J. A. Are all these consultants really necessary? *Forbes, 132*(8) (August 1983): 136–144.

Dunn, D. H. Think twice before you hang out a consultant's shingle. *Business Week* (June 13, 1982): 163–164.

Hudson, T., "Consulting: A Major HRD Role." Unpublished manuscript, University of Nebraska, Lincoln 1988.

Lippitt, G., & Lippitt, R. *The Consulting Process in Action*, 2nd ed. San Diego: University Associates, 1986.

Margulies, N., & Raia, A. *Organization Development: Values, Process and Technology*. New York: McGraw-Hill, 1972.

Robinson, D. & Younglove, B. *Making Your Career Transition into External HRD Consulting*. Alexandria, VA.: American Society for Training and Development, 1986.

Tichy, N. How different types of change agents diagnose organizations. *Human Relations, 28*(9) (September 1975): 771–779.

Turner, A. N. Consulting is more than giving advice. *Harvard Business Review, 61*(5) (1983): 120–129.

Wells, R. G. What every manager should know about management consultants. *Personnel Journal, 62*(12) (December 1983): 142–148.

Chapter 9

Archambault, R. D. The concept of need and its relation to certain aspects of education theory. *Harvard Educational Review, 27*(1) (February 1957): 38–62.

Atwood, H. M., & Ellis, J. The concept of need: An analysis for adult education. *Adult Leadership, 18*(4) (April 1987): 19, 210–212, 244.

Donaldson, L., & Scannell, E. E. *Human Resource Development: The New Trainers Guide*, 2nd ed. Reading, MA: Addison-Wesley, 1986.

McKinley, J. Perspectives on diagnostics in adult education. *Viewpoints, 49*(5), (May 1973): 69–83. Bulletin of the School of Education, Indiana University.

Michalak, D. F., & Yager, E. G. *Making the Training Process Work*. New York: Harper & Row, 1979.

Steadham, S. V. Learning to select a needs assessment strategy. *Training and Development Journal, 34*(1) (January 1980): 56–61.

Walton, R. Need: A central concept. *Social Service Quarterly, 43*(2) (Spring 1969).

Chapter 10

Donaldson, L., & Scannell, E. *Human Resource Development: The New Trainers Guide.* Reading, MA: Addison-Wesley, 2nd ed., 1986.

French, R. Teaching strategies and learning. Unpublished manuscript, University of Tennessee, Knoxville, 1975.

James, W. B., & Galbraith, M. W. Perceptual learning styles: Implications and techniques for practitioners. *Lifelong Learning: An Omnibus for Practice and Research,* 7(10) (June 1984): 20–23.

Kirkpatrick, D. L. Techniques for evaluating training programs. *Training and Development Journal,* 30(5) (May 1976): 3–17.

Lutterodt, S. A. *Principles of Instructional Design.* Columbia, MD. GP Courseware, 1983.

Michalak, D. F., & Yager, E. G. *Making the Training Process Work.* New York: Harper & Row, 1979.

Robinson, D. G. Providing training makes a difference. ASTD Region & Conference, Minneapolis, Minn., October 21, 1987.

Rockham, N. The coaching controversy. *Training and Development Journal,* 33(11) (November 1979): 14.

Shimberg, B. Testing for licensure and certification. *American Psychologist,* 36(10) (October 1981): 1138–46.

Smith, R. *Learning How to Learn.* New York: Cambridge University Press, 1982.

Chapter 11

Gilley, J. W. Practical tools for developing a comprehensive training strategy. *Lifelong Learning: An Omnibus of Practice and Research,* 10 (June 1987): 10–16.

Gilley, J. W., & Eggland, S. A. Hook, line and sinker. *Training and Development Journal,* 41 (9) (September 1987): 22–29.

Kotler, P. *Marketing Management: Analysis, Planning and Control.* Englewood Cliffs, NJ: Prentice-Hall, 1987.

McCarthy, E. J., & Perreault, A. H. *Basic Marketing: A Managerial Approach.* Homewood, IL: Irwin, 1985.

Chapter 12

Campbell, J. P., et al. *Managerial Behavior, Performance, and Effectiveness.* New York: McGraw-Hill, 1970.

Chestnut, D. How to sell new training programs to management. *Training,* 18(5) (May 1981): 45–46.

Jarkus, A. F. The uncertainty factor in human resources accounting. *Personnel,* 56(11) (Nov–Dec 1979): 72–75.

Kearsley, G., & Compton, T. Assessing costs, benefits and productivity in training systems. *Training and Development Journal, 35*(1) (January 1981): 14–18.

Langer, S. The personnel and industrial relations report. *Personnel Journal, 61*(7) (July 1982): 522–527.

Rice, O. Looking at T&D in the light of P&L. *Training, 18*(12) (December 1981): 67–68.

Shipp, T. To survive the budget inquisition, prove your training makes dollars and sense. *Training, 17*(11) (November 1980): 23–24.

Urban, T. F., et al. Management training: Justify costs or say goodbye. *Training and Development Journal, 39*(3) (March 1985): 68–73.

Chapter 13
Bratton, B. Instructional training design competencies and sources of information about them. Unpublished manuscript, University of Iowa, Iowa City, 1984.

Bratton, B., & Hildebrand, M. Plain talk about professional certification. *Instructional Innovator, 25*(9) (December 1980): 22–24, 49. (ERIC No. EJ 237 090).

Clements, R., Pinto, P., & Walker, J. Unethical and improper behavior by training and development professionals. *Training and Development Journal, 32*(12) (December 1978): 10–12.

Galbraith, M. W., & Gilley, J. W. An Examination of Professional Certification. *Lifelong Learning: An Omnibus of Practice and Research, 9*(2) (October, 1985): 12–15.

Galbraith, M. W., & Gilley, J. W. *Professional Certification Implication for Adult Education and HRD.* Columbus, OH: National Center for Vocational Education Research, 1986.

Gilley, J. W. Professional certification: The procedures established, the issues addressed, and the qualification criteria adopted by professional associations and societies." Doctoral dissertation, Oklahoma State University, Stillwater, 1985.

Gilley, J. W., & Galbraith, M. W. Examining professional certification. *Training and Development Journal, 40*(6) (June 1986): 60–61.

Gilley, J. W., & Galbraith, M. W. Professionalization and professional certification: A relationship. Proceedings of the 28th Annual Adult Education Research Conference, University of Wyoming, Laramie, 1987, pp. 96–102.

Hatcher, T. F. Professional development opportunities for trainers. *Training and Development Journal, 28*(1) (January 1974): 8–11. (ERIC No. EJ 909 754).

Lawrence, P. R. Accreditation of personnel administrators: An alternative interpretation. *Personnel Administrator, 26*(1) (January 1981): 31–35.

Lee, C. Certification for trainees: Thumbs up. *Training, 23*(11) (November 1986): 54–64.

McLagan, P., & Bedrick, R. *Model for Excellence.* Alexandria, VA: ASTD Press, 1983.

Miller, E. L. Professionalism and Its Importance to Accreditation-type Programs. (unpublished paper presented to the American Society of Personnel Administration, 1976) Ann Arbor, MI: University of Michigan, 1976.

Should trainees be certified? *Training News, 23*(5) (May 1982): 10–15.

Warzynski, C., & Noble, D. The ideology of professionalism and HRD. *Training and Development Journal, 30*(10) (October 1976): 12–17.

Webster, G., & Herold, A. *Antitrust guide for association executives.* Research Report. Washington, DC: Association Executive Press, 1983.

Chapter 14

Bratton, B. Instructional Training Design Competencies and Sources of Information about Them. Unpublished manuscript, University of Iowa, Iowa City, Iowa, 1984.

Bratton, B., & Hildebrand, M. Plain talk about professional certification. *Instructional Innovator, 25*(9) (December 1980): 22–24, 49. (ERIC No. EJ 237 090).

Bullett, F. Why certification? *Certification Registration and Information.* Washington, DC: American Production and Inventory Society, 1981.

Carlson, R. A. Professionalization in adult education. *Adult Education, 28*(1) (January 1977): 53–63.

Cervero, R. M. The predicament of professionalism for adult education. *Adult Literacy and Basic Education, 9*(1) (January, 1985): 11–17.

Clements, R., Pinto, P., & Walker, J. Unethical and improper behavior by training and development professionals. *Training and Development Journal, 32*(12) (December, 1978): 10–12.

Chalofsky, N., & Lincoln, C. I. *Up the HRD Ladder:* A Guide for Professional Growth. Reading, MA: Addison-Wesley, 1983.

Farmer, S. A. Impact of lifelong learning on the professionalism of adult education. *Journal of Research and Development in Education, 7*(4) (April 1974): 57–67.

Galbraith, M. W., & Gilley, J. W. *Professional Certification: Implications for Adult Education and HRD.* Columbus, OH: National Center for Research in Adult, Career and Vocational Education, 1986.

Gilley, J. W. Professional certification: The procedures established, the issues addressed, and the qualification criteria adopted by professional associations and societies. Doctoral dissertation, Oklahoma State University, Stillwater, 1985.

Gilley, J. W. The characteristics and developmental stages of a profession: Does HRD measure up. *Personnel Administrator, 31*(1) (January 1986): 14–18.

Gilley, J. W., & Galbraith, M. W. Professionalization and professional certification: A relationship. Proceedings of the 28th Annual Adult Education Research Conference, University of Wyoming, Laramie, 1987, pp 96–102.

Gilley, J. W., & Galbraith, M. W. Commonalities and characteristics of professional certification: implication for adult education. *Lifelong Learning: An Omnibus of Practice and Research, (11)* (1) (September 1988): 11–16.

Hatcher, T. F., Professional development opportunities for trainers. *Training and Development Journal, 28* (1) (January 1974): 8–11.

Lippitt, G. and Nadler, L. The emerging roles of the training director. *Training and Development Journal, 21* (8) (August 1967): 2–10.

McCollough, M., & McLagan, P. Keeping the competency study alive. *Training and Development Journal, 38* (6) (June 1984): 24–28.

McLagan, P., & Bedrick, R. *Model for Excellence.* Alexandria, VA: ASTD Press, 1983.

O'Mara, J. Implementation process, time and costs required to develop professional standards. Report to the Board of Directors of ASTD, Alexandria, VA., 1985.

Palomba, N. A. Accreditation of personnel administrators: Theory and reality. *Personnel Administrator, 26* (1) (January 1981): 37–40.

Professional standard committee: Report of strategy. *Training and Developmental Journal, 7* (3) (March–April 1953): 34–35.

Scheer, W. E. Is personnel management a profession? *Personnel Journal, 43* (5) (May 1964): 225–261.

Vollmer, H., & Mills, D. *Professionalization.* Englewood Cliffs, NJ: Prentice-Hall, 1966.

Whyte, G. S. The professional practitioners in the years to come. Paper presented at the 21th Conference of the Institute of Personnel Management, Washington, DC. 1977.

Chapter 15

American Society for Training and Development. *Careers in Training and Development.* Alexandria, VA: ASTD Press, 1983.

Feuer, D. *Training's* 1987 salary survey. *Training, 24* (11) (November 1987) pp 27–39.

Feuer, D. Training magazine industry report 1988. *Training, 25* (10) (October 1988): 31–41.

Gordon, J. Who is being trained to do what? *Training, 25* (10) (October 1988): 51–62.

Geber, B. Training's 1988 salary survey. *Training, 25* (11) (November 1988): 29–41.

Lee, C. Trainers' careers. *Training, 22* (10) (October 1985) pp. 75–80.

Lee, C. *Training* magazine's industry report. *Training, 24* (10) (October 1987a): 33–35.

Lee, C. Where the training dollars go. *Training, 24* (10) (October 1987b): 62.

McLagan, P. A., & Bedrick, R. Model for Excellence. Alexandria, VA: ASTD Press, 1983.

Stump, R. W. *Your Career in Human Resource Development.* Alexandria, VA: ASTD Press, 1985.

Zemke, R. Training in the 90's. *Training, 24* (1) (January 1987) pp. 40–53.

Chapter 16

American Society for Training and Development. *Serving the New Corporation.* Alexandria, VA: ASTD Press, 1986.

Bell, C. R. Future encounters of the HRD kind. *Training and Development Journal, 35* (8) (August 1981): 54–57.

Bennett, A., & Olson, G. Society's albatross and business's burden: Adult illiteracy. *Training Today,* 1987.

Lee, C. Training budgets: Neither boom nor bust. *Training, 25* (10) (October 1988): 41–51.

Gentilman, R., & Nelson, B. Futuring: The process and implications for training and development practitioners. *Training and Development Journal, 37* (6) (June 1983): 31–32, 34–36, 38.

Gordon, J. Where the training goes. *Training, 23* (10) (November 1986b): 49–63.

Gordon, J. Computer in training. *Training, 22* (10) (October 1985): 54–71.

Hale, J. Training: Preparing for the 21st century. Unpublished paper, 1987.

Jacobs, R., & McGiffen, T. A human performance system using a structured on-the-job training approach. *Performance and Instruction, 26* (3) (April 1987): pp. 24–28.

Ladd, C. Rethinking the workshop. *Training and Development Journal, 40* (12) (December 1986): 42–46.

Lusterman, S. *Trends in Corporate Education and Training.* New York: The Conference Board Inc., 1985.

Odiorne, G. Human resource strategies for the '80s. *Training, 22* (1) (January 1985): 47–51.

Olson, L. Training trends: The corporate view. *Training and Development Journal, 40* (9) (September 1986): 32–37.

Rubenstein, C. "Working it Out" *United,* September 1986.

Schwendiman, G. Background information regarding business and industrial trends: . . . Excerpts from a speech to the Annual Meeting of the Lincoln Chamber of Commerce, College of Business Administration, University of Nebraska, Lincoln, June 1987.

Society for Applied Learning Technology. Report on the Greenbrier Conference, December 1986.

Sredl, H. J., & Rothwell, W. J. *The ASTD Reference Guide to Professional Training Roles and Competencies.* Amherst, MA: HRD Press, Inc., 1987.

Zemke, R. Employee training in America. *Training and Development Journal, 40* (7) (July 1986): 34–37.

Zemke, R. Training in the '90s. *Training, 24* (1) (January 1987): 40–53.

Index

Acceptance Stage, of concept life cycle, 252–253

Accountability, 237–238

Action learning, 32

Active attention, 38

Activity strategy, 215

Adult education, definition of, 6, relationship to HRD, 17–18

Adult educators, 17

Adult learning, 124–126; principles of, 124–125; types of, 125–126

Advisor, role of career counselor, 62

Advocate, type of consultant, 178

Affective domain, 136

Alternative identifier, type of consultant, 179

American Association for Counseling and Development, 293, 296–298

American Compensation Association, 293, 296–298

American Society for Personnel Administrators, 292, 296–298, 313

American Society for Training and Development, 12, 17–19, 168–169, 309, 348, 358–359; certification efforts of, 294–295, 315–323; self-assessment questionnaire, 336–339

Analysis-for-the-Top, change agent, 184–185

Analytic models of needs assessment, 210

Andragogy, 122; definition of, 6

Applying stage, experiential learning, 140–141

Appraiser, 61

Apathy, impact on learning, 39

Archambault, R.D., 197

Argyris, C., 34

Association of Education, Communication and Technology, 312–313

Atwood, H.M., 197

Bedrick, D., 12, 27, 101, 155, 326

Beer, M., 7, 75

Behavior evaluation, 234

Behavioral career path, 66–67

Behavioral science movement, 12

Behaviorist theory, 121

Bell, C.H., 85, 354

Bell, M.R., 141

Bellman, G., 172

Bennett, A., 353

Bianco, J., 183

Blake, R.R., 122

Bowers, D.G., 79–81, 84–85, 87, 89

Boydell, T., 132–134, 149–153

Bratton, B., 284–285, 288, 312, 314–315

Brim-Donohoe, L.R., 97

Brinkerhoff, R., 232

Broker, role of career counselor, 62

Brookfield, S., 34

Broad life planning, 50

Brostrom, R., 131, 143–148

Budget Control, 113–114

Budget item center, 113

Bullett, F., 304

Byrne, J.A., 180

Campbell, J.P., 278

Career awareness, 69

Career counselor, activities of, 61; advantages of, 60; manager as, 59–62; roles of, 61–62

Career development, activities of, 52–71; approaches to 60–61; definition of, 6, 15, 48; five-stage approach to, 71–73; motives for, 48–49; and organization, 51–52; overview of, 15, 48–51; programs, 48–49; relationship to organization and individual development, 91–94; responsibility of, 54

Career development workshops, 62–63; evaluation of, 63; self-analysis approach, 62–63

Career management, 49

Career path, in HRD, 341–342

Career pathing, 65, types of, 66–67

Career planning, 49; activities of, 58; criteria of, 67–69; forces affecting, 68; purposes of, 68; reasons for, 68–69

Career resource center, 56–59; creation

Career resource center, (cont.)
of, 59; materials used in, 57–59;
purpose of, 57–59; utilization of,
57, 70
Carlson, R.A., 305
Carnevale, A., 32
Cervero, R., 308
Chadwick, R.P., 128
Chalofsky, N., 310
Change, principles of, 79
Change agent, 6, 80; competencies of,
84–85; roles of, 81–84; types of,
184–185; values of, 85
Characteristics orientation to
professionalization, 306–308
Civil Service Commission Competency
Study, 310–311
Clements, R., 317
Coach, role of career counselor, 61
Cognitive domain, 136
Cognitive theory, 121
Coleman, B., 314
Collaborative organizations, 78–79,
90–91
Collaterally identified HRD Practitioners,
23
Communicator, role of career counselor,
61
Competency model, of need assessment,
135
Competencies of instructors, 30
Competencies of instructional designers,
164–165
Competencies studies in HRD, 309–323
Competitive organizations, 90–91
Computers, in training, 358–360
Concept life cycle, 251–255; acceptance
stage of, 252–253; decline stage of,
252–254; exposure stage of, 251–253;
maturity stage of, 252–253
Concurrent validity, 230
Congruence, principle of, 7, 79
Constant STAR programs, 256–257
Constructive coping, 63
Consultant, 20–21; advantages of,
174–175; attitudes required of, 182;
competencies of, 180–182;
internal/external, 182–184; knowledge
required of, 181–182; need for,

174–175; purpose of, 186–191;
qualifications of, 174–175; roles of,
175–180; skills required of, 182;
subroles of, 180; transitions of,
172–173; types of, 182–184, 186–191
Consulting, crisis in human resources
affecting, 173; growth of, 173;
hierarchy of purpose, 186–191;
process of, 191–195; technological
development affecting, 173
Content validity, 230
Controlling, 113–116
Corporate structures, 356–358
Cost-benefit analysis, 22, 270, 280–281
Cost center, 114
Cost-effectiveness analysis, 270–274
Craig, R., 316
Critical mass theory, 26
Critical reflexivity, 33
Cross, P., 49, 124
Cummings, T.G., 79

Data confrontation, 210
Davis, L.N., 125–126
Dean, R.L., 127–128, 130, 140–141
Decline stages of Concept Life Cycle, 252,
254
Democratic models of needs assessment,
210
Departmental structure, 107–109
Dervarics, C., 12
Design, 30–31
Development, 31; definition of, 5
Developmental approach of performance
appraisal, 64–65
Developmental opportunity analysis,
274–278
Developmental orientation to
professionalization, 306
Developmental planning, 50–51
Diagnostic models of needs assessment,
210
Diagnostic phase of organizational
development, 87–88
Dialogic learning, 32–33
Director of learning, 130
Disseminator, 128, 129–130
Distraction, 39
Diversification, strategy of, 263

Division of labor, 107
Divisional Structure, 108, 110
Donaldson, L., 124, 137, 156, 161, 200, 232–233
Downsizing, 356–358
Dunn, D.A., 180

Economic factors affecting HRD, 348–349
Education, definition of, 7
Educational attainment, 352
Educational diversity, 351
Educational information, 58
Eggland, S.A., 145, 244, 248, 260–262
Ellis, J., 197
Employee request system, 55
Evaluation, 31; behavior type of, 142, 234; components of, 231–233; criteria of, 163; learning specialist, 232–233; learning type of, 141, 234; levels of, 233–237; organizational, 193–194; program, 231–232; reaction type of, 142, 234; result type of, 142, 233–234; types of, 141–142
Evaluation phase of the consulting process, 193–194
Evaluation approach of performance appraisal, 64
Evaluator, 98–99, 155–156, 229–230
Examination phase of the consulting process, 191–192
Experiential learning, 139–141; stages of, 140–141
Exposure stage, of concept life cycle, 251–253
External consultant, 182–184

Facilitation of learning, 22–23, 119
Facilitator, 130
Fact finder, type of consultant, 179
Farmer, J.A., 305
Feedback, 219–220
Feedback phase of organizational development, 89
Feuer, D., 328
Financial resources, definition of, 3–4
Follow-up phase of the consulting process, 194
Formative evaluation, 189

Franklin, J.L., 79–81, 84–85, 87, 89
French, R., 215
French, W.L., 85
Functional structure, 108–109
Future forces, 348–362; economic factors, 348–349; organizational factors, 356–362; political factors, 349–351; sociological factors, 352–356
Futurist, 362

Galbraith, M.W., 122, 215–217, 284, 287, 289, 291–293, 295, 298, 300–302, 304–306, 322, 324
Geber, B., 331, 348
General learning objectives, 135–136
Generalizing stage, of experiential learning, 140–141
Gentilman, R., 349
Gestalt theory, 121
Gilley, J.W., 2–5, 17, 60–61, 71–72, 76–77, 91–94, 123, 127, 128–130, 133, 140–141, 244–245, 248, 251–262, 284, 287, 289, 291–293, 295–296, 298, 300–302, 304–306, 308, 317, 322, 324
Goldstein, L.D., 32
Goodstein, L.D., 140
Gordon, J., 329, 353, 358–359
Governmental regulation, 349–350
Gregory, J.M., 35, 38–45
Grote, R., 56
Group problem analysis, 205–206
Gutteridge, T.G., 48, 50

Hale, J., 348–354, 356, 358–363
Hanson, M., 49, 62–63
Harper, P., 192
Hatcher, T.F., 295, 315–317
Hildebrand, M., 284–285, 312
Historical career path, 66
Hiring of HRD practitioners, 112
Hudson, T., 172, 173, 176, 183
Human relations movement, 8
Human resource accounting, 7, 281–282
Human resource concept, 5–6
Human resource development, 1; budget of, 113–114; careers in, 326–345; competencies of, 21–23, 197–282; components of, 13–15; consultant in,

Human resource development, (cont.)
172–195; employment in, 340–342;
evolution of, 8–12; future of, 347–364;
instructional designer in, 155–170;
learning activities; learning specialist
in, 118–153; managers of, 97–116;
mission of, 12–13; philosophy of, 103;
policy.of, 103–104; professional
certification in, 284–302;
professionalization of, 304–324;
purpose of, 13; roles of, 97–195
Human resource development
department, 108; budget of, 113–114;
failure of, 97–98; marketing of, 116;
policy of, 115; procedures of, 115;
staffing of, 109–112; standards of,
115–116; structure of, 108–109
Human resource development
practitioner, and adult educators, 17,
18; career of, 332–340, 341–345;
future of, 362–363; opportunities for,
327–329; rewards of, 329–332;
placement of, 112; salary of, 329–332;
selection of, 112
Human resource planning, 64
Human resource development program,
marketing of, 242–265; philosophy of,
103; policy of, 115; strategies for
designing, 103–105; support for,
104–105
Human resource management, definition
of, 7
Human resource wheel, 17, 19
Human resources, crisis in, 173;
definition of, 3–4
Humanistic theory, 121–122

Illiteracy, 353
Impact evaluation, 234–237
Impact strategy, 215
Individual appraisal models of needs
assessment, 209
Individual development, competencies
of, 29–31; definition of, 7, 15;
evolution of, 26–27; relationship to
career and organizational
development, 91–93; responsibility
for, 27–28; roles in, 28; seven laws of,
35–46

Individual self-fulfillment models of
needs assessment, 209
Industrial paradigm, 10
Information age paradigm, 11
Informational specialist, type of
consultant, 179
Institute for Management Consultants,
certification efforts of, 293, 296–298
Instruction, 29
Instructional climate, 132–134
Instructional designer, 7, 20–21, 28;
activities of, 159–163; competencies
of, 163–169; definition of, 7, 28; roles
of, 155–159
Instructional media, 226–227
Instructional methods, selection of, 138;
types of, 138–139
Instructional process, climate stage of,
132–134; evaluation stage of,
141–142; learning objectives and
activities stage, 135–138; methods of
instruction stage, 138–141; needs
assessment stage of, 134–135;
philosophy of, 127–132; stages of,
126–142
Instructional strategies, 224–225
Instructional writer, 156
Instructor, competencies of, 29–30;
evaluation of, 232
Instrumental learning, 32–33
Internal consultant, 182–184
International Board of Standards for
Training, Performance and Instruction,
30, 163–167, 296, 307, 350–351;
certification efforts, 291–292;
competencies study of, 323
Intervention, 186
Intervention phase of organizational
development, 88–89
Interviews, 200–202

Jacobs, R., 360–361
James, W.B., 122, 215–217
Job analysis, 207
Job posting system, 54–55
Johnson, R., 108
Joint problem solver, type of consultant,
179
Jones, P.R., 60

Jurkus, A.F., 281

Kahnweiler, J.B., 70
Kaye, B.L., 48, 57, 60, 129
Kirkpatrick, D.L., 63, 142
Knowles, M.S., 33, 122
Kotler, P., 243

Ladd, C., 360
Laird, D., 118
Law of the language, 40–41
Law of the learner, 38–40
Law of the learning process, 44–45˙
Law of the learning specialist, 36–38
Law of the lesson, 41–42
Law of review and application, 45–46
Law of the teaching process, 42–44
Lawrence, P.R., 285
Lawrie, J., 13, 103
Learner characteristics, 218–219
Learner materials, 227
Learning activities, 221–223; sequencing
    of, 223
Learning evaluation, 234
Learning objectives, 220–221; domains
    of, 135–137; levels of, 136–137;
    sequencing of, 223; types of, 135–138
Learning programs, constant stars, 256;
    no stars, 257; super stars, 255;
    wandering stars, 256
Learning provider, type of consultant,
    179
Learning specialist, 7, 20–21;
    competencies of, 29–30, 163–165;
    criteria for selecting, 119–120;
    definition of, 7, 28; evaluation of,
    232–233; roles of, 188–119
Learning styles, 215–218
Learning theory, 120–122
Lee, C., 287, 327, 347–348
Leibowitz, Z.B., 62
Lesson plan, 137–138, 161, 224
Lewin, D., 354
Lindeman, E.C., 131
Lippitt, G., 79, 86, 121, 173, 175–177,
    179–183, 310
Lippitt, R., 79, 86, 173, 175–177,
    179–183
Lusterman, S., 351, 354, 359

Lutterodt, S.A., 221, 223, 225, 227, 230

Manager, as career counselor, 59–62
Manager, of HRD, 7, 20–21;
    characteristics of, 102; competencies
    of, 101–102; definition of, 7;
    responsibilities of, 103; roles of,
    98–101
Margulies, N., 77, 89, 175–176
Market development, strategy of, 263
Market penetration, strategy of, 263
Market segmentation, 247–249
Market specialization, 248–249
Marketing, factors affecting, 244–245;
    of HRD, 22; objectives and goals of,
    245–247; mission of, 243–247;
    planning, 264–265; strategies of,
    262–264
Marketing mix, 250–264
Marketing plan, 264–265
Marsick, V., 32–35
Mass selling, 261
Matching process, 51–52
Materials, 223, 227–228
Maturity stage, of concept Life Cycle,
    252–253
McCarthy, E.J., 250
McCullough, M., 295, 317
McGiffen, T., 360–361
McGill, M.E., 78, 80, 85, 87, 89
McLagan, P., 12, 27, 101, 155, 306, 317,
    322, 326
McLean, A.J., 85–86
McKinley, J., 209
Media, 223, 226–227
Media specialist, 156–157
Mentor, role of career counselor, 62
Mentoring, 55; characteristics of, 56
Methods of instruction, 138–139
Mezirow, J., 32–34
Michalak, D.F., 158, 198, 200, 210, 231
Miller, E.L., 287
Mills, D., 305–306
Model for Excellence, 17–23, 168–169,
    180–181, 295, 315–323
Moir, E., 57, 59
Moore, H.A., 60–61, 133
Morgan, G., 32
Mouton, J., 122

Multi-criterion analysis, 278–281

Nadler, L., 5, 13, 23, 33, 102, 113, 155, 293, 310
Nadler Role Model, 310
National Career Counseling Association, 293, 296–299
National Society for Performance and Instruction, certification effort, 294–295; competency study, 314–315
Needs analyst, 157
Needs assessment, 22, 29, 134–135, 218–219; analytic model of, 210; competency model of, 135; definition of, 197–198; democratic model of, 210; diagnostic model of, 210; group problem analysis method of, 205–206; importance of, 198–199; individual appraisal model of, 209; individual self-fulfillment model of, 209; interview method of, 200–202; job analysis and performance review method of, 207; methods of, 200–207, 209–210; models and methods of selecting, 207–209; problem analysis model of, 134; questionnaire method of, 202–204; records and reports method of, 206–207; system discrepancy model of, 209–210; test method of, 204–205
Neilsen, E.H., 78, 81, 84–86, 90
Nelson, B., 349
Newman, K., 115
No star programs, 256–257
Nontraditional orientation of professionalization, 308

Objective observer/reflector, type of consultant, 179–180
Odiorne, G., 349, 362
Off-the-job learning activity, 16
Olson, G., 353
Olson, L., 350
O'Mara, J., 322
On-the-job learning activity, 16
Ontario Society for Training and Development, 167–168; certification efforts, 294, 296–298; competency study of, 167–168, 181, 311

Operational manager, 100
Organization awareness, 70–71
Organizational career path, 66
Organizational development, 7; characteristics of, 77–78; definition of, 7, 15; diagnostic phase of, 87–88; feedback phase of, 89; goals and objectives of, 78–79; intervention phase of, 88–89; problem identification phase of, 86; process of, 85–89; relationship to career and individual development, 91–94; relationship phase of, 86–87; solution phase of, 88; type of change agent, 184; value of, 89
Organizational efficiency, macro view of, 92–93; micro view of, 91–92
Organizational factors affecting HRD, 348, 356–362
Organizational Learning, 34–35
Organizationally identified HRD practitioners, 23
Organizing, 107
Otte, F., 48, 50
Outside Pressure, type of change agent, 184

Palomba, N.A., 313
Passive attention, 38
Passive organizations, 90
Pedagogy, definition of, 7
People-change-technology, type of change agent, 184
Perceptual learning styles, 215–217; inventory of, 217
Performance appraisal, 64–65; techniques of, 65; types of, 64
Performance deficiencies, causes of, 219
Performance planning, 50–51
Performance review, 207
Perreault, A.H., 250
Personal selling, 260–261
Perspective transformation, 33
Pfeiffer, J.W., 140
Phelps, M., 75, 78–79, 81, 84, 87–89
Phillips-Jones, L., 55
Philosophical orientation of professionalization, 305
Physical resources, definition of, 3–4

Pinto-Walker Study, 27, 295, 313–314, 317
Place strategy, 259–260
Placement, of HRD practitioners, 112
Planning, 105–107; elements of, 106–107
Policies, of HRD departments, 115
Political factors affecting HRD, 348–351
Portfolio analysis, 255–259
Predictive validity, 230
Predisposition, principle of, 79
Preindustrial paradigm, 9
Price strategy, 262
Principles of change, 79
Problem analysis model of needs assessment, 134
Problem identification phase of organizational development, 86
Procedures, 115
Process counselor, type of consultant, 179
Processing stage of experiential learning of HRD department, 140–141
Product development, strategy of, 263
Product specialization, 248–249
Product strategy, 251–259
Profit center, 114
Professional certification, activities of HRD-related societies, 291–296; benefits of, 288–289; definition of, 284–285; drawbacks of, 290–291; history of, 285–286; purpose of, 287–288; qualification criteria for, 296–298; support for, 286–287
Professionalization, characteristics orientation of, 306–308; developmental orientation of, 306; in HRD, 350–351; nontraditional orientation of, 308–309; philosophical orientation of, 305–306; process of, 305–309
Professionalization Cube, 298–301
Professionally identified HRD practitioners, 23
Program accountability, 237–238
Program demand, 218–219
Program design, 22, 30–31, 123, 220–223; stages of, 159–163
Program designer, 157–158
Program development, 223–227

Program evaluation, 231–232
Program implementation, 228
Program management, 162, 228–229
Program analysis model of needs assessment, 134–135
Programmed instructor, 130
Programming, 214
Project structure, 109, 111
Promotion strategy, 260–261
Psychomotor domain, 136
Public relations, 261
Publishing stage of experiential learning, 140–141
Pyramidal organizations, 90

Questionnaire, 202–204

Raia, A., 77, 89, 175–176
Ramirez, R., 32
Randall, J.S., 138
Reaction evaluation, 132, 234
Records and reports, 206–207
Recruitment of HRD practitioners, 109–110
Referred Agent, role of career counselor, 62
Reliability, 231
Result evaluation, 132, 234–237
Reynierse, J.H., 51
Rice, O., 274, 276
Robinson, D.G., 180, 215, 234
Rockham, N., 235–238
Rothwell, N.J., 98–99, 107–111, 115, 354–355, 361
Rubenstein, C., 354

Salary of HRD practitioners, 329–332
Sales promotion, 261
Scannell, E.E., 124, 137, 156, 161, 200, 224, 232–233
Scheer, W.E., 307
Schlossberg, N.K., 62
Schwendiman, G., 352
Scientific management, 8
Secondary passive attention, 38, hindrances of, 39
Selection of HRD practitioners, 112
Selective specialization, 248–249
Self assessment for employment, 332–340

Self-reflective learning, 32–35
Shimberg, B., 230–231
Shipp, T., 270
Smith, R., 216
Society for Applied Learning Technology, 360
Sociological factors affecting HRD, 348, 352–356
Socratic instructor, 129
Solution phase of organizational development, 88
Span of control, 107–108
Specific learning objectives, 135–136
Sredl, H.S., 98–99, 107–111, 115, 354–355, 361
Standards of HRD department, 115–116
Steadham, S.V., 207
Steinaker, N.W., 141
Stine, S., 56
Structured on-the-job training, 360–361
Succession, principle of, 79
Suessmuth, P., 112, 119, 134, 137, 149–151
Summative evaluation, 89
Super star programs, 255–256
Synergogy, 122
System discrepancy models of needs assessment, 209–210

Target marketing, 247
Task analysis, 218–219
Task analyst, 158
Taylor, H.R., 60
Technology, affecting HRD programs, 358–361
Tests, 204–205
Theoretician, 159
Thiagarajan, A.J., 139
This, L.E., 121
Through-the-job learning activity, 17
Tichy, N., 184–185
Training, benefits of, 269–270; costs of, 267–269; definition of, 7; standards of, 115–116; types of, 329
Training aids, 223
Training budget, 347–348
Training and development practitioners, competencies of, 321; outputs of, 319–320; roles of, 318
Training proposals, development of, 210–212
Training strategies, 257–258
Turner, A.N., 186–191

Union activity, and HRD, 350
Urban, T.F., 278–281
Utility, 231

Validity, 230; concurrent, 230–231; content, 231; predictive, 230
Value orientation, 353–354
Variance report, 277–278
Vollmer, H., 305–306

Walker, J., 27, 50, 51, 64–66, 67–68, 295, 313
Walton, R., 197
Wandering star programs, 256
Watkins, K., 32–35
Wells, R.G., 174
Westgaard, O., 357–358
White, L.P., 81, 82–83
Whyte, G.S., 306
Wiggs, G.D., 13, 102, 113
Wooten, K.C., 81, 82–83

Yager, E.G., 154, 198, 200, 210, 231
Yeoman, W.N., 104
Younglove, B., 180

Zemke, R., 123, 131, 352–354
Zemke, S., 123, 131
Zenger, J., 54, 67–68